LED ZEPPELIN
THE 'TIGHT BUT LOOSE' FILES

OMNIBUS PRESS

CELEBRATION II ❧ DAVE LEWIS

CONTENTS ⚶⚶⚶⚶

JOHN PAUL JONES AT THE PREMIERE OF THE LED ZEPPELIN DVD, NEW YORK, MAY 27, 2003

ACKNOWLEDGEMENTS
This book and the publication of the *Tight But Loose* magazine itself over the past 25 years has benefited greatly from the input and inspiration of the following:

Chris Charlesworth for having the initial belief, Gary and Carol Foy for much support (often against overwhelming odds!), Mike Warry for expert design and advice, and Dave Linwood for creating and maintaining the *TBL Website* with unflagging enthusiasm (www.tblweb.com).

Thanks are also due to Richard Chadwick at Opium Arts, Bill Curbishley and Andrea Thompson at Trinifold, Kevyn Gammond, Andy Edwards, Justin Adams, Cameron Crowe, Neal Preston, Ross Halfin, Phil Tattershall, Terry Boud, Kam Assi, Eddie Edwards, Julian Walker, Pete Gozzard, Gary Davies, Leo T.

Ishac, Simon Pallett, Larry Bergmann, Kevin Hewick, Steve and Jan Way, Brian Knapp, Mark Harrison, Bill McCue, Andy Adams, Billy and Alison Fletcher, Steve Jones, Dave Marsh, Anne Marsden, Laura Whitten, Gary Woolard, Steve Beale, Paul Kelvie, Keith Creek, Eric Sachs, Paul Sheppard, Dardo Simone, Grant Burgess, Bob Langley, Christophe Le Pabic, Benoit Pascal, Dave Fox, Tim Ellock,

Mark Archer, Larry Ratner, Tim Tirelli, Matt Krol, Krys Jantzen, Geoff Adamson, Andy Banks, Graeme Hutchinson, Ian Green, Roly Thompson, Alan Cousins, Rikky Rooksby, Pandora, Katherine Moore, Carolyn Longstaff, Russ Rees, Stuart Whitehead (where are you now!), Paul Hindess, Sam Rapallo, Terry Stephenson, Debbie Bonham, Jason Bonham, the late Mick Bonham, Bob Walker, David F.

Brown, Andy, Joel and Tim at *Record Collector*, Mark Paytress at *Mojo*, Mick, Sian and Dave at *Classic Rock*, Mark Blake at *Q*, Sean and Mike at Helter Skelter, Helen Donlon, Patsy Lima at Borkowski PR, Cat Hollis and Stephen at Noble PR, Pete Flatt at PPR, Erik James at Warners, Steve Jump at Badlands, Dick Carruthers at M Productions.

Fred Zeppelin, Whole Lotta Led, Simply Led, Boot-Led Zeppelin, The

FOREWORD BY JOHN PAUL JONES

For the twelve years that Led Zeppelin existed, an enormous amount of interest in the group was generated, culminating in the legacy that we know today. Of our many supporters throughout the world, few were more ardent than Dave Lewis and his *Tight But Loose* magazine. Providing comprehensive concert information, regular insights into the band and the music, as well as ongoing support for the various solo projects, and all handled with the dedication of a true fan.

I am sure that this second book will become an invaluable reference to all things Zeppelin. I know the first one helped me answer a few interview questions! So, enjoy and Rock On!

John Paul Jones

July 2003

Rubber Plants for paying tribute night after night, Steve Sauer for his excellent LZ History on line mailing service (contact Steve@LZHistory.com), Kashmir French magazine (contact zeppat94@net-up.com), Led Zeppelin fan club Italia (contact www.ledzeppelin.club it), The Underground Uprising site (www.undergroundweb.org.uk), Electric Magic site (www.ledzep-pelin.com) and Mark Ereira at the ABC Trust (www.abctrust.org.uk)

Also: Howard Mylett, Robert Godwin, Hugh Jones and Luis Rey for past Zep chronicles; Charles Shaar Murray, Nick Kent, Roy Carr, Peter Doggett, Mat Snow, Charles R. Cross, Mark Lewishon, Patrick Humphries, Simon Robinson, David Clayton, Mark Timlin for journalistic motivation past and present; and Geoff Barton for our collaboration 25 years ago in *Sounds* that kick started the whole TBL journey...

Plus Tom Locke, Dec Hickey, Phil Harris, Max Harris and James Eaton for general public house duties; Shin and Suki at the post office; Chris and Nad and the staff of The Fox and Hounds; Pete and co at the Virgin Megastore MK.

Musical inspiration during the writing this book: Nick Drake, Frank Sinatra, Miles Davis, Flaming Lips, Strange Sensation, Led Zeppelin.

To all *Tight But Loose* subscribers - thank you for your loyalty, support and patience. I hope it's always worth waiting for.

Finally, to the Lewis clan: John Lewis for introducing me to the live Electric Magic, Mervyn Lewis for lending me £30 for the Earls Court tickets, Martyn Lewis for tech know how and new generation input. To my late Mum and Dad Edith and Trevor, who heard and encouraged it from the start. To Betty and Ken and of course Jan, Sam and Adam for so much love and support and for enduring it all. This one is for all three of you.
Dave Lewis, July 2003

Back in October 1990 the concluding chapter I wrote for *Led Zeppelin A Celebration* centred on the then just released four-CD box set retrospective and *Remasters* 'best of' double package. History now repeats itself. As I complete this follow up volume, the retrospective *Led Zeppelin DVD* and live CD set *How The West Was Won* has once again raised the band's profile to a level reminiscent of the group's Seventies heyday.

The fastest selling music DVD ever, it shot straight in at number one on the US charts, and when Page, Plant and Jones reunited to attend premieres on both sides of the Atlantic, the BBC six o'clock news saw fit to cover the event, such was the furore that surrounded this monumental outpouring of material during the late spring of 2003.

When I mapped out this project nearly two years ago, the idea of Jimmy Page undertaking the task of compiling an official visual history was just another long term rumour – but that's how it's all panned out, and it's with a measure of pride that I conclude this book safe in the knowledge that Led Zeppelin's legacy is as talked about today as it was when I hand wrote the first issue of my self published magazine *Tight But Loose* nearly 25 years ago. Back then it was the expectancy of a grand return that was the talking point – and now all these years later we can view at the flick of the DVD menu just how impressive that spirited Knebworth comeback performance turned out.

The idea for *Tight But Loose* was to share and discover information.

Dave Lewis first heard Led Zeppelin when he was 13 years old. The effect has been a lasting one.

A world renowned authority on the band, he is the editor and publisher of the long running Zep magazine 'Tight But Loose' and the author of numorous Zep books - notably 'A Celebration' and 'The Complete Guide To The Music Of Led Zeppelin'.
Dave lives in Bedford with his wife Janet and children Sam and Adam.

INTRODUCTION

Led Zep didn't do fan clubs...

...and outside of the music weeklies there was little way of obtaining info. As a fan craving to know more, I undertook single-handedly the task of creating a platform of communication between Zeppelin fans across the world. Initially inspired (with some irony) by the do-it-yourself principles of the punk fanzine *Sniffin' Glue*, I put pen to paper (literally) and rattled out the first issue, placed an ad in *Sounds* and the mag was up and running.

Over the past 25 years it's been an incredible roller coaster ride. While the early issues benefited greatly from direct input from Swan Song, the demise of the band made it difficult to carry on. There then followed a ten year hiatus. As the solo albums unfolded, my enthusiasm for their work remained intact, leading to my earlier books *The Final Acclaim* and *A Celebration*.

It was the favourable reaction to the publication of *A Celebration* that inspired me to revive the magazine again in 1992. Since then *TBL* has appeared on an annual basis, with each issue evolving as a mini book scrutinising a variety of Zep topics. For more instant news updates there's the *TBL* web site (tblweb.com) - the development of which has extended my original premise of sharing information beyond my wildest expectations.

Over the past eleven years the magazine has faithfully documented the ongoing Zep saga. The unlikely liaison of Coverdale Page, Page and Plant's reunion for MTV, their subsequent world tours, John Paul Jones' emergence as a solo artist, Robert Plant's reinvention with the Priory Of Brion and Strange Sensation, the DVD and live album project. *TBL* as been at the helm of all this.

It's a task that has led me on an ongoing journey of Zep-spotting assignments. Some hilarious, some near perilous, some completely bizarre, many incredibly exciting, none of them dull.

Be it from the second row of the impressive Meadowlands Arena in New York State, atop the Kensington Roof Gardens on a bright sunny lunchtime, outside a rainy Bostanci Centre in Istanbul, inside a tent in an obscure part of Leicestershire on an October Sunday afternoon or in the book department of Borders in Oxford Street, your intrepid *TBL* reporter has constantly filed despatches from the front in a quest to present the most comprehensive Zep related coverage in the mag. Indeed, the personal trials and tribulations I've often incurred in bringing all this info to the forefront could fill a book within itself.

Celebration II unlocks the TBL Files. Alongside the story as it has unfolded since 1991, there are chapters that hone in on the significant moments in Zeppelin's history: their original BBC sessions, Zep's long asociation with bootlegs, the making of key albums such as *Led Zep IV* and *Presence*, detailed overviews of the Earls Court and Knebworth shows, plus a fresh perspective of the 1977 US tour and their final trek around Europe in 1980. Exclusive question and answer interviews with Peter Grant and John Paul Jones offer further enlightenment.

As with the original *A Celebration*, the intention is to present an absorbing reference work that chronicles the many aspects of Led Zeppelin and its related solo spin offs. It's also designed to inspire re-investigation of a catalogue of music that now stretches to nearly four decades.

So once again – with the CD and DVD player within earshot - get ready to lose yourself in a compendium of features drawn from the *TBL* files that celebrate the ongoing influence of **Jimmy Page, Robert Plant, John Paul Jones and John Bonham... collectively and individually – forever Tight But Loose, forever Led Zeppelin.**

Dave Lewis
Bedford, England, July 2003

For details of the *Tight But Loose* magazine or feedback on this book e-mail: davelewis.tbl@virgin.net
Visit the *Tight But Loose* website at www.tblweb.com

THE FIRST 'FLYER'

THANK YOU FOR YOUR ENQUIRY
REGARDING THE LED ZEPPELIN FANZINE

"TIGHT BUT LOOSE" IS PRODUCED BY MYSELF OUT
OF ENTHUSIASM AND DEDICATION FOR THE
GROUP, AND A DESIRE TO FORM A MUCH
NEEDED PLATFORM OF COMMUNICATION
FOR THE FOLLOWERS OF LED ZEPPELIN.

THE FIRST ISSUE, ALTHOUGH ASSEMBLED
ON A NON EXISTANT BUDGET, IS THE STARTING
POINT OF WHAT IS HOPED, WILL GROW INTO A
REGULAR JOURNAL AND INFORMATION CENTRE
FOR ANYONE INTERESTED IN THE GROUP, AND
THE WORLD THAT REVOLVES AROUND THEM.

"TIGHT BUT LOOSE" IS AIMED AT
YOU THE FAN, AND AS SUCH, WELCOMES
COMMENTS, QUESTIONS, OPINIONS AND IDEAS
ON ANYTHING YOU WOULD LIKE TO SEE
FEATURED IN FUTURE ISSUES.

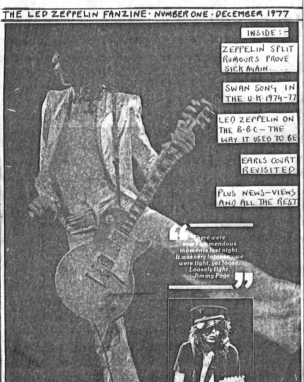

TBL: THE FIRST MOCK-UP COVER

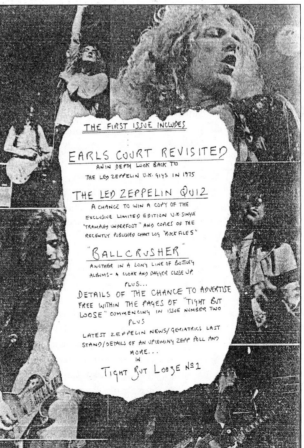

TBL ISSUE 1: THE FIRST FLYER

THE AUTHOR AT KNEBWORTH 1979

THE AUTHOR AT WHITE HART LANE, HOME
OF HIS BELOVED TOTTENHAM HOTSPUR
FOOTBALL CLUB: 2002

THANKS FOR YOUR
INTEREST — LOOK
FORWARD TO HEARING
FROM YOU...
YOUR FRIEND
DAVE LEWIS!
(DCE ZEPP FAN!)

For many years the raw, urgent recordings Led Zeppelin made exclusively for BBC radio early in their career were shrouded in myth and mystery. How these recordings came to be made and exactly when and where they were recorded was largely unknown.

What was apparent, courtesy of the many bootleg recordings that circulated in the mid-Seventies, was that that these precious sessions contained scintillating versions of tracks from their early albums, exclusive songs recorded only for radio ('Sunshine Woman', 'The Girl I Love She Got Long Black Wavy Hair', 'Travelling Riverside Blues') and, in the case of a 1971 *In Concert* recording, lengthy interpretations of 'Dazed And Confused' and 'Whole Lotta Love'.

My own fascination with these sessions dates back to the airing of that 1971 *In Concert* show. I actually taped this on the day it was first aired on Sunday, April 4, 1971 on an old reel to reel tape recorder. My enthusiasm for the Zeppelin BBC sessions was further fuelled by the various BBC session bootlegs that emerged in the mid-Seventies.

During the early days of the magazine, in February 1979, Tommy Vance aired some of the March and June 1969 sessions on his *Friday Rock Show*. This resulted in my first but by no means last detailed chronicling of these recordings in the second issue of *Tight But Loose*.

Tommy Vance went on to air the 1969 *In Concert* show at the end of the same year, adding to our still limited knowledge of the Zep sessions. Further enlightenment on the 1971 recordings came via the various CD bootlegs in the early Nineties, notably *Thank You It's Complete*, a two-CD set on the Discurious label, and the Antrabata bootleg label's *BBC Zep*, both of which contained much off mic chat and tracks not aired on the original John Peel *In Concert* show.

REFERENCE: **TIGHT BUT LOOSE 2**

1 : LED ZEPPELIN AT THE BBC

THE 1977 BBC ALBUM

In 1990 Jimmy Page sourced the tapes of the June 1969 BBC session recording of 'Travelling Riverside Blues' for official release on the *Remasters* box set. Around the same period the BBC began airing regular shows of their original session recordings from the likes of David Bowie, Queen and The Beatles. The Strange Fruit record label also embarked on a series of BBC session albums and The Beatles own *Live At The BBC* was a huge seller in 1993.

A *Led Zeppelin At The BBC* hour long special was prepared for broadcast in the autumn of 1993, and to coincide with this I was commissioned to produce a full length feature on the topic for *Record Collector*. I made contact with BBC producers Kevin Howlett and Jeff Griffin who provided me with some illuminating logs of exactly when the group's sessions took place and when they were broadcast. This clarified several misconceptions, including details of a lost BBC session cut for Alexis Korner's *Blues Is Where You Hear It* show sadly wiped from the archives, and clarification of the actual recording date of the 1971 *In Concert*. Previously this had been documented as March 25, but Jeff Griffin explained to me it had been postponed due to Plant's voice problems and was rescheduled for April 1.

Over the next couple of years rumours abounded that Jimmy Page would sanction an official release of the full Zeppelin sessions. This finally saw the light of day in 1997 when Page, working with engineer Jon Astley, restored the original tapes for release on the two-CD set *Led Zeppelin BBC Sessions*. Though severely edited, the resulting set offered a cohesive, long overdue record of the band's legendary sessions at the BBC.

REFERENCE: **TIGHT BUT LOOSE 13**

The recordings offer vital aural evidence of the way the band developed in their formative years, and what follows is a detailed report of these historic sessions. It includes the original session logs and commentary I wrote for the October 1993 issue of *Record Collector* plus an interview with engineer Jon Astley who helped restore the tapes.

It emphasises the importance these radio recordings had both in the expansion of their repertoire and in spreading the word in the UK. These BBC sessions as recorded in 1969 and 1971 offer a lasting snapshot of the development of the group during their initial years together.

From the very beginning, it was written into the constitution of Led Zeppelin that they would never conform to conventional music business practice. In signing their deal with Atlantic Records on November 1, 1968, manager Peter Grant insisted on several unique clauses, one of them being that he and the group alone would decide on the scheduling of the albums they would deem fit for release.

Jimmy Page in particular felt that his group's music was a world apart from the disposable pop in the Top 30 singles chart. Although Atlantic pressed up a promo single coupling 'Good Times Bad Times' with 'Communication Breakdown' (the first of a series of much sought-after U.K promo 45s), the band had no plans to release a single from their début album at the end of March 1969.

The lack of an official single posed the problem of how to secure radio airplay. In America, the band had already created something of a stir with a barnstorming début tour, aided by the early release of their album, which immediately became a staple on the rock FM stations. Back in the UK, initial reaction was slower. A series of club dates at choice venues like the Toby Jug, Tolworth (just 7/6d admission!) began to spread the word, but Peter Grant felt they needed to be more available to the media. A couple of TV appearances - one in Denmark, the other on a BBC-1 pilot show, *How Late It Is* - were tried, with less than successful results. At the same time, Grant used his network of contacts to negotiate a session for the influential BBC Radio One underground show *Top Gear*, hosted by John Peel.

So it was that on March 3, 1969, Page and his new colleagues, Robert Plant, John Paul Jones and John Bonham, found themselves in the auspicious surroundings of the BBC's Playhouse Theatre and duly laid down their first Radio One session. It was the start of a very fruitful relationship that would see the group return to various BBC studio locations on four occasions in the coming months.

The reason these studio sessions worked so well was that the group approached them as they would a live show. This meant that the BBC performances of songs from their first album were elongated and improvised as they were on stage. As the group's confidence grew, they employed these sessions to try out cover versions and as yet unrecorded material. There's little doubt that the exposure from these early sessions considerably aided the group's rapid rise in stature in Britain throughout 1969.

Jimmy Page was so delighted with this way of presenting the band on radio that he eventually suggested to producer Jeff Griffin that they be allowed to record one of their concerts for a live broadcast. This led them to return to the Playhouse Theatre to tape a pilot show on June 27 for what eventually became the weekly *In Concert* programme. They used the same platform again two years later for their final (and much bootlegged) BBC appearance, this time at the Paris Cinema in Lower Regent Street.

After 1971, as they established themselves amongst the world's biggest concert draws, radio performances seemed less appealing, and despite many requests for further appearances, they never returned to the BBC studios. Years later, the members of the band retained an affection for those times and Page returned to the BBC sessions for two performances ('Travelling Riverside Blues' and 'White Summer') which were included on the 1990 *Remasters* box set. Plant has continued to employ BBC sessions as a means of promotion, recording acoustic sets at Broadcasting House in 1993 and 2002.

SESSION-BY-SESSION LOG

VENUE: Playhouse Theatre, Northumberland Avenue, London
RECORDING DATE: Monday March 3, 1969, 2.30–6.00pm.
PRODUCER: Bernie Andrews
ENGINEER: Pete Ritzerma
TAPE OP: Bob Conduct
ORIGINAL BROADCAST DATE: Sunday March 23, 1969, between 3.00 and 5.00pm on John Peel's *Top Gear* (also in session on the show were Free, the Moody Blues and Deep Purple)
BACKGROUND: The group's début session came after a brief period of rest following their first US tour. It sparked off a month of intense activity that saw them play a series of club dates, record a TV slot for BBC-1, make a whistle-stop tour of Scandinavia that included the filming of a 30-minute TV special in Denmark, record another BBC radio session and film a segment for the movie *Supershow*. This month also saw the belated UK release of their début album.

The venue was the BBC's Playhouse Theatre. This trial broadcast for *Top Gear* was passed unanimously by the BBC audition panel. It also reunited producer Bernie Andrews with Jimmy Page, who had previously worked with him during Page's session days, and with The Yardbirds on their last radio appearance for *Top Gear* recorded almost a year to the day before this Zep session. "They were very loud, but very good," Bernie recalls. Tape op Bob Conduct remembers the Playhouse as being good for recording loud groups, "because the irregular shape of the converted theatre, with all its velvet upholstered seating, absorbed a lot of the volume, even when it was empty".

THE PLAYHOUSE THEATRE,
NORTHUMBERLAND AVENUE, LONDON

> *They were very loud,*
>
> *but very good.*
>
> BERNIE ANDREWS, PRODUCER

CONCERTGEBOUW, AMSTERDAM: OCTOBER 5, 1969

For collectors and Zep enthusiasts alike, the BBC sessions have long been held in great esteem. Many bootlegs have carried these performances, but uncertainty has always surrounded the details of exactly what was recorded for the Beeb, and when.

The mysterious appearance of a bootleg EP from an allegedly unbroadcast BBC session, featuring a cover version of 'Something Else' and a presumed *LZII* out-take, 'The Girl I Love'; a bootleg CD containing an unaired interview from the same source; and out-take material from the 1971 *In Concert* have all added to the confusion that surrounds the BBC sessions. Now, with the assistance of official BBC data, the opportunity at last exists to offer a full perspective on Zep's activity inside the hallowed walls of the Beeb.

What follows here is a session-by-session log with accompanying notes, designed to act as a companion to the radio programme. It reveals for the first time anywhere the accurate details of some of their most inspiring early work.

TRACKS RECORDED

1: 'Communication Breakdown' (2.58)
The first of three BBC versions of one of their early stage anthems was performed in an arrangement not dissimilar to the album take. The intro, however, found Page easing his way in tantalisingly, via a descending guitar chord, before the energy level headed for overload. The distinctive factor of the track, and indeed this whole session, was John Bonham's percussion work. His drums were superbly recorded and were very much to the fore of the mix.

There was a definite live-in-the-studio quality to the recording, the only studio enhancement being the double-tracking of Plant's vocals for the chorus. The stand-out moment came as the track moved into a slightly extended outro, with Bonham's free-falls across the kit supplemented by Page's wah-wah Telecaster effects and Plant adlibbing the line "I got to get back to my baby",

Tune In

LED ONE-HOUR RADIO SPECIAL

But the blues is spreading

and it's spreading over you

with another Wilie Dixon

song 'You Shook Me'...

From me Alexis Korner and

the Led Zeppelin, goodbye

and dare I say it, stay cool.

ALEXIS KORNER, DJ

---

before the track raced into a sudden ending. It was a vintage slice of definitive early Zep.

2: 'Dazed And Confused' (6.37)

Already building into an onstage improvisation vehicle for Page's violin-bow antics, this version of 'Dazed And Confused' was tailored to fit the time limit of the broadcast, and therefore stuck fairly rigidly to the album version. Plant mixed up the lyrics somewhat, replacing the parting shot of "Send you the bill" with "Will yer tongue wag so much when you end up in hell". Bonham was the driving force, playing off Jones' walking bass lines with consummate ease.

N.B. The original programme broadcast sheet has no record of this track being aired on the show. It definitely went out, however, during a repeat of the session, broadcast during Tommy Vance's *Friday Rock Show* on February 2, 1979.

3: 'You Shook Me' (5.15)

John Paul Jones was much more prominent on organ on this take than on the album version. There were also solo spots for Plant's harmonica and Page's guitar. Again, a live-in-the-studio atmosphere prevailed, with the call-and-response section at the finish already becoming a trademark of the new Zep sound.

4: 'I Can't Quit You Baby' (4.21)

Another relaxed interpretation of the LP version, this was a prime example of the blues-rooted emphasis Page and Plant placed on the group in their first few months together. After a fluid guitar solo, Plant steamed back in, deviating from the *LZI* version by throwing in lines from Muddy Waters' 'Nineteen Years Old'.

VENUE: Maida Vale Studio 4, Delaware Rd. London.
RECORDING DATE: Wednesday March 19, 1969, 5.30-9.00pm
PRODUCER: Jeff Griffin
ENGINEER: Joe Young
ORIGINAL BROADCAST DATE: Monday April 14, 1969, on BBC World Service's *Rhythm And Blues*
BACKGROUND: Later retitled *Blues Is Where You Hear It*, this programme was introduced by Alexis Korner and aired on the BBC World Service. Just 15 minutes long, it was usually given over to one session. Producer Jeff Griffin offered Zep the spot on the strength of their debut session. It began a hectic seven-day period that also saw them tape what would be their only live TV appearance, on BBC-1's *How Late It Is* at the Lime Grove studios, take part in the filming of *Supershow* at Staines and continue their UK club one-nighters with a home date for Plant and Bonham at Mothers Club in Birmingham.

During research for the Radio One FM special, BBC senior producer Kevin Howlett discovered that this session no longer exists in the BBC tape archive. A privately recorded medium wave recording did surface in the late Nineties.

TRACKS RECORDED
1: 'Sunshine Woman' (3.10)
"This is your friendly bluesman Alexis Korner here. Happy today because we have a storming new band for you. They've certainly been storming through their first US tour. I believe Keith Moon of The Who dreamed up their name... the Led Zeppelin."

'Sunshine Woman' was a possible group original and a slice of rock'n'blues driven by some barrelhouse piano from Jonesy

---

and harmonica blowing from Plant. Similar in pace to *Zep II*'s 'Bring It On Home', it wound up with nondescript Page Telecaster. It may have been tried in the studio during the recording of their second album but the only logged performance was on this lost BBC session.

2: 'I Can't Quit You Baby' (5.25)

"A Led Zeppelin that really swings and slow swing is hard to find but here it is," was Korner's quaint intro. The band proceeded to run down a terrific take of 'I Can't Quit You Baby'.

This version included a rare Plant ad-lib sequence beginning "I've got a fur coat for Christmas and a diamond ring". Alexis again: "Bet you never thought you'd hear that song on the BBC World Service."

3: 'You Shook Me' (6.55)

"But the blues is spreading and it's spreading over you with another Willie Dixon song 'You Shook Me'. Next week we bring you John Dummer's Blues Band. From me Alexis Korner and the Led Zeppelin, goodbye and dare I say it, stay cool." An explosive delivery of the *Zep I* standard followed, with Plant blowing away on harmonica and Jonesy prominent on organ.

VENUE: Aeolian Hall Studio 2, Bond St.
RECORDING DATE: Monday June 16, 1969, 7.30-11.00pm
PRODUCER: Session commissioned by chief producer Paul Williams. Full details unknown.
ORIGINAL BROADCAST DATE: Sunday June 22, 1969 between 10.00am and 12 midday on *Chris Grant's Tasty Pop Sundae*. Also in session on the show were Marmalade and Vanity Fare.
BACKGROUND: The first of two BBC sessions that month, this visit to the Aeolian Hall studio in Bond Street coincided with the opening of their first proper UK tour with Blodwyn Pig and the Liverpool Scene supporting. The group travelled down for this Monday session after a date at Manchester Free Trade Hall the previous night.

The session itself was to be aired on the *Symonds On Sunday* slot, a popular Sunday morning show hosted by Dave Symonds. During June, however, he was replaced by a little known stand-in, Chris Grant, who renamed the show *Tasty Pop Sundae*. His ineptness was apparent from a hilarious unbroadcast interview conducted during the session. It's also clear from his over-the-top intros that this may not have been the most appropriate time-slot for Zeppelin, especially in the company of pop/ bubblegum acts like Vanity Fare and the Marmalade.

Quite what the Radio Wonderful audience made of 'Communication Breakdown' with Plant's ad-libbed advice to "squeeze my lemon just a little bit" is anybody's guess. Had the controller of Radio One tuned in, it could well have resulted in a ban on the group, a full decade-and-a-half ahead of the Frankie Goes To Hollywood's 'Relax' scandal.

Over the years, it's this June 22 session that has produced most confusion over what was actually aired. Even with the official BBC log from the period, uncertainty remains. The BBC Programme As Broadcast sheet (PasB) for that day fails to list 'Something Else' as a broadcast item, but it certainly was aired at some point as a tape exists of the original Chris Grant voice-over. Its non appearance on the sheet could simply be an error in the log, or it's possible (though unlikely) that the track was used in a later edition of Grant's June stint.

INTERVIEW WITH BBC SESSIONS ALBUM ENGINEER JON ASTLEY
Jon Astley is an experienced producer and studio engineer. His previous credits include Eric Clapton, The Eagles and The Who, amongst many others. More recently he has concentrated on remastering back catalogue material - working on reissue projects involving The Who, Van Morrison's Them and Cream. In this interview conducted with the

author in 1997, Jon explains his involvement in the *Led Zeppelin BBC Sessions* album.

DL: How did you get involved in the project?
JA: Initially I got a call from Bill Curbishley to find out if I knew of a studio which worked late hours. Jimmy was about to undertake the mastering of the BBC tapes and all the main studios were booked. As it

turned out his specifications could be accommodated by my own home studio - so it was arranged that he would link up with my place to commence on the project. So rather than book a major studio it was all done at The Pink Room at my home in Twickenham. We did the whole thing in under two weeks.
DL: Had you worked with him before?
JA: No I hadn't, although I'd

assisted on various Led Zeppelin sessions when I was working for Olympic Studios. I think I also engineered the live mobile recording of their Knebworth shows. I remember as well a meeting with Robert during the mid-Eighties about the possibility of producing him. I actually backed out of that - I was too in awe! Years later we met again at a Who thing and he called me a coward!
DL: Were you working from the

original BBC master tapes?
JA: Well initially Jimmy turned up with a set of DAT tapes - these were OK but sounded a little dull. I was much more keen to work from the master tapes. Luckily we managed to get these out from the BBC archive. The BBC are very reluctant to let anything out but we managed to arrange a 48-hour loan of them. I was then able to transfer the original 1/4 inch tapes onto the 96K

CONCERTGEBOUW, AMSTERDAM: OCTOBER 5, 1969

TRACKS RECORDED

1: 'The Girl I Love She Got Long Black Wavy Hair' (3.00)

"It's 19 minutes past the hour of 10 o'clock... studio guests now, Led Zeppelin... Alright boys, let's get underground now... The girl I love she got long black wavy hair... the cue... Rigggght!" And that was the intro Chris Grant afforded one of the rarest Zep recordings - the sort of corny pop radio piffle that Page must have felt he had long since left behind. Nevertheless, it was providing them with prime-time airplay and must have left its mark on many listeners that Sunday morning.

This BBC recording remains the only time Zeppelin aired their arrangement of a number cut by bluesman Sleepy John Estes. It's possible that they had been working on the track that very month in Morgan Studios for their album-in-progress, Led Zeppelin II. Indeed, the riff part of the song does sound very similar to the eventual Bonham showcase on the LP, 'Moby Dick'. The fact that it never emerged officially made this session track all the more precious.

It's a typically strident mid-'69 riff-laden exercise dominated by a powerful Plant vocal and an incessant Page guitar lick (by this time he had replaced his Telecaster as his main guitar with a superb-sounding 1958 Gibson Les Paul). The rather short duration of the track - it fades less than three minutes in, with a twisting Page solo - provides a hint that this was work-in-progress, still to be fully explored.

2: "Communication Breakdown" (3.10)

"Right now... Led Zeppelin... underground sounds... 'Communication Breakdown' tell me how it is!" The frantic pace of this newly established Zep anthem was obviously infectious. It was another rousing interpretation with Plant double-tracked on the chorus, and moved into the extended outro with those 'lemon squeezing' references. Plant was joined on the final seconds of the track by Chris Grant, who screamed "Oh yeah, oh yeah, Led Zeppelin!" in his by-now customary style.

3: 'Something Else' (2.58)

Page's growing confidence during these BBC sessions is clearly evident on a rock'n'roll cover that was a staple part of their early live shows. This rendering of the Eddie Cochran classic has some barrelhouse piano from JPJ and some posturing vocals from the boy from the Midlands.

Six months in the company of his new colleagues was obviously having the desired effect on Robert Plant, whose stature was expanding by the week. I'll leave it to Chris Grant to close proceedings on the aired portion of this session: "Led Zeppelin... John Paul Jones on piano, Robert Plant on vocals, a decidedly good sound... underground sounds on Radio One."

4: 'What Is And What Should Never Be' (4.14)

Recorded on June 16 but not aired during the session, this was a taster of what would follow on LZII. The fact that they recorded another BBC session version just two weeks later suggests they weren't satisfied with the outcome of this take.

A standard run-through of the dreamy Plant inspired number they'd been working on at Olympic Studios a few weeks earlier, it's a simpler recording than the later version. There's a flanging effect on Page's solo, but otherwise the track is left unenhanced, in contrast to the heavy phasing on the subsequent BBC take and the official album version.

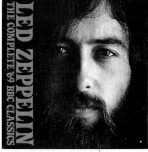

BBC SESSION BOOTLEGS

Led Zeppelin...

John Paul Jones on piano,

Robert Plant on vocals,

a decidedly good sound...

underground sounds on

Radio One.

CHRIS GRANT, DJ

---

desk that I work from.

DL: What condition were they in?

JA: Surprisingly good. These were the two track masters and they had survived amazingly well. One of the reasons we were able to complete the project very quickly was that we were working from very good source material. The 1969 tracks in particular sounded really bright.

DL: Did any of the tracks have the original DJ voice-overs on?

JA: There were some as I remember – and of course there was the Chris Grant interview. It's obvious that he was way out of his depth - we had a good laugh at that.

DL: How did you go about deciding what to put out and what to leave in?

JA: First of all we listened to everything and I produced four reference CDs. Jimmy then went away and came back with some ideas. We did

think about three CDs and including as much as possible. However that created something of a price problem for the record company. There was also talk of doing it as two CDs plus an interactive CD ROM section with some footage. That would have meant that the second CD would have run around 58 minutes. Jimmy and I then got to work on condensing it to two CDs of 70 minutes plus.

DL: Were any of the bootlegs used as a reference?

JA: Yes they were. Jimmy already had a few notes of things he was keen to hear. We were listening to the Cobra Standard CD that came out recently to get the feel of the 1971 show.

DL: What was the reasoning behind editing the 'Whole Lotta Love' medley?

JA: Space restrictions really. There

were three edits for that. We left out the 'Trucking Little Mama' section plus 'For What it's Worth'. Then we edited out the 'Honey Bee'/'Lemon Song' section. Aside from that there was very little editing on other tracks - just a couple of minor patch ups where there were drop outs in sound - one of them was in the 1971 'Dazed And Confused' though you would be hard pushed to spot it. I also EQ'ed everything to make

BACKSTAGE AT THE LYCEUM, LONDON, 1969

CG: Let's speak to John Paul

Jones. Now I believe you are

a musical arranger as well as

a composer - true?

JPJ: A musical arranger as

well as a composer?

CG: Yes.

JPJ: No!

CG: A composer as well as

a musical arranger?

JPJ: No, a musical arranger

as well as a bass guitarist.

CG: Can we do this again?

Engineer: Cut it.

OK, here we go again.

5: Group interview by Chris Grant (6.02)

Hilariously inept, this interview was conducted by Chris Grant with all four members, and opens with Page strumming the guitar. The question-and-answer session continually breaks down early on, as the engineer attempts to get the balance right and Grant fluffs the questions. For example, CG: "Ah here we go. We've got the old red light up for you boys. In the studio we've got Led Zeppelin for you. I'll reel them off - John Bonham, Robert Plant, Jimmy Page and John Paul Jones. Let's speak to John Paul Jones. Now I believe you are a musical arranger as well as a composer - true? JPJ: "A musical arranger as well as a composer?" CG: "Yes." JPJ: "No!" CG: "A composer as well as a musical arranger?" JPJ: "No, a musical arranger as well as a bass guitarist." CG: "Can we do this again?" Engineer "Cut it. OK, here we go again."

The interview wasn't broadcast, and from that extract you'll be able to tell why.

....

VENUE: Maida Vale Studio 4
RECORDING DATE: Tuesday June 24, 1969, 2.30-9.30pm
PRODUCER: John Walters
ENGINEER: Tony Wilson
ORIGINAL BROADCAST DATE: Sunday June 29, 1969 between 7.00 and 9.00pm on *Top Gear*, introduced by John Peel. Pentangle, Savoy Brown Blues Band and the Idle Race were also in session on that show.
BACKGROUND: If the effect of their second BBC session was dampened by the rather inappropriate Sunday morning scheduling, Zepp had an opportunity to hit their core audience with this session for *Top Gear* recorded just eight days later. With John Walters producing (one of his first Peel shows) and Tony Wilson arranging, this session was easily their most advanced. For the first time, Jimmy was allowed the luxury of adding several overdubs to the tracks, and the truly excellent results mirrored just how much ground the group had covered since their first BBC session in early March. "We did Led Zeppelin in mono and I still have the tape," Walters remembered. "Bearing in mind it was just an afternoon and evening in a very basic studio, it sounded great."

The group's decision to use this session to preview two brand-new recordings well ahead of their eventual release on *Led Zeppelin II* also proved a shrewd move, as it clearly demonstrated their future direction.

The reaction to this significant *Top Gear* appearance, coupled with the success of that same weekend's *In Concert* BBC recording and their appearances at the Bath Festival and Albert Hall Pop Proms, ensured that Peter Grant could fly them out to America in July for a third US tour, content in the knowledge that back home Led Zeppelin were now the most raved about group of 1969.

TRACKS RECORDED
1: 'Whole Lotta Love' (6.05)
"7.30 on Radio One and I'd like to go on with Led Zeppelin and a song called 'A Whole Lotta Love'." In sharp contrast to the *Pop Sundae* approach, that was the no-nonsense announcement provided by John Peel for the radio premiere of what would (until the emergence of 'Stairway To Heaven') become the official Zep anthem.

The officially recorded studio version remains a cavalcade of studio techniques, with its swirling use of backwards tape effects. It's therefore fascinating to compare this less elaborate but no less affecting BBC session take. The guitar riff was much less prominent here, though Page stepped on the wah-wah pedal at

JPJ GLADSAXE TEEN CLUB, DENMARK: MARCH 15, 1969

regular intervals, culminating with a full step-on for that famous solo out of the middle section. Up to that point, Bonzo had recreated the timpani parts of the studio take, and replaced the over-dubbed bongos by applying bare hands to the kit. Robert was at his preening best for the outro, throwing in ad-libs that culminated in a tongue-in-cheek reference to his Black Country origins. On the original broadcast, this prompted John Peel to comment at the song's close: "Got those West Bromwich blues? You've got to be putting me on, R. Plant!"

2: 'Communication Breakdown' (2.40)
The most direct of the three session versions, this sizzled along, aided by some vocal overdubs. The extended end section had time

---

sure we got rid of any excessive tape hiss.
DL: Jimmy obviously had the major input on the project - did Robert and John Paul also get involved?
JA: They certainly heard all the reference CDs and suggested certain points. Robert wasn't too keen on the spoken links as he felt he sounded nervous so most of those were edited out. John Paul was concerned about certain aspects of

his bass sound. I was a little worried that it got lost a few times. Jimmy told me he always requested the BBC engineers to turn up the bass. Even then it sometimes got lost. I was also aware of making sure the bass pedals came through on things like 'Stairway'.
DL: What was it like working with Jimmy in the studio?
JA: It was great. We quickly built up a good rapport and he seemed to be

very comfortable with the recording set up. It was also immensely exiting listening to these tapes again. There are times when we literally just looked at each other in amazement at what we were hearing. The Playhouse Theatre 'You Shook Me' was certainly one of those moments. There were times where Jimmy possibly felt the performances wavered with certain inconsistencies that occurred at the time

- but he weighed it up that this was how it was recorded so this is how it should be released.
DL: What are your own personal highlights from the set?
JA: 'You Shook Me' as I just mentioned, 'Travelling Riverside Blues', 'The Girl I Love'. They really stand out and I think the 1971 live set is excellent. Not having heard much else live of theirs, it really surprised me.

for Plant to ad-lib some lines before the whole thing ground to a dead halt, surprising Peel in the process. "I'd forgotten that ends so suddenly," he can be heard to comment on the original broadcast tape.

3: 'What Is And What Should Never Be' (4.20)

A much more assured rendition than earlier in the month, this version had increased vocal phasing that atmospherically captured the dreamy quality of the lyric. Aside from the few lines from the chorus that Plant inserted towards the end of Page's solo, the arrangement was very similar to the album version. The lengthy title immediately struck a chord with Peel, who commented on the original broadcast: "These are Led Zeppelin who played very well at the amazing festival in Bath yesterday, about which more later on. And this is rather curiously titled 'What Is And What Should Never Be' or something."

4: 'Travelling Riverside Blues '69' (5.10)

Page has revealed that this track was rehearsed and recorded at Maida Vale almost from scratch. If that's the case, then it was certainly one of the band's most creative sessions, as the song remains a magnificent performance, not least for Page's wonderful slide-work and Plant's pleasing vocal ad-libs ("Ahh why don-cha come in the kitchen!"). An adaptation of Robert Johnson's 1937 original complete with lemon-squeezing references, it was intended for broadcast purposes only. Years later, however, Page still thought enough of the track to seek out the original tape for official release on the 1990 *Remasters* box set (with the '69 tag removed). Aided by a promo video, their first ever, the track's standing within the Zep canon was subsequently much enhanced - and rightly so.

5: Interview With Jimmy Page (1.05) (not broadcast)

The original BBC session sheet for this day's recording also logs an interview with Jimmy Page conducted by Radio One DJ Brian Matthew. No record of it being broadcast on Radio One exsists but it may have been used for the BBC World Service. In a short accomplished interview link, Jimmy told Mathews that their new album was three quarters finished. "Were finishing off the mixing in New York and it should be out say the first week in August." (It finally surfaced in October). Page also revealed it would be called *Led Zeppelin II* and when asked to select a track to illustrate the album he chose 'What Is And What Should Never'. "It's got a bit of everything," he added.

Mathew: "You say you're going to America again - that might disappoint a lot of people here as you're getting quite a following in Britain. Everywhere I go I see posters for Led Zeppelin. Have a great trip and let's here this from the new album." The tape ended there.

....

VENUE: Playhouse Theatre
RECORDING DATE: Friday June 27, 1969: rehearsal 7.00pm, recording 8.45-10.15pm.
PRODUCER: Jeff Griffin
ENGINEER: Tony Wilson
ORIGINAL BROADCAST DATE: Sunday August 10, 1969, between 8.00 and 9.00pm for the pilot *One Night Stand* part of *Top Gear*, introduced by John Peel. Also in session on the show were the Edgar Broughton Band.
BACKGROUND: This first *In Concert* recording came about after a conversation Jeff Griffin had with Jimmy during the group's World Service broadcast. While they were enjoying the sessions, Page told Griffin it gave them only a limited time to perform, and he would welcome the opportunity for the band to capture their live show, which allowed them to expand and improvise their numbers. Griffin already had the idea for a showcase-style rock show presentation and quickly convinced the BBC that a pilot live recording be conducted with Led Zeppelin. "It was a great 50/50 arrangement," Jeff recalls. "They were keen and I obviously was. DJ Alan Black came up with the interview-plus-music idea which was based on a French rock show he'd heard. I was a bit annoyed it went out as part of *Top Gear*, but it set the wheels in motion for future live recordings of this nature on Radio One."

The date of the show was set for June 27, during another hectic week that saw them record the *Top Gear* session on June 24,

cut the track 'We're Gonna Groove' at Morgan Studios the next day (this one-time set-opener did not make the final *LZII* line-up, and remained unissued until it appeared on *Coda* 13 years later), play Portsmouth Guildhall on the 26th, then tape this show, perform at the Bath Festival on the 28th and finally put in 6pm and 9pm appearances at the Royal Albert Hall Pop Proms on June 29.

The fact that the BBC live recording showed no signs of tiredness says much for the sheer enthusiasm of the group at that time - a vast contrast to the snail's pace schedule of their later years.

Scanning the music press radio guides for that week in June 1969, it seems that the original intention was to broadcast the show live. "Led Zeppelin is to have its own one hour Radio One special on June 27," read the news story in *Disc And Music Echo*. "If successfull the show will be the first in a series of specials spotlighting the talents of major or promising groups." However, the contract drawn up for Peter Grant clearly states: "For broadcast on August 10 1969". The PasB sheet confirms that the show was aired on that Sunday in August as part of the second hour of *Top Gear*.

The Zeppelin pilot was very well received and set the seal for Jeff Griffin to push ahead with the long-running *In Concert* series, which commenced the following January.

TRACKS RECORDED

Alan Black introduction/ 'Communication Breakdown' (3.55)/ **'I Can't Quit You Baby'** (3.07)/ **Interview with Alan Black** (3.30)/ **'Dazed And Confused'** (10.48)/ Interval act - Adrian Henri, Mike Evans and Andy Roberts of the Liverpool Scene (1.55)/ **'White Summer/ Black Mountain Side'** (8.40)/ **'You Shook Me'** (10.01)/ **'How Many More Times'** (12.30)

This show remains a stunning example of the full-throttle attack of Led Zeppelin live in concert in mid-1969. From a taut 'Communication Breakdown' to a lengthy 'How Many More Times', the band (led by Page's dominant guitar work) displayed all the dynamic qualities that were establishing them as the hottest group of the moment.

The extended section of 'Communication Breakdown' included a few lines from the Isley Brothers' hit, 'It's Your Thing', and also captured some stunning Bonham bass-drum patterns. The version of 'I Can't Quit You Baby' was strung out to include some great harmonica and guitar interplay. "I don't think there was anything much restrictive about those two numbers from Led Zeppelin," said Alan Black, who went on to explain that, "Well we'll not only be hearing Led Zeppelin play tonight, we'll also be talking to them because I'd like to put a couple of questions to the two members of the group who've joined me now - on my left Robert Plant and on my right Jimmy Page."

An interesting discussion followed in which Jimmy bemoaned the lack of specialist radio programmes: "There's really only one outlet for our sort of band or Jethro Tull and Ten Years After and that's *Top Gear*, and that's only two hours in one week." "Well, we've talked a bit about freedom and creative freedom," Black concluded. "So let's use some of it tonight and perhaps if you would, you could do one of your longer numbers - feel free to do anything you like." "And when we've finished that we'll be right out of breath so we'd like to do a thing called 'Dazed And Confused'," replied Robert. Given the extended airtime, they turned in a ten-minute opus complete with violin-bow and an ending that contained some of Page's best recorded wah-wah technique.

An interval period followed with a series of sketches provided by the Liverpool Scene's Adrian Henri, Mike Evans and Andy Roberts. They enjoyed a good rapport with Zep back then and had been a support act on their début UK tour. Andy Roberts recalls a humorous incident that followed the BBC recording: "Afterwards we all adjourned to the Sherlock Holmes pub, and I remember Adrian shouting across from the bar to Jimmy Page, 'Is it true you're known as Led Wallet?'!"

The concert programme continued with the lengthy rendition of 'White Summer' that Page used on the 1990 *Remasters* set. That officially released version omitted Alan Black's quaint introduction: "Well, it's back now to Led Zeppelin. I know Jimmy Page was rather keen to do this one. It's by way of contrast. I don't know if Jimmy would like to introduce it, but I can tell you the title of the number is 'White Summer'."

Got those West Bromwich

blues? You've got to be

putting me on, R. Plant!

JOHN PEEL, DJ

KB HALLEN, COPENHAGEN: MAY 3, 1971

BBC SESSIONS: THE ALBUM
After countless bootleg releases, in 1997 Jimmy Page finally sanctioned an official double-CD release drawn from Led Zeppelin's original BBC sessions. Compiled and mastered by Page with engineer Jon Astley at Astley's Pink Room home studio.

Disc 1 contains performances from their 1969 sessions recorded on March 3, June 16, June 24 plus the live Playhouse Theatre One Night Stand show from June 27.

Disc 2 contains 78-minutes of their April 1, 1971, In Concert Paris Cinema live recording. To accommodate the running order the 'Whole Lotta Love' medley is edited down to 13 minutes.

While purists might bemoan the editing, the set still offers a generous two and a half hours of prime early period Zeppelin and finally provided fans with a cohesive overview of these historic Zeppelin sessions .

A ten-minute 'You Shook Me' was next up, featuring some solid Page guitar and a long organ solo from Jones that epitomised the creative freedom they were allowed by the programme. Finally, DJ Alan Black returned to close the set over the intro of 'How Many More Times': "Well, I could go on listening to Led Zeppelin forever. I don't know if they could go on playing forever, but it's time now to wind up so I'm going to hand you over to Robert Plant who's about to re-enact a typical Led Zeppelin stage show close, so listen carefully." Twelve minutes of spirited dynamics followed, with a version that stayed close to the album take with the inclusion of 'Oh Rosie' and 'The Hunter', but deviated into new territory with the "squeeze my lemon" episode that soon became a staple part of many Zep concerts within the 'Whole Lotta Love' medley.

This BBC presentation has remained one of the station's most requested items down the years, and was first repeated on December 28, 1979 as part of Tommy Vance's *Friday Rock Show*. That repeat, and the spasmodic airings it has enjoyed since, appeared in a truncated form with the original Alan Black interview and Liverpool Scene interlude missing. They were presumably aired from the 12" transcription discs that were cut, featuring 53 minutes of music only (see later for a full explanation of the transcription discs).

....

SESSION LOG: 1971
VENUE: Paris Cinema, Lower Regent Street, London
RECORDING DATE: Thursday April 1, 1971: rehearsal 3pm, recording 9.00-10.45pm
PRODUCER: Jeff Griffin
ORIGINAL BROADCAST DATE: Sunday April 4, 1971, between 7pm and 8pm on the John Peel Sunday *In Concert* programme.
BACKGROUND: "This is something we've waited for a long time on the Sunday repeated on Wednesday concert, and I know it's going to be well worth the wait. Would you welcome please Led Zeppelin!"

So spoke an unusually excited John Peel over the BBC airwaves on the evening of Sunday April 4, 1971. Jeff Griffin had indeed been waiting for many months to secure a return visit for the original instigators of the *In Concert* format: "They seemed to be permanently busy in 1970, but I put it to them early in 1971 and Peter Grant immediately agreed to it."

The group were commissioned for the show in March, and it tied in conveniently with a month-long UK tour that took them back to the small clubs they'd been playing around the time of their first BBC live session two years earlier. In that 24 month gap, the group's status had increased dramatically, and in America they'd graduated to selling out 20,000-seater venues. Both their second and third LPs had topped the charts on both sides of the Atlantic. And their fourth album, originally set for spring release but eventually issued in November, was eagerly awaited.

On the 1971 UK tour, they previewed three of the new songs, including 'Stairway To Heaven'. The tour took them back to venues like Mothers in Birmingham and the Marquee, and was seen as a brave move to keep them in touch with their audience. It proved to be the last chance UK fans would have to see the band at such close proximity.

For Zeppelin to return to *In Concert* was seen as a major coup at the time. But the recording was not without problems. Jeff Griffinn had originally signed them for a Thursday March 25 date at the BBC's Paris Cinema - an old wartime theatre with a capacity of under 400 and a stage that stood barely a foot off the ground. In fact, the concert has often been chronicled as taking place on that date.

The official BBC log tells a different story. Just prior to the concert, Peter Grant had warned Jeff that they might be unable to make the date due to Robert Plant losing his voice. A show at Liverpool University had already been cancelled and it was only with the aid of much medication that the singer had fulfilled the prestigious date at the Marquee on March 23. Come the day of the intended broadcast, Grant had to inform the *In Concert* team that they would have to cancel. Griffin hastily arranged for Brinsley Schwarz and the Keef Hartley Band to step in on the night, with the promise that the audience would qualify for the rearranged Zeppelin date on April 1. "And I was the luckless person who had to go out and tell the first week's audience that the band wouldn't

be appearing!" says Griffin. "When Peter rang and told us the bad news, I asked if they could possibly rearrange the date, and I was quite staggered when they agreed to do it again so soon - in fact, so many people wanted to attend the next week, I'm sure we broke every fire regulation going to cram them all in."

The hour-long presentation was duly aired three days later, and repeated (as was the custom) as part of the next Wednesday's *Sounds Of The 70s* 7-8pm slot.

This *In Concert* appearance has gone on to be one of the most bootlegged BBC sessions in history. It has appeared on countless pressings over the years - though significantly none of them have emerged in the original format in which it was aired.

There are two reasons for this. One is that the BBC tapes of the show were quickly adapted to appear as an official BBC transcription disc. These were used by the Beeb to export particular programmes to radio stations worldwide who subscribed to their transcription service. The recordings were mixed down from the original source at the BBC's Transcription Studios at Kensington House, Shepherds Bush. In fact. Jimmy Page himself oversaw the mixing of the April broadcast a month after the broadcast, on May 11. The 12" disc carried a different line-up to the aired show, with the unbroadcast encore 'Communication Breakdown' replacing 'Immigrant Song' and a voice-over proclaiming, "And now live from London, the BBC presents Led Zeppelin in concert" at the beginning.

It was this disc, with a line-up of 'Communication Breakdown', 'Dazed And Confused', 'Going To California', 'Stairway To Heaven', 'What Is And What Should Never Be' and an edited 'Whole Lotta Love' medley (spliced to finish at the end of their cover of 'A Mess Of Blues') that was later dubbed to produce the Trade Mark Of Quality bootleg *BBC Broadcast* (TMQ 71070). A later transcription pressing used for the BBC's *Rock Hour* export series in the early Eighties consisted of yet another sequence from the show, featuring 'Immigrant Song', 'Heartbreaker', 'Dazed And Confused', 'Stairway To Heaven', 'Going To California' and 'Whole Lotta Love medley'.

The second source for the bootleg packages were the original BBC tapes that presented the full version of the concert. The BBC's one hour show had been edited from a lengthier performance that omitted five additional numbers: 'Heartbreaker', 'Black Dog', 'Since I've Been Loving You', 'Thank You' and 'Communication Breakdown'. Bootlegs such as *Ballcrusher* on the Kornyfone (TAKRL 910) label plundered these tapes for the material, although it was the coming of the bootleg CD age that gave rise to the eventual appearance of an almost complete tape, as featured on the 2-CD set *Thank You (It's Complete)* (Discurious DIS 209).

The fact that Jimmy Page himself spent time mixing the tapes reaffirms the importance he placed on the concert, which captured the group at a significant stage in their career. This was the period when they introduced to their live set the more acoustically based numbers that had flowered fully on *Led Zeppelin III*. The BBC recording also offered the first-ever airing of 'Stairway To Heaven' on radio. Nobody present that evening - least of all the group themselves - could have predicted that the song would go on to log an estimated three million plays on US radio alone over the course of the next thirty years!

TRACKS RECORDED
'Immigrant Song' (3.20)/ 'Heartbreaker' (4.50)/ 'Since I've Been Loving you' (6.32)/ 'Black Dog' (4.51)/ 'Dazed And Confused' (17.20)/ 'Stairway To Heaven' (8.40)/ 'Going To California' (3.50)/ 'That's The Way' (5.25)/ 'What Is And What Should Never Be' (4.15)/ 'Whole Lotta Love' - medley including 'Let That Boy Boogie', 'That's Alright Mama', 'For What It's Worth', 'A Mess Of Blues', 'Honey Bee' and 'Lemon Song' (18.10). Encores: 'Thank You' (6.20)/ 'Communication Breakdown' (5.35)

....

ACTUAL BROADCAST
John Peel introduction/ 'Immigrant Song'/ 'Dazed And Confused'/ 'Stairway To Heaven'/ 'Going To California'/ 'That's The Way'/ 'What Is And What Should Never Be'/ John Peel introduction/ 'Whole Lotta Love' medley

"First of all I'd like to say sorry about last week. But we did 18 dates in about 6 days, or at least 20 days, and my voice just gave up

ACOUSTIC SET, LA FORUM: SEPTEMBER 4, 1970

completely. We hope it's all in condition tonight. If not, cheer, because you're on the radio." That was the introduction (later edited out) Robert Plant made to the audience explaining their nonappearance the previous week. Then Jimmy Page signalled the intro to 'Immigrant Song', with its twisting, extended guitar solo. That dovetailed into 'Heartbreaker', as was the band's custom in 1971. Like the next two tracks, 'Since I've Been Loving You' and the premiere of 'Black Dog' (arranged to feature the intro from the *LZIII* track 'Out On The Tiles'), that song was subsequently left on the cutting-room floor.

Their deletion provided the opportunity for a full airing of an 18-minute 'Dazed And Confused', with all the improvised trappings of Page's violin-bow section. A slight delay to adjust Jonesy's organ bass pedals preceded the first live radio performance of 'Stairway To Heaven', played with slight hesitancy - Page was still getting to grips with his new twin-necked Gibson, purchased specially for this number. With hindsight knowledge of how important the song would soon become, it's great now to hear it performed in such a delicate manner.

"This is the time where we like to have a cup of tea, so I think we'd better sit down instead," said Plant as introduction to the acoustic set. The BBC soundtrack was able to capture the full effect of the rush of acoustic guitars and mandolin-playing that dominated the then-unissued 'Going To California' and 'That's The Way' - the latter featuring Plant crashing the tambourine to the floor at the song's close.

A false start to 'What Is And What Should Never Be' was understandably edited from the broadcast - Plant opened the song and complained the band were in the wrong key. "Completely finished," he laughed to the crowd. "I can see the headline in Mailbag" - a reference to the lively letters column in *Melody Maker* at the time.

After they got the song right, it was time for the closing number of the broadcast. John Peel was brought back on mic for the introduction: "I'm going to sing on the next one," he joked with Plant, who also made reference to the Ray Stevens' hit of the time, 'Bridget The Midget', aping its "Do you feel alright?" catchphrase .

A full 'Whole Lotta Love' medley was delivered with the appropriate gusto, allowing the band (as usual) to indulge in all manner of rock'n'roll fun as they swung through a mixture of cover versions.

"That's all we've got time for this week, folks - next week, Ted Ray!" was Plant's humorous parting shot as induded in the original broadcast. The full tape reveals that this was actually edited in

from the very closing stages of the full concert, where they had been called back for encores of 'Thank You' and 'Communication Breakdown'.

And that concluded the BBC's 1971 presentation of Led Zeppelin. The full two-track tapes were hurriedly mixed down for the one-hour broadcast three days later, and then Page worked on the Transcription Service disc a month after that. Jeff Griffin adds: "I also remember Robert and Jimmy coming into the studio the day after the recording to supervise the editing down to one hour. It was at their suggestion that we edited slight pieces of songs, such as the medley, to tailor the set for the *In Concert* slot."

Eight years after the 1971 show, tentative steps were rumoured to have been made for Radio One to try and arrange an exclusive airing of the Zeppelin comeback show on August 4, 1979 at Knebworth. These plans eventually came to nothing, and the group's untimely demise a year later dictated that they would never again grace the national airwaves. The original Led Zeppelin at the Beeb recordings are now a precious part of the BBC archive.

I'll leave the last word to the original *In Concert* producer, Jeff Griffin: "It really was a joy to work with Led Zeppelin. Not only were they one of the most exciting live acts we ever recorded, it was their enthusiasm to do the pilot *In Concert* recording that really sent that brand of live radio on its way. When they agreed to come back for the 1971 show, I was just amazed, because their mistrust of the media was very apparent. They never felt comfortable with doing TV or talking to the press, but they seemed very at home with the BBC and we were privileged to play host to them. They were truly great sessions."

With thanks Kevin Howlett, Jeff Griffin and 'In Session Tonight' author Ken Garner for additional research and interview material.

First of all I'd like to say

sorry about last week.

But we did 18 dates in about

6 days, or at least 20 days,

and my voice just gave up

completely. We hope it's

all in condition tonight.

If not, cheer, because

you're on the radio.

ROBERT PLANT

EARLY 1969 AMERICAN PHOTO SHOOT

Bootlegs and Led Zeppelin have been synonymous for over three decades. Despite manager Peter Grant's heavy-handedness when dealing with those he caught taping their shows, the band are the most bootlegged act of all time, outstripping even The Beatles, Dylan, Springsteen and the Stones. Their final seven shows in the UK alone (five at Earl's Court and two at Knebworth) account for over 100 different releases between them. Just about every known amateur recording of the band's live gigs has made it on to CD. Given the length of their stage shows, the CD format, with its 80-minute playing time, is tailor made for presenting Zeppelin in concert, but even before the flood of digital compact format titles that emerged in the early Nineties there was no shortage of vinyl Led Zeppelin bootlegs.

Tight But Loose has carried reports on Zeppelin bootlegs since its inception. As far back as the hand written first edition I was enthusiastically reviewing the then recently issued vinyl bootleg *Ballcrusher* which documented their BBC *In Concert* show. Issue number two carried an extensive report on what was already a legendary bootleg album, *Led Zeppelin Live On Blueberry Hill*. In 1995 I returned to that 1970 recording to laud its 25th anniversary for *TBL 11*.

Whatever the legal niceties of such releases, searching out their bootleg recordings is a necessity of every serious Zep fan. Their studio albums only hinted at the creativity the group were capable of. It was on stage in live action that Zeppelin really excelled.

During the Seventies ample proof of that fact arrived with each new bootleg record, none more so than the remarkable recordings made at the Los Angles Forum from the audience on the night of September 4, 1970, during Led Zeppelin's sixth American tour. This chapter reflects on the lasting impact of that memorable bootleg recording and rounds up twelve other illicit evenings with Led Zeppelin.

REFERENCE: **TIGHT BUT LOOSE 2 & 11**

2 : LIVE ON BLUEBERRY HILL

The pioneering bootleg album, still a thrill

Led Zeppelin's impact on their initial American tours made them a prime target for the emerging bootleg recording business. The bands' skill at extending and improvising on their studio record repertoire elevated their live shows to something very different from playing their albums.

During their first 18 months on the road they cleverly interwove the basic recorded material from the first two albums with additional impromptu jams. Early examples of this included the long jam on Garnet Mimms 'As Long As I Have You', employed on many of their 1969 shows, the medley of numbers to be found within 'How Many More Times' and an improvised jam session in the middle of 'Communication Breakdown'. Then there was 'Dazed And Confused', Page's late Yardbird remnant that by 1970 was developing into a marathon 20-minute opus with differing sections, including the violin bow episode and a call and response battle between Page and Plant.

'Whole Lotta Love', the *Zep II* opener, soon became another forum for exploration, usually a platform to playfully improvise a selection of Fifties rock'n'roll classics. During 1970 they also began previewing songs from the yet to be released third album – initially an embryonic 'Since I've Been Loving You' and then, in a

bold move, the acoustic 'That's The Way', a performance that helped break the myth that Zep relied entirely on Marshall amplifiers.

Two separate teams of fans were intent on recording the Zeppelin gig at the Inglewood Forum in Los Angeles on the night of September 4, 1970, but it's unlikely they knew what Zeppelin had in store that night. Both came away with lengthy representations of the band's current state of play, recorded on reel-to-reel recorders close to the stage.

The recording that would become known as the album *Led Zeppelin Live On Blueberry Hill* was captured by a pair of West Coast bootleggers whose previous credits included Dylan's *Great White Wonder* set and The Rolling Stones' *LiveR Than You'll Ever Be*. The latter had been recorded on a Uher 4000 reel-to-reel tape recorder with 71/2ips inch reels and a Sennheiser 805 shotgun microphone. They took this set up into the Forum to record in stereo the Zeppelin September 4 performance. Unbeknown to them, a separate bootlegger known as Rubber Dubber also recorded the show and quickly issued it as a double bootleg album stamped *Led Zeppelin Live Los Angeles Forum 9-4-70*.

The more common Blimp label version (later to appear on the high profile bootleg label Trade Mark Of Quality) with a distinctive surreal cover insert also came out within weeks of the LA show. It's worth noting, however, that it was not the first Led Zeppelin bootleg to be released. That distinction fell to a vinyl album known as PB (the title derived from the chemical symbol for lead). This came packaged in a brown sleeve with the words *P.B. Live* on side one and *Recorded Live - Pure Blues* on side two, and was pressed in limited quantities around the Seattle area.

Pure Blues subsequently reached a wider market when it was picked up by the Trade Mark Of Quality label and pressed as *Mudslide*. The actual source was a soundboard recording from Zeppelin's opening night of their fifth US tour on March 21, 1970, at the Pacific Coliseum Vancouver. The 40-minute tape was notable for capturing a rare version of 'We're Gonna Groove', the Ben E King/James Beatha cover which the band used as a set opener during their early 1970 appearances. They also recorded a studio version the previous summer for possible inclusion on *Led Zeppelin II* which would eventually surface on the posthumous *Coda* album.

The UK music press of the time chronicled the constant stream of bootleg titles from the likes of Bob Dylan, The Beatles and The Rolling Stones that were being imported into the country. When reports of Zeppelin titles came to the attention of Peter Grant he was predictably angry.

In one of the few naive statements of his career, Grant was quoted in the *Melody Maker* as saying: "As far as I know there can be no Led Zeppelin tapes available. After hearing some time ago that there was going to be an attempt to bootleg some tapes of the band, I flew to America. We've managed to retrieve all the tapes and we know nothing in existence that can be issued."

When Grant heard that copies of *Live On Blueberry Hill* were being sold from a shop in Chancery Lane in London, Grant and Richard Cole, along with RAK management partner Mickie Most, paid the shop a visit. He questioned the proprietor on the Zeppelin album and with some not so gentle persuasion made sure he knew that this was one bootleg album it would be best to leave alone. In a separate incident a year later over another case of presumed bootlegging, Grant smashed the equipment being used by a team of anti-pollution scientists set up to measure noise levels at a Zeppelin show in Vancouver.

For all his muscle Grant was ultimately powerless to stop the proliferation of Zeppelin underground records of which *Blueberry Hill* was the forerunner. If you knew where to look, such artefacts were possible to come by. For this particular enchanted Zep obsessed teenager *Blueberry Hill* represented the forbidden fruit and in 1971 I was determined to track it down. Luckily the then relative newcomer to the pop press *Sounds* offered a free service for readers' classified advertisements. I scoured these columns religiously for many weeks and finally struck gold when I spotted an ad that ran along the lines: "Live albums for sale: Stones, Dylan, Zeppelin etc". The list came back and amongst the many Dylan and Beatles titles there it was - *Live On Blueberry Hill*, a dou-

ble album on the TMQ label, catalogue number TMQ 72002, and pressed on coloured vinyl, asking price £6. Back then six quid was a small fortune but it was more than worth it.

About three weeks later the postman dropped an LP size package on the doorstep. I anxiously ripped it open and there in all its glory was the genuine article: "106 minutes and fifty-three seconds of pure and alive rock" as the sleeve insert put it. Was it ever.

THE RUBBER DUBBER BOOTLEG RELEASE

The excitement of playing that double album, on blue and red vinyl, remains an unforgettable musical memory for me. It was a novelty that never wore off. Indeed, the various incarnations I've obtained since - the *Rubber Dubber* vinyl set, the various re-issues, the various bootleg CD packages - all these have only heightened the listening pleasure of that celebrated Los Angeles stop-off during Led Zeppelin's sixth American tour.

The overriding factor of the September 4 recording, regardless of which version you hear, is that it remains one of the greatest audience recordings of the era. The sheer dynamic thrust of Bonzo's drum sound, the sinewy grind of Page's guitar, Jonesy's resonant bass lines and piecing keyboards and the outstanding clarity of Plant's siren shrieks (suitably enhanced by the echo unit employed at the time), all merge into a ferocious mix that magically recreates the electricity of the occasion.

For anyone weaned the original TMQ long players, there's an authenticity in their performances ingrained in the grooves that has rarely been captured so effectively. Alongside the 1975 Madison Square Garden soundboard, the Earl's Court shows and the LA 1977 gigs, there are few finer unofficial examples of the

MADISON SQUARE GARDEN: SEPTEMBER 19, 1970

As far as I know there can be no Led Zeppelin tapes available. After hearing some time ago that there was going to be an attempt to bootleg some tapes of the band, I flew to America. We've managed to retrieve all the tapes and we know nothing in existence that can be issued.

PETER GRANT

JPJ WITH MANDOLIN, BATH FESTIVAL:
JUNE 28, 1970

Goodnight and thank you

for everything.

ROBERT PLANT

Did ya dig it?

ANNOUNCER

complete Led Zeppelin concert experience. The September 4, 1970, concert as captured on the TMQ double set was just choc full of off-the-wall surprises. There was no sign of any set list sterility back then - they just did as they pleased.

Moments to relish include:

The aural assault of 'Immigrant Song' (listed on the insert as 'From The Midnight Sun' as it had yet to be announced under its official title) exploding into 'Heartbreaker'.

The slightly menacing tone of a relatively compact 'Dazed And Confused' with Plant bursting in midway through screaming, "I don't care what people say, rock'n'roll is here to stay"

Page and Bonham linked in glorious tandem for that solo exercise on 'Bring It On Home'.

The electric finale of 'Moby Dick' ("The big B!" exclaims Plant).

The unpredictability of 'Communication Breakdown' as Zep play The Buffalo Springfield and Beatles songbooks and throw in the rarely played live *Zep I* opener 'Good Times Bad Times'.

Freshly minted nuggets from the yet to be heard *Zep III* on record such as 'Since I've Been Loving You' and the rarely played 'Out On the Tiles'.

The tentative introduction of the acoustic material, a stark and sensitive 'That's The Way' and the rare try out of Page's instrumental solo 'Bron Yr Aur', a clear five years before it was officially released.

'Thank You' preceded by the meandering organ solo from John Paul Jones and finishing with a drawn out ending featuring Page's delicate strumming.

'Whole Lotta Love' and the ensuing Zep 50's revival show and finally the breathless rendiditon of Fats Domino's 'Blueberry Hill'.

"Goodnight and thank you for everything," utters a breathless Plant at the close, followed by "Did ya dig it?" by the evening's MC.

Yes we did and still do

The greatest live album of all time? It's certainly up there with the best, official or otherwise. The reason is simple. It captures a group of musicians brimming with confidence. On stage that night in September 1970 Led Zeppelin were truly coming of age.

Live On Blueberry is also something of a yardstick for the bootlegs industry. Back then Zeppelin's recorded output was just the tip of the iceberg. On stage live was where the real action occurred and, indeed, where they really built their reputation. Peter Grant summing it all up when he told me: "Led Zeppelin was primarily an in-person band... that's what it was really about."

Bootleg recordings of the band offered a whole new level of appreciation and *Blueberry Hill* was the watershed for the subsequent flood of live Zep bootlegs that would emerge throughout the next three decades.

The whole bootleg CD market may be well out of control now, beyond any reasonable realm of quality control, but there was a time when bootlegs like *Blueberry Hill* were considered almost as important as the group's official output by fans and chroniclers alike and, if they were honest, probably the group themselves.

Maybe that's the greatest compliment that can be paid to this iconic bootleg recording. It remains as essential a part of their discography as any of their official albums.

More than three decades on *Live On Blueberry Hill* is still an absolute thrill.

TWELVE OTHER GREAT LIVE ZEPPELIN BOOTLEGS

TWINIGHT/FILLMORE WEST 1969
Immigrant

One of their earliest soundboard recordings, this 2-CD set contains material from Zeppelin's April 27, 1969, Fillmore West performance on their second US tour. It was not uncommon early in their career for the band to perform two sets at the same gig and this San Francisco showcase is one such example. It's interesting to hear how they fleshed out their set beyond their one album by attempting covers such as Garnet Mimms 'As Long As I Have You' and Spirit's 'Fresh Garbage'. Page was still influenced by the psychedelic late-Yardbirds era. There's also a laid back delivery of Buddy Guy's 'Sitting And Thinking'. Début album favourites 'Dazed And Confused' (already up to eleven minutes in length)

and 'Babe I'm Gonna Leave You' were already garnering a strong audience response. This April 27 tape has been much bootlegged and can be found on a variety of packages.

PLAYS PURE BLUES
Whoppy Cat

A superb soundbard recording of Zep's hour-long set recorded on August 31, 1969, at the Texas International Pop Festival. A ferocious display that demonstrates the exuberance with which Zeppelin won over their American audiences on those early tours. Kicking off with a short punchy run through the old Yardbirds/ Johnny Burnette stomper 'Train Kept A Rollin'', the set becomes a showcase for the *Zep I* album as they find their stride with 'I Can't Quite You Baby' and wonderful extended wades through 'Dazed And Confused' and 'You Shook Me', through to a glorious 'How Many More Times' and a breakneck-paced 'Communication Breakdown'. This is prime early period Zeppelin captured in absolute full flight.

INTIMIDATOR
Empress Valley

An excellent 3-disc presentation combining soundboard and audience sources drawn from Zeppelin's appearance at the Montreux Casino on March 7, 1970, the beginning of a long Zep association with the Montreux Jazz Festival staged by promoter Claude Knobbs. The set list features 'We're Gonna Groove' during its short lived status as their set opener and an early preview of the *Zep III* classic 'Since I've Been Loving You'. 'Thank You' is also an outstanding performance for the era.

GOING TO CALIFORNIA
Trade Mark Of Quality

Another of the early vinyl bootlegs, this excellent audience recording with clear vibrant sound features most of the performance on September 14, 1971, at the Berkeley Community Theatre in California, though it is sequenced in such a way as to present the feel of a full performance. 'Black Dog' is nothing less than a brutal assault on the senses, while on side three 'Stairway To Heaven', 'That's The Way' and 'Going To California' are expertly delivered, Jones' mandolin being well to the fore in the mix. There's also plenty of engaging Plant between-song patter which adds to the intimacy of the recording. An extended 'Whole Lotta Love' medley features blistering deliveries of 'Hello Mary Lou' and 'Mess Of Blues' and a final bluster through 'You Shook Me'. Simply a great night in California.

A CELLARFUL OF NOISE/LIVE IN JAPAN
Noise Generator

This 1971 live recording from the same era as the above provides evidence of the more relaxed approach Zeppelin adopted for Japanese audiences. Derived from a very close to the stage audience tape source on September 29, 1971, during the first of two visits to Japan, Plant is in jocular mood throughout, feeding the audience Monty Pythoneseqe comments (completely lost on the Japanese one would imagine) and even throwing in an off-the-cuff rendition of 'Smoke Gets In Your Eyes'. Despite the playfulness there's also plenty of power as they break in the new material from the soon to be released *Zep IV*, introducing 'Black Dog', 'Rock And Roll' and 'Stairway To Heaven'.

This night at the Budokan was also noteworthy for the rare live performance of 'Friends', a number Page and Plant would revive on their return to Japan some 25 years later for the Unledded tour.

LEAD POISONING/LIVE IN VIENNA '73
Cobla

After a short summer break following their 1972 US tour, Zep began a relentless touring schedule that saw them kick off in Japan, then move on through their longest ever UK tour and into Europe. This particular stop off in Vienna was another supercharged performance, demonstrating the intense level of musicianship they had had attained. The set had been radically revamped with 'Rock And Roll' as the new opener. The audience sourced *Lead Poisoning* is

LIVE ON BLUEBERRY HILL, LOS ANGELES FORUM: SEPTEMBER 4, 1970

AWARDS CEREMONY, SAVOY HOTEL,
LONDON: DECEMBER 11, 1969

an accurate representation of their mid-Seventies peak. It includes the now longer than ever 'Dazed And Confused' that made way for excerpts from Scott McKenzie's hippie anthem 'San Francisco (Be Sure To Wear Some Flowers In Your Hair)' and a masterful 'Heartbreaker' complete with a unique Page intro.

BONZO'S BIRTHDAY PARTY
Sanctuary
A 3-disc version of the much bootlegged May 31, 1973, Los Angeles Forum show, this joins various audience sources, notably the original tape used for the Trade Mark Of Quality vinyl bootleg to present the complete performance. Recorded on the night of John Bonham's 26th birthday, the band are naturally in high spirits and this is reflected in an upbeat performance. 'No Quarter' and 'The Ocean' are just two of many highlights.

FLYING CIRCUS
Empress Valley
A complete 1975 performance sourced from a superb soundboard tape, 'Flying Circus' is another essential addition to any Zeppelin collection. The night in question, February 12 1975, at Madison Square Garden proved to be one of the first blockbusting 1975 shows. Plant contacting a bout of flu and Page injuring his finger hampered the early part of this crucial comeback, but by early February they were back to near full strength and their relief at finally firing on all cylinders again manifested itself into a series of devastating shows. This is one of them. The clarity of sound vividly enhances Plant's breathy "Oh my Jesus" refrain on 'In My Time Of Dying', Jonesy's clavinet work on 'Trampled Underfoot' and Page's guitar tour-de-force on 'Dazed And Confused'. Plant gets a little hoarse towards the close but Page more than carries proceedings throughout. Plant's tongue in cheek sign off "Ladies and gentlemen of New York you are too much... and we ain't so bad ourselves" is a masterpiece of understatement.

THE ZEPPELIN EXPRESS/PHYSICAL ROCKET
Empress Valley
Perhaps the best representation of the many Earl's Court recordings. An almost complete soundboard quality recording of their final night (the end of 'No Quarter' and parts of the acoustic set comprise audience recordings), the clarity of sound illustrates how relaxed they were on this final show of 1975. Free from the pressures of the opening gigs, and content in the knowledge that their public acclaim at home was at a new height, they could just lay back and enjoy themselves.

Often seemingly oblivious to the 17,000 present they delivered an outstanding performance. The final encores showcase 'Heartbreaker' and 'Communication Breakdown' - the former siz-

zling with Page virtuosity, the latter with an ad-libbed reggae interlude - are the final evidence of a band at the very top of their game.

THE DESTROYER
Cobla Standard
Originally a much sought after vinyl box set, this April 27 1977 near complete Cleveland show has appeared on various CD sets. Performance-wise, it may lack the sparkle of the later LA Forum run but the sound quality is exceptional - taken from a well mixed soundboard tape oozing with live atmosphere. John Paul Jones' use of the thundering Alembic bass guitar is well in evidence and his meandering solo on 'No Quarter' is a joy. Overall this is a crystal clear portrayal of the band's attempt to regain their crown. Sometimes disjointed and sloppy but overall the sheer juggernaut power of '77 Zeppelin blazes though.

LISTEN TO THIS EDDIE
Silver Rarities
Taken from the legendary run of shows at the Los Angeles Forum in June 1977, this is one of the most authentic audience recordings of all time. The opening segment as the crowd scream and shout as they walk on stage and begin tuning up is a remarkable illustration of the mayhem and pure excitement they generated on this tour. From the opening bars of 'The Song Remains The Same' to the final breathless "LA goodnight!" from Plant after a rampant 'Whole Lotta Love'/'Rock And Roll', this set captures the power of the band better than almost any other live recording. Page gave his own nod of approval to this recording by employing 'Song Remains' on the *DVD*. As for the title, some say it refers to recording engineer Eddie Kramer, others claim it's a reference to Eighties guitar hero Eddie Van Halen.

THE FINAL TOUR/EUROPEAN DAZE 1980
Patriot
Zeppelin's final tour is well served on bootleg with a number of soundboard tapes circulating, and this double set captures the majority of their June 29, 1980, appearance at the Hallenstadion, Zurich. This recording holds the distinction of being the first Zep CD bootleg, appearing in the late Eighties as *Tour Over Europe* on the Twin Eagle label. This version captures their valiant efforts to cut the operation down with fine performances of 'Achilles Last Stand' and the new 'All My Love'. Left off is a rather shambolic 'Kashmir' after which Plant told the crowd, "If anybody's bootlegging that, you'll have to scratch that number as it wasn't absolutely correct!"

As a bonus, disc two includes the final three numbers from their historic final date in Berlin on July 7, 1980: 'Stairway To Heaven', 'Rock And Roll' and an unusually lengthy 'Whole Lotta Love'.

Ladies and gentlemen

of New York you are

too much...

and we ain't

so bad ourselves

ROBERT PLANT

Of all their records, Led Zeppelin's fourth album, released in late 1971, remains their most admired work, and with sales of 23 million and counting it is also far and away their most successful. Featuring both the much maligned 'Stairway To Heaven' and the widely admired 'When The Levee Breaks', the set is without question the most accessible of their catalogue and it continues to attract new listeners by the week. Few albums in the history of rock can rival its influence.

The fact that much of the album was made in a mysterious, run-down, 18th century workhouse in the middle of rural Hampshire only adds to its legacy. It's the product of a band given absolute musical freedom to do as they wished in an environment that encouraged the development of their ability to blend acoustic and electric influences within a rock framework, which they did more successfully than any other act before or since.

As a complete work it remains their most focused statement. From Page's unimpeachable riffs, through Jones musical invention and Plant's clarity of vocal to that titanic John Bonham drum sound - Led *Zeppelin IV* still emits a freshness that belies its age.

On the occasion of the 30th anniversary of the release of the album, I collated a major *Zep IV* feature for planned inclusion in *TBL 15*. With space at a premium for that issue I decided to use a more compact reappraisal of the album by fellow Zep authority Hugh Jones. The research and background info of my own piece was later used in *Classic Rock's* 100 Greatest Rock Albums feature in December 2001.

The complete text of the making of the fourth Led Zeppelin album originally intended for *TBL 15* is published here for the first time.

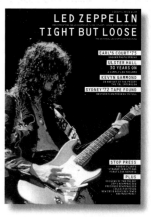

REFERENCE: **TIGHT BUT LOOSE 15**

3 : THE MAKING OF LED ZEP IV

THE ALBUM

On the evening of Saturday, September 19, 1970, the four members of Led Zeppelin took a final bow before leaving the stage of New York's Madison Square Garden. It signalled the end of a massively successful US tour, their two performances at the Garden alone netting each of them around $30,000 - not bad for six hours work. Their second album had been a fixture on the album charts on both sides of the Atlantic, racking up sales of over a million in both territories. The previous June the group's bill topping appearance at the Bath Festival had cemented their reputation on home soil. Readers of the then hugely influential *Melody Maker* had just voted them as the top act in their annual pop poll, ending years of dominance by The Beatles.

There was simply no doubt about it. Led Zeppelin were now the biggest band in the world.

Then came the backlash...

In early October their eagerly awaited new album, *Led Zeppelin III*, hit the stores. Its bold agenda in combining the familiar, trademark heavy rock dynamics with more acoustic textures confused both the public and press alike. Headlines such as "I... 2... 3 Zep weaken" were rife as this new direction confused and, to some degree disappointed, critics.

Though *Zep III* sold well initially it did not to have the across-the-board appeal of their first two albums. Never entirely at ease with the press, Page and Plant were particularly sensitive to the criticism. "The headlines are saying Zep go soft on their fans or some crap," remarked Plant to *Record Mirror* at the time. "The point is when you begin a new album you never know how it's going to come out."

For Page the third Zeppelin album signalled the beginning of a new era. "There is another side to us. This album is totally different to the others and I see this as a new direction."

Plant again: "Now we've done *Zeppelin III* the sky's the limit. It shows we can change, we can do things. It means there are endless possibilities. We are not stale and this proves it."

Brave fighting talk - but quite how their following would react long term to this new direction was at the time still in question. After the initial glow of success they were at something of a crossroads, making their next album crucial. Page later reflected: "With *Zep III* we thought we'd made a great album - in fact we knew we had. At the time, though, it was said we had started playing acoustic instruments because Crosby, Stills & Nash had just come through and we were ripping them off. I know the record company expected us to follow up 'Whole Lotta Love'. But we never made a point of trying to emulate something we had done before."

Sensibly they took their time in recording the crucial fourth album. To recharge their batteries manager Peter Grant refused all offers to tour over the coming months. This included turning down flat a cool one million dollars to appear on a New Year's Eve concert to be relayed across the world via satellite. Years later Peter Grant noted: "I got approached for the band to perform a show in Germany on New Years Eve 1970 that would be relayed to American cinemas. The offer got up to a million dollars but I found out that satellite sound can be affected by snowstorms so I said no. The promoters couldn't believe it, but it just wasn't right for us."

Aside from a day out in October to accept a clutch of gold discs from a Parliamentary Secretary for their part in sustaining the country's healthy balance of exports, the group laid low.

In late October Page and Plant returned to the idyllic cottage half way up a mountain in South Snowdonia known as Bron Yr Aur. It was here that earlier in the year they had conceived many

THE ZEP IV FACT FILE

Led Zeppelin VI climbed to the number one spot on the UK chart on Dec 4, 1971, where it stayed for two weeks before being dislodged by *Electric Warrior* by T Rex... it went on to spend 61 consecutive weeks on the chart... if you have an original UK copy of the album, it will be on the plum and orange Atlantic label catalogue number 2401012 - later copies were repressed on

Atlantic K50008... in America it stalled at number two, being held off the top spot by Carole King's *Tapestry*... two singles were issued from the album in the US – 'Black Dog' reached number 15 on the *Billboard* chart while 'Rock And Roll' fared less well, peaking at 47... 'Stairway To Heaven' was distributed as a promo single to gain radio play - this version is now highly collectable... other notable 'Stairway'

collectables include the 1990 UK promo single issued to support the *Remasters* box set - plus a special 20th Anniversary CD and single pack issued in the US in early 1992... *Zep IV* collectables include a limited edition lilac-coloured vinyl pressing issued in the UK in 1978 (now worth £40)... and a limited edition box set package distributed by the HMV chain a decade later (now worth £50)... those with deeper pockets

might be interested in the mega rare Canadian *Zep IV* multi-coloured vinyl pressing, last up for auction at a cool $2,500... you might also want to check your own copy of *Zep IV* to see if it's one of a handful of UK mispressings issued in error on the Asylum label as opposed to Atlantic - these rarities have changed hands for up to £200... cover versions of *Zep IV* tracks abound - three can be found on the official Zep tribute

album *Encomium*, namely 'Misty Mountain Hop' by The Four Non Blondes, 'Four Sticks' by Henry Rollins and 'Going To California' by Never The Bride... others include a big band rock version of 'Black Dog' by CCS and 'When The Levee Breaks' by Rosetta Stone... though you might be well advised to avoid the version of 'Rock And Roll' issued as a charity single by The Full Metal Racket including John McEnroe...

of the songs for *Zep III*. This return visit again found them ensconced around the open fire with acoustic guitars in hand preparing material for the next record.

They already had a backlog of completed and work-in-progress ideas, amongst them a lilting, Neil Young-influenced piece titled 'Down By The Seaside', 'Hey Hey What Can I Do', a semi-acoustic country stomp and, in the same vein, a song called 'Poor Tom'. 'The Rover', then an acoustic idea with idealistic lyrics, was another song waiting to be honed. John Paul Jones had been working on a brooding keyboard piece that would later emerge as 'No Quarter', while Page had began demoing a lengthy instrumental track which started off tranquil but built to a crescendo. We all know how that idea flourished.

Initially they considered a double album, and Page even toyed with the bizarre idea of issuing the album as four separate EPs. After the *Zep III* backlash they were immensely keen to lay down some fresh new material.

In December they booked initial studio sessions at Island Studios. The Basing Street location was fast becoming the most in-demand studio in London and they had recorded much of *Zeppelin III* there the previous May. Page, though, was also looking to record on location with The Rolling Stones' newly built mobile recording unit. "We started off doing some tracks at Island then we went to Headley Grange, a place we had rehearsed at. We took the Stones' mobile. It was ideal As soon as we had an idea we put it down on tape."

Headley Grange, a largely derelict 18th century manor house, was situated in deepest Hampshire. A three-storey stone structure built in 1795, it was once a workhouse known as Headley Poor for

HEADLEY GRANGE 30 YEARS ON

the aged and infirm, and in 1870 it was bought by builder Thomas Kemp who converted it to a private residence and renamed it Headley Grange.

In the wake of the 'getting it together in the country' trend that acts such as Traffic had pioneered in the late Sixties, the place began to be used as a rehearsal venue for the likes of Fleetwood Mac and Genesis. It was Fleetwood Mac who suggested the premises to Page.

Plant reflected: "Most of the mood for the fourth album was brought about in settings we had not been used to. We were living in this falling down mansion in the country. The mood was incredible."

So on a cold January morning early in 1971, accompanied by a

handful of roadies plus engineer Andy Johns (brother of noted producer Glyn Jones who had worked on the first Zeppelin album), Page, Plant, Jones and Bonham convened on the old work-house to set up and record material for their fourth album. Parked outside was the Stones' mobile studio looking not unlike some vintage army intelligence unit.

Engineer Andy Johns recalled the idea behind going there in an interview with *Guitar World*: "I had just done *Sticky Fingers* with the Stones and we'd used the mobile truck on that. So I believe I suggested using the truck to Jimmy. We had used Mick's house at Stargroves but Jimmy didn't want to stay there because Mick wanted too much money. Then Jimmy found this old mansion so we brought the truck there." They did eventually record at Stargroves the following year for the *Houses Of The Holy* album.

John Paul Jones has less positive memories of their stay at the Grange. "It was cold and damp. I remember we all ran in when we arrived in a mad scramble to get the driest rooms. There was no pool table or pub. It was so dull but that really focused your mind on getting the work done."

On hand to monitor the recordings was Ian Stewart. Stu, as he was affectionately known, was a long time backroom associate of The Rolling Stones - and had even been in an early line up of the group prior to Andrew Oldham grooming the younger band members for success. Stu was an accomplished jazz and blues pianist, and his battered old upright piano was packed alongside the Zep gear in preparation for the likelihood of a jam session or two. The relaxed nature of the whole set up deemed this inevitable.

Early on during the warm up sessions, John Bonham began banging out the cymbal led introduction to Little Richard's 'Keep A Knockin". Ian Stewart joined in the fun, adding a Jerry Lee Lewis barrelhouse piano backdrop. Jones and Page picked up the mantle, adding Scotty Moore-like guitar runs from the golden era of Sun Records. Plant soon cut in with a vocal line, but instead of tripping effortlessly into one of the many rock'n'roll standards that they performed live on stage he screamed out nondescript lyrics built around a chorus of "It's been a long time since I rock-'n'rolled". Within minutes they knew they had something, as Page remembers: "We were doing something else at the time but Bonzo played the beginning of a Little Richard track. We had the tape running and I started doing that part of the riff. It ground to a halt after 12 bars but we knew we had something - Robert came in with the lyrics and within 15 minutes it was virtually complete."

The jam session nature of the song's construction resulted in it being credited as a four man group composition, and when they played the track during their live act during European and US dates later that year, Plant introduced it under the title 'It's Been A Long Time'. When it came to deciding the final track line-up for the album they agreed this three minute and 40 seconds of stomping rock'n'roll should be titled just that. So it became universally known as 'Rock And Roll' and it would go on to be a staple Zep stage fave, taking its rightful place as an appropriate set opener from late 1972 through to 1975.

Ian Stewart was also on hand to add his influence to another jam deemed worthy of recording. This was built around the unusual ploy of making the mandolin the lead instrument over another Fifties groove, and was clearly based on Richie Valens' 'Ooh My Head', later to feature in the *La Bamba* movie. Cornball rockabilly lyrics like "I don't wanna tutti frutti, no lollipop, come on baby just rock, rock, rock" were merged with Stu's incessant barrelhouse playing, over which Page and Bonham dubbed a curious rhythmic slapping sound. Nothing more than a playful jam, they dubbed it 'Boogie With Stu' in tribute to the Stones man.

With one superior rock'n'roll jam already perfectly executed, this one was left on the cutting room floor. Three years later Page salvaged it for inclusion on the double set *Physical Graffiti* and offered a composing credit to Valens' widow. "It was obvious a variation on 'Ooh My Head' by the late Ritchie Valens which itself was a variation of Little Richard's 'Ooh My Soul'. What we tried to do was credit Ritchie's mother because we heard she never received any royalties from any of her son's hits, So what happens is they try to sue us for all of the song. We had to say bugger off to that one!"

BRON-YR-AUR

We had used Mick's house at Stargroves but Jimmy didn't want to stay there because Mick wanted too much money. Then Jimmy found this old mansion so we brought the truck there.

ANDY JOHNS, ENGINEER

as for 'Stairway', aside from the 22 artists who contributed spoof versions of the song on the Australian compilation album *Stairways To Heaven*, other bona fide covers include the Steve Harley produced version on Patricia Paay's 1975 *Beam Of Light* and Dolly Parton's hymn-like treatment of the song in 2002... the Al Stewart track 'Life And Life Only' from his *Love Chronicles* album, which features Page on guitar, is notable for having a similar chord structure to 'Stairway'... while Pearl Jam's 'Given To Fly' has an uncanny resemblance to 'Going To California'... finally perhaps the ultimate 'Stairway'/Zep tribute belongs to Gordon Roy of Lanarkshire who recently had the entire lyrics in the style of the *Zep IV* inner sleeve tattooed on his back in tribute to his late friend, as they both loved the track so much.

SANDY DENNY, LEFT, WITH JULIE FELIX:
EARLY 1970'S

So while I sang the events in

the song, Sandy answered

back as if she was the pulse of

the people on the battlements.

Sandy was playing the town

crier urging people to throw

down their weapons.

ROBERT PLANT

The mandolin was very much a feature of the *Zep IV* recording sessions. JP Jones had initially acquired it for some of the *Zep III* numbers, notably 'That's The Way'. One night in Headley Grange, Page began picking his way around that same mandolin and so began the genesis of another track.

"I picked up the mandolin, well actually it was Jonesy's mandolin and these chords just came out. It was my first experiment with mandolin. I suppose mandolin players would laugh because it must be the standard thing to play those chords but possibly not with that approach. It did sound a little like a 'let's dance around the maypole number' but it wasn't purposely like that."

Plant had written one new track, 'The Battle Of Evermore', after reading a book on the Scottish wars. He felt the track needed another vocalist to act as a foil, so they called in ex-Fairport Convention singer Sandy Denny to provide a rare cameo.

"It's really more of a playlet than a song," said Plant. "After I wrote the lyrics I realised I needed another completely different voice as well to give the song full impact. So I asked Sandy Denny to come along and sing on the track. So while I sang the events in the song, Sandy answered back as if she was the pulse of the people on the battlements. Sandy was playing the town crier urging people to throw down their weapons."

Zep and Fairport had long since enjoyed a rapport, Fairport bassist Dave Pegg hailing from the same Black Country area and being a lifelong friend of Plant and Bonham. Zep had jammed with Fairport at the Troubadour in LA on their last US tour and all the group had partied with Sandy at the *Melody Maker* poll awards in London the previous September. A month later Page

KB HALLEN, COPENHAEGEN: MAY 3, 1971

and Plant went to see Sandy's new group Fotheringay supporting Elton John at the Albert Hall. At Headley Grange Plant sang a guide vocal, leaving out the response lines for Denny to insert. Plant also claims to have played guitar on the track. The end result was an engaging folk lament and another cornerstone of the completed album.

At the time Sandy noted Plant's own prowess on the session. "We started out soft but I was hoarse by the end trying to keep up with him," she said.

Her vocal part was taken on by John Paul Jones when Zep finally performed the song live on their 1977 US tour. For their *Unledded* MTV reunion Page and Plant brought in Indian vocalist Najma Akhtar to perform with them on the track.

The acoustic guitars and mandolins were also prevalent on 'Going To California', which was very much in the style of 'That's The Way' from the previous album, and despite its title it was another number written at the Snowdonia cottage. The song included references to a Californian earthquake, though its main influence was Joni Mitchell. Both Page and Plant had long since admired her work - in fact California was the title of one of the tracks on her *Blue* album. Page commented, "Joni is able to look at something that's happened to her, draw back, crystallise it and then write about it."

In live versions of the song Plant would often throw in subtle Joni references like the night at Earl's Court in 1975 when he sung the line, "They say she plays guitar and cries and sings," adding "in parking lots...". Lyrically the song told of the unending search for the ultimate lady. "It's hard," Plant would sing on stage- "Infinitely hard...".

Another of Plant's heroes, Neil Young, provided the inspiration for 'Down By The Seaside', one of the first numbers they worked on at Island in late 1970. Written a few months earlier at at Bron Yr Aur, it mirrored Young's laid-back vocal on songs like 'Heart Of Gold'. Midway through it all went up a tempo, led by a stinging Page solo before it returning to the original country groove. With so much material at their disposal this was another track that did not fit in the scheme of things at the time, and Page later remixed it for inclusion on *Physical Graffiti*.

During their weeks at Headley Grange the band had little time for the usual boisterous antics. Tour manager Richard Cole, who more often than not took on the responsibility for relieving boredom with fun and games, noted: "There weren't any serious drugs around the band at that point - just dope and a bit of coke. Mostly we had an account at a shop in the village and we'd go down there and collect large quantities of cider. They were playing at being country squires. They found an old shotgun and used to shoot at squirrels in the woods, not that they ever hit any. And there was this lovely old black Labrador dog wandering around which we used to feed."

The dog in question would eventually provide the simple title of another Headley Grange creation, as Jones recalls: "There was an old black dog around the Grange that went off to do what dogs did and came back and slept. It was quite a powerful image at the time so we called one track 'Black Dog'."

'Black Dog', largely the product of a bass riff brought in by John Paul, was a classic monster riff exercise in the grand Zep tradition that was destined to dispel all the 'Zep go soft' claims when it blared out as the opening track of the album. "It's definitely one of my favourite riffs," he says. "It was originally all in 3/16 time but no one could keep up with that!"

Plant's acapella vocal between the riffs was an arrangement Page had picked up from Fleetwood Mac's 'Oh Well'. The almost impossible to copy rhythmic swing (a combination of 4/4 time set against 5/4) of the 'Black Dog' riff was a key indication of how far ahead of the game Zeppelin really were. Band such as Grand Funk Railroad were already being touted as the logical successor to Zep's heavyweight crown. Their monolithic riffing was completely devoid of the grace and timing compared to the likes of 'Black Dog' - a fact that would become most evident upon the album's release. Page's fade out solo was a cleverly overdubbed and triple tracked guitar pieced together by four different solos.

"The effect on those guitars was something I'd learned from Bill Hawelson," remembers Johns. "He worked with Buffalo Springfield. I plugged Jimmy's Les Paul into a direct box and from there in a mic channel."

Page again: "We used the mic-amp of the mixing board to get distortion. Then we ran it through two Urie 1176 Universal compressors." When Page was reviewing the tapes for the *Remasters* box set he recalled that the guitars almost sound like an analogue synthesiser.

The thorny and eternally topical question of legalising marijuana was the subject under discussion in 'Misty Mountain Hop'. A chunky rocker revolving around a pleasing JPJ electric piano riff, suitably enhanced by Page strident chords and Bonham's precise drumming, it's worth noting at this point the quite exemplary

ELECTRIC MAGIC, EMPIRE POOL WEMBLEY: NOVEMBER 20, 1971

We did this (Four Sticks) at Island studios. It was a bastard to mix. When I originally recorded the basic tracks I compressed the drums, then when I went to mix it I couldn't make it work. I did five or six mixes.
ANDY JOHNS, ENGINEER

MELODY MAKER AWARDS, SAVOY HOTEL, LONDON: SEPTEMBER 16, 1970

I remember sitting there thinking it sounded utterly amazing so I ran out of the truck and said, 'Bonzo you gotta come in and hear this!' He shouted, 'Whoa that's it. That's what I've been hearing!'

ANDY JOHNS, ENGINEER

percussive contribution Bonzo made to these sessions. His work on every track was superbly applied - check out the subtle dropping off the beat at four minutes 17 on this track's fade. Plant's semi-rapped vocal style here might be described as the first rock rap, predating the nu-metal movement by two decades. In doing so he exposed the problems of a certain Black Country hippy taking a walk in the park with the police looking over his shoulder.

John Paul Jones led the construction of this song. "I got up before everyone else one morning and I was sitting playing around on the electric piano. When the others got up I played them what I'd done and it went from there."

Where Zep were really beginning to score was in their ability to balance the controversial acoustic element within their more familiar electric dynamics. Another prime example of this was 'Four Sticks'. Led by a brilliantly incessant Page riff and powered by Bonham's literal use of four drumsticks - hence the title - it meandered off into a spiralling acoustic section ("When the owls cry in the night")underscored by JPJ's then pioneering use of a VCR synthesiser, and all mixed by Page to achieve maximum stereo split. "We tried different ways of approaching it. The idea was to get an abstract feeling. We tried it a few times and it didn't come off until the day Bonzo had a Double Diamond beer, picked up two sets of sticks and went for it. It was magic."

"We did this at Island studios. It was a bastard to mix," says Andy Johns. "When I originally recorded the basic tracks I compressed the drums, then when I went to mix it I couldn't make it work. I did five or six mixes." It was also reported at the time that the master tape of this track was at one point lost. Following the album's release 'Four Sticks' was re-recorded in March 1972 when Page and Plant conducted an experimental recording session in Bombay with the local symphony orchestra, the results of which remain officially unreleased.

Since their very inception Page and co had frequently plundered their blues influences to come up with new renderings of old blues tunes. To their regret and ultimate cost, they often failed to credit the source involved - most famously on 'Whole Lotta Love' which resulted in a lawsuit being brought against them by Willie Dixon. For the fourth album sessions, Plant brought in an old Memphis Minnie and Kansas Joe McCoy recording titled 'When The Levee Breaks'.

Sensibly, they did add Memphis Minnie to the eventual credits, though justifiably they also credited themselves in recreating the tune in a radical new arrangement. The end result was simply a blues rock colossus. Page: "I came up with the guitar riff and Robert sang the words which were inspired by Memphis Minnie's arrangement - though if you heard the original you wouldn't recognise the two".

Page remembers 'Levee' being a difficult track to record. "We tried to record that in the studio before we got to Headley Grange and it sounded flat. But once we got the drum sound at Headley Grange it was like boom... and that made the difference immediately. It was very exciting to listen to that drum sound on headphones."

That unique drum sound was created by positioning Bonham's drums in the hallway of the house, known as the Minstrel's Gallery. Engineer Andy Johns:

"The other guys were out having a drink and John Bonham and I were at the house. He still complained that he wasn't getting the sound he wanted. I finally had an idea. We got his drums and put him in the hallway and then hung two MI 60 mikes from the staircase and pointed them towards the kit. His kit was very well balanced internally, each drum's volume was consistent with the others. In the truck I put him into two channels and compressed the drums. Jimmy had this Italian echo unit called a Binson that used a steel drum instead of a tape - it had a real special sound and I used that as well. I remember sitting there thinking it sounded utterly amazing so I ran out of the truck and said, 'Bonzo you gotta come in and hear this!' He shouted, 'Whoa that's it. That's what I've been hearing!'"

Page was equally enthusiastic. "What you're hearing on the record is the sound of the hall with the stereo mike on the stairs second flight up. There was a lot of different effects in there. Phased vocal and a backwards echoed harmonica solo. I'd used backwards echo as far back as The Yardbirds' days." (The effect can be heard on The Yardbirds' track 'Ten Little Indians' from their *Little Games* album.)

That drum sound remains today the most sampled beat of all time - first introduced by the likes of The Beastie Boys and the house DJ's in the late Eighties, it has lit up countless rap and dance tunes in varying speeds and tempos. It remains one of the most startling percussive statements ever committed to tape.

Another number recorded at Headley Grange and over-dubbed at Island Studios dealt with the then topical subject of nuclear war. During an interview in 1971, on seeing a front page headline that read "Nuclear Test Damage Threat", Plant had this to say about the then current state of the world: "It really breaks my heart that we're all singing songs about love and peace and togetherness and really there's so little of it."

These views were reflected in the lyrics to 'Night Flight' a bright, breezy rocker. "I received a message from my brother across the water, he sat laughing as he said the end's in sight". Supplemented by Page's guitar fed through a Leslie speaker to give it a swirling effect and Jonesy's hammond organ, the track was one of the most commercial from the sessions but when it came to the final selection it was omitted from the album. Like 'Boogie With Stu' and 'Down By The Seaside' it was another track Page would revisit when it came to putting together their 1975 double album *Physical Graffiti*.

Which leaves just one song to discuss; the proverbial millstone around their necks. Couples have played it during their marriage services, radio stations still can't stop playing it (four

---

THE UNRELEASED *ZEP IV*

Talking about the fourth album to *Disc* magazine in early February 1971, Plant said: "So far we've got 14 tracks down and we did quite a bit with a mobile truck. We've got Stu from the Stones on a couple of tracks. Then there's 'Sloppy Drunk' on which I play guitar and Jimmy plays mandolin - you can imagine it being played as people dive around the maypole. With 14 tracks we

have enough for two albums but we won't put a double album out. People can appreciate a single album more as there's only eight tracks on it."

This implies they worked on a further six tracks during the fourth album sessions. Three of them, 'Down By The Seaside', 'Night Flight' and 'Boogie With Stu' were to see the light of day four years later as part of the *Physical Graffiti* double album, which leaves three

unreleased tracks. It's likely they worked on an initial version of 'No Quarter' - a much bootlegged rehearsal tape from these sessions features a fast tempo improvisation of the Jones opus that would emerge on their next album, *Houses Of The Holy*. Also from this era is an early acoustic take of 'The Rover', later worked on at the *Houses* sessions but eventually released on *Graffiti*. It's also possible they may have

attempted 'Dancing Days', another track later issued on *Houses Of The Holy* in 1973. A one-off version of this song was performed as early as their November 20 Empire Pool Wembley '71 show.

'Sloppy Drunk' was a working title for 'Battle Of Evermore' ('Sloppy Drunk' being a Jimmy Rogers blues tune covered by Page and The Black Crowes on their *Live At The Greek* album). The 45-minute

'GOING TO CALIFORNIA' DEBUT, BELFAST: MARCH 5, 1971

million logged plays and counting), would-be guitarists learn their craft by it, and the Australians, led by Rolf Harris, have made a whole parody industry out of it. Evil messages were claimed to be heard when it was played backwards. The singer allegedly hates it.

There was a time, however, when 'Stairway To Heaven' was simply the longest track on Led Zeppelin's new album. They knew it was good, but they could never have dreamt the sheer commotion that this eight-minute epic would cause over the ensuing decades. It's been both loved and loathed in equal measures.

Routined at Headley Grange, 'Stairway' was actually recorded at Island Studios in London's Notting Hill. Page had much of the

'STAIRWAY' DEBUT, BELFAST: MARCH 5, 1971

chord sequence on a demo when they first tried it out. "I'd been recording demos on a home unit called a new Vista," he said. "It was the deck from the Pye Mobile that had been used to record things like The Who's *Live At Leeds* - and we'd used it to record our Albert Hall gig. I'd been fooling around with the acoustic guitar and came up with the different sections which I married together. So I had the structure and then I ran it through Jonesy. I'd had the chord sequence pretty much worked out and Robert came up with 60 per cent of the lyrics on the spot."

Andy Johns remembers: "We did the track at Island in London. Jimmy had the tune pretty much worked out. He played acoustic in the iso booth. He was the thread that held it all together. We had Bonzo out in the main room and John Paul played a Honer electric piano."

Robert's lyrics were pieced together very quickly at the Grange. "Jimmy and I stayed up one night and we got the theme of it right there and then. The lyrics were a cynical thing about a woman getting everything she wanted without getting anything back."

Jonesy's contribution was the memorable and tranquil opening sequence. "We always had a lot of instruments lying around so I picked up a bass recorder and played along with Jimmy. Later at Island I multi-tracked the recorders to get it right."

Page made three separate attempts at the solo - and rather than deploy the usual Gibson Les Paul he returned to the battered old Telecaster (a gift from Jeff Beck) that he had used on the first Zep album. "I winged the guitar solo really. When it came to recording it I warmed up and did three of them. They were all quite different from each other. I did have the first phrase worked out and then there was the link phrase. I did check them before the tape ran. The one we used was definitely the best".

The result was one of the only guitar solos in history as likely to be whistled by milkman as air-guitared in the bedroom, such was the tracks eventual universal appeal. By the late Seventies Plant had tired of the tune and started to deride it publicly. "There's only so many times you can sing it and mean it," he said. "It just became so sanctimonious." His antipathy towards it resulted in a major backstage row with Page before their 1988 Atlantic Records 40th anniversary reunion at Madison Square Garden. Right up to them going on stage he was refusing to sing it, although he relented at the last minute.

Back in 1971 Led Zeppelin were immensely proud of 'Stairway To Heaven', and Page still views it as the apex of their career. Talking to Cameron Crowe from *Rolling Stone* in 1975, he said: "To me, I thought it crystallized the essence of the band. It had everything there and showed us at our best as a band and as a unit. Every musician wants to be to do something of lasting quality something which will hold up for years and I guess we did it with 'Stairway'."

With the recordings completed by early February, Page took Andy John's advice and flew with Peter Grant and Johns to Sunset Studios in Los Angles to mix the tracks. Just as they were flying into LA the city suffered a minor earthquake, as Page recalled: "The funny thing is that on 'Going To California' you've got the line 'mountains and the canyon's started to tremble and shake' and curiously, as we landed, there was a mild earthquake. In the hotel room before going to the studio you could feel the bed shake."

Unfortunately the mixdown did not go as planned, much to Andy John's embarrassment. "I convinced Jimmy to mix it in Los Angeles. We booked time at Sunset Sound but the room that I'd worked in before had been completely changed. So we used another room there and mixed the entire album. We came back to London and played it back at Studio One at Olympic. Anyway we put it on and it sounded terrible. I thought my number was up - but the others seemed to look to Jimmy, even though it was just as much my fault. So it had to be remixed again and that was difficult."

Page was very damning at the time: "Basically Andy Johns should be hung drawn and quartered for the fiasco he's played."

I winged the guitar solo really. When it came to recording it I warmed up and did three of them. They were all quite different from each other. I did have the first phrase worked out and then there was the link phrase. I did check them before the tape ran. The one we used was definitely the best.

JIMMY PAGE

rehearsal tape from Headley Grange which has appeared on several bootlegs, notably *Stairway Sessions* (Silver Rarities), contains fascinating work in progress run downs of 'Black Dog', 'No Quarter' and 'Stairway To Heaven'. An early demo of 'Battle Of Evermore' with only Plant on vocals, plus slightly differing monitor mixes of 'Four Sticks', 'Black Dog' and 'When The Levee Breaks', have also surfaced on bootleg. The

version of 'Four Sticks' recorded in March 1972 with the Bombay Symphony Orchestra can be heard on bootlegs such as *Complete Bombay 1972 Sessions* (Tecumseh).

As for what remains in their official archive - two complete alternate versions of 'When The Levee Breaks' plus a version of 'Going To California' definitely exist. It's also possible the two versions of 'Stairway' with the alternate guitar solos Page mentioned may have survived.

Early in 2001 there was talk of Page compiling an extended 20th anniversary edition of the fourth album with extra material - along the lines of the excellent Deep Purple anniversary series. It's a shame the opportunity to present an even fuller picture of this classic album was missed.

Maybe they are holding all that that back for the 40th anniversary...

Despite all these problems, the resulting production was one of Page's finest. Rarely again did he so precisely capture the four strands of the group on record so clearly. For all their triumphs, subsequent Zep albums often suffered from an uneven mix. Compare *Led Zep IV* to the muddy, leaden sound of their final album *In Through The Out Door*. There is just no comparison, a testament perhaps to how this relaxed style of recording, away from the distractions of the city, suited them. Maybe it would have been a wise move to have invested in their own mobile recording unit.

They had hoped to have the album out by late April but that would now be impossible. Instead Page and Johns mixed most of it again between their spring UK and European tour dates at Olympic Studios. The only mix from the Los Angeles trip that was deemed fit for eventual release was 'Levee Breaks'. The album finally went off to be cut at Trident Studios in London with more lacquers being cut at The Beatles' Apple Studios in the mid-summer of 1971.

By that time they had already began previewing numbers from the album in their new stage set. The first airing of new material occurred on Friday, March 5, at Belfast's Ulster Hall, when 'Black Dog' ,'Going To California' and 'Stairway To Heaven' were all played live for the first time. For 'Stairway' Page acquired a custom built Gibson ES1275 double-neck guitar to perform the six and 12-string passages the song requires.

The so called 'Back to the clubs' UK tour saw them return to venues such as London's Marquee where they had first established their reputation in the early days. UK listeners to Radio One's *John Peel In Concert* programme were also privy to an exclu-

ONSTAGE, USA: SUMMER OF '71

sive airing of this new material. On Sunday April 4 they broadcasted a one hour Zep live show recorded four days earlier at the Paris Cinema in London. 'Going To California' and 'Stairway' were the new numbers aired. For 'Stairway' this would be airplay number one - with another four million to follow during the next two decades.

In Europe a month later they previewed more songs from the fourth album. At an extraordinary gig at the KB Hallen in Copenhagen on May 3 'Black Dog' and 'Going To California' and

'Stairway To Heaven' were joined by the only known live performance of 'Four Sticks' ("Well try something we've never done before... there's every chance that we will fall apart," Plant warned the audience) and premieres of 'Misty Mountain Hop' and 'Rock And Roll' (introduced as 'It's Been A Long Time') during the encores.

With the album completed and having survived a riot at a curtailed show in Milan early in July, their attention turned to the design of the album cover. In these days of low-key, computer-generated graphics for modern CDs, it's difficult to understand how important artwork was back in the golden era of vinyl long players. The thick, card 12x12" sleeves were objects of desire in themselves, not to mention handy trays on which to skin up hand-rolled joints. Art-schooled Page had already set a precedent with the off- the-wall designs for *Zep I, II* and *III*. Alongside Pink Floyd and Roger Dean's work with Yes, Zeppelin were established as the forerunners of imaginative album artwork. With *Zep IV* they did not disappoint. They also won a major battle with Atlantic, their record company, by insisting that no writing whatsoever would appear on the gatefold jacket. Plant noted the battles they had to do this. "There was a lot of opposition from Atlantic about it being untitled and we wanted a cover with no writing on it and the hierarchy of the record business is not into the fact that covers are important. So we said they couldn't have the master tape until they got the cover right."

The actual photo used for the cover was discovered by Plant in an antique shop in Reading. Describing it Page said: "The old man on the cover carrying wood is in harmony with nature. He takes from nature. It's a natural cycle." The high rise flats that can be seen on the back cover were situated at Eve Hill in Dudley and were eventually demolished in 1999. The striking inside illustration, recreating The Hermit character in a set of Tarot cards, was Page's idea. A symbol of self-reliance and wisdom, it was drawn by Barrington Colby. Page later based his *Song Remains The Same* movie fantasy sequence on this same image. He also came up with the typeface for the lyrics of 'Stairway To Heaven' which appeared on the inner sleeve.

Page was also the instigator behind the enigma over the album's actual title.

"After all this crap with the critics I put it to everybody else that it would be a good idea to put something out that was totally anonymous," he explained later. "At first I wanted just one symbol but since it was our fourth album and there were four of us, we each chose our own. I designed mine and everybody else had their own reasons for using the symbol selected." Page's curious Zoso emblem has remained a vivid image ever since, as recognisable to Zeppelin fans as the Coca-Cola or Nike logos are in the world at large.

Plant, meanwhile, had this to say about his symbol: "My choice involved the feather - a symbol on which all philosophies have been based. For instance, it represents courage to many red Indian tribes. I like people to lay down the truth. No bullshit, that's what the feather in the circle is all about."

Jones' symbol was selected from *The Book Of Signs* by Rudolph Koch, a book of runes, and is said to represent a person who is both confident and competent because it's difficult to draw accurately. He recalls Page showing him the book initially. "He showed us *The Book Of Signs* and said we should each choose a symbol. So Bonzo and I did this, though later we discovered Jimmy and Robert had gone off and had their symbols specially designed, which was typical."

ZEP IV IN CONCERT: 30 YEARS OF LIVE PERFORMANCES
Over the past three decades there have been countless live renditions of the eight tracks that make up the *Zep IV* album - both from Zep and the various individuals. Here's a round up of some of the more celebrated live performances of those tracks spanning the last 30 years...

BLACK DOG
John Paul Jones
Crossing Border Festival, The Hague, Holland, October 9, 2000
JPJ reclaims his original riff idea with a startlingly aggressive instrumental delivery of the *Zep IV* opener on his debut solo tour.

ROCK AND ROLL
Led Zeppelin
Madison Square Garden, New York, July 28, 1973
The chest beating set opener of many a Zep show of the era - as captured for all time at the Garden for their *Song Remains The Same* movie now available on DVD. Definitive live *Zep IV*.

THE BATTLE OF EVERMORE
Page & Plant with Najma Akhtar
Unledded filming, London Studios, August 25, 1995
P & P turn back the years at their MTV filming concert aided by the exotic Najma who replaces Sandy Denny's original vocal part in a radical re-working.

Lacking pretension as ever, Bonzo chose three linked circles said to represent the man, woman, child trilogy. It was later suggested that the drummer's symbol bore a striking resemblance to the logo of Ballantine beer, a not inappropriate choice.

These four distinctive symbols would go on to be synonymous with the band, seen on stage equipment and adorning a million T-shirts and posters over the years. They linger still, Page and Plant using their linked symbols as the logo for their 1995/6 tour with Jones incorporating his into the artwork of his *Zooma* solo album.

The symbols were first introduced to the rock media via a series of teaser press ads in the weeks leading to the album's release, each depicting a particular symbol alongside a previous Zep album sleeve. When the album duly hit the top of the charts the press were baffled as to how to title the album with the inevitable result that it appeared under various names, the *New Led Zeppelin album*, *Led Zeppelin IV*, *Four Symbols*, *Runes* and *Zoso*, though some papers did make the effort to reproduce the actual symbols themselves. Nevertheless, Zeppelin's quest to sow confusion succeeded admirably.

The band's hectic schedule of that year continued unabated. In August they were back in America for their seventh US tour. Page was in buoyant mood and playing brilliantly. "Once the album was completed and mixed I knew it was really good," he said. "We actually went on the road in America before the manufacturing process was completed and somebody at Atlantic Records said, 'This is professional suicide for a band to tour without an album'. In retrospect that is rather amusing!"

The new material was already making an impact and Page still recalls with pride the reaction they got to 'Stairway' when they performed it at the LA Forum for the first time. "We played 'Stairway' at the Forum before the album was out and around a third of the audience stood up and gave us a standing ovation. It was then that I thought 'actually this may be a better number than I'd imagined'."

Equally successful was a three-city, five-concert first visit to Japan. Here they performed some of the most enjoyable concerts of their career - away from the glare of the press and the intensity of America, they were able to stretch out and extend their set list, throwing in off-the-cuff versions of 'Smoke Gets In Your Eyes', Cliff Richards' 'Bachelor Boy' and The Beatles' 'Please Please Me'.

After a short break, to round off a very productive year, Peter Grant booked a 16-date UK tour that nicely coincided with the eventual release of their long delayed, long awaited fourth album. The tour kicked off in Newcastle on November 11 and took in two memorable nights at London's Wembley Empire Pool.

Despite the delays and the negative reaction to the last album, it was clear that the band's popularity had not declined at all. Demand for tickets was overwhelming. All 9,000 seats for their November 20 Empire Pool show sold out in under an hour. A second was added and they could have easily slotted in a third had their schedule allowed it.

Their stage presentation now featured each of their four symbols, on Bonham's drum kit, on Jonesy's organ and on Jimmy's speaker cabinets, while Plant's feather symbol adorned the PA. Page also took to wearing a specially knitted jumper depicting his Zoso symbol. The set list now included 'Rock And Roll' in the main set, now under this title, alongside 'Black Dog', 'Stairway' and 'Going To California'.

Talking about the album to Chris Welch of *Melody Maker*, Bonzo was hugely enthusiastic. "My personal view is that it's the

EMPIRE POOL WEMBLEY: NOVEMBER 20, 1971

My personal view is that it's the best thing we've ever done. It's the next stage we were at the time of recording. The playing is some of the best we have done and Jimmy is like… mint!

JOHN BONHAM

STAIRWAY TO HEAVEN
Jimmy Page
Arms Concert, Albert Hall, September 20, 1983
An emotional return to the stage for Mr Page - as he delivers a faithful instrumental rendering of their most famous song. Even Percy would have been proud.

MISTY MOUNTAIN HOP
Led Zeppelin
Atlantic Records 40th Anniversary, Madison Square Garden, New York, May 14, 1988
One of the few successful moments during their shaky reunion for Atlantic back in 1988. Page and Jonesy spin the riff, Plant rises to the occasion and Jason Bonham gets all his dad's breaks spot on.

FOUR STICKS
Robert Plant/Strange Sensation
KB Halle Malmo April 26 2001
30 years on, the legacy continues. Witness this fresh interpretation by Plant's new band of a *Zep IV* standard. Yes the owls still cry in the night....

GOING TO CALIFORNIA
Led Zeppelin
Paris Cinema April 1 1971
As aired on the BBC and finally issued on the *BBC Sessions CD* some 26 years later. A most sensitive rendering but could it be anything else?

WHEN THE LEVEE BREAKS
Led Zeppelin
Chicago Stadium, January 20, 1975
Only ever performed live by Zep on a handful of dates on this '75 US tour - Bonzo applies the necessary echo to recreate that drum sound and Page wields a mean bottleneck. The sound of Headley Grange alive and well in Chicago.

best thing we've ever done. It's the next stage we were at the time of recording. The playing is some of the best we have done and Jimmy is like... mint!"

The culmination of the whole year's effort were the two magnificent five-hour shows in London's Empire Pool on November 20 and 21. Dubbed Electric Magic they were supported by Maggie Bell's Stone The Crows plus Bronco on the Saturday (whose line up included future Plant solo era guitarists Robbie Blunt and Kevyn Gammond), and Home on the Sunday, and on both nights Grant had booked some novelty circus acts, including performing pigs and plate spinners. The pigs - with huge ruffs around their necks - didn't really cut it; indeed, their only real contribution was an unpleasant smell in the stage area. Thankfully Zeppelin fared better.

Roy Hollingworth of *Melody Maker* was unstinting in his praise for the show. "This was an English band playing like crazy and enjoying every minute of it. They played just about every thing they've ever written. Nothing - just nothing was spared. This was no job. This was no gig. It was an event for all."

A memorable poster was produced for the event and sold for 30p - it now changes hands for over £600 on the collectors market - and the newly established Virgin Records set up stalls to sell the just released fourth album. Here and around the country, much to Atlantic's relief, fans had no trouble identifying the nameless artwork of the new record as it sailed to the number one album spot. It was a similar story in America, though it was with some irony that Carole King's multi-million selling soft rock album *Tapestry* kept it from reaching number one.

John always felt that his significance was minimal, but if you take him off any of our tracks, the track loses its sex, its potency and its power. He had a heart of gold but he never had any idea of how important he was and he was very insecure because of it.
ROBERT PLANT

ZEP 4 COMES ALIVE, BELFAST: MARCH 5, 1971

It didn't really matter - the airplay generated by 'Stairway To Heaven' ensured the album remained in the *Billboard* top forty album chart for the next six months. Peter Grant steadfastly refused to issue the track as a single, knowing that restricting its availability to the LP alone would inevitably add to its sales.

So from the adversity of the *Zeppelin III* saga, Zeppelin triumphed. As Zep historian Hugh Jones noted in a recent reappraisal of the album in *Tight But Loose*, there were now two distinct, separate entities to the group - the tight recorded unit as found on record - and the wild, often out of control live band.

"The fourth Zep album demonstated that the band were growing and changing. It also displayed how different the recorded Zeppelin were becoming from their live act. In concert you got endlessly extended solos, an ample supply of group improvisation and two to three hours of glorious excess to wallow in... Dynamics, absoloutely. Subtly? Not really.

"On their fourth album, though, Led Zep displayed unmistakable subtly, beautifully seasoning the bombast and using taste and nuance to create a recording of great depth and lasting value."

Some three decades on its influence is still paramount, not least with the three ex-members. Page and Plant attempted an ambitious remake of 'The Battle Of Evermore' with Indian singer Najma Akhtar on their initial *Unledded* MTV reunion. 'Four Sticks' and 'Misty Mountain Hop' figure regularly in the setlist of Plant's latest touring unit Strange Sensation. The latter track was also revived when Page linked up for his much acclaimed tour with The Black Crowes. On his solo tours John Paul Jones has performed instrumental versions of 'Black Dog' and 'When The Levee Breaks'.

As for 'Stairway', Plant has stubbornly refused to acknowledge it - with one little known exception. In the autumn of 1994, during his initial reunion with Page, Plant dropped his guard during a promotional TV interview appearance in Japan. He agreed, allegedly for a bet within their entourage, to perform an acoustic unplugged version of the song in the TV studio. Sat on stools in a sparse studio they reeled back the years - amazingly Plant put his whole heart and soul into the short arrangement of the song while Page almost gleefully picked out that oh so familiar tune. At that precise moment, the song was returned to its initial natural beauty, away from all the Rolf Harris nonsense and snipes from the singer himself.

Had they performed that arrangement on their subsequent *No Quarter* and *Clarksdale* tours it would simply have lifted the roof. As it is they never returned to it again - perhaps they never will.

They did attempt a version of the *Zep IV* closer 'When The Levee Breaks' on their 1995 tour, though. Perhaps tellingly they performed it in an acoustic blues arrangement, safe in the knowledge that the incredible drum sound could never be recaptured without Bonham. And 30 years on, perhaps above even 'Stairway', it's that relentless, much sampled pummelling drum sound that is the key ingredient of the fourth album. Indeed, all over the album Bonham let loose with a percussive ferocity that remains at the heart of his legacy. As Plant once observed: "John always felt that his significance was minimal, but if you take him off any of our tracks, the track loses its sex, its potency and its power. He had a heart of gold but he never had any idea of how important he was and he was very insecure because of it."

So perhaps Plant has chosen the correct path after all in his steadfast refusal to succumb to Page's long held desire to reform Led Zeppelin under that name as a going concern. Without John Bonham it really could never be the same. Listening to the fourth Led Zeppelin album, it's patently evident that this band shared a unique unbreakable chemistry.

Back in 1971, in that run down mansion in deepest Hampshire, it was that rare musical combustion of grace and power that gave *Led Zeppelin IV* a longevity that refuses to die. Pull it out now and marvel again at a truly classic rock record that will still be held in the highest esteem over the coming 30 years... and then some.

When Led Zeppelin undertook the series of five shows at London's Earl's Court Arena in May of 1975 they were at the very peak of their creative powers. Spurred on by the critical and commercial success of their sixth album, the double set *Physical Graffiti*, each show they played took on event-like proportions. The 17,000 capacity Earl's Court afforded them the luxury to showcase in the best possible setting, the sheer enormity of their stage act. Over five nights in May '75 Zeppelin delivered perhaps the most impressive series of shows of their entire career. Over a quarter of a century later, these Earl's Court performances are still held in the highest esteem.

Photographic images from the shows still light up the pages of countless Zep features and books, bootleg performances are eagerly snapped up, and the official video footage of the gigs projects the sheer magnitude and power of Led Zeppelin in full flight more than any other surviving film of the group.

Unsurprisingly Zeppelin's Earl's Court stand has been much chronicled in the pages of *Tight But Loose*. Indeed the primitive hand written first issue was dominated by a blow-by-blow account of my own experiences of the dates.

Years later, on the 25th anniversary of the shows, I produced a special limited edition *TBL Earl's Court Journal*, celebrating those epic spring shows of 1975. Much of that text is reproduced over the following pages. It attempts to analyse just why this series of concerts so effectively captured the magic of Zeppelin on stage.

REFERENCES: **TIGHT BUT LOOSE 1** (ABOVE), 15 & TBL EARL'S COURT JOURNAL

LED ZEPPELIN AT EARL'S COURT MAY 1975 : 4

PERFORMING 'STAIRWAY TO HEAVEN', EARL'S COURT: MAY 18, 1975

Why Earl's Court was the greatest series of concerts Led Zeppelin ever played

"Improvisation - guitar Jimmy Page, drums John Bonham, John Paul Jones bass guitar. Just a little world to get lost in occasionally. It only takes about 20 minutes to plot around the time signatures."
ROBERT PLANT, MAY 24, 1975

So spoke Robert Plant from the stage of the Earl's Court Arena after a performance of 'Dazed And Confused' that had spanned some 26 minutes.

Just a little world to get lost in... and almost 30 years ago there was ample opportunity to get lost in the world of Led Zeppelin as they performed five marathon concerts at London's Earl's Court.

Now there might be a school of thought that this era of three-hour plus sets represented all that was overblown about Zeppelin and indeed rock music itself in the mid-Seventies. Twenty-minute drum solos, marathon guitar solos, massive arenas and big light shows were all a long way from those innocent days of the Lyceum Ballroom and the Marquee, and such excesses would soon inspire the back-to-basics punk and new wave explosion that was around the corner.

But Led Zeppelin at Earl's Court was absolutely of its time; a

ZEP-MANIA IN LONDON

This is part of the vast queue which built up at London Earl's Court last weekend, prior to the box-office opening for Led Zeppelin's concerts there on May 23, 24 and 25. The queue started on Thursday night and, by Saturday morning, it stretched all round the building and was nearly a mile long, but by 4 p.m., the queue had dispersed, with everyone present having secured tickets.

However, all seats have now been sold and no further applications can be accepted. The 10,000 tickets which were made available on the previous have also been sold, as have 11,000 seat order tickets. In fact, there were 100,000 postal applications, and in many cases money is having to be refunded. Promoter Mel Bush said there is no chance of Zeppelin playing any additional concerts.

ROBERT AND MAUREEN AT THE EARL'S COURT PARTY: MAY 25, 1975

moment in time that captured the very essence of the power and influence the group held over its audience at this point in their career. Those of us who were lucky enough to be there - and indeed those that have since carefully studied the case history of Earl's Court via the numerous bootlegs - will testify to their brilliance on those memorable May days. The sheer scale of what Led Zeppelin had become seemed to inspire an arrogance within the group that in turn led to their performing a series of shows that, as Plant was keen to explain, mirrored every colour of their musical spectrum. "We intend to take you through some of the colours... we've explored the prism and we've developed music along the lines of colours, some of them bright and some of them dark," he told the audience on the final night.

Arrogant or not, the sheer gargantuan scale of Earl's Court was perfect for Zeppelin in 1975. It was the ultimate demonstration of just how far they had progressed in the space of six and a half years; from humble post-Yardbirds beginnings to massive acceptance in America and their standing as Britain's most successful group of the era. It also cemented the loyalty of their British fans.

Unlike The Beatles, Led Zeppelin were not and never would be mainstream heroes. Their music was never intended for an across-the-board audience. They were a cult, albeit a massive one, and like all cults they were a secret society, one that in their case attracted young, long-haired, mostly male followers who read about them avidly in the music press and took them very seriously indeed. The national tabloid press never understood them and, by and large, ignored them, it being assumed by the editors of such papers, probably correctly, that their readers simply weren't interested.

Similarly, Led Zeppelin never appeared on TV or in the singles charts, manager Peter Grant having long ago decided that such popular media exposure was both unnecessary and, indeed, somehow demeaning. It was a doubly wise decision, not only placing Zeppelin on a pedestal occupied by no-one else but also creating the necessary vacuum in which the Led Zeppelin cult could flourish: a variation on the old showbiz maxim 'keep 'em wanting more'.

In today's maze of mass communication, in which access to rock performers ranges from MTV to MP3 downloads, it seems extraordinary to consider that for a large part of the audience at Earl's Court the only previous visual image they would have had of Led Zeppelin was from the pictures that appeared in the weekly music press. There were no videos in 1975 and even the pictures of the group that appeared on the covers of their albums were slyly obscured.

Though with a nod towards whimsical irony they named their music publishing arm Superhype, the massive success they now enjoyed had been built the hard way, on sheer word of mouth, on handed-down enthusiasm for their live concerts and the quality of their albums. If you were a Zeppelin fan there were no half measures. It was an all encompassing passion. Every album they released - and every move they made - became a part of your life. To be part of their world was to be part of a very special elite, and Earl's Court offered the perfect platform for every lucky attendant to revel in that status.

It's significant that at the time there was very little carping about their decision to play just three London dates in 1975. Fans accepted that the whole Led Zeppelin operation had become too large for a UK tour around the usual, theatre-style venues. To use

a now familiar maxim - Led Zeppelin no longer played concerts, they staged events. Plant had hinted as such in interviews early in the year. Talking in January to Bob Harris on the BBC's *Whistle Test*, the only TV show on which Zep might appear, albeit never live, he stated: "What we want to do in England, if we can find the right venue and I think we possibly can, is turn it into something of an event and go to town on it in true style."

In a clever advertising strategy that incorporated British Rail and their 'Zeppelin Express', the concerts were promoted in adverts that displayed the links to London's Earl's Court arena via BR's Inter City train services, thus explaining how Earl's Court was easily accessible from all parts of the country. The difficult bit was actually obtaining the tickets. The three original dates sold out within a day of box offices opening around the country on March 15.

A further two dates for the preceding weekend of May 17/18 were added and they too sold out instantly. This prompted the noted critic and film maker Tony Palmer, in a very perceptive feature in *The Observer* magazine on May 18, 1975, to state that: "Statistics are always misleading. With Led Zeppelin statistics are irrelevant - except that they are truly astonishing. Last night they gave the first of five concerts at London's Earl's Court arena. Total seats 85,000. No pop group in history, no entertainer, no film star, no opera singer has ever attracted such an audience."

There are many reasons why Earl's Court represented an all time high for the group.

For a start, unlike the rather nervous, tentative approach to Knebworth four years later, Led Zeppelin approached the run of Earl's Court concerts at the very top of their game. When the dates were announced in mid-March the group were on the final stretch of their first American tour for two years. The tour had encountered problems early on in January when Page injured a finger just prior to the opening dates and Plant contracted flu in the chilly midwest. The first gigs were compromised by these setbacks but by the time they reached Madison Square Garden on February 3 they were back on the rails, the fingers on Page's left hand having recovered sufficiently to enable him to play 'Dazed And Confused' for the first time this tour. Eleven days later, at the Nassau Coliseum, they turned in a superb performance, 'No Quarter' taking on the improvisational free-form approach that would light up Earl's Court. Towards the end of March they hit a real roll, putting together a string of consistently excellent performances, notably in Long Beach, Vancouver and Seattle. By now they were inserting a version of 'Woodstock' in the 'Dazed' interlude, another highlight of the forthcoming Earl's Court run.

The American tour wound up with three performances at their spiritual home, the LA Forum. During these dates there was a hint of Earl's Court fashion on parade, with Plant adopting the dark blue Miss Selfridge cut-off blouse and Page premiering the dragon-emblazoned suit trousers. On March 27, as the band shuffled off stage for the final time in America that year, Plant excitedly exclaimed: 'If there's anyone here from England - well we're coming back, baby!'

Another key ingredient to the success of Earl's Court was the stage presentation overseen by technician Ian Knight. The vastness of the 17,000 capacity arena offered the perfect opportunity to bring to the UK the so-called American show, all 40 tons of it, including a custom built 80 x 40 foot stage set up with black backcloths shielding over 300 flashbulbs that would ignite simultaneously

EARL'S COURT FACT FILE
The 40 tons of Showco PA airlifted from Dallas to Earl's Court included

100 speaker cabinets linked to 40 microphones, 200 spotlights, four supertrooper spotlights, eight CSI spotlamps, all powered by generators capable of an output of 20,000 watts, enough to illuminate every neon sign in London's West End.

Background music played over the PA as the audiences filed in before the Earl's Court shows included Steely Dan's *Katy Lied* album and Supertramp's *Crime Of*

The Century.

The security guards on duty to man the gangways and aisles were supplied by the Sturico Security company.

Official merchandise on sale included the Earl's Court T-shirt depicting the Earl's Court ad (mine came off during ironing within a month!) and the excellent programme which now commands a £50 collectors price. Unofficial

merchandise sold outside the arena included a variety of posters, scarves and badges plus a now much sought after unofficial programme.

It was so cold in the empty arena at the soundcheck prior to the first date that Bonzo wore his overcoat throughout rehearsals. Electric fires were also installed in the caravan dressing rooms.

Press and complimentary invites for the shows came in the form of a

full colour Physical Rocket ticket marked First Class - these were also used to gain entry at the end of show party on May 25.

Five prominent DJs were given the task of introducing the band on stage at each show - lining up as follows: May 17 Bob Harris, May 18 Johnnie Walker, May 23 Kid Jensen, May 24 Nicky Horne, May 25 Alan Freeman. Each were given a special souvenir goblet in appreciation by

EARLS COURT ARENA
(OPPOSITE WARWICK ROAD EXIT EARLS COURT TUBE STATION)

MEL BUSH by arrangement with PETER GRANT presents

LED ZEPPELIN

BLOCK
35

Friday, May 23rd, 1975
at 8-0 p.m. (Doors open 6-0)

3rd Tier Stalls £2-00

ROW SEAT
D 163

FOR CONDITIONS OF ... SEE OVER

TO BE RETAINED

Statistics are always mis-leading. With Led Zeppelin statistics are irreverent - except that they are truly astonishing. Last night they gave the first of five concerts at London's Earl's Court arena. Total seats 85,000. No pop group in history, no entertainer, no film star, no opera singer has ever attracted such an audience.

TONY PALMER,
THE OBSERVER MAGAZINE:
MAY 18, 1975

ON STAGE, EARLS COURT: MAY 18, 1975

Peter Grant.

Songs ad-libbed by Plant between numbers over the five shows included Neil Young's 'Old Man', Little Richards' 'Rip It Up', Robert Johnson's 'Judgement Day', and their own 'Friends' and 'Livin' Lovin' Maid'. John Paul Jones also played some bars from the 'Teddy Bears Picnic' before 'Stairway To Heaven' at the May 17 show.

The following were all name checked by Plant during his between song patter over the course of the five shows: Chris Welch, Charles Shaar Murray, Roy Harper, Neil Young, Robert Johnson, Elvis Presley, Boz Scaggs, Scott McKenzie, Noddy Holder, Bob Dylan, Ian Campbell folk group, Jet Harris & Tony Meehan, Bob Marley & The Wailers, The Osmonds, Tim Rose, Greta Garbo, Richard Burton, Denis Healey, DJ Alan Freeman, footballer Jimmy McCalliog, football referee Jack Taylor, roadies Mick Hinton, Ray Thomas, plus Peter Grant, Carmen Plant, Jason Bonham, Bonzo's dad, and the mysterious Reginald Pinner.

According to press reports The Osmonds were guests at one of the Zeppelin shows and they returned the compliment by inviting John Bonham and familly to see their show at the same venue the next week.

ZEPPELIN LIFT-OFF!

A ROCK extravaganza hits London this weekend when Led Zeppelin play the first of their five concerts at Earls Court — the band's only British appearances this year. Zeppelin will be playing this Saturday (May 17) and Sunday. And they have promised to present, for the first time in this country, their full American stage act — including lasers, a giant video screen and a 350,000 watt light show.

Earls Court is the largest concert hall in Europe. A total of 85,000 fans will see the band — the other three concerts will be on May 23, 24 and 25.

Bonzo refused to join us because he was getting £40 with Tim Rose. I had eight telegrams sent to the Three Men In A Boat pub in Walsall where Noddy Holder was our roadie... nobody would believe The New Yardbirds...

ROBERT PLANT, MAY 24

as they returned to the stage for encores. Then there were the pioneering laser effects, designed to pierce through the air just as Page branded the violin bow during 'Dazed'.

Also ahead of its time was the use giant Ediphor video screen suspended high above the stage, at cost of £10,000, that allowed every one of the 17,000 present a clear view of the action. There were concerns over the acoustics of the hall, promoter Mel Bush having been on the end of criticism when David Bowie had played the venue in 1973 (though there were no such problems when Slade played the same venue a week later). Having learnt from that experience and the fact that Zeppelin employed the best sound system in the world, courtesy of the Showco team from Dallas, he was confident that everyone in the audience would hear and see the group in the best possible setting.

Then there was the set list. Initially developed for the American tour to present a cross section of their progress to date, it included material from the newly released *Physical Graffiti*, 'Sick Again', 'In My Time Of Dying', 'Kashmir' and 'Trampled Underfoot' all offering live evidence of the potency of a new record that included 15 recordings spread across a double album. If Earl's Court represents a live peak, then *Physical Graffiti* stands alongside it as their definitive recorded statement. On stage, numbers such as 'Trampled Underfoot' and 'Kashmir' developed beyond their studio counterparts to take on a new life of their own, just like previous great Zep live creations. The only disappointment was that they did not introduce more numbers from the album on stage, 'The Wanton Song' being dropped after a few airings early on the US tour and 'Custard Pie' not making it out of rehearsals.

They also reinstated the acoustic section last heard in America in 1972. Gathered together closely at the front of the stage, seated on chairs, the group offered 'Going To California', 'That's The Way' and 'Bron Yr Aur Stomp', bringing an intimacy to the proceedings that belied the huge setting and accentuating the rapport between artists and audience.

Then there was the reinstating for Earl's Court only of 'Tangerine', performed as a four-part harmony piece - "We can do 'Bus Stop' by The Hollies next time" quipped Plant on May 18 – and the overall sequencing of the show, whereby marathons such as 'No Quarter', 'Moby Dick' and 'Dazed And Confused' were strategic placed so as to sustain the momentum. 'Moby Dick' may have been long and indulgent but there were no mass walkouts. It was accepted it for what it was, an integral part of Led Zeppelin and a showcase for Bonzo and his craft. 'Stairway To Heaven' was now the rightful finale to every show and still sung by Plant as though he meant every word.

It would have been easy for them to simply re-enact the US set list for these UK shows. The fact that they actually came up with an exclusive repertoire says much for the high regard they placed on these Earl's Court concerts. Never before had they had such a vast array of material at their disposal, and never before (or again) would they present it so intelligently.

L ed Zeppelin's shows at Earl's Court were among their most photographed ever, justifiably so since in 1975 they were certainly at their most photogenic. Zeppelin's reputation may have been built more on their music than the clothes they wore but they didn't ignore the sartorial side of things completely. The mystique that developed from their lack of media exposure led to an element of mystery about their actual appearance. Magnified by the use of a video screen, the way they looked and dressed at

Earl's Court became ingrained on the minds of those in attendance and in turn by the appearance of countless shots that have appeared in books and magazines ever since.

Page's dragon suit and flailing black hair radiated a demonic quality evident in his every twist and turn across the stage. The suit reflected Page's other worldly image as never before. His face covered in a tangled mass of damp curls, his fingers leaping from fret to fret, he seemed so fully immersed in his playing that it was difficult not to be overwhelmed by the sheer charisma of a genius of the electric guitar in his absolute element.

Equally in his prime was Jimmy's foil, Robert Plant. The singer dominated proceedings over the five nights with a confidence and cheeky arrogance that reflected the whole upbeat camaraderie within the group. Aside from one night when he pulled out the wraparound, long sleeved attire he'd used on the US tour, he chose a Miss Selfridge cut-off that exposed plenty of chest and wore his blonde hair long and loose. His vocal strength required none of the stimulus of the electronic harmoniser that was predominant in later years.

Always a more than competent master of ceremonies, at Earl's Court Plant took on the added role of group raconteur, conjuring up various witticisms and telling a series of little stories about the group's history: "Bonzo refused to join us because he was getting £40 with Tim Rose," he said on May 24. "I had eight telegrams sent to the Three Men In A Boat pub in Walsall where Noddy Holder was our roadie... nobody would believe The New Yardbirds..." and about Earl's Court itself: "It's such a pleasure to be playing to so many peoeple in England all at one time - we

JPJ AT EARL'S COURT: MAY 18, 1975

couldn't make Nottingham Boat club this time" (May 17) and "The equipment you see now amassed above our heads in a rather precarious position took three weeks to get through customs, so were really pleased not only to be here and able to play but to have all the equipment to give you our best" (May 18).

There was a high quota of soccer references: "Jimmy McCalloig's has left the stage" (May 24) and "The Welsh, who nearly beat Scotland yesterday!" (May 18), and a few typical

---

WHAT THE PAPERS SAID

PETE MAKOWSKI/SOUNDS:
"In six and a half years Led Zeppelin have grown to be the biggest band in the land and judging by the excellence of their performance at Earl's Court, one of if not THE most exiting live act in the world. I guess I came on the right night. It's difficult to describe the magic or atmosphere of that Sunday - it was one of

those gigs that will remain scarred on my brain forever."

MICHAEL OLDFIELD/MELODY MAKER:
"It's not very often that the opportunity of experiencing the very best of something presents itself, and when it does come along it's inevitably only appreciated in retrospect. Yet before Led Zeppelin had got too far into their set at London's Earl's

Court on Sunday it became obvious this was the ultimate definitive rock performance. So much so that it's inconceivable that another band could do so well. In the space of three and a half hours they covered virtually every variation in rock, and left no doubt they could triumph with any style they omitted."

CHARLES SHAAR MURRAY/NME:
"Apart from The Who and the

Stones I can't think of many bands who could have put on anything like it. During moments like 'Trampled Underfoot' it seemed the whole stage was just going to fall forward and crush everybody in the hall."

RODDERICK GILCHRIST/ DAILY MAIL :
"In its field, this is one of the most astonishing examples of pure theatre I've seen anywhere. There are

moments during Zeppelin's colourful, sometimes psychedelic non-stop show when Jimmy Page's searing guitar carried by 20,000 watts of power, cuts right through the senses like some fast-acting drug and virtually blots out everything but the music. Led Zeppelin - number one in rock - and how they raised those eerie wastes of Earl's Court to frenzy."

swipes at the press: "Charles Shaar Murray wherever you are - keep taking the pills" (May 25). There was mention of their children: "Tonight there is a lad watching his dad who is a remarkable drummer. He is better than 80% of rock group drummers today. So Jason Bonham this is your dad John Bonham!" (May 24) and "Well, Carmen here it is, a song to a little girl who sits there probably wondering what it's all about. In fact to all our kids who come and see us and sit and go 'oh really'. But what's it all about so where is the bridge. Well Carmen, here's your chance to find out where the bridge is and if you know, will you let us know after the show?" (May 25). The group were about to go into self imposed tax exile and Plant was obviously none too happy at the high earnings tax he and the group were obliged to pay, so Chancellor Denis Healey didn't escape his sharp tongue: "Somebody voted for someone and now everyone's on the run" (May 25) and "You know Denis - no artists in the country anymore - he must be 'Dazed And Confused'!"

Listening to these comments almost 30 years later adds much to the period feel of Zeppelin in 1975. Robert Plant talked a very good show every night in Earl's Court adding much to the rapport between the group and their audience.

As for Jones, his fashion sense was as bizarre as ever, risking Plant's caustic wit with that fancy Spanish jacket complete with onions on the shoulders and sporting a pair of platform shoes that Noddy Holder would have been proud of. His playing, particularly on 'Kashmir' and 'No Quarter' was exemplary, even by his high standards. Rarely if ever did those two compositions sound as impressive as when they were performed at Earl's Court.

a show and we were expecting trouble with such a huge audience. But everything went really well. I also thought the video screen was well worth doing. It cost a lot of bread but you could see close-ups you'd never be able to see normally at a concert."

So they had the confidence, they had the look, they had the lights, they had the set list. All they had to do was deliver. And deliver they did.

Opening night, Saturday May 17, was a little nervous and tentative at first. After Bob Harris' "Welcome back to Britain" introduction, Jimmy spent the whole of 'Rock And Roll' trying to keep his lead intact. This prompted Plant's opening comment: "You wouldn't believe that after all the trouble to get this unearthly monster with us, the first number gets blown and all it is is a sixpenny jack plug."

The guitar problems led to Page using his Lake Placid Fender Strat for a couple of numbers, a guitar that was also in evidence during the May 23 show.

After this somewhat shaky start they quickly regained confidence and the new numbers from *Physical Graffiti*, 'In My Time Of Dying' and 'Kashmir' set the standard. The latter's Eastern-sounding riff rose into a thick, booming sound that reverberated throughout the entire arena. As the tapes of the shows so vividly reveal, that booming sound was very much an Earl's Court characteristic, a sound so solid that when Page laid down a chord you could practically lean on it.

By the evening's end the early nerves had all but evaporated, to be replaced by a relaxed atmosphere which found JPJ playfully

'MOBY DICK' AT EARL'S COURT: MAY 1975

Tonight there is a lad watching his dad who is a remarkable drummer. He is better than 80% of rock group drummers today. So Jason Bonham this is your dad John Bonham!

ROBERT PLANT, MAY 24

A beardless Bonzo, retaining his sideboards and sporting a new smarter haircut, looked well up for it, respondent in embroidered T-shirt. His no-nonsense cut and thrust approach to the familiar Perspex drum kit was the driving force of Earl's Court. Interviewed by Chris Welch just after the gigs he was obviously proud of the way his band handled these UK dates. "I really enjoyed those concerts," he admitted. "I thought they were the best shows we've ever put on in England. I always get tense before

offering a few bars of 'The Teddy Bears Picnic' as Robert introduced 'Stairway To Heaven'.

The second night saw them settled into the run. 'Over The Hills And Far Away' developed into an early set template on each successive night. Loaded with rock steady authority, with Page at his most spontaneous, supplemented by Bonham and Jones holding down the bottom line, hinting at the rhythmic tempos they would develop for 'Candy Store Rock' on *Presence*. Page's double-

---

CHRIS WELCH/MELODY MAKER:
"It was a splendid return, proof that Zeppelin have their strength and imagination intact and a great zest for fresh challenges. It's looking good for the next six years of Zeppelin history making."

ROBIN DESNLOW/THE GAURDIAN:
"It was Page who above all matched the music to the efforts. Moving

from style to style, apparently effortlessly knocking Clapton off the 'guitar king' slot, he produced a virtuoso performance. There were admittedly dull passages of random noise and overlong improvisations in the three hours, but overall Zeppelin had done more than enough to justify their reputation."

ANTHONY THORNCROFT/ FINANCIAL TIMES
"The group were on their best behaviour with singer Robert Plant reporting on what they had been doing in the last two years since the last concerts with a graciousness approaching the Queen's Christmas message. Perhaps they are more popular than The Beatles. Could any artist, contemporary or historical in any musical field, improve on their

achievements of packing Earl's Court five times with many more disappointed? When I first saw Led Zeppelin over five years ago they were a very good rock band. Now they must rate a paragraph in any social history of the twentieth century. They are no longer judged in mere musical terms but as an entertainment industry phenomenon."

JAN ILES/RECORD MIRROR:
"If ever there was a concert that you could brag about seeing to all your friends it was the one Led Zeppelin performed at Earl's Court last Sunday. It tuned out to be a nocturnal delight and one that should be remembered for eons to come."

J PAGE, EARL'S COURT: MAY '75

neck guitar poses during 'The Song Remains The Same' would give the attendant photographers plenty of famous images while 'The Rain Song' saw the guitarist draped in blue light, casting another memorable portrait, a solitary figure in the spotlight ringing out a jangle of familiar notes.

The outstanding performance of May 18, though, was 'No Quarter' as immortalised on the subsequent Red Devil vinyl bootleg. Never before had JPJ immersed himself in this showpiece with such subtlety and grace, the defining moment being the point where he came out of the classical sequence, at around 3' 45", to play a cluster of descending notes that rippled from the grand piano and into the Earl's Court air.

The acoustic section found Plant at his loquacious best, unfolding tales of the origins of 'Going To California' ("So we went to Wales and when we got there we wrote songs about California") and 'That's The Way' ("So we were sitting on a grassy bank looking across the unspoiled countryside"). 'Dazed And Confused' was also developing its own unique Earl's Court quality. Page's delicate, melodic guitar passages leading into 'Woodstock' remain an evocative reminder of the times that still brings on the chill every time I hear the tape 25 years on.

During 'Whole Lotta Love' they kicked into the rhythm of 'The Crunge' as they had done briefly the previous night but now further developed Plant's echoed "I'm just trying to find the bridge" lines. A crunching 'Black Dog' brought show number two to a close after some 195 minutes on stage.

A week later they were back for a Friday night special. In between they had fared pretty well in the press, garnering memo-

> *So we went to Wales and when we got there we wrote songs about California.*
>
> ROBERT PLANT

PERFORMING 'THAT'S THE WAY', EARL'S COURT: MAY 1975

rable front page cover stories in both the *Melody Maker* and *NME*. However Charles Shaar Murray's slightly less than complimentary review irritated Plant enough for him to throw in a couple of digs on stage.

But they were just so up for it, as evident right from the moment when Plant gave out an excited 'Immigrant Song'-style "Ah ah" squeal as Bonzo and Jimmy did the usual pre-song warm up. Following 'Rock And Roll' and 'Sick Again' Plant attracted huge cheers when he explained: "Last week we did a couple of warm up dates for these three nights, Friday, Saturday, and Sunday. We believe that these were the first three gigs to be sold

out so these must be the ones with the most energy stored up because you've been waiting..."

The freewheeling on-stage energy was evident throughout, with Plant at his most gymnastic vocally, throwing in verses from 'You Shook Me' at the close of a thrilling 'In My Time Of Dying', and keeping up his Healey references with a "Bye bye Denis" during the song's close. Before 'Kashmir' Plant explained he'd just had a vaccination in preparation for their impending exile... "'Ready for when we go hunting in the jungle for new words and new songs for a new album". He and wife Maureen were due to leave the country on Monday.

It's worth mentioning that this particular version of 'Kashmir' did not go entirely to plan - they missed the cue after Robert's "Woman talkin' to ya" ad lib, coming in a few bars late - an illustration that these shows, like many others, had their fair share of musical mishaps born of tendency to leap before they looked - but Zeppelin live on stage was never about perfection. It was that air of unpredictability that made them such an engrossing live experience.

During 'Dazed And Confused' they brought back a revival of the previously much deployed 'San Francisco' insert. 'Stairway' was introduced with the cryptic shot at *NME* scribe Shaar Murray. They left the stage to the hum of feedback and the swirling lighting effects provided by the mirror balls suspended above the stage, another nightly Earl's Court ritual.

So to the Saturday night of May 24, 1975. A combination of my familiarity with the much bootlegged soundboard tape - not to mention the fact that I was lucky enough to be in the second row - has elevated this show to a night I will never forget. It remains one of the greatest gigs the band ever played, certainly the most accomplished I ever witnessed.

At the helm was Plant's rapport and enthusiasm, and Page's joyously deranged playing. Witness Plant's heartfelt "This is for our family and friends and the people who've been with us through the lot" speech before a particularly melodic and caressing version of 'Tangerine', and superb phrasing during 'That's The Way'. Witness Page's absolutely out-there-and-who-knows-where-it's-heading solo on a ferocious 'Trampled Underfoot', the ending of which somehow collided with 'Gallows Pole'.

And then there was 'No Quarter'. If the May 18 version stands as the definitive JPJ exercise, this May 24 version saw Page staking his own claim on the proceedings, emerging from the dry ice to layer on a series of solos, each quite exquisite in their delivery and command. Add on a truly memorable 'Dazed' with the best version of 'Woodstock' ever played live, plus an affecting 'Stairway' and a galvanic 'Whole Lotta Love'/'Black Dog' and you have the definitive Zeppelin in-concert experience. Hey and England beat Scotland 5-1 into the bargain! Not that Bonzo cared that much: "I think football's a load of bollocks," he bellowed, ambling up to the mic as they came back for the encore.

By Sunday, the final show, the party was nearly over and both group and audience seemed to sense that this was to be something of a swan song. Confirmation came when Plant said: "Welcome to the last concert in England for a considerable time. There's always the Eighties." How ironic that statement was to prove.

There were still many great moments to savour before the final exit: another refrain of 'You Shook Me' during 'In My Time Of Dying', Plant playfully scat singing ad lib lines of 'Friends' and 'Mystery Train' before 'Bron Yr Aur Stomp'; the San Francisco

---

"Think of 1980 - It's *The Song Remains The Same* soundtrack or nothing. 1990 - *The Song Remains The Same* or nothing. And now it's the same. I've always wanted to put out a chronological live album of Zeppelin stuff - there's some incredibly good stuff - but I just can't get the others to agree, so I've stopped trying."
Jimmy Page
Classic Rock, March 2000.

IMAGINE THE EARL'S COURT BOX SET...
It would seem from those comments that the long mooted idea of a multi-CD, chronological, live Zeppelin set being officially released was off the drawing board in 2000. And until the situation is resolved, bootlegs will have to suffice.

Nevertheless, it's fun to speculate on its hypothetical contents. Back in the summer of 1995 I used

the Earl's Court shows as a basis for an imaginary 4-CD set for a feature in *Record Collector* magazine (issue 191).

In reality it won't happen of course, not least because it's doubtful that the group have the complete tapes of all the shows in their archive anyway.

Since the emergence of the world wide web, other artists have used the internet to issue historical live sets,

notably The Who and King Crimson. Wouldn't it be great, I thought, if Jimmy Page collated such a set from the best available sources (board or audience) and offered it as a net only release in the style of the Crowes/ *Excess All Areas* live album?

Without making it too much of a big deal of it, true fans could gain access to this historical material and bypass the bootleggers in the process.

Whatever the likelihood of it ever happening, there is huge scope to produce a complete overview of the five Earl's Court shows spread over four CDs, combining the best versions of the regular repertoire with a selection of the unique items performed at these shows in the same way that Deep Purple's *Made In Japan* album was expanded to a three-CD *Live In Japan* commemorative set.

BACK FOR THE ENCORE, EARL'S COURT: MAY 18, 1975

insert returning during what would be the final live Zeppelin version of 'Dazed And Confused'; then on into the home straight with an emotional 'Stairway' preceded by Plant's moving reference to his daughter Carmen. Fittingly they added some extras for this final flurry: after the usual 'Whole Lotta Love'/'Black Dog' they returned to the stage again to perform 'Heartbreaker', Plant shouting out "Any requests" in a manner he would repeat at Live Aid ten years hence. They stayed on stage to decide what to do next, and at the suggestion of a cameramen pulled out 'Communication Breakdown'. It said everything about the spirit of Earl's Court that this final statement carried a final twist, Plant ad libbing lines from the never before played live 'D'yer Ma'ker', aping the reggae style of the then emerging Bob Marley. The extended middle section featured a spontaneous series of instrumental stops and starts between Page, Jones and Bonham.

"Well it's been about three hours and forty-five minutes. It's time we went back to listen to some Bob Marley & The Wailers. Thank you very much for showing us we're still alive and well. And it's goodnight from me and goodnight from you. Good night and watch out for the holy grail."

There was a party inside Earl's Court after the final show attended by all the group and various guests including Jeff Beck, Chris Squire from Yes, Alan Freeman and Bob Harris. Music was supplied by Gonzalez and Dr Feelgood. The next day Plant left England for Agadir with his wife Maureen, subsequently meeting up with Jimmy in Marakesh for a spate of travelling that would inspire 'Achilles Last Stand'. The plan was for the group to reconvene in Paris in August to prepare for a series of outdoor dates in America due to commence in San Francisco later that month.

The events of August 4 would change all that. Holidaying in Rhodes, Robert and his wife were seriously injured when their rented car spun off the road.

It was the first of a series of misfortunes that would dog the band for the rest of their career. The glory days were over.

In retrospect those glory days ended as the four of them left the Earl's Court stage for the final time late on the evening of May 25, 1975.

It remains a milestone in their history. Sure there other great stints of concert greatness, those early runs at the Fillmore, Japan 1971, the spring dates in Europe in 1973 and the riotous six shows at the LA Forum in 1977, but what sets Earl's Court apart from any other period was the perfect timing of it all. The group and everyone involved in their organisation really were at the peak of their powers.

Over the five nights their performances crystallised their ability to play incredibly tight and still sound so loose and informal, balancing a delicacy and brutality of rock emotion that has never been matched.

For many years video footage from Earl's Court remained in their archive – the most talked about and desired artefact of fans the world over. Tantalising glimpses were issued officially on the 'Whole Lotta Love' promo and 'Kashmir' CD-ROM. Finally, some 28 years after the event Page did include 49 minutes of footage mixed from their May 24 and 25 shows on the official 2003 *DVD*.

Can it really be 28 years ago? "It's been a lifetime and yet a second," commented Robert on May 18. Led Zeppelin never bettered the triumph of Earl's Court. Sadly they were never allowed the opportunity to equal it. Truly they were the days of their lives. And our's too.

Great Britain - it's been five glorious days... and if you see Denis Healey... tell him we've gone.

ROBERT PLANT, MAY 25

So, having analysed the five shows, here is my imaginary four-CD selection. It offers four and a half hours of definitive Earl's Court 1975 Zeppelin, 29 live performances selected in chronological order over the five shows. Within this there are nine instances where different versions of the same track, thus offering the opportunity to compare how the songs evolved on successive nights, and it's all sequenced with relevant between song patter from Plant that captures the unique atmosphere of the Earl's Court season.

CD 1:
Material from the first two shows:
Rock And Roll (3min 51 sec)/Sick Again (4.51)/The Song Remains The Same (5.20)/The Rain Song (7.40) - all from May 17.
In My Time Of Dying (12.23)/

Kashmir (10.05)/No Quarter (21.26)/Moby Dick (12.50 edit) - all from May 18
CD2:
Material from the third show:
Over The Hills And Far Away (8.00)/Tangerine (4.20)/Going To California 5.50/That's The Way (7.45)/Dazed And Confused (32.00)/Stairway To Heaven (12.35)
CD3:
Material from the fourth show:

No Quarter (22.51)/Tangerine (4.00)/That's The Way 6.06/Trampled Underfoot 9.05)/Dazed And Confused (33.21)
CD4:
Material from the final show
Over The Hills And Far Away (7.50)/In My Time Of Dying (10.05)/Kashmir (9.07)/Going To California (4.53)/Bron Yr Aur Stomp (5.40)/Stairway To Heaven (10.43)/Whole Lotta Love (6.35)/Black Dog (6.50)/

Heartbreaker (5.58)/Communication Breakdown (5.03)

So there you have it: 270 minutes of unchallengeable evidence that Earl's Court was the greatest series of concerts Led Zeppelin ever performed.

Earl's Court was a landmark in rock'n'roll presentation and it paved the way for the big arena shows that are commonplace now. I see Robert and Jimmy occasionally and we always have a warm conversation about those days.

MEL BUSH, PROMOTER

PERFORMING 'BLACK DOG', EARL'S COURT: MAY 1975

THE TBL EARL'S COURT INTERVIEWS

THE PROMOTER

Mel Bush has been one of the leading UK concert promoters and managers for over 30 years. His handling of the Earl's Court shows was much admired by Peter Grant. Mel is still very active in the business, promoting and managing a variety of artists including David Essex, Vennesa Mae and Bond.

TBL: When did you first work with Zeppelin?
MB: I did some early shows with them in the Bournemouth area. We did a show at the Royal Ballroom in Bournemouth. I came up with naming the venue Starkers - which was a sort of tongue-in-cheek comment of the free spirit of the times.
TBL: How easy was it to work with Peter Grant?
MB: Very easy indeed. It was a pleasure to do business because he was so organised. We quickly came to the arrangement of the 90/10 deal - ie 90% for the band and 10% for the promoter which as you probably know became the standard for the era.
TBL: How did the opportunity to present them at Earl's Court come about?
MB: By that time they were a huge attraction and I knew Peter wanted to present them in the biggest and best setting that particular year. I was the first concert promoter to use Earl's Court a couple of years before with David Bowie and Slade. So when Peter was considering venues to use he got in touch. Once it was all up and running we came to a good arrangement about the ticket prices which Peter was always keen to keep at a reasonable level.
TBL: Can you remember how much the deal was?
MB: No it was a long time ago - all I can say is that it was very substantial for the time though the actual cost to present all the lights and PA was also astronomical.
TBL: Who came up with the idea for the Zeppelin Express link up with British Rail that was featured on the posters?
MB: That was mine and Peter's. We realised that by coming by train you could literally get into Earl's Court from any part of the country. So we co-ordinated it all with British Rail and called the trains the Zeppelin Express. On the day of the gigs we had all these Inter City trains full of Zeppelin fans from all parts of the UK. It all added to the event - and that's how I approached promoting Zeppelin at Earl's Court. This just wasn't another gig - it was a real event. The poster was designed by Martine, a graphic artist I knew in Bournemouth. None of us realised of course that it would go on to become one of the most collectable posters in rock'n'roll history. I recently put one up for auction for the Eddie Kidd fund and it raised £1,800.

TBL: Were you surprised how quickly the original three dates sold out?
MB: We knew there was going to be a massive demand but it was just phenomenal. I know there was some criticism of how we sold the tickets but there wasn't a lot else we could do. I was at the Earl's Court box office managing the crowds the day they went on sale. We did feel by opening it to personal callers the true fans would be bothered to make it. We then added two more dates which did give a lot more people the chance to get to see it.
TBL: Were you worried about how they would cope with the hall's acoustics - I know there was some problems with the sound at David Bowie's 1973 Earl's Court show.
MB: We had learn't a lot form doing the Bowie gig. I don't think I realised how big the place was until we got in there but if anyone could make it work then it was Zeppelin. At the time they were far and away the most acomplished band in terms of rock presentation. The guy they had doing the sound, Benji Le Fevre, was really good. They also spent a lot of time preparing the show and working with the lasers which again were very innovative for the time. They spent a good week in pre-production and getting used to the venue's acoustics.
TBL: Did they seem nervous backstage before the first show?
MB: Not so much nervous - there was real anticipation and the adrenalin was really flowing. I think we all knew this was something special and the atmosphere was just electric. To hear 18,000 fans chanting "Zeppelin, Zeppelin" before they came on was just so exiting The whole set up with Zeppelin - the limos, the security, the whole entourage thing - it was just a vast powerful organisation. Everything they did had such a presence about it.
DL: Any particular stand out memories from the shows?
MB: Every night was amazing. They were just so powerful. The whole chemistry of the four of them - a fantastic singer in Robert, Jimmy's guitar playing and John Paul Jones' immense musicianship and perhaps most of all I remember John Bonham. He was such a talent - the best drummer in rock'n'roll without a doubt. It was such a loss when he died. When he died I remember thinking how he drove the whole Earl's Court event along with his enthusiasm and power.
TBL: Did you ever get the opportunity to work with them again?
MB: Sadly not. I did try and get them on an outdoor thing I was trying to arrange a couple of years later but it fell through and of course Freddie Bannister had the licence for Knebworth which they did. I went to that and it was also great. I really would have liked to do something with them again and I think I would as I got on well with Peter, but sadly it was not to be.

TBL: Final thoughts 25 years on?
MB: Earl's Court was a landmark in rock'n'roll presentation and it paved the way for the big arena shows that are commonplace now. I see Robert and Jimmy occasionally and we always have a warm conversation about those days. I'm still very active in the business with Venessa Mae, David Essex and I'm just bringing Santana over. I like a lot of the current bands like Travis, but you just don't seem to get the lasting bands anymore. I was lucky to promote some fantastic artists - David Bowie. Queen, Roxy Music, The Who, Thin Lizzy. Great acts. I'm just so proud to have been associated with so many acts that have become part of rock'n'roll history. Led Zeppelin, though, really were the greatest rock'n'roll band in the world - and in my view they proved it once and for all with the performances they gave at Earl's Court.

THE PHOTOGRAPHER

Barry Plummer was a freelance photographer whose work was most frequently seen in *Melody Maker* during the Seventies. His photos from Earl's Court are still

BONZO, EARL'S COURT: 1975

much in demand by agencies and magazines throughout the world.
TBL: Had you photographed Zeppelin on many occasions before Earl's Court?
BP: Yes a few times. I was at that reception when they received an award by the Board of Trade and I also shot them at the Bath festival which was really good. In fact one of my photos of them backstage was used in *Mojo* recently. I also did those shots at Southampton in 1971 when they performed on that stage with a carpet (see page 59 of *The Concert File*). Another occasion from that era was at Manchester University for the *Music Paper*. Unfortunately hardly any of the live stuff from then was used as it got sent to an agency and seemingly lost. There are shots backstage from that gig which have been used in various books. I remember knocking on the dressing room door to ask if I could take some photos - Peter Grant said "What do you think boys?" and Plant said OK as long as I didn't use a flash. Luckily I had

some police surveillance film which was a bit grainy but got me the shots I was looking for.
TBL: How many nights did you shoot at Earl's Court?
BP: I did two nights and I think it was the first weekend of shows but to be honest I can't be sure. I was only down for one but Rob Lynton the PR had another spare press ticket for the next night so we went again.
TBL: How many numbers were you allowed to photograph?
BP: This was before the stipulations of doing only the first three numbers so luckily it was virtually the whole show. There were about four or five of us - Rob Ellis, Michael Putland and I think Pennie Smith and each of us was given twenty minutes at a time throughout the show. I seem to remember there were video cameras scooting about so we had to go on a gang plank each time to shoot up at the stage
TBL: What camera equipment did you use?
BP: A Nikon F2 camera with a 20 mill lens. It wasn't quite a fish eye but it enabled me to get the whole stage covered, particularly on the shots of the encore with the neon sign ablaze.
TBL: How many rolls of film did you use?
BP: At least six x 36 exposures on black and white and then four x 36 in colour. The colour shots were a little over exposed when the neon Led Zeppelin sign was lit during the encores. I actually discarded quite a lot of them when I was printing them up - I also sent about 30 negs to a Japanese publication which I never saw again. It's funny looking back but the colour shots were never in much demand. It was mainly the German and French magazines who dealt in those. I used to do really well out of the colour stuff I did on The Osmonds and David Cassidy which were used by the teen mags. Of course nowadays Zeppelin pics are always being asked for so I wish I'd photographed more of their gigs than I did!
TBL: What do you remember of the performance?
BP: Fantastic - definitely one of the best gigs I ever saw. You tended to concentrate on getting the photos

right rather than the performance you were witnessing but at Earl's Court there was this great wave of power that just washed over me.

The lasers were also really impressive - that sort of effect was pretty new back then and it was a stunning moment when Page emerged with the violin bow. You could feel it was really gelling on stage. I still play their stuff in the car - things like 'Kashmir' remind you of that power that was so evident at Earl's Court.

TBL: *Which of your Earl's Court photos do you think stand out?*
BP: I really like the one that was coloured for the Ross Halfin *Photographers Led Zeppelin* book (see page 232). The shot of Page that *Classic Rock* used in their Greatest Guitarists feature - and the group shot that was on the cover of their Zeppelin special last year. Earl's Court was definitely the best set of pictures I got of the group. I did both Knebworths but I was disappointed with the results. I didn't really have a good position for those. There was a real good feeling about Earl's Court and I think that was captured in the shots I got.

THE JOURNALIST
During his time writing for *Melody Maker* **Chris Welch** chronicled the group's career from day one. Indeed, he was the first journalist to interview Jimmy after he'd formed Led Zeppelin. He remains a loyal supporter of their work - even though a critical review of *Houses Of The Holy* was unappreciated by the group. As a result his press credentials were withheld and he watched the opening Earl's Court show from half way up a gangway aisle...

TBL: *You attended the first night at Earl's Court - I seem to remember in your Zeppelin biography you mentioned something about a mix up over your tickets?*
CW: There certainly was. When my wife and I arrived we were told there were no press tickets for the *Melody Maker* so I had to go and get a couple from a tout. We actually ended up sitting in the aisle which was OK for me but a bit insulting for Maralyn my wife!
TBL: *Was it a premeditated move by Peter Grant not to provide tickets for the Melody Maker because the paper's press coverage had been*

less than enthusiastic at times.
CW: It was never quite proved but I know Robert in particular took umbridge to my review of *Houses Of The Holy*. I didn't like 'The Crunge' or 'Dy'er Mak'e'r'. I couldn't see how they fitted in with their style. Those, of course, were two of the numbers that Robert liked. The *MM* had been particularly supportive of the group from way back and I certainly still held them in high esteem.

But as we know they were very sensitive to press criticism. My job was to be a critic and at times that meant criticising what I didn't like. It's a shame they couldn't see that, especially as no paper did more to publicise them early on.
TBL: *Not having press tickets did not stop you giving the concert a rave review in the next week's edition.*
CW: Absolutely not. They were outstanding that night. A brilliant performance. The whole presentation with the lasers etc was electrifying. They really did seem to be enjoying themselves and the new material from *Physical Graffiti* added a whole new dimension to their show.

I mean 'Trampled Underfoot' was just sensational.
TBL: *Do you know Robert had a sly pop at you in one of his onstage spiels during the second show – "Been away a long time gotta impress... got that Chris?"*
CW: Yes I did get to hear about it He was always one for getting in his dig at the press when he felt like it though I think it was a good natured banter rather than any serious grudge. On the whole I enjoyed a great relationship with them.
TBL: *Was the Earl's Court show the best Zeppelin gig you saw?*
CW: One of them for sure. I guess my personal choice has to be when I saw them at the Carnegie Hall in '69 because I ended up jamming with them on stage!

Earl's Court, though, was a real peak. They had such impetus in their playing. Looking back now the fact that I didn't have a privileged press seat and sat amongst the fans only added to the event for me. I really did view them that night as a fan which I genuinely was... and of course 25 years on still am.

Been away a long time

gotta impress...

got that Chris?

ROBERT PLANT, MAY 18

PERFORMING 'IN MY TIME OF DYING', EARL'S COURT: MAY 1975

In general *Presence* is viewed as a lesser part of the Zep studio album canon. I consider it to be one of their most vital and *Tight But Loose* has long since championed the cause of this album. In *TBL 12* I unravelled the tangled web of events that led to the construction of the album and in *TBL 15* re-appraised the merits of the record 25 years on from its original release.

An amalgamation of those features are produced for this chapter which once again brings the case for *Presence* to order. As far as Jimmy Page is concerned the verdict is not in doubt. Asked by interviewer Nick Kent in 2003 to name his favourite Zeppelin album he replied, "A personal favourite for me will always be *Presence*. I love that album because it was done at a totally negative time but the music was still superbly positive." Read on to find out why.

REFERENCE: **TIGHT BUT LOOSE 12 & 15**

"It was an April morning when they told us we should go"

IN THE PRESENCE : 5
OF PURE ROCK'N'ROLL

A few weeks after Led Zeppelin completed their 1975 US tour with three sold out dates at the LA Forum, Jimmy Page, Robert Plant and Peter Grant met in New York to discuss the group's future plans. This visit also saw Page begin work on the soundtrack for their yet to be completed movie, Plant filmed a rare TV interview with JJ Jackson for screening on *Midnight Special* and the pair attend a reception for Monty Python.

The meeting with Grant and their accountants confirmed something they had known for a while. A period of tax exile was essential for them to protect their vast earnings. Grant quickly established a base for his operation, renting promoter Claude Knobs' house in Montreux. A touring plan was drawn up that would see them return to the US to play a series of major outdoor dates in August and then move on to South America before returning to perform in Europe in early 1976.

Page and Plant wanted to spend time travelling together during the summer before the American dates. In May they returned to the UK to prepare for the forthcoming Earl's Court stint. During those shows Plant threw in more than one barbed comment regarding their upcoming forced exile. "Somebody voted for someone and now everybody's on the run. You know Denis (Healey, then Chancellor of the Exchequer)... no artist in the country anymore... he must be Dazed And Confused!"

Led Zeppelin played their final night at Earl's Court on Sunday May 25, Plant commenting, "This is our last concert in England for some considerable time. Still there's always the Eighties." His parting shot was equally to the point. "If you see Denis Healey tell him we've gone!" The next day Plant and wife Maureen flew to Agadir. Three weeks later Jimmy met up with him in Marrakesh where they spent several nights at the local folk festival. They then travelled down to the Spanish Sahara looking to go to Tafia. Confrontations between Spain and Morocco at the time prevented them from going much further in that part of the country. So they travelled by car back up through Casablanca and Tangier, meeting up with the rest of the group in Montreux. A date was set in mid-August for them to meet up in Paris to begin rehearsing for the US tour which would commence on August 23 with two massive dates at the Oakland Stadium in San Francisco.

Before then Plant and family took a holiday on the Greek island of Rhodes, planning to join Phil May of The Pretty Things. Page went to Sicily to view a farmhouse once owned by Aleister Crowley and returned to London for work on the film. "We were all going to meet up five days later... then there was the accident and we were just stopped in our tracks."

The accident that would dictate a whole new direction occurred on Monday August 4. A hired Austin Mini, driven by Plant's wife Maureen, left the road and crashed into a tree. On impact Robert suffered multiple injuries to his right leg and elbow, Maureen a broken pelvis and fractured skull. Plant's children suffered minor injuries and Jimmy's daughter, who was with them, escaped with bruising. Plant was taken to a Greek hospital where with the aid of an interpreter he tried to explain who he was. "I had to share a room with a drunken soldier who'd fallen over. He kept uttering my name and singing 'The Ocean' - it was bizarre". Luckily Jimmy's girlfriend Charlotte got word to Richard Cole in England who immediately flew out with two Harley Street doctors in a private jet owned by the civil engineer Sir Robert McAlpine.

THE ALBUM

Meanwhile, in Utah on the morning of August 5, promoter Bill Graham had been enjoying a boating holiday. A plane flew over his boat with a skyline message reading "Bill, call urgently". Returning to the shore he took the call which turned out to be from Peter Grant explaining that because of Robert's accident they would have to cancel the forthcoming dates. Graham immediately flew to San Francisco to supervise the refunding of 110,000 tickets for the sold out Oakland Stadium shows at a reputed personal cost of $130,000. Additional dates lined up for Kansas City Louisville, New Orleans, Tempe, Arizona, Denver Atlanta and the Rose Bowl Pasadena for September 6 were also cancelled.

Cole arranged for the Plant family to fly back to England via Rome. Knowing a stop-over in the UK would adversely affect his tax status, a plan was hatched to move Robert to Jersey. Heavily encased in plaster, Peter Grant ensured his flight would be as comfortable as possible. "I bought the seats in the front and then had them removed. There was a bit of a row, but I got the captain to make sure we could unscrew the seats before we took off. That way Robert got the space he needed."

After recuperating at a house owned by noted Jersey lawyer Dick Christian, the entourage moved out to Los Angeles. Rather than spend the time wallowing in self pity, it was decided they would use this period to record a new album.

Robert's own morale had been severely tested during the weeks since the accident and having to leave his wife behind made him understandably depressed. "Time goes very slowly when you get up every day and you can't kick a ball... kick a roadie or even your drummer."

He and Page rented houses in Malibu Colony where they

IMMEDIATE RELEASE/ AUGUST 8, 1975

LED ZEPPELIN AUGUST-SEPTEMBER TOUR POSTPONED FOLLOWING AUTO
ACCIDENT OF LEAD SINGER ROBERT PLANT AND HIS FAMILY ON GREEK ISLAND.
From: Danny Goldberg

The August-September tour of English supergroup, Led Zeppelin,
has been postponed following an auto accident on the small Greek island
of Rhodes in which Zeppelin lead singer Robert Plant and members of
his family were injured.

The accident took place on Monday afternoon, August 4th. Due to
the nature and extent of the injuries sustained by Plant and his
family, and the inadequate medical facilities in Rhodes, a number of
the London staff of Swan Song, Led Zeppelin's record company, flew to
Rhodes in a chartered jet equipped with stretchers, blood plasma,
and two doctors from Harley St., England's finest medical center.

Plant and his family are currently under intensive care in a
London hospital. Earlier today, physicians there diagnosed his injuries
as multiple fractures of ankle, bones supporting the foot, and elbow.
Following this diagnosis, it was announced by Led Zeppelin manager,
Peter Grant, and Zeppelin attorney, Steve Weiss, that the August-
September American tour was postponed, as was the October tour that had
been scheduled for the Far East. Additionally, there is the possibility
that the scheduled November tour of Europe and December tour of Japan
may also have to be postponed.

Within the next couple of weeks, doctors expect to have a better
idea of when Plant will be recovered and able to perform again.

Plant's wife, Maureen, also in the car, suffered a lengthy period
of concussions, and has broken her leg in several places. She has four
fractures of the pelvis and facial lacerations. Plant's son, Karac 4,
suffered a fractured leg and multiple cuts and bruises. His daughter,
Carmen 7, has a broken wrist, cuts and bruises.

The band was due to begin rehearsals for their forthcoming U.S.
tour, in Paris on August 14. 110,000 tickets to two shows at the
Oakland Stadium were completely sold out on Aug 4. Among the other
concerts which were postponed were those in Los Angeles at the Rose
Bowl, Kansas City, Louisville, New Orleans, Tempe, Arizona, Denver,
and Atlanta.

began writing. Plant was accompanied by sound man Benji Lefevre. "In the end I did begin to get out a bit. We rented a pink Cadillac. It was a crazy existence really." A freak storm wiped part of the beach away not far from Plant's residence. "I woke up and went down to the beach to find ten feet of it just swept away. I thought that's all I need." He'd already vowed not to sing 'In My Time Of Dying' again (which he didn't keep to). "Now I was beginning to think I shouldn't have written 'The Ocean'!"

On September 14 the entourage showed up at the Renaissance Pleasure Fair in Navato, 30 miles north of San Francisco. Plant was carried round in a sedan chair. They were eventually joined in LA by John Paul Jones and John Bonham. Full scale rehearsals were soon underway in SIR Studios in Hollywood.

The material they were constructing had an immediate edge to it – with no room for keyboard experiments and the like. It was back to basics. Page did bring in a few riff structures he had kept under wraps for some time (notably the riff pattern used on the then unreleased 'Walter's Walk' which was layered on to 'Hots On For Nowhere') but mostly they started from scratch. The slow blues 'Tea Far One' began as a bluesy skit with Plant singing the lines to 'Minnie The Moocher'. Old standards such as 'Stop Me Talking' were also used to warm up the rehearsals. With little material pre-planned, the lyrics for these new songs were heavily influenced by recent events. The lengthy 'Achilles Last Stand' was built around the travels Plant had experienced with Jimmy back in the summer. His depressive state in Malibu gave rise to the venomous theme of 'For Your Life'. "That was a bitter treaty with rock'n'roll," he commented later. "The girls who in 'Sick Again'

CHICAGO STADIUM: JANUARY 20, 1975

JERSEY: DECEMBER 10, 1975

had been wonderful were now suddenly... well they were hung on the balance of a crystal paying through the nose."

Another new song 'Hots On For Nowhere' mirrored Plant's anger with Page and Grant and what he saw as their initial insensitivity to his situation ("I've got friends who would give me fuck all!"). As ever the quest for their roots was never too far away - this time in the guise of 'Nobody's Fault But Mine' - an old Blind Willie Johnson tune from the late Twenties, given a new dynamic twist by Page's guitar technology. As well as the familiar Les Paul he also began using a Lake Placid Blue Stratocaster (notably on 'For Your Life').

Talking about the strangeness of the times Plant remembers, "I was just sitting in that wheelchair and getting morose. 'Tea For

One' was very personal. I couldn't get back to the woman and children I loved. It was like... is this rock'n'roll thing really anything at all?"

On a lighter vein there was 'Candy Store Rock'. "That was a saving grace and me being Ral Donner. The guy who wanted to be Elvis... and now was. The bridge section is pure Ral and Jimmy's guitar playing is incredible. The whole band moved into another gear on that. Bonzo's and Jonesy's rhythm playing went beyond mere pop music beyond jazz and rock'n' roll. It was just inspired."

Of course being in Los Angeles offered the usual road fever attractions. They ventured out to see Donovan's Santa Monica show and met up with Paul Rodgers and Boz Burrell from Bad Co. Jimmy checked out Michael Des Barres new band Detective and a deal was set up for them to sign for Swan Song. There were familiar reports of Bonham's bad behaviour on the LA club circuit and drugs were never very far away.

By late October they were ready to record. Knowing the American tax situation was now likely to catch up with them they ventured back to Europe, selecting Musicland Studios in Munich as the place to record.

Once there Plant's sense of humour was duly revived. "It was a bit claustrophobic in Musicland as the studio was in the bowels of the Arabella Hotel. There was a whore house on the fourth floor and I kept being pushed into the lift in the wheelchair where I'd fumble for the fourth floor button. I could never quite reach it though, being stuck in that chair so I ended up on the ground floor where Bonzo would be making stew out of the tape operator's shoes!"

Once underway (they were a week behind schedule when one of them turned up late) the Munich sessions went supremely well under the guidance of engineer Keith Harwood. In just a mere 18 days they had the whole thing complete. Page: "We hardly went out from the studio. 'For Your Life' was made up there and then on the spot. So was 'Hots On Far Nowhere' and the structure for 'Achilles'. I built it piece by piece and got it in one. I'm really pleased with the solo on 'Tea For One'. It's so held back. Seven minutes long and at no point does it blow out."

There was a moment of drama when Plant slipped over a wire in the studio landing on his bad ankle but luckily he was OK. "I've never known Jimmy to move so quickly. He was out of the mixing booth and holding me up, fragile as he might be. It was a bit rash of me to be bopping about but the track we were doing was so brilliantl!" With The Rolling Stones due in to begin recording after them Page asked Mick Jagger for two extra days to finish the project - putting in one 14-hour session to finish the overdubs before their time was up, much to the Stones amazement. "That was the ultimate test of that whole lifestyle. It was incredibly fulfilling."

The new album was completed the day before Thanksgiving. The next day Plant called the Swan Song office in New York to tell them the news - even suggesting they should title the album *Thanksgiving*. That idea was later dropped in favour of *Presence* after consultations with Hipgnosis on the artwork.

With the album completed it was back to the serenity of Jersey. However the performing bug was definitely returning. On December 3 Bonzo and John Paul Jones sat in with Norman Hale, the resident pianist at Beehan's West Park, a local niterie. Hale was a former member of The Tornados. They promised to return the next week with the whole band. So on December 10, Led Zeppelin made a surprise 45 minute appearance at the club with Hale on piano. Their last show at Earl's Court had been seen by some 17,000. Just

BEEHAN'S PARK WEST: THAT IMPROMPTU GIG

Led Zeppelin's last live show had been in front of 17,000 at London's Earl's Court in May. Just 350 witnessed the next, an unexpected return to the stage in Jersey on the night of December 10, 1975.

The venue was Beehan's Park West, a local night spot on the island. Bonzo and Jonesy had performed there a week earlier and

brought Page and Plant back the next week to jam with local pianist Norman Hale, a former member of The Tornados. The 45-minute performance consisted of rock'n'roll classics mixed with some of their own material. For the occasion Page brought along his Lake Placid Stratocaster that had been on hand for the Earl's Court shows and in use during the Musicland sessions for *Presence*.

Speaking a few weeks after the gig Plant commented: "No one really knew who we were and we had this great piano player. After about 15 minutes of Eddie Cochran and Little Richard songs we got right into a long blues thing. Suddenly all the stops and dynamics we subconsciously activate on stage came out. We were very happy with each other."

Judging from what Plant had

hinted, it's interesting to speculate on the set list. I would reckon at least one *Presence* track would have been included - could that 'long blues thing' have been a stab at 'Tea For One'? The newly recorded 'Candy Store Rock' would have fitted into the Fifties theme of the evening. A speculative guess at the set list for this one off occasion might line up as follows:

'Something Else'/'Blue Suede

Shoes'/'It'll Be Me', 'C'mon Everybody', 'My Baby Left Me', 'Tea For One', 'Candy Store Rock', 'Money', 'Weekend', 'Louie Louie', 'Whole Lotta Love', 'Whole Lotta Shakin' Going On' and 'Rip it Up'.

For Robert Plant the Beehans show was a key moment in his recovery process. "You see the possibility of performing and who can avoid it, you know? It was like rock'n'roll night at this dance hall

ADVERT FOR A RUMOURED ZEP APPEAR-
ANCE AT THE MARQUEE, LONDON IN MAY
1976. THE MYSTERY BAND TURNED OUT TO
BE THE PRETTY THINGS WITH JOHN PAUL
JONES GUESTING.

INTERVIEWS FOR *PRESENCE*, SWAN SONG OFFICE, LONDON: MARCH, 1976

350 witnessed this return to something like active duty.

This impromptu appearance fuelled rumours that they would soon be back on stage. Plant however was still in the early stages of a full recovery. In Paris on New Years Day he took his first steps unaided. "It was one small step for man," he said soon after, "and one giant leap for six nights at Madison Square Garden."

In January he was in New York giving interviews looking very fit with a restyled haircut. "I know it's a real punk thing to say but it's just good to be alive. This is the longest, most pensive period of my life. I had no choice but to question everything after the accident. My mind, which at first was taken up with repairing the physical, was then taken up with the musical. As such there's a lot of determination on this new album."

Page and Bonham were also over for the trip - a boisterous Bonzo bursting on at the end of Deep Purple's show at the Radio City Hall to proclaim to the crowd in an inebriated state, "Hi, I'm John Bonham from Led Zeppelin and we've got a new album coming out soon!" With the glint now firmly back in Plant's eye, the entourage journeyed to their old hunting ground of Los Angeles checking out, amongst others, the all girl group The Runaways. With the infamous cover art now complete, Jimmy returned to the UK to give a round of promotional interviews upon the album's early April release. "The whole testimony of the new album is that it proved to us once and for all that there was no reason for us to split up. I can't think of many groups who have been going as long as we have who still have that spontaneity about them. I'm very optimistic about the future."

In the UK the album went gold on advance sales alone and was the fastest selling album in the Atlantic group's history up to that point. It was an instant number one. In the US it made the biggest leap in *Billboard's* then chart history moving from 24 to the top spot in its second week of release. By and large it was also favourably received by the critics and fans alike.

On May 23 Page and Plant were back on stage at the LA Forum jamming with Bad Company for an encore performance of 'I Just Wanna Make Love To You'. "I want to get back on stage so much," said Plant after the show. Despite constant rumours during that summer of 1976 Grant declined all offers, awaiting Plant's full fitness in the new year. The attention instead turned to the long awaited release of their *Song Remains The Same* movie and soundtrack. These events seemed to somewhat overshadow the *Presence* album and as the album's sales drifted off, it seemed the majority of fans were content to store the strange looking sleeve away, preferring the thrill of the film and its accompanying live album.

When it came time to rehearse for their 1977 tour though, it was the number that in his *Sounds* review Jonh Ingram said would be "a motherfucker live" that they immediately got to work on. 'Achilles Last Stand' went on to become a centrepiece of their comeback US tour which commenced in the spring of 1977. "*Presence* was our stand against everything. Against the elements and chance," Plant told the *NME's* Roy Carr from the Manticore rehearsal studio.

With such enthusiasm for the new album, it's somewhat surprising that they hardly plundered their seventh album for live material. Only 'Nobody's Fault But Mine' and 'Achilles' were adapted for live performance. Perhaps Robert felt that some of those songs were too personal to perform repeatedly. It's a shame that the riff numbers, such as 'Royal Orleans' and 'Candy Store

I know it's a real punk thing

to say but it's just good

to be alive.

ROBERT PLANT

---

that was like some place ten years gone by in the best English tradition. Bonzo said, 'Come on man, lets plan on going' and I said. 'Look I can't even walk for God's sake. Don't embarrass me. I can't hobble across the dance hall and go on to the stage.' He said we would go through the side door and then up the back steps. And with amazing grace that's what I did and found myself plunked on a stool. But I was

really shy. Every time I went to hit a high note I stood up. Not putting any weight on my foot, but just sort of standing. Oh they got some great photos.

"You know those guys in holiday areas with cameras who come and take your photo and then you have to call in the next day and show up at the pier where they will present you with whatever snaps they took the night before and you find out

how silly you look or how drunk you were for an extortionate price? I gave the guy a free hand to shoot like crazy... shoot all these shots of Led Zeppelin in this antiquated ballroom. It was a really exciting experience - rock'n'roll in the most basic sense.

"Of course I'd made sure I stayed behind Bonzo wedged between the piano and the drums, but then I felt myself edge forward a little bit... then after the third number I was

wiggling the stool past the drums and further out. And once we got going we didn't want to stop. They kept flashing the lights on inside the place, 'Get them off stage, they've done enough!'

"Bad Company played the same gig after us - so this tiny little dance hall is getting the pride of English musicians for nothing. Just for the hell of playing."

Spontaneous though it was, the

Beehan's Park West show was one of the most significant events in what had already been a momentous year. It was an occasion when they realised that after all the traumas of the previous months, they still had the desire and inclination to perform in front of an audience. But it would be another 18 months before all four would return to the stage in Dallas for the opening night of their 1977 comeback tour.

BONZO, CHICAGO STADIUM: JANUARY 20, 1975

Rock', were never given the opportunity to develop in a live setting. It was to be a situation they would repeat with their next album *In Through The Out Door*. Their reticence to approach newly recorded studio material in the latter touring era was perhaps an indication of the unrest within the group that lay below the surface.

In retrospect they have mixed feelings about *Presence*. The forced circumstances of its construction is still held in high esteem by Page but Plant now seems less enthusiastic for it. "*Presence* was the most difficult record in my career to come up with. I spent the whole process of preparing and delivering the songs from a wheelchair. The whole thing was quite a strain and I think that's reflected in my vocals because they sound tired."

For Jimmy Page though it was a watershed. "All our pent up energy and passion went into making it what it was. That's why there was no acoustic material there. The mechanism was perfectly oiled. We started screaming in rehearsals and never stopped."

Presence was on extraordinary chapter in their career. A soap opera of events surrounded its emergence as they turned inner turmoil into something constructive. The atmosphere that surrounds the whole record is one of urgency and fight. It needs to be listened to with the knowledge of just exactly what they were going through at the time. Then its true power is undeniable. This isn't the Led Zeppelin record for musical diversity. But it is the record for sheer out and out muscle and thrust.

The urgency and spontaneity made little time for the experimentation of the past. So there were no boogies with Stu, no hat's off to Harper's. No funk or reggae parodies. No mellotrons or synths.

The result of the basic/bass/drums/guitar/vocal approach was to give the record a very live feel – leading to the conclusion that in my view *Presence* is the nearest they got to capturing over a complete album the unpredictable edge and power of their onstage performances within a studio

Presence in retrospect
So how does it stand up all these years later. Still intensely powerful. Still very focused. The stuctrual grace of 'Achilles Last Stand' still retains all it's majesty led by Bonham's staccato drumming and Page's cascading guitar overdubs.This track remains one of the defining statements of their entire catalogue. 'For Your Life'

> *Presence was the most difficult record in my career to come up with. I spent the whole process of preparing and delivering the songs from a wheelchair.*
>
> ROBERT PLANT

POST ACCIDENT: AUTUMN, 1975

has an undeniably dark edge as it grinds through its six minutes duration. The Page solo is one of his very best - perhaps THE best, unfolding with incredible venom. 'Royal Orleans' is of lighter mood. Page Jones and Bonham show they are still masters of the simple gargantuan riff over which Plant unfolds the humorous story of road fever, name checking love god Barry White along the way.

For all the early blues musings on the first two Zep albums, they never dressed up an old blues tune more inventively than when they rewrote Blind Wille Johnson's 'Nobody's Fault But Mine'. Lemon squeezing delta dealings merges with Page's sonic guitar technology. In the Ral Donner skit 'Candy Store Rock', we find them just turning themselves on playing on a 50's groove in the manner they approached the countless off the cuff juke box faves they pumped into those' Whole Lotta Love' live medleys.

The pure intuitive swing of 'Hots On For Nowhere' reflects its live in the studio construction and as Charles Shaar Murray noted in his *NME* review of the time brings to mind "What Glenn Miller would have sounded like had he played in a murderously heavy four piece rock band".

That leaves the understated downbeat 'Tea For One', a slow blues reflecting Plant's hurt at being away from his family. Blessed with the final Page guitar flurry – a beautifully brooding laid back affair.

Presence was Led Zeppelin's lesson in immortality. In a year that had seen them taste immense success in both the US and the UK, they suddenly found themselves in a postiton of rare vulnerabilty and out of it made a record that once again saw the original catalyst of the group back at the helm. *Presence* is stock full of Jimmy Page's guitar rages. Rarely before or for that matter since, has he dominated an album so convincingly. For that reason alone it's a vital part of the story. It may never enjoy the high profile of *Zep 4* or *Physical Graffiti* but all these years on *Presence* still portrays the real heart and soul of Led Zeppelin more vividly than anything else they released.

The mystery of *The Object* and that bizarre sleeve
In the January 17 issue of *Melody Maker*, a news report suggested that the forthcoming Led Zeppelin album would be titled *Obelisk* and was due for release on February 20. Although they were a good six weeks out with the release date, and the eventual album title, the rumour of *Obelisk* gave hint to the actual sleeve design. For the sleeve would feature an obelisk (dictionary defined meaning: monolithic shaft of stone, square or rectangular in section with pyramical apex or simiar shape) or as Swan Song would dub it "The Object".

The first visual evidence of this was leaked to *Sounds* in early March. "US adverts for the new Zeppelin album look like a scene from an early Sixties breakfast cereal ad" is how they described the illustration. By now the album had been officially titled *Presence* and Atlantic's marketing team were advising of the delays in a press release as they tried to co-ordinate their sales campaign, stating that "Led Zeppelin oversee all and every detail of the production of their albums to ensure the end result is nothing short of excellent". Finally, on April 6 1976, the full extent of the bizarre gatefold sleeve was revealed alongside the seven new compositons it housed.

Zeppelin had created a series of enigmas with their controversial and striking sleeve designs. For *Presence* they went right out on a tangent. The idea was conceived by Storm and Po of the Hipgnosis design team who'd worked on the *Houses Of The Holy* sleeve. The concept came about after a group meeting between Hipgnosis, Peter Grant and George Hardie (a fine art designer who had worked on the first Zeppelin sleeve). It was apparent to Storm and Po that Zeppelin projected an almost unseen presence of power - the brief was to translate that presence into a visual illustration.

Storm takes up the story. "What we came up with was the idea of placing an item from one time or another into a surrounding from another time. So we chose all those pictures from the Forties and Fifties and contaminated them with the presence of the black obsessional object. The black object stands as being as powerful as one's imagination cares it to be and we felt Zeppelin could rightfully feel the same way about themselves in the world of rock music. So, in those scenes *The Object*, as we dubbed it, was essential to all parts of the society. And those people in the scenes were trying to discover what *The Object* was - and how its presence was felt.

"The front and back pictures were shot by us. The back cover girl was the same child model we'd used in the *Houses Of The Holy* shoot. All the inner spread photos were lifted from US magazines such as Life and Look. The object was pointed on by Richard Manning - Jimmy Page actually asked us to alter the shape of the design of it and the title *Presence* was their suggestion. I think the whole sleeve concept was very appropriate for Zeppelin. The band are a very powerful band, musically and socially, and the black object is a definite thing of power. Its pervasive presence and mystery appealed very strongly to them."

Jimmy was in agreement with most of their ideas. "It came out of that conversation when Hypgnosis said we had a very positive force. The fact that four people can create an effect. There's definitely a presence there - and that was it. They came up with *The Object* and wanted to call it *Obelisk*. I held out for *Presence*. You think about more than just a symbol that way."

In designing *The Object*, Hypgnosis were commissioned by Swan Song to have around 1,000 of them made as a three dimensional promotional items. Not all of them were welcome in the Zeppelin households.

The mystery prompted Rolling Stone reporter Cameron Crowe to call the London Swan Song office. He reported the following:

black... and twisted and obviously worse for wear and tear since its original appearance in 2001. To look at it on the pictures decorating the new Led Zeppelin album it would seem *The Object* is now back in the year 1950 or thereabouts.

Robert Plant has contemplated *The Object* perceiving in it the messages that others might discover in The Pyramids of Egypt. 'It's been ever present throughout time,' he told us. 'We just took one moment in time in which to illuminate its presence in society.'

"*The Object* may not be welcome everywhere - it appeared recently in the home of John Bonham who told us this story. 'While I was away my wife received one of these *Objects* in the post and put it on the table. There was tape machine running, recording the children singing, and when they played it back, there was another sound on the tape altogether so there's something to think about. In fact Pat put it outside the house, we won't have it in the house at all.' So be forewarned! If Led Zeppelin's music is sounding a little strange to you lately it may be because of that *Object* on the cover. If so, follow the lead of John Bonham's wife and put the album sleeve out of the house."

In the UK this speculation was taken up by *Sounds* who asked readers to write in with their own explanations. One can only marvel at the eccentric reaction all this *Object* scrutiny prompted. It was another episode in the grand Zeppelin guessing game. Did it really mean something, or was it all part of their playful desire to add to the mystique?

Whatever it was, you can hardly imagine anyone getting worked up about a sleeve design in this miniatured CD jewel box

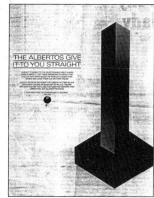

JPJ, CHICAGO STADIUM: JANUARY 20 1975

"Richard Cole answered the phone 'I've no idea what it all means. I'm not sure they even know. Hold on for Robert". Cole clamped his hand over the phone and returned to the receiver. 'This is great.' Plant came on and exclaimed, 'I'm glad people are wondering what it means. The most I can say though is that everybody should work it out for themselves - it's not hard to work out especially for our Kubrickian fans.' Plant's comments seemed a clue that *The Object* is Zeppelin's miniature modified version of the monolith featured in Stanley Kubrick's *2001: A Space Odyssey*. Designer Aubrey Powell denied this. 'Didn't think of that - I just had a tremendous feeling when we took it to them that this design was absolutely right for the band at this point in time.' Back to Plant 'Whatever you want to say, it says it. *The Object* can be taken in many ways. Let's just say we like plucking these mysteries out. We used symbols on the fourth album. They're fun and add to the music. But there's not much fun in knowing everything is there?"

The Kubrick 2001 theme was also taken up by an hilarious *Earth News* radio special broadcast in the US at the time of the album's release. Here's some of that dialogue: "*The Object* is

age. Back then these things seemed to matter as anyone weaned on double gatefold sleeves in the Hypgnosist/Roger Dean/Island era will testify.

However, just when it seemed we were all about to get mixed up in the pretension of all this *Object* lark - it was firmly debunked by popular satire rockers of the time Albertos Y Lost Trios Paranoias.

In a superb spoof on the artwork of the official Zeppelin UK ads, the group advertised their new album with the illustration of "The Thing" - an upright version of *The Object* all under the slogan "The Albertos Give It To You Straight".

After seeing that, I can imagine the likes of the more down to earth Bonham reversing his decision to keep that obelisk out in the garden, laughing out aloud at this scam and explaining something along the lines of "I think *The Objects* a load of bollocks".

Great art or a load of bollocks? The mystery of *The Object* (if indeed there was one) certainly kept us all bemused and amused long after the album had drifted from the charts during the late summer of 1976.

Led Zeppelin's 1977 tour of America was the pivotal episode in the rise and fall of the band. Against a background of doubts about Plant's fitness following a car smash, a backstage entourage spiralling out of control, the health of the increasingly frail looking Page and manager Peter Grant's messy divorce, the band barnstormed their way through America, anxious to reclaim their crown as the world's number one rock attraction. It would prove to be their last hurrah in the US.

With so much off-stage baggage it wasn't surprising that on stage the performances were an erratic mix of the bizarre, the chaotic and masterful.

When they got it right, as they did during a week of memorable June concerts at their old stamping ground the Los Angeles Forum, the results were spectacular. The early optimism of the 'Blueberry Hill' era may have been long gone but when the chemistry of the four found itself again, the sheer power of the band remained undiminished. Audio evidence of this can be heard on the famous *Listen To This Eddie* bootleg.

Ultimately the tour would be remembered not for the erratic quality of the shows but for riotous scenes at a chaotic abandoned date at rain-lashed Tampa stadium, the controversial backstage violence at Oakland and the sudden tragic death of Plant's five-year-old son back in England, which brought the tour shuddering to a premature halt.

Despite – or perhaps in spite of – all this, the 1977 US tour has long held a deep fascination for Zep devotees. My initial attempt to cover the jaunt appeared in *TBL8*, and in 2002 I wrote a lengthy overview of the tour. This feature, revisited again for this book, attempts to summarise and investigate the almost schizophrenic state of play inside Led Zeppelin at the time. In hindsight Led Zeppelin's 1977 American campaign would signal the beginning of the end. It could never be the same after this tour.

REFERENCE: **TIGHT BUT LOOSE 8**

6 : THE 1977 US TOUR –
THE BEGINNING OF THE END

PERFORMING 'BRON YR AUR STOMP' MADISON SQUARE GARDEN: JUNE 1977

The date: Tuesday, June 21, 1977. The venue: The Inglewood Forum, Los Angeles. The occasion: The 35th show on Led Zeppelin's 1977 American tour. Robert Plant is in familiar semi-naked chest and tight jeans, still the absolute king of cock rock, arrogantly stalking the stage. Even after a two year absence he exhumes awe-inspiring confidence, re-affirming his status as THE rock front man.

"Nobody's fault but myyyne," he taunts the frenzied faithful, placing particular emphasis on the final word of this, a track from the band's last album *Presence*, a record less well received than previous outings but with Zeppelin mere records are now not enough. Seeing them live is the real deal.

Over to Plant's left is Jimmy Page, a waif like figure, clad in a dragon suit that would be scorned by emerging punk rockers should he choose to wear it back home in the Kings Road. Here it matters not. It's the regal uniform expected of the man who has been described as the grand sorcerer of the electric guitar. He twists round to face the singer with low-slung Gibson Les Paul armed and ready to execute an ear splitting solo. On cue Plant screams out "Oh Jimmy... Oh Jimmy!" and it's the signal for him to weave his magic. He does not disappoint. That he has not slept for three nights, that he has sustained himself solely on a liquid diet of banana daiquiris causing deep concern to those close to him, matters not at all as he conjures a glorious noise from the six strings he scrubs.

Behind him John Bonham and John Paul Jones absorb the stinging electricity out front and back it up with a steadfast rhythm that never wanes. The complex stop-start patterns of the song are mere fodder for them. That they have not played together onstage for some two years again matters little. The pair easily maintain the partnership forged back in days when Zeppelin toured endlessly.

As the song winds to a climatic close, Plant swings back into action, takes up the mic, strikes the archetypal front man pose and screams out the final lyric...

"N-n-n-n-n-nobody's fault." BLAM! With telepathic continuity, Page, Jones and Bonham slam down the final flurry of notes and 18,000 fans erupt.

This is Led Zeppelin 1977, still, after eight years, the world's number one rock attraction. Still so far ahead of whoever might be residing below them at number two as to render it a case of absolute no contest.

Within mere weeks, though, their very existence will be threatened as this mammoth tour is curtailed amidst off-stage violence and tragedy. For Led Zeppelin it will signal the beginning of the end.

Nobody's fault? Perhaps, but over the preceding 18 months the signs had been there. Rumours of Satanic pacts may have been described by the band as sheer nonsense but the facts stack up that from 1975 onwards a sense of prevailing doom seem to follow them around.

Before all the madness, it was anticipated by one and all that the 1977 American tour was to be the one to get it all back on track, as Page had explained late in 1976. "It's changing now... playing live, that whole stimulus has been missing and, Christ, when we did that first rehearsal we could have eased into it by playing familiar stuff but we went into the deep end by trying out 'Achilles Last Stand'. It just clicked all over again."

At the time both Zeppelin and rock culture itself were undergoing fundamental changes. For Zeppelin the optimism of the early Seventies was clearly wearing thin. The enormous demand to see them, coupled with the touring cavalcade that surrounded them, was taking its toll. Their every move was scrutinised: every album had to top the previous one; attendance records set on one tour were there to be broken for the next; the pressure was relentless.

Their last proper live appearances were the acclaimed five-night stint at London's Earl's Court in May 1975, a series of dates that followed yet another record-breaking American tour. With their double set *Physical Graffiti* racking up a million sales plus on the both sides of the Atlantic, Zeppelin's staggering six and a half year reign at the top showed no signs of waning. After an early summer break, manager Peter Grant booked them back to the US for a series of outdoor shows scheduled to open with two dates at the 90,000-capacity Oakland Coliseum in San Francisco.

Then it all began to go horribly wrong. On August 4, 1975, Plant was holidaying on the Greek island of Rhodes with his family and Phil May of The Pretty Things. He was due to meet up with Page in Paris a couple of days later to begin rehearsals for the tour. He never made it. Early that afternoon the hired car his wife was driving spun out of control on a narrow road and ended up against a tree. Plant sustained multiple fractures of his ankle and elbow and his wife Maureen was also seriously injured. The Plants were hastily airlifted back to the UK and then Robert holed up in Jersey to maintain his non-residential status and avoid paying UK taxes. Here the band decided to channel their energies into recording a new album. With Plant slowly recovering they relocated to Malibu and then returned to Europe for a three-week recording stint at Munich's Musicland Studio

The resulting album, *Presence*, was issued the following spring. Despite initial huge sales it was destined not to be one of their long-term best sellers. The direct, hard-hitting nature of the seven recordings failed to connect with a fan base more accustomed to the diversity and experimental edge of their previous work.

With Plant still recovering there was no chance of supporting the album's release with a tour, though fans did get to see them live that year on film. The lay-off encouraged them to complete their much delayed movie project *The Song Remains The Same*, a bizarre mix of fantasy sequences and live footage from three-year-old performances at Madison Square Garden which was released to somewhat muted reaction in the fall of '76.

What their still adoring public really wanted was to see the band live in the flesh. As ever America was where the dollars were - and their most fervent fans. Manager Peter Grant surveyed the then changing face of the UK scene and saw a climate where 'dinosaur' acts such as Zep were public enemy number one for the emerging punks. Comments such as "I don't have to hear Led Zeppelin - just looking at their record covers makes me want to be

sick" from The Clash's Paul Simonon confirmed the contempt in which they were held by this new movement.

Surprisingly, and to their credit, far from ignoring the punk scene Zep met it head on as they moved their operation to the Manticore rehearsal studios in Fulham in the early weeks of 1977. One of the band's rehearsing nearby just happened to be Generation X, led by bottle-blond Billy Idol, and the two groups exchanged good humoured banter when they met, Plant even offering him the use of the latest Zep stage show toy, a vocal harmoniser. "Here you, try this," he said to Idol. "It can make you sound like the Everly Brothers." The bleached one duly wailed an acapella version of 'Whole Lotta Love'. Soon, Led Zep's well-established penchant for a good night out led to first hand experience of punk rock when they spent a couple of evenings at the Roxy Club in Soho.

Early in January 1977 Page and Plant ventured into this punk HQ to see The Damned and Eater. Page later talked to drummer Rat Scabies, leading to rumours that he would be up for producing their debut album (the job went to fellow dinosaur rocker, Pink Floyd's Nick Mason). Page was quoted as saying The Damned had been "fantastic". Their album would be a firm fave on Page's hotel playlist during the upcoming US tour.

The following week Plant took Bonham along to see The Damned. Slightly worse for wear Bonzo wavered on stage to proclaim, "Get this drummer off stage. He's better than I am." Jeers of "Fuck off" from the crowd greeted him. Noticing the NBC camera present he shouted out, "Who wants to see a camera get smashed?" before being ushered way. The same night he allegedly tried to chat up a young lady by informing her of his fame and fortune, to which she replied, "I don't care who you are. Getcha bleeding hands off me!"

Whatever the cultural differences between these diametrically opposed generations of rockers, Plant was determined to seek harmony with the new movement. Talking about The Damned, he said, "Ask me if it reminds me of when we were starting out... well it doesn't, it reminds me of when we were rehearsing this afternoon. There's that same feel for the music."

Whilst in the Roxy Plant eyed Sex Pistols' singer Johnny Rotten but there was no grand meeting of the gods of old and new wave. Year's later Rotten, aka John Lydon, would request Plant's office for the lyrics to 'Kashmir' for an intended live performance by his group Public Image.

For the moment these admirable attempts at being friendly old uncles of the old wave to the emerging punks fudged the issue. Unimagined problems lay ahead for Zeppelin and by the end of their forthcoming US tour the new order would be well established, courtesy of chart and media presence from the likes of the Pistols, Jam, Stranglers and Clash.

Back in the early weeks of '77 rehearsals at Manticore studios continued to inspire the regrouped old wavers. Another visitor during this period was Steve Marriott, then in the throes of reforming The Small Faces. "We ended up the two of us singing Muddy Waters songs. He's still the master of white contemporary blues," commented Plant at the time. Other nights out on the town included a visit to the Golden Lion in Fulham to check out The Tom Robinson Band, in the company of former Hendrix drummer Mitch Mitchell.

During the weeks of rehearsals they completely overhauled the set list. Conscious of having no new album to plug, *Presence* itself now being a year old, they looked to offer a generous overview of their whole catalogue. 'The Song Remains The Same' was installed as the set opener. The previously unplayed *Graffiti* romantic epic 'Ten Years Gone' was tried and they also decided to reinstall an acoustic segment into the show for the first time in the US since 1972. "[It was] a unanimous group decision that Jimmy and I made," said Robert. They also came up with an arrangement of the *Zep IV* standard 'The Battle Of Evermore' with John Paul Jones singing the Sandy Denny vocal parts. "I'll never know how I agreed to that!" admitted Jones later. "It was a case of 'Oh Jonesy will do it' which happened quite a lot."

Perhaps significantly, only two numbers from *Presence*, 'Achilles Last Stand' and 'Nobody's Fault But Mine', were honed

BONZO, OVER THE TOP, MADISON SQUARE GARDEN: JUNE, 1977

It's changing now... playing live, that whole stimulus has been missing and, Christ, when we did that first rehearsal we could have eased into it by playing familiar stuff but we went into the deep end by trying out 'Achilles Last Stand'. It just clicked all over again.

JIMMY PAGE

BACKSTAGE, TAMPA STADIUM: JUNE 3, 1977

THE TOUR DOCTOR

for this tour, which suggested an overall displeasure with the set. It was certainly written during a period of turmoil and Plant may have felt that some of the material was too personal for live performance. Nevertheless, Page and Plant stressed its importance in overcoming a very difficult period. "*Presence* was our stand against everything," commented Page at the time. Plant voiced similar sentiments: "It was our stand against the elements, against chance. We were literally fighting against existence. It did seem everything was about to crumble. We didn't know if whether it would be the same, should we get back together."

As they approached what would be a gruelling tour, spread over five months, a giant question mark loomed over the band's state of health. Page's dependence on drugs was a major cause for concern. Tour manager Richard Cole noted in his book a meeting with Grant in late 1976 during which the fearsome manager questioned Jimmy's well being. Page had suffered various domestic traumas during 1976, squatters having occupied his London house, and he'd incurred the wrath of film maker Kenneth Anger for failing to deliver an appropriate soundtrack for the infamous *Lucifer Rising* movie.

Images from the '77 tour show Page wafer thin in the white dragon suit, long straggly hair covering his gaunt features. Page admitted early in the tour that he was using a blender to prepare his food. "I do have a blender... I prefer to eat liquid food, something like a banana daiquiri and I put powdered vitamin in. I am not into solid foods very much. I can't remember when I last had a steak. I know I'll never turn down some alcohol so a banana daiquiris with all the food protein is the answer. It got me through the last tour."

Once on the road there were contrasting reports about his health. Close sources reported Jimmy to be virtually drug-free, Plant stating that it was the first time in years Jimmy had been straight, adding that it was just like the old days. Straight or not, the Zep entourage included their own doctor, Larry Badgley, a veteran of two previous Zep tours and one Rolling Stone jaunt, and a graduate of Harvard.

John Bonham's persistent homesickness raised its head again over the coming months, and his drinking and erratic off-stage behaviour would again need monitoring. Grant, too, had his own problems, not least the fall-out of painful divorce from his wife Gloria. When *NME* printed a report that Grant had become a recluse, morose and unapproachable, delegating task to assistants, they were forced to print a hasty apology after he threatened to sue.

"It's funny but you could feel it," recalled Cole in his autobiography. "There was something very bad around us. It was all the drugs I suppose. It wasn't the same going out in '77. It felt wrong."

Whatever the doubts, Grant planned a huge campaign, knowing that financially the tour had the potential to be the biggest grossing series of shows in entertainment history. As ever the question of security was paramount and Grant and Cole went to great lengths to protect the group, perhaps too far, employing John Bindon, a well-known London face with a reputation as the toughest man in London. Bindon was a TV and film tough guy actor who'd appeared in Nicolas Roeg's *Performance*, in the role of simpleton thug Moody, which he carried off with some relish. He was also in the TV crime series *Hazel*. An associate of the London underworld, he would later stand trial for murder.

Plant had been building up his leg strength by training with his beloved Wolverhampton Wanderers. Only the ever-reliable JPJ seemed 100% fit and ready - his only worry was how he would handle the weight of his newly built three-necked guitar he would be using to perform 'Ten Years Gone'.

The US itinerary itself underwent no fewer than six revisions. It was due to start in Fort Worth on February 27 but they had to postpone it all when Plant contracted laryngitis, the first sign that this tour would not be plain sailing. The delay thwarted UK promoter Mel Bush in his quest to coax Zeppelin to top a one-day festival at Wrotham Park in Potters Bar. Grant finally settled on a 49-concert schedule in three segments running from April to August. Even by their own standards the statistics were staggering. A total of 1,300,000 fans would see them perform, the smallest crowd being 10,000 in Dallas, the largest 95,000 in Philadelphia. As usual there would be no support act and the shows would be billed simply as "an evening with Led Zeppelin", an idea Grant took from the vaudeville acts of the Thirties and Forties.

The delay reduced their rehearsal time, all their equipment having been airlifted in advance to the States. Page: "We didn't have any instruments for a month. All the equipment was shipped over here five days before we were due to go. I didn't play a guitar for a month. I was terrified at the prospect of the first few shows."

As they lined up at the Dallas Memorial Auditorium on the evening of April 1, 1977 for their first live show in nearly two years, many questions were still to be answered. Would Plant's injured foot take the strain? Would the long gap between rehearsals affect them adversely? Would America still crave for Led Zeppelin as they had in previous years?

They needn't really have worried. From the moment Page slashed across the double-neck Gibson to pick out the opening chord of 'The Song Remains The Same', it was more than evident that America's love affair with this group was far from over. Afterwards Plant was euphoric: "It was emotional last night," he told Robert Hilburn of the *LA Times*. "I tried to keep a positive attitude in the months after the accident, but even after I was able to walk again I didn't know how the foot would hold up on stage. Even the rehearsals didn't prove it to me. I was so nervous before we went on stage last night that I almost threw up. I could feel the tenseness in my throat for the first couple of songs. I kept telling myself to loosen up. The whole show possessed an element of emotion that I've never known before. I could just have easily knelt on the stage and cried, I was so happy. You can't pretend last night's concert was the greatest thing we've ever done but there was something between us after that long gap that in certain songs we

THE OFFICIAL '77 VIDEO
For some of the larger indoor shows the band's performance was projected on to a giant video screen. Dates at the Silverdome in Pontiac, the Summit in Houston and the Seattle Kingdome were known to be filmed in this way. The latter video from their July 17 show is the only video footage known to still exist. The whole show was video taped and subsequently stored in their archive. To promote the *Remasters* releases in 1990, clips of 'The Song Remains The Same' and 'Achilles Last Stand' from this video were aired on a special MTV Zeppelin documentary. Images from the Seattle video were also used in the promo the video put together to accompany the track 'Over The Hills And Far Away'. Snippets of the '77 show were also included in the 1997 'Whole Lotta Love' promo.

Filmed from three main camera angles, the action is limited and although the gig in question was not one of the best nights from the tour, it does contain some stunning images of the band in all their 1977 on-stage glory.

Parts of it have surfaced on bootleg videos. However, Page did not consider the quality of this footage good enough for the official 2003 DVD set.

It's funny but you could feel it.

There was something very bad

around us. It was all the drugs

I suppose. It wasn't the same

going out in '77. It felt wrong.

RICHARD COLE, TOUR MANAGER

BACKSTAGE TAMPA STADIUM, FLORIDA: JUNE 3, 1977

It's been said these shows now are events more than concerts and I suppose that's true. But what's the option. I guess we must carry a bit of the legend with us, but you don't have to over try or it becomes clinical and clear cut.

ROBERT PLANT

really got hold of it - to go far beyond where we have before.''

Plant's upbeat mood was maintained throughout the tour but he was uneasy about the mayhem that surrounded them: "I see a lot of craziness. Somehow we generate it and we revile it We are trying to put across a positive message but some people react in such an excitable manner and they miss the meaning of it. I don't know why the fans throw firecrackers. I think it's horrible. That's the aspect that makes you wonder wether it would be better to be half way up a tree in Wales."

Their early April shows attracted 76,000 fans to four shows at the Chicago Stadium. On the second night Page dressed as a storm trooper with jack boots and a peaked cap. Plant's high spirits and relief at being back on stage was most apparent in his between-song spiels. Introducing Bonham's drum solo 'Moby Dick', now retitled 'Over The Top', he told the audience: "Bonzo is a diplomat for peace and good relations He hasn't been to jail yet although he's been here four for five days."

During the third Chicago concert Page's health faltered when, 65 minutes into the set, he was forced to leave the stage and the show was abandoned. His playing had been erratic from the start and after performing 'Ten Years Gone' Plant told the audience, "Jimmy has got a bout of gastro-enteritis which isn't helped by firecrackers, so were gonna take a five minute break."

Eventually road manager Richard Cole came on to announce the end of the show. Next day a recovering Page told *Circus* magazine: "It's the first time we've ever stopped a show like that. They think it was food poisoning. We are not a rip-off band but the pain was unbearable." Describing the then upbeat morale of the band he noted: "Led Zeppelin is a stag party that never ends. This is no last tour. It would be a criminal act to break up this band." He was back on course for the next night when Plant commented: "Jimmy was feeling ill last night but it was only a false pregnancy so that's alright."

Wind and rain at Chicago's O'Hare airport delayed the band's take off in their luxury Boeing 727 hired especially for the tour and the next night's show in Minneapolis was delayed by over an

hour. After the show there occurred a backstage spat between the good Dr Badgley and Page over a supply of methaquaalude that was missing. The doctor allegedly cornered Page and cross examined him about the missing drugs. "Accusing me! Who the fuck does he think is paying his salary," was Page's sharp retort.

The next night in St Paul it was reported that 24 fans were arrested for disorderly conduct as around 100, without tickets, attempted to rush the gates. A similar incident occurred at the Cincinnati Riverside Coliseum where a reported 1,000 tried to gatecrash the show. In a surprisingly little publicised incident a fan was actually killed at the second show in Cincinnati after falling from the stadium's third level. On April 17 Zep performed in Indianapolis at the Market Square Arena, the same venue where Elvis Presley would play his final show in June.

The early spring shows had seen some erratic performances, the long lay off having evidently taken its toll. And the set list was still gruellingly long. Jonesy's epic 'No Quarter' now included a lengthy semi-classical solo that often meandered to 20 minutes in length. Page's old Yardbirds solo 'White Summer' was reinstated as a prelude to 'Kashmir'. They had dropped the long term stage favourite 'Dazed And Confused' and in its place Page performed a guitar virtuoso solo spot, dragging all manner of effects from his Gibson, including the violin bow trademark and an arrangement of the Hendrix version of 'Star Spangled Banner'. Bonham's 'Moby Dick' drum solo was yet another half hour long haul, appropriately dubbed by Plant as 'Over The Top'. Fans at the shows recall the unrest during these long pieces with many treating them as unofficial intervals.

Where the group still excelled was in the potent rockers, songs like 'Trampled Underfoot', 'Heartbreaker' and 'Communication Breakdown', which were still performed with the vigour and verve of earlier days. 'Stairway To Heaven' remained as the rightful finale of every show, with Plant still performing it like he meant it and Page turning in a consistently devastating solo.

THE '77 BOOTLEGS

Led Zeppelin's 1977 American tour is well served on bootleg. Of the 49 shows they played, over 30 have appeared on bootleg CDs. At the time cassette recording facilities were rapidly improving and plenty of fans managed to smuggle in equipment to record shows from out front.

The most revered bootleg from this era is a recording of the com-

plete show from their opening night at the Los Angeles Forum on June 21. This has appeared on various bootleg CD labels over the years, notably Silver Rarities and The Diagrams Of Led Zeppelin, under the title *Listen To This Eddie*, apparently a reference to Eddie Van Halen.

Often cited as the best live unofficial Zep CD, it's a scintillating audience recording capturing all the

excitement and exuberance of that special night.

The legendary Japanese bootleg label Tarantura packaged all six LA shows in a remarkable and much sought after 12 CD box set package titled *A Week For Badgeholders*. This now commands a four-figure sum among collectors.

The June 23 LA show is also a Zep bootleg favourite, originally issued as a two-disc vinyl set as For

PERFORMING 'THE BATTLE OF EVERMORE', MADISON SQUARE GARDEN: JUNE, 1977

The first leg ended in record-breaking style when on Saturday, April 30 they clocked up another milestone at the giant Silverdome in Pontiac, Michigan, where some 76,229 witnessed the show. This set a new record, later to feature in the *Guinness Book Of Records* for the largest attendance at a single show, marginally beating the previous best of 75,962 for a show at the same venue by The Who in December, 1975. This gig alone netted a cool $792,361. For once there was little crowd disturbance, prompting a Pontiac police chief to comment: "We were pleasantly surprised. This is the first time in five big shows at the Silverdome that we've had no problems with crowds rushing the turnstiles."

After the show Richard Cole picked up a cheque for $800,000 - not bad for a little under three hours work.

Following the Pontiac date the band returned to the UK for a two-week break. Page flew to Cairo for a short holiday. In a much misreported story at the time, his decision to go was influenced by watching a TV programme hosted by Omar Sharif about the mysteries of the pyramids. Unsure of whether to go to Cairo, Page's mind was made up when footage of a Zeppelin airship was screened flying above the pyramids. "I thought that's it I'll go. It seemed a strange coincidence that the bit of footage should come on as I was thinking about going."

On May 12, Page, Jones and Plant, together with Peter Grant, attended the prestigious Ivor Novello awards a the Grosvenor Hotel in London to pick up an award for Led Zeppelin's Outstanding Contribution To British Music.

Four days later London's *Evening Standard* reported that Led Zeppelin singer Robert Plant had been arrested at Hartsfield Airport, Atlanta, for pulling a knife and being drunk. It was a case of mistaken identity, a 19-year-old youth having impersonated Plant while the real thing was horse riding in Wales at the time. A retraction and apology appeared in the *Standard's* May 17 edition. That afternoon Plant met up with the rest of the band at Heathrow as they flew out for what would be an incident-packed second leg of the tour.

The opening date in Birmingham, Alabama, saw them really begin to gel on stage. John Paul Jones had now having taken delivery of his newly constructed three-neck guitar and Page's guitar solo before 'Achilles Last Stand' included a segment of the Southern anthem 'Dixie' in recognition of their visit to the Deep South. While in Texas their paths crossed those of label mates Bad Company, resulting in plenty of hotel high jinks and Bad Co guitarist Mick Ralphs joining the band on stage in Fort Worth for an encore jam on Jerry Lee Lewis 'It'll Be Me'.

At Zeppelin's next stint of gigs in Landover near Washington DC, Peter Grant was invited to dinner at the Russian Embassy, following which a group of delegates attended the show. Years later he recalled: "They met the band before the show, and then Jonesy played variations from Rachmaninov during 'No Quarter'. It blew them away!"

June brought six night stints at both Madison Square Garden and the LA Forum which were to have followed a massive festival date at the Tampa Stadium in Florida. This venue had been the scene of a major triumph on their 1973 visit to the States when they had broken The Beatles' Shea Stadium record by playing to 56,000. However the morning of Friday June 3 opened with black skies and major problems.

Grant: "This was a big mistake. We were flying to the gig and Cole showed me the ticket for the gig, which clearly stated come rain or shine. This meant there was no rain date, a situation where we could reschedule if it rained. It got worse. On arrival at the site we saw they had a canvas roof instead of a metal one which we demanded. So when we got to the site there was something like 10,000 tons of water resting over the drums. I had to make a decision about them going on - you can imagine the pressure. There was 70,000 waiting so we had to go on. I let them go on even though there was this big cloud looming. After 15 minutes it started pouring. I quickly actioned Robert to wind it up and we ran off stage."

The band had managed only the opening segment of 'Song Remains The Same'/'Sick Again' and 'Nobody's Fault But Mine'. For the assembled crows this wasn't enough. A major riot ensued, with 50 fans injured and 19 arrested in the ensuing chaos. Around 4,000 stormed the barricades chanting "we want Led Zeppelin".

The next day Grant instructed promoters Concerts West to print a full-page apology in the Tampa area newspaper as he felt the group were not responsible for the debacle. They duly obliged with a statement that read: "You did everything that you could and wanted to do so much more. You are the best and deserve the best - not the worst treatment."

Security was stepped up for their next run of shows at Madison Square Garden: six in all running from June 7 to 13 with a

Badgeholders Only and later issued on a variety of CD labels.

All of the LA shows were recorded by Mike Millard, a local taper, who committed suicide in 1980.

The Destroyer is another high profile unofficial release from the '77 tour. It exists in two different recordings - a crystal clear soundboard from the April 27 Cleveland show and in an audience recording

from the April 28 show, the latter first appearing on the market in a vinyl box set that resembled a typewriter carry case. Other notable '77 CD bootleg releases include *Kingdome Come*, a recently surfaced new recording sourced from the video and the cynically titled *A Fighting Finish*, a double set from an audience recording of their final American show at the Oakland Stadium on July 24.

LED·ZEPPELIN

UNITED STATES OF AMERICA 1977

THE TOUR T-SHIRT

CHICAGO STADIUM: APRIL 6, 1977

'77 TOUR FLASHES

NEWSFLASH: JANUARY 29, 1977: OKLAHOMA CITY, OKLAHOMA
"Led Zeppelin fans staging a three day vigil to buy tickets for the forthcoming show here resorted to desperate measures. As the cold became more intense they began tearing down fence poles to feed the fires they had built with metal cans."

NEWSFLASH: JANUARY 30, 1977: HOUSTON, TEXAS
"In South Houston today, police had to call in fire trucks to hose down 3,000 Led Zeppelin fans who tried to stampede Warehouse Records to buy tickets for the band's April concerts. Store officials instructed the successful buyers to hide their tickets and leave by the rear entrance of the store to avoid them being stolen by the crowd."

NEWSFLASH: MARCH 17, 1977: CHICAGO, ILLINOIS
"Thirty young men including several juveniles were arrested by police today during disturbances around Chicago Stadium as thousands of people sought to buy tickets for a concert by the English rock group Led Zeppelin. Their forthcoming tour consists of 40 cities with a projected gross somewhere in the altitude of ten million dollars."

NEWSFLASH: APRIL 17, 1977: MIAMI, FLORIDA
"Up to 1,000 Led Zeppelin fans waiting in line to buy tickets broke through the gates and began vandalising the Orange Bowl Stadium. Police had to use tear gas to break up the melee and 16 policemen were injured as a result."

gross of £1.2 million. No act up to that time had ever created such demand. Thankfully these shows were relatively incident free and the band could relax in what had always been a favourite stomping ground. The only blot on proceedings occurred when Page was hit on the hand by a firecracker during one show and forced to vacate the stage. Luckily he was uninjured and able to continue.

At the first show Plant dedicated 'In My Time Of Dying' to the British monarch, it being the Queen's Silver Jubilee day back in England. "Tonight is the beginning of Queen Elizabeth II's Silver Jubilee and that's a heavy one so we'll do this for Liz." Backstage visitors included Mick Jagger and Keith Richards and actress Faye Dunaway, the latter excitedly taking photos out front. These New York show heralded same minor set changes: 'Over The Hills And Far Away' from the *Houses Of The Holy* album was revived, and the *Zep II* standard 'Heartbreaker' also made a welcome return.

While in New York they visited Trax disco downtown, meeting up with Ron Wood and Keith Richards. Jimmy also called into the see The Rolling Stones recording at Atlantic Studios. John Paul was spotted shopping at the Rizzoli bookshop and Plant took time out to play soccer in Central Park and also bought a Lincoln Mark VI with red interiors to be shipped back to England. For the curtailed Tampa show and the first New York date the band flew in their families, combining the shows with a visit to Disneyland. "We just brought them in for the weekend. This is not the kind of lifestyle that lends itself to us taking them with us," Plant noted somewhat diplomatically.

Peter Grant recalled this week of shows as a key moment. "One very clear and positive memory I have was when I realised just how much it had come to mean. We announced the New York dates via Scott Muni's radio show and it was instantly sold out. The tariff for those Garden shows showed the bill for advertising as virtually nil. It was the demand from the street and the fans that astounded me. There was no hype, no MTV or anything... it was pure demand. At that point I really did wonder how much bigger this could get. From those humble beginnings in '69 to this in a space of just seven years. It was astonishing."

Off stage in New York Plant took the opportunity to do a few interviews. Talking to Ray Coleman for *Melody Maker* he mused on their future: "It's been said these shows now are events more than concerts and I suppose that's true. But what's the option. I guess we must carry a bit of the legend with us, but you don't have to over try or it becomes clinical and clear cut. We have to bring out our best every time because the kids expect it but we don't want to produce it with a stiff upper lip. It's got to be tight but loose. That's probably the title of the next album. When will it be? Who knows? We haven't started thinking about that yet but we may work on it in the autumn. Then again after this marathon tour we may all want to go home and lie horizontal for a while."

From New York, the band travelled to the west coast for the final part of the second leg. On the plane over was Dave Schulps of *Trouser Press* magazine who conducted a much-delayed interview with Page in the Beverly Hilton. "Page looked remarkably thin and pale, his sideburns showing a slight touch of grey, his skin exhibiting a wraith-like pallor. I found it hard to believe this was the same person I had seen bouncing around at Madison Square Garden a week earlier." Shulps noted Page spoke in a half mumble and whisper, which matched his physical appearance. His memory was all intact, however, and the resulting interview, which ran in three consecutive issues of the magazine in the fall,

were amongst the most illuminating Page ever gave, assessing his entire career up to that point.

Although Bonham complained of food poisoning and Jonesy had a touch of back trouble, they turned in a fine performance at the San Diego Sports Arena, a prelude to six momentous shows at the LA Forum. "LA is our spiritual home. We've drawn a lot of inspiration from this town," Plant stated upon arrival. Their rapport with the Californian audiences stemmed right back to their early days, appearing at the Whiskey on Sunset Strip. Within only a year they had graduated to performing at the 18,000 capacity Inglewood Forum, returning again and again every tour to mass acclaim, with this 1977 run taking in an unprecedented six shows.

After all the heath troubles, crowd disturbances and curtailed performances Zeppelin breezed into Los Angeles for one last time and played some of the finest concerts in their history. Back to reclaim their rightful crown among the rock aristocracy, it was a glorious send off. Plant sang with renewed vigour, maintaining the party mood with repeated jokes about badgeholders - a reference to the many (predominantly female) guests hanging out backstage.

The set, although still far too long, contained many moments of spontaneity: the return of 'Trampled Underfoot' on June 22, an unplanned 'Rip It Up' segment tailed on to 'In My Time Of Dying' on June 25, Jerry Lee Lewis 'It'll Be Me' played as a rare encore on June 25, acoustic interludes of Muddy Waters 'Just Can't Be Satisfied' and their own rarely played 'Dancing Days' on June 27. Also of note was an unplanned jam with Keith Moon on June 23. Moon ambled on quite casually to join Bonzo on his 'Moby Dick' solo, then returned for the encore, offering the audience his views on rock'n'roll and attempting to sing 'C'mon Everybody' before Plant and Page arrived for a cathartic 'Rock And Roll'.

Backstage visitors in LA included Rod Stewart, Beach Boy Dennis Wilson, and Swan Song signing Detective with Michael Des Barres.

While in Los Angeles the acute paranoia prevalent among the entourage reared its head again. When Grant ordered a full audit of the band's expenses, some $10,460 appeared unaccounted for. The incident echoed the robbery of over $200,000 from a safe deposit box at the Drake hotel in New York in 1973. Cole: "I thought 'Not again' thinking about the New York robbery. I thought what with all the drugs I may have made a blunder." As it turned out the cash discrepancy was traced back to $10,000 Cole was to have picked up from a promoter in Houston but the arrangements had been changed.

On the last night at the Forum Plant bid the audience farewell: "Thanks to the badgeholders of California" and they romped through 'Whole Lotta Love' and 'Rock And Roll', took to the limousines and were soon on their way back to English sanity. Though they didn't know it, Led Zeppelin's eight-year love affair with Los Angeles was at an end.

The final leg of the tour was to have seen them play a further 11 stadium and arena shows to a total audience of nearly 500,000. In the event they never got past the fourth gig.

On July 17, 65,000 packed into to the giant Seattle Kingdome, home of the Seattle Sounders, for a show that highlighted the increasingly distant atmosphere at this type of event. The three-week break had broken the momentum of the New York and LA shows, and a lacklustre performance coupled with poor sound and an unruly crowd made for an unsatisfying evening. There was mixed critical reception in an area they had previously enjoyed a great rapport. Maybe the punks were right. The sheer scale of this 'enormadome' show highlighted that for Zeppelin it was all getting out of hand. Jones: "It did begin to feel like a sound check in the dark. The audience was so far away. You couldn't see them or hardly hear them."

A show at the more manageable 18,000 Activities Centre in Tempe, Arizona, found them in a somewhat downbeat mood, Page electing to drop his 'White Summer' solo from the set.

In late July the Californian sun beckoned again with two massive weekend festival-style outdoor dates at the Oakland Coliseum. After performances from Rick Derringer and Judas Priest, Zeppelin took to the elaborate stage, a mock up of

PETER GRANT BACKSTAGE, TAMPA STADIUM: JUNE 3, 1977

We have to bring out our best every time because the kids expect it but we don't want to produce it with a stiff upper lip.

It's got to be tight but loose.

ROBERT PLANT

NEWSFLASH: APRIL 19, 1977: CINCINNATI, OHIO
"Led Zeppelin, a British rock group again brought violence in its wake when about 1,000 fans tried to gate crash a Zeppelin show in Cincinnati last night. Police arrested 100 youths during the mini riot which was punctuated by thrown bottles and fights."

NEWSFLASH: JUNE 1, 1977: NEW YORK
"Rumours of a Led Zeppelin tour scheduled to begin in the fall of 1979 spanning 30 dates has sparked off an unprecedented appeal for ticket information. Unhappy fans when told that tickets were not yet available as the tour had not even been confirmed resorted to sending plastic explosives to Tickertron offices across the USA."

WITH KEITH MOON, LOS ANGELES FORUM: JUNE 23, 1977

I could never in good

conscience book them again.

For these people to assume

that might makes right is

totally wrong.

BILL GRAHAM, PROMOTER

Stonehenge that years later would return to haunt them in *Spinal Tap*. This early evening set was an improvement on their recent performances with Page suitably dressed in the black dragon suit he'd worn at Earl's Court in 1975 and Plant strutting the stage in a T-shirt emblazoned with the words 'Nurses Do it Better'.

Backstage after the show it all began to go drastically wrong. There were two violent incidents. The first involved Peter Grant and John Bindon. As they left the stage Jim Doeney, a member of promoter Bill Graham's crew, allegedly asked Grant if he needed help. Taking offence to this Bindon assaulted Downey by banging his head on the concrete. The second, more serious incident involved a security man named Jim Matzorkis. Matzorkis was taking down a wooden plaque with Led Zeppelin's name on it to put away for the next show. Peter Grant's son Warren asked him for the sign and was rebuffed. This got back to Grant who approached Matzorkis with Bindon and John Bonham. "You don't talk to a kid like that," Grant said and asked Matzorkis to apologise. Bonham kicked him in the groin. Matzorkis fled the scene.

Bill Graham would later tell *Rolling Stone* that Grant's employees then searched for Matzorkis. During the search it was alleged Graham's production manager Bob Barsotti was hit on the head with a lead pipe. Graham said he tried to speak to Grant to resolve the situation. Grant asked to speak to Matzorkis again. Graham agreed as long as there was no more violence. "I went over to the trailer where Jim was hiding. I said 'Jim. It's okay, it's me' then I stepped in. I said 'Jim this is Mr Peter Grant, the boy's father'. Before I could finish the sentence Peter blasted Jim in the face." He

then forced me out and locked the door. I tried to get in but his people blocked the door. Matkoviz made his way to the door but by then his face was bloody mess. He was then taken to East Bay hospital."

Graham added that a Zeppelin representative told him the band would not take the stage the following day unless he signed an agreement indemnifying the group against damages resulting from the Matzorkis incident. Graham signed the paper after taking advice from his lawyer, who assured him the document was not legally binding.

On the Sunday Zeppelin finally appeared on stage some ninety minutes late. In the light of the events the show was remarkably good and included a rare acoustic version of 'Mystery Train'. Plant even thanked Bill Graham as they left the stage.

But Graham was devastated. "I could never in good conscience book them again. For these people to assume that might makes right is totally wrong," he said.

The next day Grant, Bonham Cole and Bindon were arrested by a SWAT team and held in an open jail for a few hours before being released on bail. Graham's security team also wanted revenge. There was a plan to fly 25 of them into New Orleans with guns. Luckily it never came to that.

John Paul Jones remembered the arrest. "There were police everywhere. I had all the family with me and I'd rented a motor home. We went down to the service elevator out the back on to the freeway and away from the trouble and on to Oregon."

In early 1978 Grant, Bonham, Richard Cole and John Bindon pleaded *nolo contedere* to the assault charges arising from the Oakland brawl. All four were found guilty and given fines and suspended sentences. Since they were not required to appear in court, the civil suits brought against them were never heard. Graham was furious at the lenient sentences. "They'll never learn," he said. He would later relent, and was involved in the less than successful 1988 Zeppelin reunion for the Atlantic Records 40th birthday bash in New York.

Years later Grant was full of remorse. In his biography of the late Zep manager, Chris Welch documents an incident that occurred when Grant read Bill Graham's account of the Oakland incident in his own autobiography. Grant was deeply upset. "I don't want to be thought of as a bad person," he tearfully told his friend Ed Bicknell, the manager of Dire Straits.

Amidst all the fall out from the Oakland incident the tour was set to roll on. The next date occurred four days later at the Superdome in New Orleans where they were to be given the freedom of the city. The entourage flew into Louisiana and booked into their hotel. Then Robert Plant received a phone call from England. His five-year-old son Karac had died from a viral infection.

Accompanied by Cole and John Bonham, Robert flew home immediately. It was the wrong goodbye.

Cole: "In 1977 there was something wrong. It should never have happened like that, and afterwards it was never the same. The whole thing just erupted. It was like somebody said, 'Here you fuckers ... have this.'"

Robert and Bonzo went to ground. Jones stayed in the US on holiday and Page was next seen jamming with Ron Wood at a charity event in a local pub near his Plumpton home. He also gave a series of interviews to dispel rumours that the band would split up. He was defensive of the Graham incident: "I wasn't there when it happened but I've often wondered what the need is for really heavy bouncers," and of suggestions that bad karma surrounded the band. "It's just the wrong term to ever use and how somebody can level that at us shocks me," he said. "The whole concept of the band is entertainment. I don't see any link between that and karma – it's nonsense."

For Plant the whole tragic episode signalled clear up time. Years later he acknowledged 1977 as the year it all stopped: "Addiction to powders was the worst way to see yourself, a waste of your time and everybody's time. You make excuses to yourself about why things aren't right or about what's happening to your potential. You lie to yourself first and rub your nose later. It was time to get out.

"I went away for a year. I wouldn't go out. I used to patrol the grounds of my house with a shotgun because the press were

PERFORMING 'THE SONG REMAINS THE SAME', USA: 1977

around. When you've gone through something like that and come out the other end, all the godhead shit and the affectations of a rock star pale away. You tend not to take yourself too seriously."

The band did eventually regroup, initially for rehearsals at Clearwell Castle in May 1978 before flying to Stockholm to record their final album *In Through The Out Door*. In 1979 they performed two massive shows at Knebworth. As emotional as these events were musically, they appeared erratic and tired. In an intelligent move, perhaps influenced by the punk ethic, they faced up to the new decade with a radically stripped down tour of Europe in 1980.

Since the 1977 debacle, Plant refused to consider going back to America. Grant knew they had to go back if they were to reclaim their world crown. Coming back from the 1980 European tour Plant relented and Grant began arranging a tour campaign entitled 'Led Zeppelin - The 1980's Part One'. Some 21 shows were announced, commencing in Montreal on October 17 and closing with four shows in Chicago in November. The lessons of 1977 were being heeded. Superdome shows were out - they needed to re-establish contact with their audiences as they had in Europe during the summer.

Sadly it was not to be. Tragedy dealt the final blow on September 25 when, following a massive drinking binge, John Bonham was found dead at Page's Windsor home where the group had convened to begin rehearsals. It was all over. They could not continue as they were.

Fate dealt lousy hands to other participants in the ugly climax

OAKLAND: JULY 23, 1977

to that ill-stared 1977 tour. In 1991 promoter Bill Graham died in a helicopter crash. John Bindon, after being acquitted on a murder charge, died aged 48 of cancer in 1993. Richard Cole was slightly more fortunate. After being sacked by Grant and told to clean up he was arrested in Italy terrorism charges and was languishing in jail when he heard news of Bonham's death. "'One of your group's dead' I was told and I immediately thought, 'Oh poor Pagey'. I couldn't believe it would be Bonzo..."

He did eventually clean up and live to tell his remarkable tale in his biography *Stairway To Heaven: Led Zeppelin Uncensored*. Sober for 15 years, he now enjoys a healthy involvement in the LA music scene.

The ultimate tragedy of Bonham's death sealed Led Zeppelin's fate. In retrospect the last American tour, with its staggered itinerary and massive arena and stadium venues, became the blueprint for which the likes of Bruce Springsteen, The Rolling Stones and U2 would base their multimillion dollar tours during the Eighties and Nineties. Back then, though, Grant and Zeppelin were making their own rules as they went along. The unwieldy scale of just how big the Zeppelin experience had become was encapsulated over those 44 1977 shows.

More than any other tour they undertook this 1977 North American tour was an astonishing trawl. In turn triumphant, reckless, and chaotic, it was an extraordinary flexing of sheer musical muscle. Twenty-five years later the stories, images and performances from that year continue to haunt Led Zeppelin's legacy for all time. The summer of 1977 was the moment Led Zeppelin truly went over the top. They never recovered.

MADISON SQUARE GARDEN: JUNE 1977

Ask any British Led Zeppelin fan lucky enough to have seen the group perform live where and when they saw them and the answer is invariably the same: "At Knebworth in 1979."

Knebworth was the last gathering of the clans, an astonishing show of devotion by the faithful in a musical climate dominated, according to the music press anyway, by punk and new wave. In the modern era of mass communication, Oasis and Robbie Williams can draw huge crowds to the same field outside Stevenage, but in Led Zeppelin's day the publicity for the event comprised just a few full page press adverts. It was another masterstroke of timing by Peter Grant. His boys had been away from the UK stage for over four years. What better way to put them back in the spotlight than to play to the biggest audience possible in one location? As he told me years later: "I said fuck doing a tour. We're the biggest band in the world so we'd better get out there and show them we still are. I said Knebworth was the gig and I felt we could sell out two nights. I was absolutely confident."

Led Zeppelin in 1979 was a very different outfit to the one that had last walked off a UK stage after the triumph of Earls Court in 1975. Long lay offs and assorted tragedies had taken their toll. Clearly under-rehearsed, the performances were musically uneven but as an event Knebworth was pure Zeppelin theatre and it put them right back in the spotlight. It should have been the springboard for further world domination but a little over a year later it was all over. For the thousand of fans in attendance seeing was believing. Issue 3 of *Tight But Loose*, published soon after the shows, duly reflected my own blind devotion of the time - a view of the proceedings through rose tinted glasses. More objective was a retrospective view presented in *TBL 14* that marked the 20th anniversary and which is reproduced here. It attempts to summarise how Zeppelin, in the throes of recovery, came out to meet their post punk audience and reclaim their crown. The nostalgic recollections from those out in the field would suggest they succeed.

REFERENCE: **TIGHT BUT LOOSE 3 & 14**

7 : L E D   Z E P P E L I N   A T   K N E B W O R T H   1 9 7 9

In the days of the "No Led Anything" I witnessed - at close quarters - Robert Plant enjoying a rare mental flash-back to the glory days of Zeppelin. Backstage in the Retford Porterhouse club, where his new found pick-up band The Honeydrippers were about to play, one of the local stage hands approached him. "Robert, I saw you at Knebworth and it was just amazing," he said.

At the time Robert was doing his best to disassociate himself from the past but now and again he allowed himself a moment of reflection. This was such an occasion. His eyes lit up. "Yeah, I suppose it was amazing looking back. Even now I can't believe so many people came to see us."

On another occasion, talking to Tom Hibbert in the March 1988 edition of *Q*, he observed, "Knebworth was an enormous incredible thing. I patrolled the grounds the night before the first gig - I went out in a jeep - and people pushed the stone pillars down with the metal gates attached because they wanted to get in early. Those gates had been there since 1732, and they just pushed them over. It was a phenomenally powerful thing." These comments were in sharp contrast to certain later interviews in which he dismissed the event.

To really understand what Knebworth 1979 represented you really had to be there, and being there enabled us to see and believe. We, of course, now accept that it was not their greatest musical performance. Too many internal troubles had taken their toll.

What Led Zeppelin at Knebworth really represented was the absolute power they still held over their audience - and the sheer devotion of that audience. And this, don't forget, was mid-1979 with the UK in the grip of the post-punk era.

For many in attendance it was their first ever concert experience. For many it would be the only time they would get to see Zeppelin perform live. For that reason alone it holds a special affection in their live history. The first show in particular, with so much riding on it, was perhaps the most important they ever played.

Upwards of 200,000 came to pay homage that first Saturday in August twenty years ago. They came not because MTV or VH1 told them to, not because the much hyped release of a new album had inspired them (in a rare marketing bungle the new Zeppelin album actually came out a week *after* the gigs), and not because the support bill held any real attraction (in retrospect it was the worst support bill ever assembled for a Knebworth festival). No-one had read about it on a web site, which didn't exist at the time anyway.

They came, as Peter Grant was proud to explain to me, off the back of one simple advert and on the strength of a ten-year repu-

tation that had cultivated the country's biggest musical cult following ever.

It couldn't happen now of course, not in the overplayed media circus that currently surrounds every major pop or rock phenomenon. Today it would be simulcasts on Radio One, with online Internet chats beforehand, free tickets to be won in the *Sun's* Bizarre column, credit card bookings and corporate hospitality tents in every direction. The music business has changed beyond all recognition.

Led Zeppelin at Knebworth was the last great musical event of the Seventies. Despite the grand scale of it all, there was an innocence about the whole affair - a sense of belonging to something, a blind devotion to being, as Plant put it, "On a blind date".

And yes, seeing was believing. The irony of course is that we never got the opportunity to see how it might have developed. Led Zeppelin at Knebworth could have been, and should have been, a new beginning. As it was it turned out to be their last goodbye but being there to unknowingly wave them off was, for all in attendance, a truly unforgettable experience.

This special retrospective focus on Led Zeppelin At Knebworth attempts to capture some of the atmosphere that prevailed throughout that late summer of 1979. We've got the pictures... we've got the eye-witnesses, we've got all the facts you need to know. It's a nostalgic feast that just might, for a few pages, take you there... and this time the sleeping bag is not required...

Led Zeppelin 1979: The state of play

It's fair to say that the Led Zeppelin that approached the Knebworth Festival in 1979 was a very different group from the one that had triumphed so convincingly at the 1970 Bath Festival, the scene of their last major outdoor UK date.

In 1979 Led Zeppelin was a group in the throes of recovery. The tragic curtailment of the 1977 US tour following the death of Robert Plant's son put their whole operation on hold. The likelihood of the group ever performing again was under serious threat as Robert retreated to his Midlands home. For months he questioned his role and his future. Close confidants believed him when he said he could never return to the group.

Slowly matters did improve. After much persuasion, notably from John Bonham, Plant finally agreed to reconvene with the group in May 1978. Rehearsals at Clearwell Castle in the Forest Of Dean did see them working on new material again but it was still all very tentative at that stage. As John Paul Jones noted: "Getting back together at Clearwell was a bit odd. I didn't really feel comfortable. We were not in good shape mentally or health wise."

Cameo appearances with the likes of Dr Feelgood and Dave Edmunds boosted Plant's confidence and after rehearsing in London the group flew to Stockholm in early November for a series of sessions at Abba's Polar Studios which would result in the *In Through The Out Door* album.

It's no secret that Jimmy was not at his strongest during these Polar sessions. It was John Paul Jones who led the group through this period mainly, as he put it, "Because I was often the first and only one in the studio". The sessions may have been a little tense but they did come away with ten numbers ready to be mixed down. The mixing of the album took place in early 1979 at Page's Plumpton home studio, at which point he began to take up the reins again.

With a new album ready for release all that was required to seal their return to active duty was a return to live performances. There were rumours that they would work themselves in via a series of low-key gigs in Europe and there was also talk of them playing unannounced club dates in the UK. Due to Plant's reluctance to return there, America was definitely not on the schedule at this stage.

The dilemma they faced was which way to take it. The whole operation had become just too big. Page's experience from the 1971 club tour ruled out any small dates. They had played the biggest indoor arena in the UK (Earl's Court) four years earlier. As Peter Grant saw it, they had to come back in the grandest style possible. Knebworth was the answer and after negotiations with promoter Freddie Bannister the August 4 date was scheduled

with a second date on hold. The demand for tickets for the first date was enormous, leading to the second date being added. Their fee for performing was reported to be the largest ever paid to one single act at that time.

During the spring of '79 they participated in a couple of on-stage jams - Plant with local Midlands band Melvin's Marauders; Page, Plant and Bonham with Bad Company in Birmingham. After visiting the Knebworth site in early June for a photo call they got down to a period of rehearsals at Bray Studios in Berkshire. The story starts here...

Pre-Knebworth: The Knebworth photo call

In early June all four members of the group convened on the Knebworth site for a formal photo session with the Hipgnosis design team. It consisted of various face-on and side-on group portraits with the four of them standing in an adjoining field to the Knebworth arena site. Two sets of photos were taken with the group wearing different attire for each session.

The more familiar shots have both Page and Plant wearing ties. Page's is thin, the style favoured by new wave artists of the time, a definite attempt to adopt a more contemporary look. The alternate shoot has Plant in an open necked shirt and Jones wearing one of those bizarre Spanish jackets similar to the one he had worn at Earl's Court. The sessions themselves were not without incident. First Jimmy had problems with his hair, having been driven by Richard Cole in his open top Austin Healy. To spice things up two strippers were hired to ensure the band had a smile on their face. There are several out-takes from the shoot which

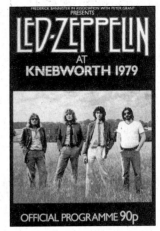

WARMING UP IN COPENHAGEN: JULY 23, 1979

clearly shows them acknowledging the entertainment. Such a jape was bound to lead to some infamous Zep frivolity and there exists somewhere an outtake from the session which shows Robert with his pants down, clearly revealing the reason for his "Percy" nickname! I once saw this for sale at a fair for £500.

After the shoot various touches were applied to the photos. Allegedly Jimmy could be seen with his flies undone which had to be retouched and Bonzo requested a few inches off his paunch. The rather dull skyline was then replaced by a backdrop from a Texas location. Eventually the face-on portrait shot was used for the Knebworth programme and accompanying poster while the side-on shot was used inside the programme and as an official Swan Song hand out photo. This 'outstanding in their field' photo became one of the most enduring images of the latter Zeppelin era.

Pre-Knebworth: The Bray rehearsals

Bray Film Studios was chosen as the location for pre-Knebworth rehearsals. Notable as the studio where Gerry Anderson's *Space 1999* was filmed, more recently it had been used for shooting the sci-fi film *The Alien*. The group spent three weeks in Bray on and off. Aside from working on a variety of old faves, four new numbers, 'In The Evening', 'Hot Dog', 'Carousalambra' and 'Wearing And Tearing' were also worked on. The latter was being considered for release as a special Knebworth commemorative single but time ran out on that idea. The track was subsequently dropped from the set and the album - but it would later resurface on *Coda*.

Extensive lighting effects were tried out in Bray, including the laser pyramid effect Jimmy would use during the violin bow solo. Video footage was shot of the rehearsals, including one scene in which Bonzo demonstrated the art of folding a T-shirt, drawing on his former menswear salesman skills. This scene was later considered as a possible still for the *Coda* sleeve. Three photographs have been published from the Bray sessions - all of which find them in various states of undress due to the heat. Two can be seen in the Knebworth programme - a topless Plant and a topless Jones in shorts seated at the piano. On Page 137 of the *On Tour* book there's a terrific group shot running down 'Achilles Last Stand' - with Jonesy in Hawaiian shirt and white shorts, Plant in red shorts and Jimmy looking very thin in white shorts.

To spice things up two strippers were hired to ensure the band had a smile on their face.

The Bray interview

Journalist Jim Taylor caught up with Robert outside the studio in mid-July. He reported: "With a strictly No Admittance sign on the locked stage door we were not going to get a sneak preview of the show Zeppelin were rehearsing for Knebworth. Robert Plant got out of his car – dressed in bright yellow T-shirt, army green trousers and plimsolls."

Why are you here Robert? "Well it's just a nice big room where we can fit all our equipment in. We only play when we want to. Zep has been going eleven years but I still need to get on stage and play."

Then why haven't you played in England for four years? Plant shrugged. I pointed out since that last UK performance a musical revolution had taken place. Punk has set out to destroy the barriers created by superstars like Zeppelin. Plant did not see it as competition. "Something had to happen while we were resting. People may think we are conventional now. But we are still a law unto ourselves."

The set list at Knebworth will contain old standards, according to Robert, because "fans won't know the new numbers".

The Robert Plant Radio One *Rock On* interview

On June 9 Radio One's *Rock On* programme broadcast an exclusive interview with Robert - his first in two years. It was conducted by DJ Trevor Dann backstage at London's Palace Theatre following a Dave Edmunds concert he had attended.

Robert gave little away, deflecting the questions with sometimes ambiguous answers. "I think the music will speak for itself. It will stand up there as it always has done. Things always change with Zeppelin, that's why after two years we can still get together and play. We are what we are when we walk on to the stage and play. It's not a question of are we heroes anymore? Heroes are in books, old books."

The Jimmy Page *NME/Melody Maker* interviews

On Friday, July 20, 1979, Jimmy gave two pre-Knebworth interviews to the *Melody Maker* and *NME*, both of which made cover stories on the August 4 editions. Both interviews hint at the pre-Knebworth nerves Jimmy may have been suffering.

The accompanying photos reveal a rather drawn image of the man. The Chris Salewicz interview feature in the *NME* was very perceptive, painting a sometimes unflattering but realistic view of the guitarist on the day. He notes Page being very comfortable talking about extra curricular activities outside the group (his trip to Cairo) but less so when discussing the band.

He notes that throughout the interview Page drank pints of lager and smoked Marlboros (fashion note: he wore the green jacket worn at the Knebworth photo call and the white patterned shirt worn on stage at Kezar stadium in '73). It was the hottest day of the year and he constantly brushed sweat away from his brow. Salewicz challenged him on a number of topics - amongst them the possibility of Zeppelin doing smaller gigs, like The Clash?

"We did all that around the time of the fourth album and got criticised for it. The supply and demand thing is a problem. So from then on we were faced with a dilemma. But then again, it becomes a challenge to see if we can make it work on a large scale. Don't get me wrong, I'm the first to admit it can get too large, but something like Knebworth is a challenge because you know it's worked in the past. When we'd finished the album we were trying to work out where we could get in and play. But then we thought 'Are we running away from something?'

"I'm looking forward to Knebworth. We've done a lot of rehearsing and checked things out. We've been down to the site and worked things out relative to the site. It's like a natural amphitheatre so I would imagine it's actually quite a good gig to be at. I went to Blackbush but that was a bit of a sea of bodies.

"When we finished the album I knew at the time it didn't matter if it didn't come out for nine months because I knew I could rely on the fact that Led Zeppelin hadn't dated - the identity of the band is still there. I had my reservations at one point about playing a date like Knebworth. But in the end it all went hand in hand with the LP.

"I was worried whether we could still gel together. Having felt something special towards this band for so long I still wanted that to be there. But when we got together a few times to play we could still see that it was... well a very good feeling.

"The LP really is a bit of a bi-product. To me Knebworth is far more important. People can buy the album and we won't see how they're reacting to it. But I will at Knebworth. The LP's a frozen statement which can always be referred to, but Knebworth's going to be different.

"At this point in time we just want to get back into playing music. And we will be doing other dates. I don't know about England. We've been talking about playing Ibiza - just getting in there and playing. Just so we've got a chance of trying out new ideas, new riffs and arrangements."

Salewicz: "Do you not think that Led Zeppelin has become part of some huge thing that's got totally out of hand?"

"Well if it has it certainly won't in the future 'cos we'll be playing places like Ibiza."

Salevicz: "Jimmy tells me he has to go in five minutes. There are many other things I'd liked to have asked him. What he and the other band members done for the last eighteen months or so? Whose records has Page been playing recently? Why doesn't Swan Song sign any hot new acts? As it is I only had time for one more. Does he feel isolated and cut off? He claims not to feel that now, though he admits to having been in a pretty weird state around the time of the fourth album."

"It can do very odd things, to you the whole guitar hero bit. Look at Peter Green - that's an obvious example. I don't think I'm doing too badly."

The Knebworth support bill

"The line-up we had hoped for was Fairport, Dire Straits, Little Feat and Joni Mitchell." That's what Jimmy had to say about the support bill in his *Melody Maker* interview. As it turned out none

I'm looking forward to Knebworth. We've done a lot of rehearsing and checked things out. We've been down to the site and worked things out relative to the site.
JIMMY PAGE

TALKING UP KNEBWORTH - SWAN SONG OFFICE, LONDON: JULY 20, 1979

YOU'LL NEVER WALK ALONE. LEAVING THE STAGE: AUGUST 4, 1979

of those acts were available. Promoter Freddie Bannister took several weeks to sort out the line-up for the two dates and both went on sale with only Zeppelin as the officially named attraction.

Artists rumoured to be playing included Bob Seger, The Boomtown Rats, Aerosmith, BB King and Van Morrison. Eventually Fairport Convention were confirmed for the August 4 date and Chas & Dave, Southside Johnny & The Asbury Dukes and Todd Rundgrens' Utopia for both weeks. Fairport's appearance on the August 4 show was their penultimate before disbanding (at least for a while). After opening the this show they went on to play a second show of the day at their annual Cropredy Festival - later to be frequently visited in years to come by one R. Plant.

At one point The Marshall Tucker Band were also confirmed to appear but they dropped out at the last minute with Commander Cody & His Lost Planet Airmen stepping in. The second on the bill spot was eventually taken by The New Barbarians, a part time pick-up band fronted by Ronnie Wood and Keith Richards. They had planned to perform at both gigs but they had to scrap the August 4 date due to Rolling Stones' recording commitments. Barbarians aside, the confirmed line-ups lacked any big name attractions and carried a very second division feel about it. How Chas & Dave got involved is anyone's guess. It would seem Peter Grant had little input and perhaps shrewdly let Bannister assemble a line-up that was going to pose little threat to Zeppelin. For the thousands of punters in attendance it made for a very long and often tedious wait before they got what they came for.

The Copenhagen warm ups
As was often their custom before a major tour, Peter Grant advised the group to undertake two warm-up dates before the big comeback at Knebworth. Copenhagen in Denmark was chosen as the venue and two dates were booked at the 2,000 capacity Falkoner Theatre. On Monday, July 23, the Zeppelin entourage flew out to set up for their first show in exactly 24 months. There were major production problems in assembling the new lighting, the rig proving too big for the arena which resulted in a blown generator and delayed the gig by nearly two hours.

Eventually they performed a very rusty show based on the set list they would employ at Knebworth. Covering the gig for *Sounds*, Erik von Lustbaden described the show as "Dazzling, staggering and sometimes awful. Describing Jimmy's 'White Summer' he observed, "Another Page solo, all without any backing. I went for a piss, bought a bar of chocolate, ate it, had a sit down, made some notes, went back in and he was still playing it!"

The second show the following evening was not sold out, probably due to the low key nature of the affair. This gig was slicker, though delays did occur in the setting up of JPJs three-necked guitar for 'Ten Years Gone' ("It'll soon be 'Eleven Years Gone!'" - Plant)

Setting the scene for the expected press backlash *NME* covered the gig and the review by Eric Kornfeldt was one of the most vitriolic of their career. Under the headline Dazed'N'Abused he wrote: "They appeared sloppy and under-rehearsed, bewildered and lost. It was like watching a fully automated factory producing an endless string of chords that neither musicians nor audience cared about." Bet Grant had that one hidden from Robert.

The Knebworth set list
The Knebworth set list was an interesting combination of the 1977 and 1973 set lists, offering a lengthy and diverse selection of numbers. There was a somewhat safe leaning towards the 1977 list with well over half the set remaining from that last tour.

'The Song Remains The Same' was retained as the set opener; 'Celebration Day' returned to the set for the first time since 1973; 'Black Dog' was recalled to the main set for the first time since 1973 (it had been an encore in '75/'77); 'Nobody's Fault But Mine' and 'Over The Hills And Far Away' were as per 1977; 'Misty Mountain Hop' returned after a six year absence; 'Since I've Been Loving You' and 'No Quarter' were as per 1977; 'Ten Years Gone' was performed as per '77 but only at the opening date probably due to the problems in setting up the three-necked guitar and

bass pedals; 'Hot Dog' was taken from the new album; 'The Rain Song' was played in its own right and not as part of the 'Song Remains', as previously deployed in 1973/5; 'White Summer-Black Mountain Side' led into 'Kashmir' as per 1977; 'Trampled Underfoot' was in the main set as on some of the 1977 dates; 'Sick Again' was played in its own right and not as part of the opening segment as it had been in '75/'77; 'Achilles' was played as per 1977; Jimmy's violin bow solo which had preceded 'Achilles' in 1977 was shifted further on to herald the introduction of the new 'In The Evening'; 'Stairway' was the finale as per 1975/77.

The encores were 'Rock And Roll' and 'Whole Lotta Love' played in a newly revamped, compact arrangement incorporating the new riff section and on August 4 only 'Heartbreaker'. On August 11 the encores were 'Rock And Roll' into 'Whole Lotta Love' which for this date included the 'Boogie Chillun' lines, and a finale of 'Communication Breakdown' played for only the second time since the last Earl's Court show in May '75.

The honeymoon and birth!
For newly-weds Paul and Margaret Weaver the August 4 date also served as the beginning of their honeymoon. After tying the knot at Braintree, they turned up still in their wedding gear to enjoy the show, their honeymoon suite being nothing more than a tent on the camp site.

Now that's what I call dedication! Wonder how Margaret and Paul will be celebrating their 20th wedding anniversary? Anyone know of their whereabouts?

It was also reported that an expectant mother had to be rushed off from the arena to give birth to a baby boy.

Knebworth merchandise
There was plenty of official merchandise on sale over both dates. Despite the thousands sold, good condition items are hard to come by and now command high fees on the collectors market. Current price guide is as follows:

- Original T-shirt with Knebworth print on sale at £3.50, now worth £40
- Original sweat shirt Knebworth print on sale at £8.50, now worth £50
- Original T-shirt with Zeppelin stamp print on sale at £3.50, now worth £50
- Original sweat shirt with Zeppelin stamp print on sale at £8.50, now worth £60
- Full colour group shot poster on sale at £1, now worth £75
- Baseball hat on sale at £3, now worth £40
- Knebworth logo button badge on sale at 50p, now worth £10
- Zeppelin stamp design button badge on sale at 50p, now worth £10
- Official programme on sale at 90p, now worth £50
- There were also unofficial T-shirts and a bootleg programme produced. The latter sported a red Knebworth logo cover and sold for £1. This currently commands a £100 fee in good condition.
- Special road crew T-shirts were produced - a crew neck grey shirt with the Knebworth logo - the video crew also had special shirts with a yellow Zeppelin logo on the back. Plant wore one of those at the November Goaldiggers soccer event at Wembley.

I also joined the merchandising game by producing two limited edition "TBL at Knebworth" T-shirt designs. There was a yellow run of 10 and a second run of 100 in a white design with the Knebworth logo. These were advertised in *TBL3*. Members of the audience can be seen wearing these during the John Bonham *Alright Now* TV appearance in March 1980.

BONZO AT KNEBWORTH: 1979

It's gotta be better

than Earl's Court.

ROBERT PLANT

Backstage at Knebworth

The group arrived in Knebworth on the evening of August 2 to conduct the sound-check. John Bonham's son Jason was in attendance and performed with them on 'Trampled Underfoot'.

It was reported that Jimmy requested to see the memorabilia of Sir Edward Bulwer Lytton who had lived there in the 1800s - Bulwer apparently had an interest in the occult.

The group and entourage were booked into the nearby Roebuck Inn a few minutes from the site. Robert, however, took umbrage to the kids hanging outside and moved to the nearby Blakemore.

On the first date Robert wandered around the backstage area with daughter Carmen and wife Maureen. Jimmy arrived by helicopter in the late afternoon with his then girlfriend Charlotte. His father was also in attendance. John Bonham was also accompanied by wife Pat and JPJ had his wife Mo and three daughters Cindy, Tammy and Kiera in tow. Other guests included Bad Company's Mick Ralphs and Boz Burrell, Chris Squire from Yes, John Cooper Clarke, Judy Tzuke, Cozy Powell, Lemmy from Motorhead and Earls Court promoter Mel Bush.

The attraction of Keith Richards on the second date brought forth various new wave and punk stars to the liggers enclosure - notably Mick Jones and Topper Headon from The Clash and Sex Pistols' Steve Jones and Paul Cook.

Plant: Knebworth's master of ceremonies

He may have been nervous, but when it came to the between-song patter, Robert Plant talked a very good show at Knebworth. This was the era when what he had to say on stage often mirrored the state of play inside the group. At Knebworth his comments were often witty ("I told Pagey one or two people might turn up"), sometimes offbeat ("It's gotta be better than Earls Court"), sometimes defensive ("So we went to Munich and made an album called *Presence* with one track on which Charles Sharr Murray really liked... and he's still taking the pills"), occasionally emotional ("This song is for so many people who've helped us over the years, no people more important than yourselves who came here on a blind date") and at times self depreciating ("Can you do the dinosaur rock!").

This approach did much to enhance the rapport between the group and its vast audience. It was one of the last occasions he would fully display this master of ceremonies technique - the more flippant "D'yer feel alright" drawl became more commonplace in the Nineties. A shame, because Robert was and still is at times a very good between-song raconteur.

The performances in retrospective: Some home truths

They came, we saw - they conquered. Basically that was how I summed it up some 20 years back in *TBL3*.

In retrospect with the benefit of hindsight provided by the tapes, the bootlegs, the CDs, the videos... the question now to ask is 'Was it really that good?' Well yes... and no.

Some of it was breathtaking, some musically woefully inept and sometimes it wavered between the two in the space of a few minutes.

The set list by and large offered a good cross section of material somewhat biased towards the '77 set but as we had not had the pleasure of hearing that live this was no major problem. The opening segment of 'The Song Remains' into 'Celebration Day' worked very well. The actual presentation was quite startling. The giant screen behind them was very innovative for the times and one of the most enduring memories of the event; in fact of their entire history.

In hindsight, and with the scrutiny of the videos and tapes, the performances lacked the excitement of the '75 and '77 eras. Compare the fluency and inventiveness to the solo on the LA Forum June 26, 1977, version of 'Over The Hills And Far Away' to the waveringly nervous delivery on both Knebworth versions; not that surprising considering the lay-off but they really should have been better rehearsed.

Am I alone in also finding the post 1975 performances of 'No Quarter' rather jaded? The relaxed air of improvisation so evident at Earl's Court had all but evaporated to be replaced by an altogether laboured and less satisfying arrangement.

For much of the shows the sheer chemistry of the four got them through, Bonham's incisive playing, driving 'Nobody's Fault But Mine' with all the necessary power. Jimmy overall was very nervous, which all too often affected his co-ordination. Robert seemed to gain in confidence as the set developed, and by the end his on-stage bravado was back to its best.

The same cannot be said for his vocal strength. All too often he allowed the purity of his vocal to be clouded by the use of harmoniser effects - often producing an over pitched squeal (witness parts of 'Misty Mountain'/'Hot Dog'/'Whole Lotta Love'). I'd question the use of that harmoniser effect (as did JPJ when I interviewed him in *TBL13*), which often spoilt the overall sound of his vocals post-'77.

The inclusion of 'White Summer' brought a nostalgic air to the proceedings, and the delivery of 'Kashmir' carried the necessary pomp that had made it a highlight of the Earl's Court shows.

As for that other marathon epic, the sheer grandeur of 'Achilles Last Stand' prompted Page and Plant to pull out all the stops in one of the best performances of the era as can vividly be seen in the official DVD.

Also on the plus side 'Ten Years Gone' and 'The Rain Song' proved they had lost none of the emotional edge that balanced out the dynamics. 'In The Evening' was a revelation, for once all the nervousness was washed away as they sailed through this important premiere. 'Stairway' was acceptable, though again lacked the instrumental rollercoaster ride of '77.

The Knebworth revamp applied to 'Whole Lotta Love' was, alongside 'In The Evening', the other illuminating moment of the set - with its 'You Need Love' refrain and that dynamic riff section that would remain a part of the Page/Plant set nearly 20 years hence.

Analysing the Knebworth shows in this way certainly reveals the shortcomings of the 1979 Led Zeppelin but it also highlights the fact that when they were good they were still very good indeed. It remains a great shame they could not build on the more positive aspects of the Knebworth comeback. There were enough moments during the shows that proved that a Led Zeppelin in the Eighties still had new places to go. Further exploration of that potential was what was really required.

Just imagine if the Eighties campaign had led to the revamping of 'Kashmir' and 'Trampled' in a similar manner to the way they had tampered with 'Whole Lotta Love', or had given them the freedom to bring in 'Carousalmbra', 'Fool In The Rain', and 'Wearing And Tearing'. Perhaps they could have essayed unplayed studio numbers such as 'Candy Store Rock' and 'Royal

Melody Maker were fairly kind, but elsewhere they suffered...

"Ghosts Of Progressive Rock Past" read the headline in the *NME* as the then influential Paul Morley noted that "Led Zeppelin did not do enough to live up to their legend - what they did do was to prove they're a clever, conceited, old fashioned rock'n'roll group who still have drastic lapses in taste and discipline. They are not heroes - they are survivors. They have a lot to do to surpass their own past work and much more if they to be properly innovative and speculative."

Robert obviously read all this because he was particularly defensive in some of his on-stage comments on the August 11 date - perhaps too much so. "Well it didn't rain, but it rained on us from one or two sources in the week - well we're gonna take it and stick it right where it really belongs."

This stance riled the once supportive Nick Kent. Reviewing the second show in the *NME* he wrote: "For the first half one couldn't help but be impressed by Zep's overdrive, at times they were breathtaking. But the mixture of Robert Plant's frequent snipes at their less than totally adulatory press coverage and the elongated virtuosity of the likes of 'No Quarter' ultimately left me cold and bored. Zep are like a behomoth - impressive but something from the past - almost a museum piece. Trouble is real inspired rock'n'roll is never only anything and Knebworth 2 proved that with a vengeance."

Phil Sutcliffe was somewhat kinder in his *Sounds* review: "Consider what would you feel if you saw a dinosaur coming down the street? Surprise, fear, fascination, awe, excitement? All of these things. It's by no means all bad to be a living fossil. And

BONZO ZOOMS IN: AUGUST 2, 1979

ROBERT ARRIVES FOR THE SOUNDCHECK, KNEBWORTH: AUGUST 2, 1979

Well it didn't rain, but it rained on us from one or two sources in the week - well we're gonna take it and stick it right where it really belongs.
ROBERT PLANT

JOHN PAUL JONES AND THE GX1, KNEBWORTH: 1979

Orleans', or reintroduced an acoustic set sandwiched between 'Ten Years Gone' and 'The Rain Song'. The scope was still all there...

Knebworth would then have been viewed as the starting point of something new and inventive - not the nervous, rather tentative attempt to step back into the limelight.

At Knebworth, all those years back, the sheer enormity of the event clouded all these issues. We thought we had seen the second coming and on some levels we had. Musically, though, there was still plenty of catching up to do. And though we didn't realise it, so little time left in which to achieve it.

What the papers said

Never the best of bedfellows with the rock press I would imagine they feared a critical mauling in the UK, particularly in the light of the changing face of the UK music scene. *Record Mirror* and

from the impartial Zeppelin watcher's point of view it's futile to demand that they change, that they be anything other than their old selves. So at this second Knebworth show it has to be acknowledged that within terms which bear little comparison to the Clash, Talking Heads or Ian Dury, this was a passable Led Zeppelin concert."

That telephone

It was one of those then deluxe grey models and it sat proudly on JPJ's new GX1 Yamaha keyboard. But why? *Sounds* cryptically noted that it might be employed as a hot line to Jimmy Page so that Jonesy could ask him what song they might be playing at any one time. Perhaps on the other hand it was there to provide JPJ the opportunity to ring through to the Stevenage Tandoori for a speedy take-away to be delivered during Jimmy's violin bow solo!

Sept 20 1979

There have been some misconceptions reported in the press concerning Led Zeppelin and Knebworth, which as the concert promoter I would like to clarify.

Firstly, before anyone knew what the total ticket sales for the two concerts would be, at my request, Led Zeppelin voluntarily reduced their guarantee by a substantial amount and were willing to accept an alternative arrangement in order to help ensure the best possible concert for the patrons and payment to all concerned, in the event there was insufficient funds to pay everyone. Peter Grant, manager of Led Zeppelin, was particularly concerned that all acts appearing at the concert be paid. Unfortunately, because of a large increase in production and staffing costs, increased V.A.T. amongst other reasons, this very substantial reduction by Zeppelin, while very helpful and very much appreciated was unfortunately not sufficient.

Secondly, at all times Led Zeppelin, the manager and his staff have been completely co-operative.

The group's performance at Knebworth, was in my opinion, really tremendous and their popularity, as shown by their album being No 1 throughout the world speaks for itself.

Finally it would be a privilege and pleasure for me to promote another Led Zeppelin concert in the future and hope to have the opportunity of so doing.

Signed Frederick Bannister
Director, Tedoar Ltd.

So why did we retire abruptly? In a word - fear. Peter Grant was in such a terrible state, both mentally and physically, we thought he was on his way out and would be delighted to take us with him.

FREDDIE BANNISTER, PROMOTER

As it turned out it was nothing more than a bi-product of the JPJ humour. Some roadie had plonked it there during the Bray rehearsals and that's where it stayed.

The after show interviews / the lost promo album
Following the final Knebworth show, Robert and JPJ conducted two radio interviews from the Knebworth site - one for Australian radio, the other with long time Zeppelin supporter JJ Jackson for K LOS radio in Los Angeles.

There was a plan for Swan Song in America to use part of the JJ Jackson interview to publicise the *In Through The Out Door* album. To that end a promo interview album entitled "Robert Plant and John Paul Jones Talk about Led Zeppelin Past Present And Future" was planned and allocated a number (Swan Song PR 342). A colour cover was designed depicting the famous Knebworth photo call side-on shot.

However the project never reached fruition and was shelved. Vinyl copies of the promo album are known to exist - well known Zeppelin collector Robert Godwin picked one up at a record fair in the in the mid-Eighties. A handful of mock-up sleeves were printed. Three of these came on to the market via an ex-employee of Swan Song's marketing department, one of which was sold for £3,000, making it one of the rarest Zeppelin collectables of all time. With the finished promo vinyl record that fee could easily double.

After the event: The Freddie Bannister dispute
There was a dispute between Grant and promoter Freddie Bannister about the attendance figures. Backstage disagreements also caused a delay in The New Barbarians appearing on the second date. The query over tickets sales forced Grant to send aerial pictures to a Nassau monitoring lab to establish the true extent of the attendance. From the pictures Grant claimed 218,000 were counted from the photos supplied for August 4, and 187,000 the second week. The license was for only 100,000. Bannister allegedly claimed that only 104,000 attended. For the second show Grant brought in his own staff to count tickets and man turnstiles.

The disagreements about payments and attendance figures eventually forced Bannister's Tedoar company into liquidation. This allegedly left unpaid bills of £50,000 for the police and £2,000 to Stevenage Borough Council.

In his book about promoting the Knebworth festivals, *There Must Be A Better Way*, Bannister goes into some detail about his troubles with Grant. He states there was difficulty in selling the second show and that the tickets sold totalled only 40,000. He also states that he was forced to sign a disclaimer letter clearing up misconceptions about the promoting of Zeppelin which Grant later had printed in full page adverts in *NME* and *Melody Maker*.

It all makes for some unsavoury reading - with Bannister saying his dealings with Grant over Knebworth forced him to retire. "So why did we retire abruptly? In a word - fear. Peter Grant was in such a terrible state, both mentally and physically, we thought he was on his way out and would be delighted to take us with him."

Knebworth owner David Cobbold was also fined £150 by North Herts Council for alleged breaches of the festival licence, overrunning the time restrictions and noise problems. At one point it did look as though the level of complaints from the local authorities would put future festivals at the site in doubt. However the following year Captial Radio promoted the event with The Beach Boys headlining.

The Knebworth video and audio filming
Both Knebworth shows were professionally recorded on The Rolling Stones' mobile studio with George Chkianz engineering and filmed for the backdrop video screens that were used on both dates. The screen was one of the major success of the event. Nowadays big screen projection is commonplace at major outdoor events but back then it was in its infancy. Peter Grant had experimented with screens at the Earls Court gigs and used a company called TV International to shoot some of the 1977 US dates. The same company were used for Knebworth under the direction of Chris Bodger.

There was a plan for the footage to be used in a TV special - which is one of the reasons why the group wore the same clothes on both dates. Nothing came of that although the August 11 'Hot Dog' clip was quickly edited for use as an in store promo trailer for the new album. A clip of 'Heartbreaker' shot from one camera face on was aired during Atlantic Records' 40th Anniversary show in May 1988. Full versions of 'Kashmir' (August 11) and 'Ten Years Gone' (August 4) were later used by MTV during their November/December 1990 *Remasters* promotions. In 1990 the 'Over The Hills And Far Away' *Remasters* promo video featured shots from Knebworth (August 11) and in 1997 clips from both weeks were used in the 'Whole Lotta Love' promo video produced to accompany the UK single release of the track.

The Knebworth video bootleg
In 1991 a full length bootleg video of the Knebworth August 11 show began circulating in collecting circles. The video was garnered from the screen shot footage filmed by TV International. Unfortunately it was lacking in quality with most versions suffering major colour drop out and somewhat fuzzy reproduction.

Nevertheless it was a welcome visual reminder of the day. The appearance of the video did go some way to dispel the Knebworth myth as it clearly shows the group's occasional ineptness during the performance. Overall, it does capture some of the atmosphere of the event - particularly the crowd shots that appear before the encores.

The first editions came in a numbered box with a colour cover. It's since been bootlegged many times over and good to fair quality prints are hard to find.

Knebworth cine film
Some enterprising fans did take it upon themselves to shoot cine film of the event (portable video cameras were virtually unattainable at that time). An excerpt of 'Kashmir' has been circulated - silent footage shot from the side of the stage about half way back. A closer, three minute excerpt is also in circulation.

Other known footage includes Andy Bank's privately shot cine film from August 4. This has clips from the camp site, the arena during the day, Zeppelin on stage shot from about half way back (amply demonstrating the impressive images of the screen) and some of this was used in the official DVD.

The Knebworth bootlegs
The first audience recorded bootlegs to appear arrived in early '80, with the two- volume Knebworth Fair double vinyl sets on the K&S label. Both sets offered highlights from the August 4 show. The advent of CD bootlegs brought forth the three-volume Knebworth set on Flying Disc and the wrongly dated November 11 1979 double set on TNT.

Tarantura really went to town on their 6-CD set capturing both dates in superb hard-back-book-style package. This commands a $900+ price on the collectors market.

RETURN TO KNEBWORTH: JUNE 30, 1990

IN THE AFTERNOON, KNEBWORTH: AUGUST 4, 1979

All four 1979 concerts were presented on the now hard to find 9-CD set from Antrabata titled *'79*. This came in a deluxe binder package. In 1993 the Big Music 5-CD box set *Through The Years* included two Knebworth extracts – 'Ten Years Gone' from August 4 and 'Kashmir' from August 11. These performances were taken from the MTV extracts aired in 1990, and were reproduced with excellent sound quality. Those video recordings have appeared as bonus cuts more recently on *Dinosaurs In The Park*, a 3-CD set on The Diagrams Of Led Zeppelin label. This comprises of the complete August 11 show with a disappointing hiss and muddy video-track sound quality, plus the aforementioned excellent quality MTV excerpts and, curiously, an excellent quality video recording of the 'Heartbreaker' August 4 encore. This poses the obvious question: are there more Knebworth recordings of this quality yet to surface? It would be great to hear more of the event in this clarity.

Peter Grant on Knebworth
"We didn't want to start all over again so I said, 'Fuck doing a tour. We're the biggest band in the world so we better get out there and show them we still are'. I said Knebworth was the gig and I reckoned we could sell out two dates. I was absolutely confident.

"The performance was a bit rusty. We'd been to Copenhagen to get the sound sorted out - that was always one of my strategies to warm up in Europe. I thought the laser bow light show was most effective. Jimmy worked really hard with the lighting guys to get the exact order he would project the bow outwards to make sure the laser effects were spot on. That was a fantastic moment watching that from the side of the stage." (As told to Dave Lewis in 1993.)

Knebworth revisited - 11 years on
On Saturday, June 30, 1990, Robert Plant and Jimmy Page returned to the site of their last Zeppelin UK appearance when they participated in The Silver Clef Award Winners concert at Knebworth.

As the latest recipient of the award, Robert was a late addition to a bill that included Cliff Richard, Genesis, Dire Straits, Pink Floyd and Paul McCartney. Speculation was rife in the week leading up to the event that Jimmy would join him. Introduced by Radio One DJ Gary Davies - "A singer who is no stranger to big crowds, he played here to 380,000 eleven years ago" - Plant and his then touring band took the stage in the late afternoon. After running down 'Hurting Kind', 'Immigrant Song', 'Tie Die On The Highway', 'Liars Dance', 'Going To California' and 'Tall Cool One' he brought Jimmy on for an enthusiastic romp through 'Misty

Mountain Hop' and a superb first ever live performance 'Wearing And Tearing' - the number they were considering as a commemorative single to be sold at Knebworth back in 1979. They rounded off a hugely enjoyable reunion with a rousing 'Rock And Roll'.

Their hugs and handshakes at the end indicated that a full reunion was not too far away. On the evidence of that spirited Knebworth return they should have got back together the very next week. As it turned out it took another four years.

Postscript: Post Knebworth
After the gigs there was the album to look forward to. It arrived in a brown paper bag with six different sleeves on Monday August 20. I had the great fortune to have an advance copy waiting for me on tape on arrival back from the second date. I played it to death of course - and it was 'In The Evening', 'Carousalmbra' and 'All My Love' that really stood out. Looking back now it was a patchy affair with some severe loss of inspiration apparent at times. No matter, despite the reviews (Geoff Barton in *Sounds* really going to town), it sold well here and very well in the US.

Aside from their appearance at the *Melody Maker* awards and the guest spots at the Kampuchea gig, not much else happened. The much rumoured Christmas gigs never occurred, and neither did Jimmy's hinted-at Ibiza Bull ring shows (that must have been a Page interview wind up). At last, in early 1980, reports of their rehearsals at London's Rainbow fuelled speculation that a proper series of UK gigs was on the agenda.

Tight But Loose 3, the Knebworth special, duly appeared in the autumn of '79 to be followed by the upgraded, more professional looking *TBL4* in the spring of the next year. This benefited considerably from some terrific input from the Swan Song office and the supply of Knebworth photos taken by Mick Bonham, even though Jimmy complained there were too many pics of Robert!

Subsequently they made that rejuvenated trek around Europe in the summer (a fantastic experience for me, I attended five of the shows) and with the announcement of their first US tour dates since '77 in the autumn, it really did look as though this activity would usher in the Eighties Zeppelin era.

Tragic events dictated otherwise. Knebworth was to take on new status as our last live UK experience. How thankful I am twenty three years on that my memories of that event remain so positive. I and thousands upon thousands came to pay homage. It was an unprecedented show of acclaim for the group - ultimately the final one in their homeland. Thankfully the *DVD* recaptures some of that magic.

"THANKS FOR ELEVEN YEARS." LEAVING THE STAGE, KNEBWORTH: AUGUST 4, 1979

KNEBWORTH PHOTO CALL: JUNE, 1979

THE KNEBWORTH SOUNDCHECK

A letter I received from David F Brown in Australia led to the emergence of some previously unseen visual images from Led Zeppelin's soundcheck at Knebworth on the evening of August 2, 1979.

Now myself and the then members of the *TBL* crew were on the Knebworth site as early as 7am on that particular day, determined to soak up the action and secure the best possible vantage point for the show. We spent most of the day watching the road crew set up the stage and in the late afternoon saw and spoke to Robert as he drove in for the soundcheck. We also saw Bonzo speed in around 6pm.

Unfortunately we then fell victim to the security guards who, with the soundcheck looming, were instructed to clear the park of all those who were not there in an official capacity. We had to drive to an adjoining field about two miles away from the arena where we could here the muffled sound of them on stage, but not much else. How I wish I'd hidden in one of the many bushes and trees that surrounded the site to gain access to the soundcheck! From where we were forced to move it was very difficult to make out what was being performed.

David F Brown had a much better view. Being well used to the Knebworth House layout he easily gained access to the arena, taking with him his Fujica 35 mm camera.

I'll let him take up the story...

"It was easy to get into the arena as the public footpaths that led to the church were only about three hundred yards from the back-stage area. I was able to settle for a position near the stage. Initially the roadies tested the sound by playing a Little Feat album. John Bonham arrived with his son Jason dressed in the same Ludwig T-shirts. John Paul Jones arrived with some friends in a Bad Company T-shirt. Jimmy arrived by helicopter with Peter Grant - he was last to arrive as the rest of the band were already on stage. Robert had a white T-shirt on and red shorts (see the Knebworth programme for this attire, or page 137 of the *Led Zeppelin On Tour* book).

"I was also lucky enough to attend the after show party held in Knebworth House. The party was held in the picture gallery. Bonzo was in attendance, wearing a black cloak - Jimmy made a very low key exit. I managed to pluck up courage to ask him for a light. Peter Grant came in later. I recall he and some friends moved into the dining hall to hold court. I think there may have been some substances going down at this point as David Lytton Cobbold looked a worried man. I don't think there was any love lost between Grant and the Cobbold family. Being so close to what was a very important comeback for Zeppelin was incredibly exiting. The photos that I took were not technically brilliant but they do capture the band warming up for what would prove to be their last UK shows in front of one of the biggest audiences ever assembled for a rock gig - Oasis included!"

These Knebworth soundcheck images really do capture the pre-gig atmosphere of the occasion quite superbly. What emerges is the confident aura that Robert seems to project, in contrast perhaps to the more tentative Page. With Jason on hand and the Big G watching from the wings - the whole Zeppelin family atmosphere is perfectly captured. They knew that a big occasion loomed and they knew what had to be done.

A little over 48 hours Led Zeppelin would take the stage in very different circumstances - with upwards of 200,000 fans awaiting their every move. On this Thursday evening in the cool August air it was just Led Zeppelin - a few roadies and sundry others knowing that this run-through was a prelude for perhaps the most important appearance of their entire career. This was truly the calm before the storm... before Knebworth got what it came for.

Two days later they'd be back on stage in front of tens of thousands of fans.

Knebworth soundcheck picture spread *(pages 66 - 67)*

Left to right, top to bottom:
01: Jimmy and Peter Grant and his son Warren arrive at the site
02: Bonzo and son Jason arrive
03: Warren Grant and Jimmy walk past a helicopter
04: Bonzo chats to Jimmy
05: John Paul Jones arrives with Atlantic excec Phil Carson
06-07: Robert surveys the site

08: Robert surveys the sound from a lighting tower
09: Robert jams on guitar
10: Robert talking to members of the Lytton Cobbold family
11: Soundchecking Hot Dog
12-17: Soundchecking In The Evening.
18: Jonesy soundchecking Hot Dog
19-25: Soundchecking Sick Again

01

02

03

06

07

08

11

12

13

16

17

18

21

22

23

04

05

09

10

14

15

19

20

24

25

8 : THE COLOUR FILES

1: *MELODY MAKER* POLL AWARDS, SAVOY
   HOTEL, LONDON: SEPTEMBER 16, 1970

2: BONZO, BACKSTAGE, BATH FESTIVAL:
   JUNE 28, 1970

3: JOHN PAUL JONES, BACKSTAGE:
   CIRCA 1971

4: PERFORMING 'DAZED AND CONFUSED' AT
   BATH: JUNE 28, 1970

5: EMPIRE POOL WEMBLEY: NOVEMBER 20,
   1971

5

1

2

1: BONZO, MADISON SQUARE GARDEN:
   JULY 28, 1973

2: JPJ NEWCASTLE CITY HALL:
   NOVEMBER 30, 1972

3: JPJ & BONZO, KEZAR STADIUM:
   JUNE 2, 1973

4: PERFORMING 'THE BATTLE OF
   EVERMORE', OAKLAND COLISEUM,
   CALIFORNIA: JULY 23, 1977

5: PERFORMING 'STAIRWAY TO HEAVEN',
   EARL'S COURT: MAY 1975

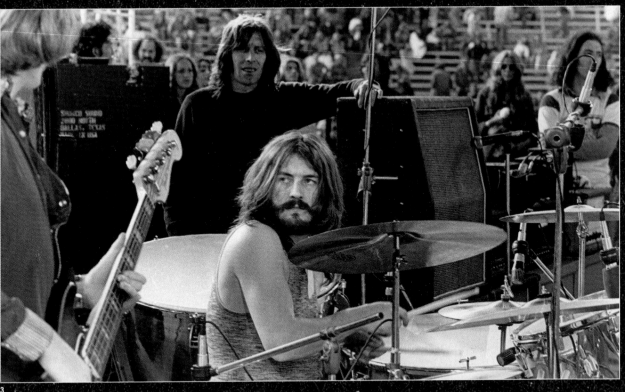

3

5

1

2

1: PERFORMING 'THE SONG REMAINS THE SAME', MADISON SQUARE GARDEN: JUNE, 1977

2: BONZO, MADISON SQUARE GARDEN: JUNE, 1977

3: PERFORMING 'THE RAIN SONG', OVER EUROPE, 1980

4: PERFORMING 'TRAIN KEPT A ROLLIN', AHOY ROTTERDAM: JUNE 21, 1980

5: PERFORMING 'IN THE EVENING', KNEBWORTH: AUGUST 4, 1979

6: JOHN PAUL JONES PERFORMING 'NO QUARTER', KNEBWORTH: AUGUST 4, 1979

7: JIMMY AT KNEBWORTH, AUGUST 4, 1979

5

7

6

1: REUNION AT THE ATLANTIC 40TH
   ANNIVERSARY, MADISON SQUARE
   GARDEN: MAY 14, 1988

2: COVERDALE PAGE: 1993

3: PERFORMING 'STAIRWAY TO HEAVEN',
   ARMS CONCERT, ROYAL ALBERT HALL:
   SEPTEMBER 20, 1983

4: *OUTRIDER* ERA: 1988

5: PLANT AND PAGE ON STAGE, SHEPHERDS
   BUSH EMPIRE: MARCH 25, 1998

6: PAGE AND PLANT PHOTOSHOOT: 1998

5

6

1: JOHN PAUL JONES ACCEPTING THE INTER-
NATIONAL ARTIST AWARD FOR LED
ZEPPELIN, *AMERICAN MUSIC AWARDS*,
LOS ANGELES: JANUARY 30, 1995

2: JOHN PAUL JONES *ZOOMA* TOUR: 1999

3: JIMMY PAGE ATTACKING THE THEREMIN,
USA: 1995

4: ROBERT WITH STRANGE SENSATION, 2002

5: PHOTOSHOOT TO PROMOTE *DREAMLAND*:
2002

5

Led Zeppelin's final tour – a low key 14 date trek around Europe in the summer of 1980, garnered little press coverage and reaction at the time. In the UK it earned one solitary review. The fifth issue of *Tight But Loose* more than fulfilled its premise to form a platform of communication for the group's fans when I produced a 10,000 word feature of events in Europe based on the five gigs I was lucky enough to attend. It was by far the most comprehensive coverage of the tour produced at the time.

Ironically that issue was wrapped and sent to the printers the very day the news came through that John Bonham had died. I painfully rewrote the introduction for an issue that finally appeared as a tragic, unscheduled tribute to the late drummer.

Being in close proximity to them all during the gigs I saw, there was a real sense of rejuvenation among the band and entourage. Even if the performances were an uneven blend of the great, good and mediocre, it was viewed as the tonic they all needed in rebuilding Led Zeppelin as a working band. Had they got to America in the fall, a whole new impetus may have driven them through the next decade. We will never know.

This newly written overview of the *1980 Tour Over Europe* attempts to summarise the last days of Led Zeppelin as they attempted to recapture the spirit of happier times. It hopefully further illuminates on a period that has been largely under reported and rarely re-appraised since.

REFERENCE: **TIGHT BUT LOOSE 5**

9 : LED ZEPPELIN OVER EUROPE 1980

The train kept a rollin', for one last time

Not even the eternally optimistic Peter Grant could have predicted the American reaction to the release of Led Zeppelin's comeback album *In Through The Out Door*. Up until the summer of 1979 the American recording industry was experiencing one of the worst ever slumps in its history, but the shipping of the Zeppelin album on August 22 changed it all that. Dave Glen, the then Atlantic Records general manager, was quoted as saying "It gave the whole industry a shot in the arm."

Within four days of its release, Atlantic had received an additional 900,000 orders for the album and by the end of September it had shipped almost three million.

Not only that, but Atlantic also had to fulfil orders for one million copies of the previous eight Zeppelin albums, a situation that resulted in the band occupying a record breaking nine places on the Billboard top 200 album chart for the week of October 27 with every album in their catalogue represented. *In Through The Out Door* itself enjoyed a seven week stint at the top of the US chart. Although the album sold less fervently in the UK it still enjoyed two weeks at the top and became the seventh Zeppelin album to enter at number one in its first week.

Despite the emergence of the punk and new wave movements and some decidedly lacklustre reviews for their two Knebworth comeback shows, Zeppelin's popularity remained sky high on both sides of the Atlantic, a fact confirmed at the end of the year when readers of the then still influential *Melody Maker* voted Zeppelin top in seven categories of their annual readers poll.

The problem the band and Peter Grant were presented with was what to do next. In the interviews leading up to Knebworth, Page had stated they were considering playing a bull ring in Ibiza. That may have been a vague idea but it never came to fruition.

In truth there was still an element of concern within the band. Whilst Jones, Plant and Bonzo had busied themselves turning up to collect their *Melody Maker* awards and then performing on stage at Christmas as a part of Paul McCartney's benefit concerts for Kampuchea, Jimmy Page was conspicuous by his absence. Page was unable to attend the awards ceremony as he was in the witness box at the inquest of the death of his photographer friend Phillip Hale who had been found dead at Page's Plumpton home in October. A verdict of accidental death was recorded. The autopsy, though, revealed lethal traces of cocaine and alcohol, and death was caused by inhalation of vomit. Page sold his Plumpton home and eventually bought Michael Caine's old house in Windsor. Little did he realise that history was to repeat itself within a few months when his fellow band mate would be found dead in similar circumstances.

Page's well being had been in question throughout the previous year. His involvement in the recording of the *In Through* album was minimal compared to the *Presence* sessions which he had driven so effectively. By his own admission he let go of the reigns, allowing Jones and Plant to lead the creative process at the sessions in Stockholm. "I wasn't really keen on things like 'All My Love'," he admitted later. "I just thought it wasn't us. In its place it was fine but I wouldn't have wanted to have pursued that direction in the future."

As the new decade dawned, there was a feeling among the four of them that getting back on the road would consolidate them again as a band.

Despite worries about Page and the erratic behaviour of long serving tour manager Richard Cole, Peter Grant set about putting together a new tour schedule. The success of the *In Through* album was ample proof that America was begging for them but the stumbling block was Robert Plant. Following the tragic curtailment of the US tour in 1977, Plant was adamant that he did not want to return to the US. Grant knew that for the band to thrive he would have to coax the singer to reverse that decision. Fearing that playing in the UK would only put them under more media pressure, Grant used a ploy that had had held them in good stead right from the beginning. In line with their Scandinavian beginnings in 1968 as The New Yardbirds, Grant decided to steer them away from the UK and into mainland Europe on a short tour that would visit Belgium, Holland, Switzerland and Germany.

Early rehearsals took place at London's Rainbow and the New Victoria Theatre. A series of photos from these rehearsals show Page gaunt and wafer thin in marked contrast to the now shorn and healthy looking John Paul Jones and the vibrant Plant, also with shorter hair, smiling and preening around in a Brazil soccer shirt. Bonham, while still carrying the excess weight of recent years, appeared upbeat for the photo shoot. During the rehearsals they ventured out to the local London haunts such as The Golden Lion in Fulham and went to see The Jags at the Marquee.

Perhaps tellingly, few new songs were worked on for their new revised stage act. Of the numbers performed in Europe only one additional song from the new album - the sublime 'All My Love' - was deemed road worthy, despite Page's misgivings. They did decide to bring in a nostalgic rerun of the old Johnny Burnette stomper 'The Train Kept A Rollin'' which they had played as a carry over from The Yardbirds on their early tours. With John Paul Jones planning to take the GX1 keyboard equipment on the tour there was definite scope for the lengthy keyboard led *In Through* track 'Carouselambra' which may have been rehearsed but never materialised. As it turned out the GX1 proved too large for the reduced stage set up.

The set very much resembled the Knebworth list and although it was cut down to less than two hours, it seemed to indicate their unwillingness to approach new material and experiment with the enthusiasm of the old days.

In playing mainly 2-4,000-seater venues it was an intelligent decision to reduce the on-stage operation and set list. Out went the marathon 'No Quarter', Bonzo's 'Moby Dick' and the elongated 'Dazed And Confused' guitar solo piece, and in came a reduced lighting rig minus the lasers. The Europe gigs would herald a new, slim line Zeppelin. The final rehearsals took place at Shepperton in May. As Plant recalled, "I think we had learned a lot from bands like XTC and people like that. I was really keen to stop the self-importance and the guitar solos that lasted an hour. We did decide to cut everything down."

The tour underwent various revisions. It was due to begin in late May then reverted to a June 14 start at the Paris Palais des Sports, but in the end opened in Germany. Finally promoter Harvey Goldsmith in association with the German promoters Lipmann, Rau and Scheller finalised a 14-date stint over three weeks that would cross Belgium, Holland, Switzerland and Germany under the slogan *Over Europe 1980*. Alongside the changes to their act, there were changes in tour personal. Richard Cole's increasing drug problems led him to being dropped from the entourage. Phil Carlo from Bad Company's road crew was brought in to run the tour, along with Billy Francis from Rod Stewart's organisation. There was no official UK press notification of the tour and consequently little press coverage of the gigs.

On Tuesday, June 17, Led Zeppelin came out to face the Eighties at their opening date at Wesfalenhalle in Dortmund. With a radically cut down PA and a performance that clocked in at one hour and fifty minutes there was a sense of immediate rejuvenation. "It's just like 1968," was Plant's excited comment as they came off stage following the closing of 'Stairway To Heaven'. Page, whose thin frame was emphasised by the baggy suit that hung loosely from his body, seemed animated and positive, even greeting the audience to introduce 'Black Dog' - a novelty that became a nightly ritual on the tour. A rare encore arrangement of 'Whole Lotta Love' with 'Heartbreaker' snuck in between capped a remarkably buoyant opening night. "Good night - dinosaurs rule!" was Plant's caustic parting.

The next day the band flew to Cologne, booking in at the Intercontinental. Morale was high. "It was brilliant," was Plant's assessment of the Dortmund show.

In the 4,000 capacity Cologne Sporthalle they again impressed. Page, seemingly at home back on the road, played up to the crowd with all the old poses.

'All My Love', the only really new song added to the show, emerged as a throwback to past delicate arrangements that transcended successfully from album to stage. A nostalgic speed run through 'Communication Breakdown' inspired another triumphant closing Plant retort to the audience. "So this is what it's like being in a rock'n'roll band."

Considering his reluctance to undertake any lengthy touring, Plant was in good spirits throughout the dates. His frequent comments of "Eye thank yew" in the style of old musical hall comedian Arthur Askey captured his exuberant mood in the same way that he had milked the 'badgeholders' reference on the 1977 US tour. There was also little doubt that Page was applying himself with renewed vigour. However if the spirit was willing his execution wasn't always spot on.

Page's 'White Summer'/'Black Mountain Side' solo became the one real indulgent part of the set - often at odds with the enthusiastic and rowdy European audiences. On more that one occasion he was forced to stop playing the piece and appeal to the crowd for calm.

The set list itself stayed closely within the perimeters of their '77 tour and Knebworth line ups. 'The Train Kept A Rollin'' was the one real revelation, deployed as an opener perhaps to reflect the feeling of rejuvenation they sought. Of the new tracks 'In The Evening' worked well as an early set stomper, the rather lame studio cut 'Hot Dog' did sound more effective in a live setting as a clap-along hoe down. 'All My Love' was the opportunity for Jones to shine with that baroque classical solo and was also one of Plant's best moments. 'Stairway To Heaven', despite Plant's reticence to perform it, was carried by Page's continued love of the song. Bonham shook off the pre-gig nerves nightly to provide the swing and kick that drove their sound. Whatever misdemeanours he got up to off stage, he was still the unflagging crucial element that underpinned their sound.

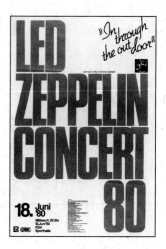

I was really keen to stop the self-importance and the guitar solos that lasted an hour. We did decide to cut everything down.

ROBERT PLANT

Tour of Europe 1980

GUEST

JPJ, DORTMUND: JUNE 17, 1980

PERFORMING 'WHOLE LOTTA LOVE', BRUSSELS: JUNE 20, 1980

I just want to play and play.

I get off so much on the

feedback this group gets

and of course somewhere

along the line we want

to do an album.

JIMMY PAGE

Plant's positively amiable mood was in keeping with the image they were so anxious to project. However, his constant reliance on the harmoniser vocal effect they had brought in for the 1977 US tour seemed to diminish his once unassailable vocal power – notably on tracks such as 'Black Dog' and 'Heartbreaker'.

By the seventh gig at the Stadhalle, Vienna, a pattern of inconsistency was evident. Performances in Belgium and Rotterdam carried the early momentum, the latter gigs included a strong UK presence in the audience, but the shows at Bremen and Hanover displayed the band's shortcomings – performances of 'Trampled Underfoot and 'Achilles Last Stand' often sounding hurried and flawed. The Vienna show on June 26 brought the first real controversy. During Page's 'White Summer' solo he was struck by a firecracker and promptly left the stage. An announcer appealed for calm and they eventually reappeared for 'Kashmir' and the show recovered.

More worrying was the incident that occurred three songs in during the next night's gig at Nuremberg. Being back on the road had clearly affected John Bonham. His natural dislike of being away from his family coupled with the nervousness he suffered before gigs led to erratic drinking and eating habits that took their toll dramatically during this show. From the start Bonham complained of being unwell. Page hinted at the problem when introducing 'Black Dog': "Two of us are not at all well – stomach trouble but we'll do our best as usual. The next number reflects how I'm feeling and the other member." Plant announced the next song, 'In The Evening', but it was evident something was wrong, a technical problem, according to Robert. In the event, the song was never started as Bonham collapsed at his drums and was rushed to the local hospital. The gig was abandoned.

Bonham had overeaten. As Grant explained: "We had trouble in Nuremberg with Bonzo. When he collapsed they wrapped him in a blanket and he said, 'How do I look?' and I said, 'Like fucking Father Christmas.' He said, 'Don't make me laugh. It bloody hurts.' But as he'd eaten something like 27 bananas before the gig it's not surprising."

With a day to recover they were back on stage in Zurich for a much improved show, blighted only by mistakes during 'Kashmir'. A stunning 'Heartbreaker' found Page running through the solo with all the aplomb of the early Seventies.

The next night's show at Frankfurt's Festhalle also saw them firing on all cylinders. The larger venue and partisan crowd (including plenty of US serviceman stationed in the city) and the presence of Atlantic Records boss Ahmet Ertegun seemed to spur them into a performance that indicated they could take America on again with conviction. The crowd's enthusiasm did again prompt Page to ask for calm during 'White Summer'. The home straight saw them fly through a blistering 'Whole Lotta Love' complete with 'Frankfurt Special' insert and a stomping encore blast of Barret Strong's 'Money' with Atlantic's Phil Carson on bass. Even 'Stairway To Heaven' was performed with due care, with Plant ad-libbing "I keep chopin'n'changin'. I keep chopin'n'changin'."

The whole atmosphere of this night mirrored the big business operation of the glory American tours. Back at the Plaza Hotel, Grant talked with Ertegun about a new five album/five year deal.

Plant was on peak form. "This is beginning to make Knebworth look a little puny," was his boastful after show comment. In retrospect this Frankfurt show was the last truly great live performance of their career.

Carlos Santana was another impressed observer. The next night Page returned to the venue to catch the Santana show and ended up on stage again for an encore jam on 'Shake Your Money Maker'.

On July 2 the entourage decamped to Mannheim for a two-night stint at the canvas-roofed Eisstadion. The audience again included many American servicemen which made for a noisy and at times unruly atmosphere. Plant repeatedly made pleas for calm down the front.

After the show Page hung out at the Mannheim Hoff hotel signing autographs. "I just want to play and play. I get off so much on the feedback this group gets and of course somewhere along the line we want to do an album," he told the *TBL* editor. Later Bonham and visiting Bad Company drummer Simon Kirke held court in the bar where Kirke played Beatles tunes on the piano.

The band's past ties with the city of Munich ensured a host of well wishers would be there to greet them on their arrival at the Munich Hilton for their Saturday night gig. It was a place they knew well from their stay when they recorded the *Presence* album in the basement studio adjoining the hotel. The only UK journalist to review the show, *Melody Maker's* Steve Gett, was also in attendance. The vastness of the Munich Olympichalle venue must have prompted Peter Grant to think of the prospect of returning to the big arenas in America. This penultimate show was a fairly average performance, the main talking point being an encore jam that saw Bad Company's Simon Kirke add a second drum kit to the stage. The five man Zep with two drummers then blasted through 'Whole Lotta Love' with its 'Boogie Chillun'' medley. The venue prompted Page to comment afterwards: "Munich was the nearest feeling to that of the big American shows. There was a lot of energy and it was really exciting."

All the band celebrated the show afterwards at a local night club. Bonzo reflected on the tour's progress. "Overall everyone is well chuffed with the way it's gone. This one's been a bit of a gamble. We want to keep working and there are all sorts of possibilities. And of course we want to work in England. We'll have to talk about that when we get back."

On Monday July 7 Led Zeppelin took the stage for the final night of the tour - and ultimately what would be their final ever show.

The 135-minute performance summarised their current state of play, an uneven mixture ranging from sloppy to experimental. 'Since I've Been Loving You' sounded tired and obsolete but the improvisation on an extended 'Trampled Underfoot' recalled the mid-period glories. 'Achilles Last Stand' was strangely absent from this show, the only occasion they hadn't performed it since the 1977 US tour. Like virtually all their 1980 shows this final gig was captured by the bootleggers. Listening now to what would be there last moments together as a band is an eerie and moving experience, not least because of the striking content of the final performances of 'Stairway To Heaven' and 'Whole Lotta Love'. Both were delivered in unique arrangements. 'Stairway' clocked in at over fourteen minutes, half of which was given over to a rambling and mesmerising Page solo. It was easily the longest on the tour.

Similarly unusual was the version of 'Whole Lotta Love', somewhat appropriately the last ever song the original Zeppelin quartet performed live as a band. It began with Page aping the intro of The Who's 'Anyway Anyhow Anywhere' and led on to a rare, totally medley-less arrangement that clocked in at 17 minutes. A mid-section jam saw Jones beefing up the funk riff over which Page teased with the theremin and then opened up the wah-wah effects. Plant kept up the pace with suitable primal screams and Bonzo pounded away relentlessly. These final moments saw them drifting off into their own little world, almost oblivious of the audience. It was as if some sixth sense intuition was telling them that this would be their very last chance to play together and they didn't want it to end. Perhaps there was an underlying fear that it could never be this good again. Sadly it had to end. "Eye thank yew. Thank you very much Berlin. Thank you very much everyone who's worked for us and put up with us and all those sort of things, and er... goodnight!" A last embrace and they were gone.

For Peter Grant there was one more challenge. He knew he still had to confront Plant on the issue of going back to America. Throughout the three weeks in Europe he had looked for the right moment. "I knew Robert was getting worried about it on that tour. He'd look across at me and wonder why I wasn't saying anything about it. As we got off the private plane at Gatwick coming back

Over Europe tour would prove to be their swan song, 14 performances that exposed all the strengths and weaknesses of a band still in the throes of recovery. Despite the highs, there was still a nagging inconsistency to their playing that gave rise to the notion that their best days might be behind them. Perhaps significantly the most impressive gigs were in the bigger arenas such as the Frankfurt Festhalle: the big occasion was where they functioned best.

The American tour might have given them the impetus to rebuild their confidence to the levels of their early Seventies triumphs but it was not to be. On reflection Jones and Page remain adamant that they could have taken it further.

"It was positive," recalled Jones. "As far as I'm concerned we just needed to get on the road in America and in the studio. I still felt we had a lot to offer. I certainly felt no desire to do anything outside the group. We were still up for it. We were keen to make our mark in the Eighties as we had done in the Seventies but it was not to be."

Page: "We were going back to the States and I think we would have been further revitalised after getting back on the road because that would have been the first really big tour we'd have done for quite a while. I'm sure that would have been the stimulus to get back in to the studio and record again. John Bonham and I had discussions that the next Led Zeppelin LP would be riff heavy and really rocky."

Robert Plant recalls the final days with less enthusiasm: "I was developing my own independence and I didn't feel tied to them any more. But I wanted to be there because there was still a

> *Overall everyone has been pleased with the way this tour has gone. It was a bit of a gamble but it's worked well. We want to keep working and of course, we want to do England.*
> JOHN BONHAM

VORST STADIUM, BRUSSELS: JUNE 20, 1980

from Europe and we were walking across the tarmac, Robert looked at me and said 'All right Gee but not for longer than thirty days'. I said, 'Okay I'll call you in a few days.'"

It was the green light for what Grant and everyone involved hoped would signal a new era. So he began putting together an American tour which would cover the Midwest and East Coast in the autumn of 1980 and then return for shows on the West Coast in 1981 with the UK to follow. In line with Robert's request, Grant set up a 21-date itinerary to open in Montreal on October 17 and finish on November 13 after four shows in Chicago. It would be dubbed "Led Zeppelin - The '80's, Part One".

The tragic events of September would dictate otherwise. *The*

lot of love there. I just didn't want to do anything a minute longer than necessary if I didn't like it. For the last album Jonesy and I did work a lot more on things but by the time we got through the 1980 tour Jimmy was back in a commanding position. The band didn't exist the minute Bonzo had gone to me. Sometimes I still shout up there at that mass of blue and go 'That was not a very good trick.'"

Without Bonzo there was no Led Zeppelin - "No Led anything," as Plant was insisting to journalists the next year. *The Over Europe* tour was the final low key ending.

The train could not, and did not keep on rolling.

**THE LAST MOMENTS OF THE LAST GIG,
BERLIN: JULY 7, 1980**

As far as I'm concerned

there is no more

Led Zeppelin,

no more Led anything.

The band no longer exists.

ROBERT PLANT, MARCH 1981

Following John Bonham's death and the announcement that Led Zeppelin no longer wished to continue as they were, Robert Plant began facing up to a life without Zeppelin, retreating to his Midlands home to consider his options. He did think about giving up singing and, like his long time friend and former Band Of Joy colleague Kevyn Gammond, take up a career in teaching.

Gradually he began to pick up the pieces. During the latter Zep era Plant had played a few low key gigs with his Midlands musician friends. Local band Little Acre were one of many outfits he had befriended over the years. When one of their ex-members Andy Silvester suggested to Robert he take to the road for a series of ad hoc R&B gigs he jumped at the idea. Billed as The Honeydrippers (after an old blues instrumental by Joe Liggins) they played a series of shows around the Midlands and North during the spring of 1981. It was a scenario he would repeat some twenty years later when he turned his back on his renewed partnership with Page to form a similarly low key Midlands based outfit dubbed Priory Of Brion.

Over several Honeydrippers performances, I was able to view at close proximity the change of perspective that Robert Plant underwent in those opening months of 1981. The plan was to file back an on-the-road Honeydrippers report that would appear in *TBL 6*. At Robert's own request this was shelved. He felt that making The Honeydrippers a big deal would distort his intentions. "It's just me having a blow so let's leave it at that," is how he dismissed it at the time. Years later I came across the original text and the transcript of a rare interview given to a local university mag. The text was reprinted in *TBL 12* in early 1997.

It's now reproduced here – an illuminating insight into Robert's state of mind at the time. This is how it was back in the days when, as the singer admitted there was "No Led anything". Just an attempt by the former singer with the biggest band in the world to come out and start living in the performing world again– albeit in very different circumstances.

REFERENCE: **TIGHT BUT LOOSE 12**

THE HONEYDRIPPERS : 10 REVISITED

...the patches are already coming off the jackets!
ROBERT PLANT

The first time I heard anything about The Honeydrippers was a few days after their début gig at a Stourbridge wine bar. Among my daily crop of mail, I received a cutting from a Birmingham newspaper. "Led Zeppelin's Plant Stages Return" proclaimed the headline. It went on to report that Robert had hitched up with a group of local R&B musicians under the name The Honeydrippers and had played in Stourbridge on March 9, followed by an appearance at Keele University the next night.

My initial reaction was distress. Pleased as I was that Robert was back on stage, a quote attributed to him after these gigs made me realise, perhaps for the first time, the stark reality that the dream really was over. "As far as I'm concerned there is no more Led Zeppelin, no more Led anything. The band no longer exists."

The Honeydrippers were evidently Robert's initial attempt at exorcising the past, a move not all that surprising since throughout it all he had made a point of never losing sight of his Midlands roots. It was therefore only natural that he would surround himself with local musicians and return to the kind of small club venues he was accustomed to in The Band Of Joy. It was the very opposite of the high-flying but sheltered world of Zep on tour.

On April 12, 1981, The Honeydrippers continued their low key gigs with a date at the Kelvington County Club, Middlesboro.

Carolyn Longstaff and Sarah Brewin, two regular *Tight But Loose* readers, filed me a full report and pictures. It was startling to see Robert with such short hair, and equally bizarre to see him in such small places. I was finally able to view the phenomenon for myself when The Honeydrippers played at the Retford Porterhouse on May 4. Swan Song had tipped me off about this gig yet, surprisingly, the date was billed in the music paper gig guides. With word already spreading of Plant's return to action under The Honeydrippers monicker, a healthy crowd had gathered by the time fellow *TBL* staffer Tom Locke and myself found the venue on a bleak May Bank Holiday Monday.

The last time I had seen Robert sing live was to thousands of fans on the Over Europe tour the previous year. That only a few hundred would witness this Retford performance seemed remarkable. The fact that the amps and monitors were all stacked on beer crates made me realise this was a long way from the days of the PA experts Showco Inc. of Dallas, Texas.

Robert was ushered into the club via a fire exit door around about 6pm. Having become accustomed to Plant's image as a flamboyant front man, I remember being very conscious of a distinct change of character in this 1981 model. Gone was the self-styled carnal rock god. The flowing locks and bangles seen in the world's biggest stadiums were replaced by a pre-1968 length hair and a penchant for slick zoot suits. Here was a man just glad to be among friends, singing the songs that had fuelled his original ambitions to be a successful singer back in the mid-Sixties.

There were no Zeppelin songs performed during The Honeydrippers tour of early '81; no familiar on stage preening either, just plenty of rhythm and sweat and a few nods in the direction of where many Zeppelin influences originally surfaced.

On May 18, Plant and Co took the road to Pontypridd deep in the valleys of Wales, coincidentally six years to the day of the Earl's Court show. At an afternoon soundcheck at the Treforest Teachers' Training College, I watched Robert coax Robbie Blunt in a soulful version of the Al Green standard 'Can't Get Next To You'. Already one could sense a keen rapport between the pair. After the evening show, Robert held court in more familiar manner backstage. The inevitable questions about Zeppelin, put to him by well wishers and interviewers alike, were fielded casually but carefully. Back then I think the sheer enormity of what Led Zeppelin had achieved had become clouded in the tragic circumstances of their forced demise. The pride, though, still shone through.

Particular instances I remember include his disgust at the way Atlantic had altered the colour of the original sleeve of a pristine new copy of *Led Zeppelin II* he was autographing. At the Sheffield Limits Club, looking through a copy of the *Over Europe Viva Japanese* magazine, his eyes lit up and he eagerly thrust the pics of John Paul Jones towards his new colleagues, proclaiming "Look at Jonesy – Billy Fury or what!"

THE HONEYDRIPPERS WHOS' WHO

Robert Plant: Vocals
Former singer with Led Zeppelin, Hobbstweedle, The Band Of Joy, Listen, The Crawling King Snakes, Delta Blues Band, Black Snake Moan, The Banned, New Memphis Bluesbreakers and Andy Long And The Original Jurymen.

Robbie Blunt: Guitar
Worked with ex-Band Of Joy guitarist Kevyn Gammond in Bronco - also with Michael Des Barres in Silverhead, Stan Webb, Steve Gibbons Band and Little Acre.

Andy Silvester: Guitar and backing vocals
Gigged with a variety of Midlands bands, notably Little Acre.

Ricky Cool: Harmonica/ saxophone and backing vocals
Well known on the Midlands R & B scene with his bands Ricky Cool and The Icebergs and The Rialtos.

Jim Hickman: Bass/backing vocals
Midlands based musician previously worked with Andy Silvester amongst others.

Kevin J O'Neal: Drums/backing vocals
Previously gigged with Ricky Cool and the Rialtos.

Keith Evans: Saxophone
Also played in The Rialtos.

LIMIT CLUB, SHEFFIELD: MAY 26, 1981

I next caught up with them a week later when Robert Plant went back to the Nottingham Boat Club, scene of one of the "Back to the Club" shows in 1971. In the tiny confines of this old wooden hut The Honeydrippers delivered a blistering set. Earlier in the afternoon, Robert had strayed onto the club's balcony to talk to the fans queuing below. It was typical of the scale of this tour. Out went the limos and luxury hotels. In came the communal group van and overnight stays anywhere they found themselves.

In Sheffield the whole band, plus yours truly and supporting female cast, booked into a huge pub guest-house. A night of

riotous behaviour ensued, with doors coming off hinges, marathon card games and a large consumption of gin. I clearly remember the rather glazed former singer with the biggest group in the world turning to me as he slugged from the bottle to state, with a mischievous grin: "Well, you've followed me all these years and it's all ended up here in a pub hotel room in Sheffield."

The Honeydrippers tied up this three days a week tour with a show at Bradford University on May 27. The cramped stages at previous shows, coupled with his own wish to forget the past and with it the image he once projected, had ruled out any major Plant stage preening up to that point. The Bradford stage, however, was fairly spacious. I distinctly remember Robert doing a very 'Trampled Underfoot' style stage dance before spinning round in quintessential fashion during a run down of The Beatles' 'Day Tripper'. When he realised what had spontaneously happened, he checked himself and returned to the more conservative R&B stance. A rare slip of the new found image.

The relaxed college environment here made for a couple of other memorable sketches. Before the gig Plant slipped away from The Honeydripper entourage to watch live coverage of Liverpool's successful 1981 European Cup defence against Borussia, in a TV room alongside a host of students. The presence of the star of the ensuing show went virtually unnoticed among the gathering. When he passed by the entrance area, he even took a brief stint on the door collecting tickets for his own show!

There were plans for The Honeydrippers to make a further round of appearances in the summer and, indeed, a London debut was announced for Dingwalls Club on July 14, together with a handful of other shows including Birmingham's Romeo and Juliet Club and Leeds Warehouse. These shows were advertised openly, *NME* going as far as to plug the London show with a vintage Earl's Court photo. Perhaps this put unnecessary pressure on Robert for no sooner were they announced than they were swiftly cancelled.

This decision signalled the end of The Honeydrippers Mark 1, though Plant had developed a musical kinship with guitarist Robbie Blunt and back in Kidderminster they began demoing ideas for songs together. By August several completed songs were at the ready-to-record stage. Auditions for musicians to help record the first ever Plant solo album brought forth Paul Martinez on bass, and keyboardist Jezz Woodroffe. Cozy Powell was listed as the initial drummer, and later Phil Collins was called in to complete the album.

All roads from there on led to Monmouth and Rockfield Studios. The following June, Robert Plant's first solo album *Pictures At Eleven* was the second best selling album in the UK.

"Zojo was a great bloke, but he ain't here now"

On the end of a cassette recorded at The Honeydrippers' Pontypridd show, there lies a long lost Robert Plant interview. In the dressing room after the gig Plant held court with his entourage, chatting with students and friends. One of the students, it turned out, ran the local college rag magazine and asked Robert for an interview. He agreed to do it there and then.

Within the confines of the dressing room, Robert answered the questions with much humour. There's an early dig at David Coverdale as a would be imitator, some years before the 1988 war of words, which is now somewhat ironic in view of Jimmy Page's subsequent collaboration with the man. Equally ironic is Plant's subtle reference to Jimmy in his reply about the fourth album symbol. Note also his underplaying of the Zepp legacy and off-hand comments of how "the patches are already coming off he jackets" as he put it.

I don't know if the college rag mag ever used this interview. Whether they realised it or not it was something of an exclusive. Apart from a few radio interviews in 1979, it represents Robert's only question and answer session with any section of the press between 1977 and 1982.

This then is the full transcript of that back stage interview, conducted on the night of May 18 1981 at the Treforest Technical College in Pontypridd, South Wales. The scene is a packed dressing room and the tape picks up the last words of a conversation I was having with him.

RETFORD PORTERHOUSE CLUB: MAY 4, 1981

LIVE AT R&J's
ON
TUESDAY 7th. JULY
The
Honeydrippers
FEATURING
ROBERT PLANT · RICKY KOOL
ROBBIE BLUNT · ANDY SILVESTER
KEVIN O'NEIL · JIM HICKMAN
KEITH EVANS
Tickets £2 IN ADVANCE £2.50 ON THE EVENING
★ BARS OPEN 9-2a.m.

CANCELLED GIG POSTER

It all started as an idea to stop boredom setting in on an old dinosaur who was sitting at home not doing a great deal.
ROBERT PLANT

RETFORD PORTERHOUSE CLUB: MAY 4, 1981

D. Lewis: (on spotting a poster for the gig): "I could do with one of those actually."

R. Plant: "Here we go... *Tight But Loose*. Across the front page... £1.75 to members £2 on the night. (Turning to interviewer) OK fire away... how did all this start?"

Interviewer: "Yes how did it all start?"

DL: "If we're going with an interview I'll get my player out here too."

RP: "Oh this is only like a rag thing. It all started as an idea to stop boredom setting in on an old dinosaur who was sitting at home not doing a great deal. My pals said fancy having a blow so we've had ten blows."

INT: "And how many more have you got to do?"

RP: "We've got another five to do, then we'll revamp the whole thing. Go back to our separate corners have long farewells I suppose."

INT: "Did you know all this lot years ago?"

RP: "Yeah, I've known 'em for years, they're all pals. They have their own band they work on at weekends. We just work Monday, Tuesday and Wednesday. Just casual."

INT: "It's alright for some! What about the choice of numbers, is it all their own stuff?"

RP: "No, they're all standards."

INT: "Oh sure... but you know..."

RP: "Choicewise? It's a combination job, whatever anyone feels like playing."

At this point the interviewer gets interrupted by the news that someone has just tried to get backstage, claiming that they were

Interviewer: Sorry about that. Numerous people trying to impersonate me.

Robert: I know what you mean. I saw David Coverdale last night.

doing the rag interview.

INT: "Sorry about that. Numerous people trying to impersonate me."

RP: "I know what you mean. I saw David Coverdale last night." (Laughs all round)

INT: "I'm glad I got that on tape!"

RP: "No, I'm only kidding. Sorry David!"

INT: "I hope this reaches Whitesnake. Does it worry you playing numbers that half the audience can't remember?"

RP: "No. That's half the challenge really because they come along expecting something else and they get something they had no idea they were going to hear. I mean the numbers are all good, even though they come from a different point in time. So, it's a young audience basically that we'll get to begin with, plus a few die-hards who were around when mono was in force. It's a good choice really and if it initiates a few kids to what got us fired up in the first place... the bonds in the Sixties and Seventies then it's good."

INT: "Two inevitable questions... you don't have to answer them if you don't want to."

RP: "Do I go with women?" (Laughs all round)

INT: "No, no... I could ask that as well I suppose. Was it a conscious decision not to play any Led Zepp?"

RP: "Yes"

INT: "Fine. And the other one. What about the fact that the audience are here for you rather than for you and the group. Or would you disagree?"

RP: "Well, I think that's a cross we have to bear to begin with. But as time goes on everyone will make their own little niche in it all. It's awkward because in a way I feel bad about it, though I shouldn't feel bad about it because it's inevitable. You can introduce someone at the beginning and there's a mild ripple of applause but by the end it's very warm. There's no room for comedowns in a short life."

INT: "I know what you mean and I'm only 18.

RP: "Lucky bugger!"

INT: "Looking at the thing as a whole and not just Led Zeppelin but everything else. How do you react to a thing that's primarily aimed at an all male audience? At least it seems to be all male audience tonight that picked up on it."

RP: "One per cent were female tonight. That's a bright light somewhere! I can't understand why after all those years I've danced with no shirt on... I mean everything changes I've got a shirt on now... but I'm stunned by that.

I think what's happened is that guys are working and have a routine and want to express themselves come along to gigs like the ones we used to do and really get themselves into it physically that chicks just veered out of the way. I mean I don't think Bowie or Bryan whatshisface..."

INT: "Bryan Ferry."

RP: "Yeah... are that much better looking than me. It's just that all their gigs are full of chicks and mine's all geezers!"

At this point a female fan backstage cuts in: "The reason so few females come to your gigs is that the blokes sell their tickets to their mates."

RP: "Well, we played Knebworth the first week. We had upwards of 180,000 in one day and I bet you there were 10,000 chicks. I had a helicopter check!"

INT: "And the final inevitable question after that totally innocuous one: is there going to be the same albatross hanging over you and John Paul Jones and Jimmy Page as there was for The Beatles, the inevitable Led Zeppelin reunion or is Led Zeppelin totally dead and gone?"

RP: "I think we are fortunate because we were never that good that it was gonna be... it wasn't like The Beatles... they were like everything, they encompassed everything really. It was a total audience from 65 to 15 or 5 or whatever whereas we had a sort of niche. So whatever happens... I don't think it can happen really because there are loads of bands coming along and taking the majority of our audience away already. You know the patches are already coming off the jackets."

INT: "Oh I don't know... what about the amount of people who have Zojo (sic) and everything else on the back of their jackets?"

RP: "Well Zojo was a great bloke but he ain't here now."

POSTSCRIPT

The Honeydrippers moniker was retained by Robert for the infrequent R&B club gigs he undertook during the rest of the Eighties (amended, humourously, to Moneydrippers and Skinnydrippers for gigs in Wolverhampton and Monmouth respectively).

He also recorded a mini-album of standards under the title The Honeydrippers Vol One. A volume two was scheduled, with material such as Roy Head's 'Treat Her Right' and Screaming Jay Hawkins 'I Put A Spell On You' rumoured to be in the can. Anxious not to be seen as on American version of Shakin' Stevens (as Robert put it), however, no further Honeydrippers records emerged.

The last time I saw Peter Grant in the Eighties he was ushering his boys off stage after the penultimate Led Zeppelin concert on the *Over Europe* tour in Munich. A decade later I found myself face to face with him again at London's Marquee Club when we both attended a showcase gig by Bonham, the band formed by Jason Bonham. He may have lost a little weight but he still projected that commanding, fearsome presence that had ensured his artists were never messed with. I had a quick conversation with him and Atlantic exec Phil Carson – I had previously mentioned to Phil that I was working on a Zep reference book to be titled *Led Zeppelin: A Celebration*. Mr Grant obviously heard me mention this to Phil because within days he was on the phone to me.

"Do the band know about this book?" he asked me rather indignantly. Peter insisted all the chapters were seen by him. This procedure was duly put in place. What was interesting about all that was how Peter still referred to "the band" as if Zep was still a going concern.

That pride and sense of preservation for the group was evident throughout the astonishing two days I spent with him in 1993. I sent Peter a copy of the *A Celebration* when it was published. He thought it was a commendable effort and we kept in touch from then. I did try to coax him into attending the 1992 London Led Zeppelin Convention but he eventually opted out. I then made numerous requests to Peter to agree to an interview for the *TBL* magazine. It took around six months of calls and faxes and postponements before a date was finally agreed on. In June and October I spent two days in his company.

PLANNED FOR: **TIGHT BUT LOOSE 9**
UNPUBLISHED

PETER GRANT : 11
THE TBL INTERVIEW

The interview brief was for a complete overview of his management career and it went incredibly well. The plan was to publish the interview for *TBL 9* in 1994 but that deadline passed when Peter asked to view the transcribed text. The interview was put on the back burner. The last time I saw Peter was in July 1995 at Wembley Arena for Page and Plant's final UK show. I asked if he could make time to update our initial interviews so I could publish a final version in *TBL 11*. Before that idea could be fully pursued Peter died suddenly of a heart attack on November 21, 1995.

The original interview is published here for the first time. It's without doubt the longest interview Peter ever gave. It touches on all aspects of his remarkable career and I believe it stands as a fitting testament to the importance of his role in re-writing the rule book of band management and establishing Led Zeppelin as the biggest act of their era.

His pride and satisfaction at what he achieved is apparent throughout. Note, too, the occasional hint of regret at some of the more unsavoury incidents he was involved in and the deep sense of loss he felt when it all slipped away following John Bonham's death.

He was undoubtedly the vital fifth element of the chemistry. He was unquestionably the man who led Zeppelin. This is his last major interview.

DL: Let's go back 25 years to the summer of 1968. The Yardbirds fell apart with their last gig at, I think, Luton Technical College.
PG: Well, as I recall we never played a gig after that American tour so really it fell apart in America. Jim McCarty wasn't in the best of health and we had to use a session man. I think the top of it all was when a date came in to do the Image Club for $5,000. That was a lot of money. Jimmy wanted to do it and Chris, but the others didn't want to. There was a big row in the Holiday Inn. And I drafted out a letter giving Jimmy the rights to the name which they all signed.
DL: So you don't remember the gig in Luton?
PG: No, I can't remember that. What I can remember distinctly is driving Jimmy around Shaftesbury Avenue near the Saville after the split. We were in a traffic jam and I said to Jimmy, "What are you going to do. Do you want to go back to sessions or what?" And he said, "Well, I've got some ideas." He didn't mention anybody. I said what about a producer, and he said, "I'd like to do that too, if you can get a deal." So I thought great let's do it.
DL: Was it always the idea Jimmy would carry on with The Yardbirds.
PG: Well it was, but we took the name New Yardbirds so as to get

some gigs. I remember going to see Keith Altham and him turning down an interview with Jimmy at the time for the *NME*, which to this day he still regrets.
DL: So in August '68 Jimmy started forming the new line-up?
PG: Let me tell you how it happened. Chris Dreja was keen to be in it. Jimmy had seen Jonesy on a session. I knew Jonesy with Jet Harris years back. Jonesy said to Jimmy count me in if there is a band going. And later Chris went on to photography. I was managing Terry Reid who incidentally had a dreadful father I had to deal with. Jimmy was keen on Steve Marriot, too, but he wasn't approached then. But I know Jimmy was keen on Terry and one day we came out of Oxford Street and bumped into Terry and it was at that point that he told us he didn't want to do it and suggested Robert Plant.
DL: So that's when you went to see Robert in Hobbstweedle.
PG: Yeah – me, Jimmy and Chris went up there. This big guy with a University of Toronto sweat shirt appeared to let us backstage

and I remember Jimmy saying "Crikey they've got a big roadie!" and he comes back and it turns out to be Robert! Jimmy loved Robert straight away.

DL: When it comes to a drummer I know various names were mentioned, including BJ Thomas from Procal Harum.

PG: Well we definitely approached Aynsley Dunbar. I knew him well and he was a great drummer – but he went off to Zappa's band.

DL: Jack Bruce told me a while back that he was asked to join on bass?

PG: Not that I know of. I can't remember that at all.

DL: What about Steve Winwood?

PG: He was thought of for the vocals but he was never approached.

DL: But then Robert suggested Bonzo.

PG: Well, I was away with The Jeff Beck Group. I was on tour in San Francisco. And Jimmy rang me up and says, "I saw a drummer last night and this guy plays so good and so loud we must get him. He plays so loud promoters won't even book him!" So I came back and started sending the telegrams that formed the famous story. It was at least 30.

DL: I remember 40 being quoted.

PG: Well, I'll tell you a lovely story from the time. They had been rehearsing at the weekend and he came to see me on the Monday and said, "Mr Grant I might have dropped a clanger. I was meant to go to the Isle of Wight to play with Chris Farlowe this week". I said, "Why didn't you tell me. It was for Rick Gunnel, a heavy duty promoter." And he says, "I've already had the 40 quid last week as I needed it." So I said I'd phone Rick and sort it and I did and Rick told me to forget it and we left it at that. Both him and Robert were a bit naive in those early days.

DL: So John was in and what about Chris?

PG: Well he left just before John Bonham arrived. He didn't really want to do the tour and Jonesy was called in.

DL: There was never a chance it was going to be a five piece then?

PG: No not then. The only time we talked about a five piece as I recall was after the first couple of tours. There was talk of adding a keyboard player and I can remember that Keith Emerson was mentioned. And there was also a thing that Brian Lane, the manager of Yes, was paranoid that we were going to nick Chris Squire as a bass player and move Jonesy to keyboards. But that was never a serious proposition.

DL: So the line up was complete and there was that original rehearsal in Gerrard Street. Can you remember being there for that?

PG: No I wasn't there. The first time I saw them play was in Scandinavia. I remember standing on the side of the stage and being amazed. And Bonzo was only on fifty pounds a week and I recall him coming back afterwards and offering to drive the van for another fifty!

DL: The early dates on that first tour. Can you remember how many gigs they played. Do records exist?

PG: Well, funnily enough I do remember coming across an itinerary recently amongst my records. Most of my stuff is in storage but I did find a year's itinerary for 1969.

DL: Was Copenhagen the first ever gig?

PG: As I recall.

DL: Was it pretty apparent it was going to happen for them in a big way?

PG: Oh instantly. I mean you've jumped ahead a bit here because when I made the handshake deal with Atlantic there was no band. Just Jimmy.

DL: Had you spoken to Jerry Wexler when you went out on that first tour the New Yardbirds Scandinavian tour?

PG: The word had gone out.

DL: Weren't there other companies in the running like Pye?

PG: Oh Pye. Yes they laughed me out of the office. And Mo Austin at Warners we talked to. Mo knew Jimmy from session work. Let me tell you how Jimmy was viewed amongst these people. Jimmy and I were walking down 5th Avenue on tour with The Yardbirds. And this limo screeches to a halt backs up and out gets Burt Bacharach - white tuxedo and beautiful woman in the back - and greets Jimmy enthusiastically. He remembered him from those sessions. All the important guys in the US biz knew of Jimmy. But with Pye I went to see Louis Benjamin and I asked for - the figure was £17,500 - and he said you've got to be joking.

DL: What about EMI and Harold Davison?

PG: Harold Davison was good at getting visas and we did use him. But Harold and Tito Burns were around when I first signed The Yardbirds. Simon Napier Bell told me to get rid of Jimmy Page because he would be a problem. When I spoke to Jimmy he told me all the trouble they were having with the money. Not getting paid for months of work. I soon changed all that.

DL: In setting the deal with Atlantic, Dusty Springlield often gets mentioned as putting in a good word.

PG: Yes she does. The story is that she was down at Jerry Wexler's house and he told her about this new group that were in the offing with Jimmy Page and John Paul Jones and when she said she'd worked with Jonesy on arrangements and such, Jerry was knocked out.

DL: So there was no music to be heard before the deal was signed?

PG: No. We signed on the strength of JImmy's name largely. We did eventually play Atlantic the album and I recall them saying they wanted to remix it and Jimmy said what are they talking about. But I said it's just politics. Tom Dowd was there and Jimmy foxed him with a few technical questions. That was an early battle we won.

DL: What about Glyn John's role?

PG: He did try and rope himself in as producer but he was really only the engineer. It was Jimmy's idea to use reverse echo that Glyn copied for the next Stones album. All the creative ideas came from the band.

DL: Were you shocked at how little time that first album took to record?

PG: Yes I was. It cost £1,800 including the cover - and a rostrum for John to play on which gave us that great sound.

DL: Were you actually at the sessions?

PG: The early ones yes. It was tremendous.

DL: Going back to Atlantic - were you worried that the label was not as established here as in the US?

PG: Not at all. It had such a fantastic reputation and Cream had been on the label. When word got around we did have a bit of trouble getting support slots in the States because our reputation was already spreading.

DL: Didn't they really crush Iron Butterfly on that first tour?

PG: Well, what happened was that Bill Graham really liked The Yardbirds and I had a good relationship with Bill which as you know deteriorated sadly at the end. So with a new band you have to go on second at the Fillmore and he got us on with the Butterfly. I knew a girl who worked with the band and she tipped me the nod that they'd signed the contract, which I'm sure they did without knowing it was us they were going to be up against. And sure enough the kids were still shouting 'Zeppelin Zeppelin' as they walked on after our set. One up to us.

DL: Why did you form the Superhype company?

PG: We didn't sign direct to the label - we had a production company. The title came from Jimmy being aware of the hype that surrounded us at the time. So I did a tongue-in-cheek number and called Superhype Music Inc. We sold off the publishing company some years later. The whole deal with Atlantic gave us various clauses that we were able to use to our favour.

DL: What's your version of how the name came into being?

PG: It was going to be Lead Zeppelin. I played around with the letters, doodling in the office and realised Led looked a lot simpler and it was all that light and heavy irony. Jimmy came up with the name, remembering it from Keith Moon.

DL: So you signed as Led Zeppelin on November 1, 1968.

PG: The good thing was in those days you weren't dealing with giant corporate companies like now. The Ertegun brothers and Jerry Wexler owned the company and we shook on a deal. That's how it was back then. Ahmet was the finest record man of all time and every time we negotiated and he said, 'Peter shake on it', you knew it was done.

DL: In England the early reception to the band was only lukewarm.

PG: At first but not for long. I mean the final thing with no singles was when we did the Marquee and offered BBC2 the chance to

---

It was going to be Lead Zeppelin. I played around with the letters, doodling in the office and realised Led looked a lot simpler and it was all that light and heavy irony. Jimmy came up with the name, remembering it from Keith Moon.

PETER GRANT

film it and they didn't even turn up. I went out early afternoon from our office in Oxford Street to Wardour Street and thought, "Fuck me what's this queue?" There were about 200 already lined up. That's when I knew that we just wouldn't need the media. It was going to be about the fans.

DL: Who was in the road crew initially?

PG: Richard Cole who had worked with me in The Yardbirds and Clive Coulson who was working for an Australian we loaned our Hammond organ off. Those were the main two when we went out to the States. Clive, of course, later road managed Bad Company.

DL: Didn't you miss the first US gigs?

PG: Yes I did. I had to tell them to fly out on December 24 and I caught up with them at the Fillmore West. Robert always tells that tale that I said if we don't make it here then there was no hope because The Yardbirds had a good following at the Fillmore. I was talking to Maureen Plant recently and she recalled how I'd met her at San Francisco... this waif-like figure. She was due to meet with Robert at the same time I was meeting up with them.

DL: The first album came out quickly once you were there.

PG: Yes and we'd had a few white labels go out. WBCN in Boston had it because JJ Jackson supported us. I'd known him with The Yardbirds. Stations like that and KASN had the album.

DL: What else do you recall about those first tours?

PG: Well, that poster with Julie Driscoll reminds me of a situation. I remember Georgio Gomelsky being backstage and telling me what a dame Julie was with her finesse. She promptly came offstage and flopped on the chair saying, 'It ain't half fucking hot out there!" So that put paid to that theory of Georgio's. Great singer

lars from the guys in the queue. So I took my rings off joined the line and as I came for my turn I shouted "Gotcha!' and took him back to the dressing room and had him empty his pockets and took every last dime and nickel from him. He didn't do it again.

DL: Though you shied from TV, those radio sessions for the BBC went down very well.

PG: Yeah, I knew Bernie Andrews. I'd dealt with him with Bo Didley on *Saturday Club*. Anyway I reckon I knew how to handle the BBC. We agreed to do that live concert. I told Jimmy it would be good. Mind you I didn't know it was going to be bootlegged! Alan Freeman repeated it last year as I recall He was great to us you know. Always played us on his Saturday show. He was always the first one at the Beeb to get a new Zeppelin album. Last week on his *Rock Show* he played 'Black Dog' and then went straight into a track from Robert's album. Wonderful man.

DL: So you remember doing the *Supershow* film?

PG: That was a mate of Jimmy's who buttonholed us into that. I wasn't that keen. I didn't even go down to the filming. As for the French TV – that was another difficult one. They never knew how to get the sound right in a TV studio. The thing I remember about France was that Eddie Barclay party when we didn't play because we couldn't get the gear in the place. Jimmy only wanted to go so he could meet Bridget Bardot. Anyway we didn't play live but all the papers gave us great reviews next day presuming we had. That was a laugh.

DL: Do you remember John using two bass drums?

PG: Disaster! Just too much. I know when he got that first 28 inch bass drum, that maple kit. We had it in for a Boston Tea Party gig

BACKSTAGE WITH JIMMY, DENMARK: MARCH, 1969

mind was Jools.

DL: These are some shots from the Kinetic Playground.

PG: We started there at $7,500 and ended up at the end of the year with two days at $12,500 a night. At that place some people tried to lay some amps on us. Jimmy told Richard to tell 'em we didn't like them but what he had us do was connect the new speakers into his old Orange and Fender gear! Typical Led Wallet! I remember we caught a guy fiddling there. It was a date with Jethro Tull. Ahmet was there and I went out front to see what the crowds were like. The box office was on a corner. This guy was taking five dol-

and I recall saying to the promoter John Law watch the drummer - you won't believe it and John goes and drops the sticks several times and blows it for me!

DL: Here's a photo of that kit from a mid-1969 show.

PG: Yeah that would be at what they called Summer Stock. We used to play in the tents.

DL: Is it true that you and Jimmy were a little unsure about Robert being a suitable singer during the first couple of US tours?

PG: No, not really. He did lack a bit of confidence at first and I used to hide all the negative reviews we had. But come mid '69 he was well in the swing of it.

DL: By the end of '69 the gold disc awards started appearing.

PG: One of those award ceremonies we held in Sweden at a sex club. There's all of us getting the awards and on the floor a couple are having it away. The press didn't quite know what to make of that!

DL: It was a constant touring schedule in that first year but it certainly paid off.

PG: Yes. We went to the States a lot that year and we did loads of festivals. We had a fall out with Blood Sweat & Tears. They wouldn't come off. So I stood on the steps and nobody got through until they cleared off. But I used to say to the boys on those bills go out there and tear the place apart, take the roof or canvas off. I don't want to see you afterwards unless you succeed. That normally got the required response. It was on one of those festivals I had an hour long chat with Janis Joplin backstage. I've got a picture of that somewhere. Also I recall a row with Chicago Transit Authority or whatever they were called.

DL: When *Zep II* came out 'Whole Lotta Love' nearly came out as a UK single. What's the story behind that?

PG: It was down to Phil Carson. He came to the office and told me he'd pressed 500 and they had been shipped to Manchester. I said, "Look we don't do singles". He was a bit pushy in those days. I said, "Have you told Ahmet?" and promptly called him and there were red faces all round. Our contract stated we had the last say on such decisions.

DL: Do you recall the press release about it where you stated Zeppelin would be recording a special single instead of releasing 'Whole Lotta Love'?

PG: I think that was a cover up. We never ever went in just to record a single. That was the golden rule. No singles. I could never understand why he only pressed 500 - I mean thanks for your confidence in us Phil!

DL: Early in 1970 you filmed the Albert Hall gig. Why didn't that ever reach the screens?

PG: We filmed that and I think some of the Bath Festival. We did it with Stanley Doorfman and believe it or not he used the wrong speed film and it came out too dark. So that was no use.

DL: Did he film in Iceland?

PG: No, I never went to that gig. One of the few I missed. No, it was Bath but I stopped it.

DL: Were you conscious that *Zep III* signalled a change of emphasis musically?

PG: It was an extension. In Jimmy's mind it was an expansion of the music. I remember they were mixing 'Gallows Pole' at Island Studios and Chris Blackwell came in and just couldn't believe how good it was.

DL: What about the Bath Festival in 1970?

PG: That was great. I went down to the site unbeknown to Freddie Bannister and I found out from the Met Office what time the sun was setting and it was right behind the stage and by going on at eight in the evening I was able to bring the lights up a bit at a time. And it was vital we went on to match that. That's why I made sure Flock or whoever it was got off on time. Not that we had anything to lose as we'd been paid £20,000 up front! Bath was a turning point in terms of recognition for us. It was great and I remember Jonesy arriving by helicopter with Julie Felix and Mo and we had to get the Hells Angels to help us get them on site. I'd made a contact with the Angels in Cleveland in America with The Yardbirds so we had no bother with them.

DL: So you were now the number one band - as voted by readers of the M*elody Maker*.

PG: We had that awards ceremony for helping British payments abroad. They wanted to give us the Queen's Award for Industry and I turned it down. It was too establishment for Led Zeppelin. We had that string quartet come down and I told the press they were the guys that played on the album!

DL: With the fourth album do you remember the mixing problems?

PG: Well I know we had mixing problems with the third album and I remember Jimmy and I going down to Memphis in the middle of a tour to put that right.

DL: What was Headley Grange like?

PG: That was magic for me because I knew the area really well

because I'd been evacuated there in the war. Jimmy now lives about four miles out.

DL: Tell me how you came to do the small clubs tour?

PG: What happened was that *Melody Maker* and all that lot were saying Zep were getting too big for their boots with their US tours, so I said to the lads let's go and do a small tour and everyone was up for it so we did Nottingham Boat Club etc. Then it's "Oh aren't Led Zeppelin selfish to do those dates denying the fans access." You couldn't win.

DL: Then you had that riot in Milan.

PG: One thing you have got to remember is the great training I'd had as a tour manager before Zep. Gene Vincent, Chuck Berry, Jerry Lee, Bo Diddley. I worked with all those guys - and I'd also done four months in Italy with Wee Willie Harris back in the Fifties. So I knew what a dodgy place it could be. So I got all the money up front and made sure we got the air tickets back in advance. Just as well because when we got to the gig there were water cannons and tear gas. Everybody just went mad.

So we had to flee and I'm not that good at running but Mick Hinton and Richard got us out and we barricaded ourselves in the medical room and stayed there till it all cooled down. Years later I bumped into the promoter of that gig at the Cafe Royale and I went in the toilet to have a piss and this guy saw me and pissed all down himself because he thought I was going to have him. I'd forgiven him by then though. You can't account for the actions of the Italian police.

DL: I think it's evident that your experience before Zeppelin was pretty crucial and something that not many people recognise.

PG: It still surprises people. Last year we had Rick Mayall down here performing and I went along and he was in awe when he heard I'd worked with all those rock'n'rollers. We stayed up till two o'clock telling stories backstage like the time Jerry Lee Lewis threw Brylcream all over the audience.

DL: You had a good relationship with Claude Knobs and the Montreux Festival didn't you?

PG: Yes we did. One time we did it it was so packed I had the idea of feeding the sound outside on to the lawn where loads of fans who couldn't get in had congregated. Claude loved that.

DL: And of course you went down a storm in Japan.

PG: I can tell you exactly when we first went (Peter pulls out his passport). It was on September 19 and then in 1972 we were admitted September 29 and left October 8 the second time. There you have it. We had a single entry visa. And we went on to Hong Kong. The first time we went the Japanese company insisted they record it. There was this 6-track transistorised board. Jimmy was a bit worried about this so the deal I made was that they could record it if we could have the tapes and take them back to England and approve it. So Jimmy listened to them and found them to be terrible. So he took the tapes back and wiped over them and used them again. So it was goodbye Live In Japan.

DL: After Japan in '71 you did the Empire Pool.

PG: Yeah it was a chance to do something different and we had the circus acts and the pigs and we had them dressed up in policemen's helmets. One of them shit backstage and I turned to Robert and said, "Don't worry he's just nervous - it's the first time he's played a big gig!" We thought the pigs would save it. Good times those. Maggie was on the bill and played wonderfully and we were great too.

DL: The fourth album came out with the symbols on much to Atlantic's alarm.

PG: We had trouble initially but Ahmet believed in us. Again it was a case of following our instincts and knowing that the cover would not harm sales one bit. And we were right again.

DL: Then to Australia in '72.

PG: Don't ask me about that police bust because I slept through it. Warner's had a deal with Air India and we got a round the world trip for 500 quid and we got to Perth and it was so hot. Fantastic gigs though. New Zealand was the biggest public gathering in the history of the Island.

DL: About the same time you pulled that stunt on the Midem Invitation replying to their Invitation for Mr. Zeppelin to play their festival with a full page ad in *Music Week*.

PG: Do you know music publishers today still ask me about that

Bath was a turning point in

terms of recognition for us.

It was great and I remember

Jonesy arriving by helicopter

with Julie Felix and Mo and

we had to get the Hells Angels

to help us get them on site.

PETER GRANT

HOLDING COURT, *IN THE CITY* CONVENTION, MANCHESTER: 1992

One of the pigs shit backstage and I turned to Robert and said, "Don't worry he's just nervous – it's the first time he's played a big gig!"
PETER GRANT

one, guys who could have only been kids in those days. When I was at the *In The City* event people were coming up to me from Chappells and such like and saying how they loved that advert.

DL: It said everything that here was a band selling millions of albums [yet] totally misunderstood by the industry establishment.

PG: Quite right. I mean Bernard Chevy was a prat. I just never replied to his letter. I just took the ad "Mr. Zeppelin regrets".

DL: '72 was a golden era really particularly for touring, though the US tour seemed to be overshadowed by the Stones touring at the same time.

PG: Yes, that really shook me into getting a publicist. We had BP Fallon and later Danny Goldberg. I remember Beep on the UK tour. We played at Greens Playhouse. Beep had the make-up and the glitter on and managed to get himself a good kicking outside the gig. John Bonham came up with a classic line. We came off stage and there's Fallon looking worse the wear and John shouts over, "Look who bopped the beep!" But that's the humour that we enjoyed, even if it was a bit cruel and all those books miss that.

DL: Looking back at the period, did you have much trouble getting them to do what you suggested. Did they get fed up with the touring?

PG: Well, there were always battles. I had to be firm. But it was like my philosophy with every album that we should treat each one as a first album. You know... pay that much attention to the advertising, the sleeve etc. They were always fantastic though. But part of the success was that we never hung out at the Speakeasy or wherever. We got together when we needed to and then did our own thing. That's why I always tried to make sure we didn't overdo the touring during the school holidays - so the guys could see their children. We didn't live in each other's pockets.

We always delivered and everybody played their part. Of course there were odd rows. It's like what Bonzo said to Robert, "All you've got to do is stand out there and look good. We'll take care of the music!" There were rows, one bloody amazing one in Japan when Robert came off stage with a split lip. It was over some dispute over some money from some tour. He still owed Bonzo some petrol money - 70 quid or something - but that's how it was.

DL: Did the excess and indulgencies get in the way?

PG: Not as much as was reported. I made sure they always got on stage. But it's really the funnier stories that nobody prints. Like the time we played a trick on Bonzo during 'Moby Dick'. Normally in the solo he switched from sticks to playing with his bare hands. One night we hid the sticks and he's shouting out to Mick for the sticks and is expecting the boys to come back out and tie it all up. The arms are getting weary. And he's looking at me and I know where they are and he's going "Where the fuckin' hell are they?" so I point out front and he glances at the mixing desk and the three of them jump out waving! Eventually they came round and get on stage by which time Bonzo has recorded the longest ever version of 'Moby Dick'!

DL: We move on to the spring of '73 and *Houses Of The Holy*.

PG: Do you remember those ads we took: 'Does things to people' and 'The effect is shattering'. Well we found those pictures in an old junk shop. I had to use them. Actually my big artistic input on that album was the wraparound band which we put on to shut

There were rows, one bloody amazing one in Japan when Robert came off stage with a split lip. It was over some dispute over some money from some tour. He still owed Bonzo some petrol money – 70 quid or something.

PETER GRANT

MELODY MAKER POLL AWARDS, SAVOY HOTEL, LONDON: SEPTEMBER 16, 1970

Atlantic up. It was another wordless cover as you know. Got the idea from those lavish books that have wraparound covers.

DL: Summer of '73 and it's those massive crowds at Atlanta and Tampa.

PG: Yeah and into the *Guinness Book Of Records*. I'd love a copy of the version that mentioned my achievement of getting 90% for Zeppelin in another paragraph under our attendance record. My son Warren told me about that. The thing with Tampa is that I didn't tell them really how big it was going to be but when we drew up Robert was going, "Fucking hell G where did these people all come from?" And I just said "Don't worry son. I know you're still on probation with the band but you'll be alright." I was confident they could handle it. In fact I knew they would rise to the occasion.

DL: Why, and more to the point, how had their audience grown so fantastically from '69 to this mammoth gathering in 1973?

PG: It was the pacing of it. We didn't go to Madison Square Garden straight off. It was gradually built up in all those states like North Carolina. It's like we built it up into an event. In fact that was when I came up with that 'An Evening With Led Zeppelin' tag. I know it was corny but it was like the old Thirties stage line. I guess that was a by-product of my days as a 14-year-old stage hand. I'd learned the trade. When I told them that's how it should be billed they all giggled a bit but I was proved right again Those big promoters like Jerry Weintraub loved it. It was an event.

DL: This photo of an arena from the era kind of sums it up.

PG: That could be Nassau. We had the triangle mirrors then. I remember we hated that effect. In fact in the end they came off one night and kicked the shit out of it! And years later when Robert had the crash he was nursed by the daughter of the designer of the mirrors much to our embarrassment! We were always looking for new effects and Iggy Knight who was now with us by then was great. I once came up with an idea I'd seen from the old stage hand days of using a real fountain behind the set to project the light. We were seriously considering this idea until we realised it would mean using fifty tons of water.

DL: On the '73 tour you finally shot some film that was to be used.

PG: We were in Boston in the Sheraton. Jimmy knew Massot. We'd been on about the failure of the Dorfman film. So we got Massot and Ernie Day over and started filming. It turned out to be pretty traumatic to say the least. They filmed three nights at the Garden and never got one complete 'Whole Lotta Love'.

DL: Is that why you did the additional scenes and fantasy sequences?

PG: We did always plan for it to be more than just the concert film. There's one piece I came up with. During 'Dazed', where Jimmy is playing really fast and the camera goes through his eyes to the black cop sequence. That was to show that beyond the concrete wall and all this intense music, life was going on around us. So that filled a gap.

DL: Why did Joe Massot get taken off the project?

PG: We knew Peter Clifton because years back he'd come to us to do a film and showed Jimmy and I a load of clips in a viewing theatre off Wardour Street of Hendrix that he had shot. This was with a view to him salvaging the Dorfman film. But we didn't want to do that. So we searched for this Australian Clifton and found he lived in Holland Park and offered him the salvage job of the Massot mess. I'm afraid with Joe it really wasn't what we had intended.

DL: Did Clifton do a good job?

PG: Well yes, with the resources that he had.

DL: Did you shoot some stuff at Shepperton - recreating the stage set up?

PG: Yes, but we didn't shout about the fact.

DL: Were you happy with the end result of the film?

PG: Some of it but what did we know about making films? There was that famous throwaway line that I had about it being the most expensive home movie ever made. That was the truth. If it had been totally hopeless we would have shelved it. I did enjoy the premieres and meeting with all the film media. And Robert and I did the *Whistle Test* interview. They took us out to lunch beforehand and plied us with the best claret, then it was onto the boat. I thought it would be a small cruiser but it turned out to be an 800 passenger thing called the Swanage Queen.

The other thing about the film was the debates we had with Frank Wells at Warners over the titles. We wanted to bring in Po [Hipgnosis designer Aubrey Powell] or somebody to do them again and we had a meeting with all the Warner big shots where Frank says something like, "We won't run out on you Peter" and I replied "I know because I won't let you get out of the fucking door!" It got sorted OK in the end.

DL: How serious was it in late 1974 when John Paul Jones told you he wanted to quit the band?

PG: Oh, very serious. He turned up at my house one afternoon and told me he'd had enough and said he was going to be the choirmaster at Winchester Cathedral. We had this heart to heart during which we recalled a time in Australia when I got very insecure and thought the band wanted to blow me out. Anyway it turns out John said he thought it was the other way round - that I was going to blow them out. Anyway I said if you want to leave, well you've got to do what you've got to do. But I said think about it. So we invented that press story saying he was overtaxed. There was a bonus to all this because the studio time we had booked at the Grange for Zeppelin we gave to Bad Company who had just formed.

DL: Did the others get to know about Jonesy's unrest or was it kept low key?

PG: It was kept low key. I told Jimmy of course who couldn't believe it. But it was the pressure. He was a family man was Jonesy. By that time the security thing in the US was getting ridiculous. We started getting death threats - in fact straight after the '73 tour following, the Drake robbery, there was a very serious one. Some crackpot letter from Jamaica stating what was in store for us when we toured again. It got very worrying. That's how we lost a little of the camaraderie after that when we were in America because there were armed guards outside the hotel rooms all the time. I think we even talked about wearing bullet-proof vests at one time. Bonzo told me to order extra large ones for him and me! We did laugh at it but it was a serious problem. The thing is outside the States it was fine. In Europe on that last tour we cruised through it.

DL: So you slowed down the touring and general work rate a bit.

PG: Well Jonesy came back refreshed and ready to go again and we did finish the film off and set up Swan Song.

DL: But you turned down Knebworth and a satellite show to be beamed from Munich.

PG: We turned down Knebworth more than once. I think we turned it down in '75 too. I'm sure I have a telegram somewhere from Harvey Goldsmith offering us £225,000 but I said no. As for the satellite show I know we turned that idea down around 1970 when we were in Oxford Street with RAK. It was to be a New Year's Eve show but the Met Office tipped me off that a snowstorm could easily affect the quality. I think they offered a million. But the thing is Led Zeppelin was essentially an in-person band. That was where it was for us as simple as that. As for Knebworth we never agreed to do it in '74. Bannister jumped the gun.

DL: And during this time they were making the sixth album.

PG: With 'Kashmir, I remember Bonzo playing me the demo of him and Jimmy running it down first. It was fantastic. Funny thing is when it was first finished it was decided it was a bit of a dirge. We were in Paris and we played it to Atlantic and we thought it was a dirge so Richard was dispatched to Southall in London to find a Pakistani Orchestra. We put the strings on and Jonesy got it all together and the end result was just exactly what was needed. He was a master arranger.

DL: Was it around the Swan Song launch in '74 that you met Elvis?

PG: I think it was Jonesy and Richard who met him that year. Richard had a watch and they had a swap and Elvis gave Jonesy a watch with an East Coast and West Coast face. I think I met him the next year.

DL: What was that like?

PG: It was incredible. I've still got the badge in the cabinet over there - 'Elvis in Person On Tour 444'. What happened was we were about 10 or 12 rows from the front. They did a number and it was all over the place and Elvis goes "Stop, stop, stop" and he turns to the audience and says, "We're gonna do that again because we've got Led Zeppelin in the audience and we want to look like we know what we're doing up here." I just went cold - it was the near-

> *We turned down Knebworth more than once. I think we turned it down in '75 too. I'm sure I have a telegram somewhere from Harvey Goldsmith offering us £225,000 but I said no.*
>
> PETER GRANT

est I've had to snuffing it! I mean what a compliment. And we went back and that's when I sat on Elvis' father! There was this huge suite and I was talking to Ronnie the drummer and I sat on Vernon. He was perched on the end of the settee and I just didn't see him. Jerry Weintraub told me we'd only get a 20-minute stay and we were up there for two and a half hours.

Bonzo and Elvis had been talking about hot rods. This thing about how much kick back you can get. And John was calling him El and he says "I've had one El that kicked back real hard" and he pushes Elvis' shoulder and knocks him back and all the minders jump up. Elvis laughs and says, "What did you do that for?" and John replies, "Well I gotta tell you El, I was in reverse at the time!" When we said goodbye I apologised for sitting on his dad and Elvis looks me in the eye, clicks his fingers and says "Stick around son - you might get a permanent job". Brilliant. He said how much he'd liked the band. It was then he gave me the badge I noticed one of the minders wearing - Elvis 444 - and I said that was the number of our offices in New York so Elvis promptly tells the minder to give me the badge. Wonderful night.

DL: In 1975 the tour in America kicked off with Jimmy injuring his hand.

PG: Yeah we kicked off in January. That was the start of the non-residency which we were only told about three weeks up front. Our accountant Joan Hudson told us of the massive problems we would have if we didn't go. It was an 87% tax rate then on high earners. Disgusting really. I think Jimmy caught his hand at Haywards Heath or something. There was another time in San Diego might have been '73 when he sprained his finger on a fence.

When we said goodbye I apologised for sitting on his dad and Elvis looks me in the eye, clicks his fingers and says "Stick around son – you might get a permanent job".
PETER GRANT

BACKSTAGE, KEZAR STADIUM: JUNE 2, 1973

DL: How did you come to choose Earl's Court for the '75 UK shows?

PG: That was to keep faith with the fans. Mel Bush did a great job with that series. That Physical Rocket idea we got from Australia when trains from the south islands were chartered in. Earl's Court was fantastic. Nobody sat behind the stage. We had the screen and the whole Showco set up. It took half a jumbo jet to get it over. Mel Bush did a super job in promoting those gigs. He presented us with souvenir mirrors afterwards depicting the advert. Mel told me that we had enough ticket applications to have done 10 shows that month.

DL: The Earl's Court video still exists doesn't it?

PG: Jimmy's got them all. He took my copy when he came around to the house one day. They could be used I suppose if there ever was a video release. I just never really rated the idea of Zeppelin on the small screen. Times have changed now, so maybe it would look OK now.

DL: Did you look back and see Earl's Court as the last of the glory days?

PG: Perhaps. We had that second tour in the US lined up as we were going to be away from England all year. I was in the south of France when I heard about Robert's crash. A nightmare. We were trying to run the operation from a house in Malibu which was a crazy idea. There was a lot of tension about that period, all holed up in houses we didn't really want to be in. In fact John moved out to the Hyatt hotel.

DL: And then to Munich.

PG: It was an uphill struggle. It was difficult in the writing and rehearsing stage and then we were pressured to record it quickly. It's not one of my favourite albums but there again it's got 'Achilles' on which is a masterpiece. 'Tea For One' sums that period up for me really. That was Maureen's song. She used to come out at weekends and Robert was pretty depressed.

DL: What about the sleeve?

PG: Well the idea was to put into perspective whether the obelisk was real or just an illusion. The only time it becomes real is on the inner sleeve when you can see the shadow. On the sleeve it looks a bit stuck on. Talking of sleeves did you know the Spanish banned *Physical Graffiti* with the picture of the nun on the inner sleeve. They stamped 'censored' on it. Have you seen *The Obelisk* objects we had made.

DL: Yes, one came up at Sothebys last year.

PG: Yes I remember all that stuff from Jimmy going in. Stephen Maycock knows I've got a lot of stuff. I know there's a market for Zep memorabilia. Do you remember Gully, our big Welsh guy? He was in Italy with Roger Chapman wearing the '77 Zeppelin tour jacket and a doorman offered him 300 quid for it on the spot and it was in rags!

DL: So the exile ended in the spring of 1976. Do you recall all those rumours of the band playing the Marquee again?

PG: Vaguely. We were getting a lot of offers then. But we weren't ready to do it. It was getting a bit worrying. There were problems with Jimmy with squatters in his house. With Bad Company the deal was I'd always try and get to the important gigs and I had to go out to sort some problems out that year and my wife was just fed up with it all and walked out on me. It was not a good scene at all. Plus Jimmy's health was suffering. There were definite drug problems with one of two people, including myself.

DL: How did you approach the '77 tour?

PG: It was hard really for me because I had to leave the kids and my divorce was starting. John Bonham was also uptight that year and we took Rex out to be his whipping boy. John Bindon came out, who was friend of Richard's. I'd decided I wasn't going to do much clubbing and John was an aide who ended up looking after Jimmy quite a lot.

DL: John Bindon died recently.

PG: I didn't know anything about that until the *Evening Standard* rang me for some quotes. I was very surprised but I hadn't seen him in years. He worked for Ryan O'Neal at one point, looking after Tatum.

DL: Was he the right guy to have at the time?

PG: He had a lot of good points. He took care of my situation and Jimmy. Unfortunately the only problem we had was in Oakland. But you have to remember he worked under the direction of our

American security who were all serving police officers. We had the same guys every time.

DL: Let's discuss a couple of '77 incidents – the Tampa rain cancellation.

PG: A big mistake. Possibly one of our biggest and all because we never realised there should be a rain date. It had been dreadfully wet for days in the area with rain like you've never seen. That was the situation where, if an outdoor show was rained off a rain date was booked and you did it the following day. Now somehow we missed the detail on this one. It wasn't until we were on the plane flying from Miami to the gig that Richard shows me the ticket which says on it 'An Evening with Led Zeppelin June 3; come rain or shine' i.e. no rain date. I storm off to blast Terry Bassett from Concerts West. Steve Weiss, our lawyer, should have caught it in the contract. I should have sent Richard out to check the place but he'd been sorting out some trip for Robert and Jonesy to visit Disneyland with the kids. All sorts of trouble.

If Richard had gone he'd have seen that they'd set up a canvas roof instead of a metal one which we always demanded. So when we get to the site there was something like 10,000 tons of water resting over the drums. So now I have to make a decision about them going on. You can't imagine the pressure. When they're about to go on the rain has stopped. There's 70,000 fans gathered and we've got to get it on somehow. So I decided to let them start. Nearby overhead there's this big dark cloud looming. I thought at this rate it will be us who'll be leaving under a big black cloud and sure enough after three numbers it starts pouring. I quickly actioned to Robert to wind it up and off we run.

were in the clear for all to see.

DL: To keep on the same theme, wasn't there a problem of some missing money during the middle of the tour?

PG: 10,000 dollars actually. There was a query over some of the expenses Richard had handled but it all turned out to be accountant error thank the Lord. I mean if it had been just a 1,000 dollars I could have lived with it - it might have been down to Hinton putting something on his expenses but $10,000 was a bit different The thing is it wasn't my money or Richard's it was the band's and I was paid to be responsible for it.

DL: And then you got to Oakland.

PG: Oakland was another nightmare and very heavy. It was a flashpoint situation that got out of hand. It could have got a lot worse. It was just a very regrettable incident. But we were up against Bill Graham's security guys with their gloves filled with sand. We didn't want to get into that. There were wives and children with us. We'd brought the kids on tour for that part of the leg. It was just after we did that *Daily Mirror* special story. One dear memory of '77 and a very positive one was when I realised just how much it had all come to mean. It was during our stay at the Plaza in New York which we used as a base to fly out to the surrounding gigs and our stint at Madison Square was still some weeks off. Every night outside the hotel there were scores of fans surrounding the limos and it was just amazing.

Then we announced the New York dates via Scott Muni's radio show. Woosh! All tickets gone. The tariff for that Madison stint showed our advertising reading nil. It was the demand from the street and the fans that astounded me. There was no hype, no

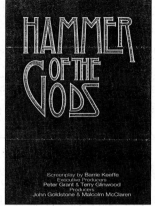

SYNOPSIS FOR THE PLANNED GRANT BIOPIC

WITH PLANT, HYATT HOUSE, LOS ANGELES: JUNE 1973

Oakland was another nightmare and very heavy. It was a flashpoint situation that got out of hand. It could have got a lot worse. It was just a very regrettable incident.

PETER GRANT

One funny aside to this is Robert telling me later that as he's coming off stage my son Warren shouts to Robert to pick up a frisbee he's thrown on. As you can imagine Robert told him in no uncertain terms to leave it there! Getting out was a nightmare too, and we had to wait at the airport for John's wife Mo who had travelled out in a separate limo which had spun off the road. It was another typical '77 mishap all round. Now we would have firmly got the blame for all this and there was a council meeting coming up after the weekend so I put our view forward which was the truth. I took a double page ad in the *Tampa Times* or whatever it was stating that in no way were we to blame and that Concerts West were taking responsibility. The way we rushed it through is that I knew Colonel Tom Parker's son-in-law ran an ad agency so we got him out of bed early on Sunday to get the ad in for first thing the next morning. So no matter what the council said we

MTV or anything like now. It was pure demand. At that point I really did wonder how much bigger this could all get. From those humble beginnings in '69 to this in the space of seven years was just astounding.

DL: It seems though within all the chaos that they still made some great music. There were some magic nights musically in '77.

PG: That's right but that's how it was. I remember the first time Weintraub saw Jimmy on a tour. He says to me, "Is that guy gonna live!" He was faking a bit was Jimmy which he often did for a laugh with the others. But on stage was where it happened for Jimmy. And Jonesy was doing incredible versions of 'No Quarter'. You must have that *Badge Holders Only* bootleg with that on.

DL: There's some very good tapes of the 1977 tour going about.

PG: I'm not surprised because Benji lost some desk tapes one night. I never did bollock him for it, just put it down as one of those things. In fact in the early Eighties I was disappointed and hurt by his plan to become Robert's manager which all went wrong in the end. I used to phone up and I'd never get a return call or any communication. Silly really. I must also tell you about our meet with the Russians that year. Utterly amazing. I was invited to dinner at the Russian Embassy and all the guests came to the gig. I think it was in Landover. They really knew their stuff. I was in the limo of one of the wives and she says, "What's the sound like for your group?" and I say "Very good" and she adds that when they saw the Stones last year there was no bottom to their sound because all the amps were hung. Amazing.

So then they met with the band beforehand and during the gig instead of watching in the box they all want to sit on the side of the stage. Jonesy then plays variations from Rachmaninov during 'No Quarter' and the Russian guests are just blown away. We planned to go to Russia but after Robert's tragedy we had to scrap it. Shame as we could have been one of the first rock acts to go. Elton John went instead as you probably know.

DL: Then the '77 tour was cancelled when Robert's son died.

PG: We were in New Orleans. Robert phoned me from Scotland just after the funeral. I couldn't t get back as I was trying to sort out the cancellations. In New Orleans the radio stations played Zeppelin 24 hours on the day we were meant to play as a tribute. Robert phoned me and I just said let me know the situation when you're ready. He obviously needed a break.

DL: Did you think it could be the end?

PG: No though I didn't think Robert would say he didn't want to sing 'Stairway' again which is what he kept saying at rehearsals.

IVOR NOVELLO AWARDS, GROSVENOR HOTEL, LONDON: MAY 12, 1997

After that I knew it would take a while after the tragedy but I knew he would come back to the fold.

DL: Wasn't it around early '78 that you had a heart scare?

PG: Yes it was and that really did worry me but after some recuperation it got better. It was all down to pressure. My divorce really did knock me for six.

DL: They eventually emerged at Clearwell to rehearse in May 1978.

PG: That was after a long uphill battle to get him to work again. Robert kept saying he'd do it and then back down. But Bonzo was a tower of strength. We had a meeting in the Royal Garden Hotel and they started talking about Bad Company and Maggie and all that with their Swan Song hats on and I said, "What the fuck are you talking about? You should worry about your own careers". So I suggested Clearwell because Bad Company had been. So Robert says he'd just like to do some jamming so that's what they did. And it was OK. I went down there. Things were looking up.

DL: Why did you choose Polar studios to make the next album?

PG: Abba came to us and offered it. It was actually a slog to do it. We used to get the noon flight out on Monday and then return the Friday for the weekend. It was cold and dark all the time. They were difficult conditions but Jonesy was great on that. He put in so much effort. But that was Led Zeppelin as four people again bonding together to lift each other up.

DL: The scene was set for a return and you chose Knebworth rather than a proper tour. In retrospect was that the right decision?

PG: Absolutely. We didn't want to start all over again so I said "Fuck doing a tour. We're the biggest band in the world so we better get out there and show them we still are." I said Knebworth was the gig and I reckoned we could do two dates. I said to Bannister, "This is the biggest fucking band in the world and we can do two dates." I was absolutely confident.

DL: I remember that the advert just had their name on.

PG: Yeah it should have said full supporting cast but he left that off but it didn't matter. We did have a bit of a row over the attendance but I had it photographed from the helicopter that first week and sent it to Nassau to be analysed. There was 210,000 in there give or take 2% they told us. Well we got paid in full. There was some battle over VAT, I recall. I think it was 180,000 the second week. We had the photograph of the aerial shot hanging in the office. There were some very good Knebworth photos. There's a great pic of Robert and Carmen backstage that was used in a few magazines.

DL: That photo session for the Knebworth publicity beforehand seems to have been quite eventful.

PG: I wasn't there – the story that I recall is Jimmy moaning about his hair because Richard had driven him up in his Austin Healey with the top open. His hair was all in knots when he got there. Another bollocking for Richard. Oh and then Bonzo complained the pictures captured his love handles and they had to be airbrushed out. The sky was too dull and we had to overlay a sky scene from a shot of Texas to give it some colour! The traumas we went though to get one picture correct.

DL: There exists a photo from that session of Robert with his trousers down revealing er... the original Percy.

PG: Really? I'll have to find that one for my own book when comes out!

DL: What did you think of their performance at Knebworth?

PG: It was a bit rusty. We'd been to Copenhagen to get the sound sorted out – that was always one of my strategies to warm up in Europe, usually Scandinavia. I must tell you for that laser violin bow effect Jimmy was up for hours rehearsing with the lighting guys the exact order he would project the bow outwards to make sure the laser effects were spot on. That really was a fantastic moment watching that at the side of the stage. And backstage in the day it was great seeing all the families come in. We had a special Ligger enclosure marked as such. We banned *Sounds* though, which was a typical move when the press got up our noses.

DL: And then six sleeves for *In Through The Out Door*.

PG: Yes the brown bag. My idea which Robert years later in the Hipgnosis book said that line about it being "All power to pomp". Do you know I don't have much to do with him. In fact I haven't seen him since Jason's wedding but he was on Radio One the other day with Simon Bates. He said Led Zep was four great musicians and a very heavy manager. I had to laugh! He's still such a wag is Robert. Getting back to the sleeve Jimmy came up with that great idea of the watercolour on the inner sleeve from one of Scarlet's books. But then Atlantic went and spoiled it by telling everybody. We wanted it to be a surprise. Still, whatever sleeve it had it still sold a bucket full which pleased us greatly of course and seemed to bolster the US record biz at the time.

DL: How did you come to the decision to go to Europe in 1980 with such a stripped down set up?

PG: That came out of discussion with Jimmy really. We said let's forget the 320 lamps set up and go back to 120 lamps, a back-to-basics sort of thing. And Robert kept insisting at the time that he wouldn't go back to America. Do you remember at Knebworth he sang the wrong words in 'Stairway'? Unforgiveable really. He was in a difficult frame of mind. And then there was all that speech on stage. "We're never going to Texas anymore... but we will go to Manchester" and all that and as he's saying it he's eyeing me out at the side of the stage. So we did the Europe tour but before it we had this big meet down at my house that went on all night. But all the others said it was down to me to get Robert to agree to go back to the States.

I mean we just had to go if we were to carry on really. That was where a sizeable amount of the market was, simple as that. So purposely I played it down with Robert, and Bonzo would tell me he'd say to him "How come G hasn't said anything to me about America yet?" I never said a thing. But I have an outstanding memory of coming off the Europe tour and landing in the Falcon jet in England and walking across the tarmac and Robert coming up to me and saying "OK I'll do it but only for four weeks". So I said I'd give him a call in the next few days and we were able to set up the autumn tour. We were fully operational again.

We did have a bit of a row over the attendance but I had it photographed from the helicopter that first week and sent it to Nassau to be analysed. There was 210,000 in there give or take 2% they told us.

PETER GRANT

DL: In Europe you used Phil Carlo and dropped Richard.

PG: I'd paid for the doctor's visits and all that and it just wasn't getting better. He had a massive problem so I thought the only way to shake him up was to blow him out so I told him I wouldn't want him in Europe and he says, "You can't do it without me" but I said well we've got to. He was shattered and he spoke to Jimmy but I made the decision. The next we hear he's in Italy with some dreadful girl. But I can't take away what he did for us in the peak years. He was always there and always reliable. He was always employed by me. We needed him for America so I thought this would shake him up but it didn't seem to do much good.

DL: Did you think Europe had gone well?

PG: By and large very well. We had that trouble with Bonzo in Nuremberg but I must tell you another Bonham funny that occurred there. They wrapped him up in a red blanket in the ambulance. So they strapped him in with this belt and he says, "How do I look?" and I said "Like fucking Father Christmas!" and he says "Don't make me laugh. It bloody hurts" But he'd had 27 bananas that night so it's not surprising he was ill!

DL: So you arranged for the US tour to be titled *Led Zeppelin The 1980s Part One*.

PG: I knew we couldn't cover everywhere in four weeks because Robert's schedule was always two days on then one day off. But I reckoned that once Robert got over there and got into the swing he'd be OK so it was a Part One of what I hoped would be further visits. We had a meeting at Blakes to get it organised and set the first dates up. It was looking good.

DL: And then you got the fateful call on September 25.

DL: So then you announced the statement.

PG: We had to do that to end all the speculation.

DL: And then came the aftermath.

PG: Yeah... it was the beginning of the period of blackness. I remember John joking with Simon Kirke about how the job was his type of thing after they had done the jam in Munich and there was that great headline in the *Melody Maker* - 'Led Zeppelin Uber Alles'. And I reckon he though he was going to get the job. We were getting calls from people like Carl Palmer. And Atlantic, not Arhmet, but the corporate people were baying for a live album - a terrible time.

DL: You did release *Coda*.

PG: That was an agreement we struck with Ahmet. It was both to fulfil the contract of albums and also done as a separate deal. When I made that deal with Ahmet we did owe an album or two but the deal was a separate thing which we had a meet with the three of them and Pat to sort out. And Jimmy said he'd hoped we had enough to release an album and Ahmet was great and paid an advance even knowing that it was sub-standard and we couldn't find enough material for a decent set then the advance would be refunded. In fact the contract for that was called the Omega contract. You see in Germany in Frankfurt we had verbally agreed to renew our contract within the next year. We shook hands on that one. We did many a deal with Ahmet on trust and the paperwork would follow many months later. It's interesting that Ahmet was the only one who has ever said to me that I mourned too long over John. Maybe he was right.

DL: If it had gone into the Eighties how do you think their career

BACKSTAGE AT KNEBWORTH: AUGUST 4, 1979

THE SONG REMAINS THE SAME PREMIERE, LEICESTER SQUARE, LONDON: NOVEMBER 4, 1976

PG: Benji phoned me. It was such a tragedy. People forget what a family man Bonzo really was. He was such a family man. In Zurich earlier in that year my children Helen and Warren had come out with Jason. And I remember John talking to Warren on the safety need on motorbikes because they were all into motorcross then.

DL: How did you personally cope in the first few days?

PG: It was on the radio in Philadelphia within three hours. We didn't know how. Helen told me Mitchell Fox who worked for us had been on the radio talking about it, which angered me. After the funeral the boys all went to Jersey. But we had all that trouble with the *Evening Standard* saying dreadful things.

DL: Was there ever a notion that you could carry on in some format?

PG: Never. They came back from Jersey: I booked a suite for afternoon tea at the Savoy. And they all looked at me and asked what I thought. I said it just couldn't go on because it was the four of them and they were all relieved because they had decided the same.

DL: Do you think if you had suggested to them that a replacement be sought they would have abided by that?

PG: No. It would have been totally out of character. You have to realise that for Led Zeppelin to make that music it needed the four of them to do it. And now one was gone.

would have gone?

PG: I'm sure we d have gone into the mega stadium circuit that everybody does now like five nights at Wembley Stadium. It would have probably have slowed down and I'm sure there would have been solo albums. In fact let me tell you a story about the time Robert came in to see me in the mid-Seventies. He asked if I would support him if he wanted to do a solo album. I said of course, and then went on to ask who he imagined would play guitar on it. "Umm," he said "I suppose I'd have to have Jimmy." "What about bass?" "Well again" says Robert "It would have to be Jonesy". "And drums?" "Gotta be Bonzo I guess". "Why do you want to do a solo album Robert?" I said. He never mentioned it again!

DL: Jimmy did the *Death Wish 2* soundtrack in late '81

PG: Another nightmare. Michael Winner rang me and asked me if Jimmy would do it. Jimmy was on holiday in a narrow boat up the Thames. Now if you recall the first *Death Wish* ends with Charles Bronson in Chicago at the airport. So when Jimmy rang me he agreed to do it. And Jimmy says "Yeah let's do it" thinking that it will be set in Chicago. He says, "Yeah I could do a blues album that would be really great." Then we had draft contracts and all that and eventually we see a rush video of the new film and it's a bloody street gang scenario set in New York! We stalled it a bit but even-

Robert asked if I would support him if he wanted to do a solo album. I said of course, and then went on to ask who he imagined would play guitar on it. "Umm," he said "I suppose I'd have to have Jimmy." "What about bass?" "Well again" says Robert "It would have to be Jonesy". "And drums?" "Gotta be Bonzo I guess". "Why do you want to do a solo album Robert?" I said. He never mentioned it again!

PETER GRANT

REFLECTING ON IT ALL: 1990

tually came up with the goods but Michael Winner wasn't happy.

He sent some heavy down to my house to get the contract signed but he was wasting his fucking time doing that. I just left him outside all night. It got done in the end - in fact Jimmy always worked better with a deadline. I saw Winner a few weeks ago at the National Film Festival. He told me he keeps a unique letters file and still has one in it that I sent him back then. It was one that informed him that I'd filed his last letter to me in my own silly letters file!

DL: How actively were you involved with managing their separate careers in the early Eighties?

PG: By 1982 I just wasn't up to it. Mentally and everything. I'd just had enough. I did negotiate Robert's five album solo deal. Shook hands with him on that. I always remember when we got the slick of the *Pictures At Eleven* sleeve there was a problem with the lettering. I phoned Robert and told him and we got it put right but he made me laugh because he said, "I didn't know you got so involved in all the cover designs and stuff" which says something for all the battles we had with sleeves in the Zep days. It was me and Jimmy who did the sweating then.

DL: Were you surprised that none of them wanted to work together in some format, for instance Robert and Jimmy?

PG: Well I think there was an agreement that if they did get back together any solo deal would be declared null and void but they never really had the need. Actually Robert and I did have a bit of a falling out and I said the best thing would be for him to manage himself. In fact I think Tony Smith got involved with him for a while. But you've got to realise Robert always wanted to be the boss of the band anyway. He finally got his own way. I must say though that Bill Curbishley has done an excellent job in managing Robert in recent years.

DL: Phil Carson also managed him.

PG: Dear Phil yes. He was probably getting his own back for when they had him on stage in Japan playing bass in 'C'mon Everybody' and they played it so fast he came off with his fingers bleeding! In fact if I recall rightly Robert got Clive Coulson our roadie to sing on that number. (This is documented on the 'C'mon Everybody' CD from Osaka 28/9/71). Phil was the man from Atlantic and sometimes took too much of the limelight. As you know first hand when you were doing your book. You and I had a slight run in over Phil blabbing a bit too much. I know we got it sorted fairly quickly but that's the sort of thing that can happen. In fact it was my daughter Helen who brought it to my attention.

DL: And then Swan Song wound up. Were you sad?

PG: In a way but on reflection it was too much for us to take on what with me trying to manage Bad Company and Zepp. There were just not enough hours in the day. That's why I passed on managing Queen in '75. I'd love to have done it but there just wasn't the time.

DL: Do you regret getting bogged down with the label.

PG: Not really. What I regret is not getting someone in to run it properly. We kept getting it wrong or I did. This all really brings home the situation I found myself in with the label and my home life. I tried to run it like a nine-to-five job, driving up to London for three hours every day. It just wore me out. Then I'd get home and Danny Goldberg or Steve Weiss would be on the line [from America]. It was too much. If I could have done a David Frost and jetted between New York and here it might have been OK. But that was never on. That's not to say I didn't enjoy the success we had. I thought Bad Company were the perfect band for the label.

I even negotiated Paul out of a deal he had with Island, which meant the first few albums didn't come out here on Swan Song. I sorted that out with Chris Blackwell. But that whole 'Can't Get Enough' era was so fresh. We had Maggie doing quite well and The Pretty Things. I have that framed *Billboard* chart with all our artists listed one week in early '75. It was just that even to do Zep justice was a 24-hour job. Dave Edmunds and people like that I just didn't have the time to oversee. Dave had Jake Riviera anyway which brought its own set of problems. Of course we also missed a few by not getting to hear the demo tapes. Clearing out the office we found loads, including Paul Young with The Q Tips.

DL: What about that singer songwriter Mirabia you signed?

PG: That's a perfect example of people making decisions I wouldn't have made and me having to support it. That was a Goldberg investment that I persuaded Ahmet to bankroll. Similar to when I got him to take the Lord Sutch album Jimmy and Bonzo played on years earlier. Of course that wouldn't happen nowadays with record companies.

DL: And then Jimmy went to work with Paul Rodgers.

PG: That was initially my idea because he's a great singer. The only problem is he is such a difficult man to deal with and I think that's what went wrong in the end with The Firm. Of all the artists I've known he's even more difficult than Chuck Berry. Paul seems to have come storming back with the Muddy Waters album. I heard he was great on a Radio One session last week.

DL: Any thoughts on Live Aid?

PG: It was fairly dreadful really in my view because they were obviously unrehearsed. But it was nowhere near as bad as the Atlantic 40th show. Actually I was really upset that I didn't get an official invitation for that show. I may not have gone but that's not the point. Phil Carson apparently felt I wasn't healthy enough. I think Ahmet expected me to be there, not realising I did feel a bit left out to say the least. Then there was all this thing about Robert not wanting to sing 'Stairway' again. At least Jason got his wish to play with them all.

DL: Did you know much about that get together in Bath in early '86?

PG: I only heard the rumours. Nothing more.

DL: In the mid-'80s both Jimmy and Robert played Zep songs live. What was your view of that?

PG: Let's face it, people want to hear them. I mean I remember being there when Jimmy did that 'Stairway To Heaven' version at the Arms. Amazing. Freaked out Simon Phillips a bit though.

DL: What about Jason's wedding?

PG: That was great. Seeing everyone and all the wives. We all had a great time.

DL: And Jason has his own career now.

PG: Well he hasn't had the best advice and it's a great shame. They've got a new line-up and it's happening a bit now. They come down here now and again to rehearse because one of the new singers is from down this way.

DL: How did you get involved with the *In The City* convention last year?

PG: I'd seen it in *Music Week* and I rang up Elliot, Simply Red's manager who was organising it and I'd spoken to Ed Bicknell and they all wanted me to do it and so I did. I did that celebrity interview with Paul Morley. Someone tipped me off that he was going to do a number on me. I sorted him well and truly. He thought I was an old fart and he came unstuck. But it was great and I met so many people and the good thing is so many new managers keep in touch. It's nice to share that knowledge.

DL: And you went again this year.

PG: Yes, I didn't do any of the interviews but I sat on an interesting forum called 'Do we need lawyers?' which was quite fun. They said to me, "Are you retired?" and I said if something really special came along I'd think about it and within 30 seconds somebody's mobile phone went and Paul Russell from Sony shouts out, "There's an offer now, Peter!" and somebody else says it must be Robert and I said, "Oh no not a second time!"

DL: What's your view of the two new box sets?

PG: At least this time I've been sent them because the first one didn't even come my way from Atlantic. I got it from other means. It does look very nice and the 10-CD set is a wonderful package but the mistakes that you pointed out are very sloppy. I'm sure Jimmy will be furious because he and I always took so much time over the covers. You must remember the delay on *Houses* because we couldn't get the colouring right. It was from a black and white photo and we had to colour it. It also annoys me that nobody contacts me about these things now. If I had been involved I would have made sure it had been presented properly. Jimmy's done such a great job with the music. He's gone to such efforts to remaster those tapes and then for Atlantic to get the detail wrong is not good at all.

DL: Can you see there being a live set released at some point?

PG: It's a possibility – the tapes do exist without doubt. But there are so many bootlegs out there now perhaps there's just no need for it.

DL: Would you ever get involved in management again?

PG: It would have to be something very special. I still get the tapes sent to me. I do a lot of local charity gigs here and I've been the senior judge on a local *Battle Of The Bands* contest. I did have an interest in Goodbye Mr. McKenzie but they wanted me to manage them for North America and I just couldn't do it. Then there was a 10-year-old guitarist, Thomas McLaughlin, an amazing player for his age. Ahmet came over to see him. Trouble is he was one of those with an impossible father. You know "All I want for my boy is to hear him on Radio One being a star!" I mentioned that to Brian May and he said that was the biggest mistake anyone could make!

DL: Are you surprised Led Zep did not reform when all that speculation was rife a couple of years back?

PG: Not really. It would have been a vast earner and it would have outsold anyone including the Stones but would they have been any happier? I know Jimmy was keen but Robert didn't want to do it. But let's face it, it wouldn't be the same. It they had done it that invaluable Zeppelin mystique would have gone forever.

DL: What do you think of Robert's current album?

PG: He's singing great that's for sure but I saw him on that Jools Holland TV thing. I was actually watching that with Maureen Plant down here in the dressing room of Jason's gig. I thought he looked a bit dishevelled in that. I must also say he can still be a little bitter. That comment when he was on the bed with Paula on the *Big Breakfast* about Jimmy getting on a better deal than him was a bit naughty. He can get like that though but that's Robert - larger than life as I found out so many times.

DL: And Coverdale Page?

PG: Great to see Jimmy playing like that again. I'm just very surprised they didn't tour America when the album came out. They seem to have missed the boat on that one. There was a big buzz about it. They should have gone out and booked 7,000 to 10,000 seaters. If they put those tickets on sale a month before the album comes out surely you're going to sell at least half the tour out on the strength of Jimmy's legend alone and then tie the rest when the album comes out. I did speak to him recently. They're going to Japan but where it goes from there I don't really know. Do you know they recorded the album in an analog situation? It doesn't really surprise me because he knows how to get a good studio sound.

DL: Do you know Jimmy will be 50 in January?

PG: Yes he is but he's nocturnal. He'll play on as long as he wants to, simple as that. The man is such a creative artist. He might look a bit older but it he wants any tips on dieting he can always call

me because I've been on a diet all my life!

DL: Have you seen the Richard Cole *Led Zeppelin Uncensored* book?

PG: I've heard about it and read extracts. It disappoints me when John is spoken about in that manner. It was personal stuff. He's clean now is Colesy. He worked with Lita Ford. Apparently she dumped him because he was too dull and straight which shows how things have gone full circle

DL: Looking back at the heavy reputation you were labelled with in the Seventies - was it justified?

PG: In lots of ways yes - but I was paid to protect the boys assets in every way. I was always fair though and went by my instincts. It does make me laugh that all these years later that reputation still survives. I was with an EMI music publisher recently who was telling me how he'd got into Knebworth for free when the gates went down. So jokingly I raised my voice and demanded the £7.50. Amazingly he starts reaching for his wallet thinking I'm serious! Ready to balance the books all these years later! I had to laugh at that one.

DL: Did Zeppelin retain a lot of their money?

PG: Yes we did. Much more so than many bands simply because we never took a vast entourage out with us. Everyone who came on tour with us had a function. All the deals I did with Showco and the travelling and things like the deal I got to use the Starship... it all protected the profits. I'm not saying we didn't spend a lot individually because we all did but as for the overall earnings we played it clever for a very long time.

DL: Final summary then. Now you're in semi-retirement would you say you're content?

PG: Yes and I'm quite healthy now. I did have a lot of head trouble. Once in '78 I had a collapsed heart and then in the Eighties things weren't good. There does seem to be a lot of respect for what I and the band achieved and it's very rewarding to know that. And wherever I go it does seem everybody wants to talk about that legacy we created which is quite amazing considering it was all those years ago now.

DL: How would you sum up the four personalities that made Led Zeppelin?

PG: Robert was the perfect Leo and frontman larger than life and incredibly vibrant particularly when we really made it in the US. Jimmy was and still is the master craftsman. It was his vision initially that really made it happen. Jonesy - incredible musician, the vital link and in perfect liaison with John Bonham. And John was and always will be the ultimate rock drummer. It's been said hundreds of times but it was a chemistry - a perfect chemistry.

DL: Let me put you on the spot by throwing some personal highlights at you. So what for instance were the most memorable gigs?

PG: Well I think Earl's Court was tremendous... The first time we played in Boston... the first Tampa.

DL: The best tour?

PG: Certainly the first tour because it was just so exciting and we knew we had something.

DL: What about best album - and favourite tracks?

PG: *Physical Graffiti*. Undoubtedly. It was the first one on Swan Song. And tracks? 'Kashmir', 'Houses Of The Holy' and 'Thank You' spring to mind.

DL: What about the best deal you struck?

PG: They were all good! But I've got to say that it's more the ones I didn't do like Woodstock. We were asked to do it and Atlantic were very keen and so was our US promoter of the time, Frank Barsalona. I said no and instead we did a weekend I think in Boston and got rave reviews. At Woodstock we'd have just been another band on the bill.

DL: So finally sum up what the Zeppelin years represented for you.

PG: The most fantastic live music one could ever possible wish to hear. Billions of laughs - great times. Great camaraderie - even during the traumas we could always laugh afterwards... and there were never any grudges. The fact that it still means so much to so many people is fantastic.

There's still a mystique about Zeppelin and that's really down to how we played it back then. To be associated on any level was a privilege because Led Zeppelin really were the biggest and best. Working with them for me was a time of total magic.

STILL FEARSOME, 1993

There's still a mystique about Zeppelin and that's really down to how we played it back then. To be associated on any level was a privilege because Led Zeppelin really were the biggest and best. Working with them for me was a time of total magic.

PETER GRANT

In 1993 all hopes of any conceivable type of Zeppelin reunion seemed well off the agenda.

Page and Plant were both wrapped up in respective projects – Page with his surprisingly effective link up with David Coverdale and Plant touring with a new band on the back of the release of his excellent *Fate Of Nations* album.

All that changed when Plant received an offer from MTV to participate in their hugely successful *Unplugged* TV series – in which showcased artists were asked to perform sans electric instruments in a purely acoustic setting. This formula had been responsible for big selling accompanying albums from the likes of Eric Clapton and Nirvana.

Plant considered the idea, and in an abrupt about-turn called Page and asked if he'd consider participating with him for this MTV recording. "When the MTV offer came I really felt I couldn't do the Zeppelin numbers outside of a live gig on my own," said Plant, "so I felt it was the right time to ask Jimmy and it was really fortuitous." Events moved fast. Page flew to Boston to see Robert on tour and the pair agreed to do it. In December Page played a series of contracted concerts with Coverdale in Japan and Plant duly completed his tour with dates in South America. By February they were rehearsing together in a Kings Cross studio – working with tape loops to rekindle the old fire. The first visual evidence of the reunion occured in April when they played a short set at the Buxton Opera House at an Alexis Korner tribute concert.

From the start two decisons were taken. The first was to turn the *Unplugged* offer into something more elaborate. Rather than a straight acoustic performance they decided to re-interpret the classic Zep catalogue and call it *Unledded*, bringing in Plant's rhythm section of Michael Lee on drums and Charlie Jones on bass. They also enlisted an ambitious array of additional musicians, including an Egyptian Ensemble and the London Metropolitan Orchestra.

REFERENCE: **TIGHT BUT LOOSE 10**

12 : PAGE & PLANT – UNLEDDED FOR MTV

NO QUARTER, THE ALBUM

REHEARSING 'GALLOWS POLE', LONDON STUDIOS: AUGUST 24, 1994

The second was that there would be no approach to John Paul Jones. Plant saw it as a way of avoiding this being viewed as a Zeppelin reunion and they both felt from the start that just the pair of them was enough to contend with. "We were gaining so much momentum from the loops and working with Charlie and Michael," said Page at the time. "Quite honestly, I for one wasn't thinking of John Paul Jones. I was thinking about what we were getting together. It was its own thing before all of that started to be an issue." The mistake they made was not informing their former band mate directly. It was less than gracious behaviour and would tarnish what was an otherwise much welcomed career move.

Alongside filming sessions in Wales and Marrakesh, Page and Plant booked the London TV Studios on the South Bank for two specially staged concerts in front of an invited audience comprised of personal guests, MTV competition winners and *Tight But Loose* readers. It was a great privilege to be asked by their office to supply the then current list of of subscribers to the magazine whose names then went into a ballot with the successful names drawn being invited to the recording. The subsequent August 25 and 26 TV recordings were both emotionally charged affairs. After so many years apart it was an immense thrill to be present to see them reinvent the Zep catalogue. It was the first of a series of memorable Page and Plant occasions that would unfold over the next four years.

TBL issue 10 carried extensive and exclusive coverage of the entire MTV *Unledded* project. The on-the-spot as-it-happened report of the two August MTV shows is reproduced here. It captures first hand reaction as Page and Plant turned back the clock. As the press ads of the time accurately said: "Many acts could be unplugged... but only one could be unledded."

Jimmy Page and Robert Plant had taken most of August 1994 to film the long-mooted MTV project, the end results of which would appear as an MTV *Unplugged* special in October. Location trips to Marrakesh and Wales would now be rounded off with two live performances before an invited audience at a secret London location set for the nights of August 25 & 26.

Feedback from those close to the project had been very positive. The filming in Marrakesh had gone very smoothly with the airing of three new songs – two untitled and one dubbed 'City Don't Cry'. In Wales, despite the rain they had managed to film some excellent footage with 'When The Levee Breaks' proving particularly inspiring. A dress rehearsal for the London shows on Wednesday had also gone remarkable well according to those in attendance. Confirmation of the deployment of a full orchestra and an Egyptian string and drum section certainly whetted my appetite – it all sounded almost surreal.

DATELINE: THURSDAY AUGUST 25

Festival Pier 5 pm, the meeting point at which invited fans were advised to attend. From here we would be escorted to the location. In another queue are 50 MTV/radio station competition winners flown all expenses paid from the US. They line up excitedly amongst the other lucky fans. It's a long wait and security is very tight, with everybody subjected to a metal detector test for obvious reasons. Interestingly enough, the billing for tonight's show on the ticket is: "An Evening With Page And Plant"; Friday's reads: "Plant and Page" and the laminated passes have Page Plant at the top... and Plant Page at the bottom – a subtle method of solving the 'who gets top billing wrangle'.

Around ten to eight Alex the MTV coordinator does some cheer leading warm ups. "Let's hear it for Rex King!" shouts Alex and an appropriate cheer goes up for the long term Plant/Page aide who is marching around the stage checking last minute details - an appreciative cheer for the man responsible for many of us being here tonight. Minutes later with the camera angles tested and the subtle lighting set, a short no-nonsense announcement precedes what we've waited fourteen years to hear. "Please welcome Robert Plant and Jimmy Page" ... and it's a thunderous welcome.

Robert Plant strides on stage from the left followed by Charlie Jones and Michael Lee, Jimmy enters from behind a black curtain on the right and immediately takes off his suit jacket to reveal a Knebworth style blue shirt.

Looking slightly nervous but ready to do what's to be done they confer briefly in the centre of the stage like newly-weds after signing the register. For this particular remarriage the ceremony is about to begin.

"Good Evening... Let's get, er, plugged in then," remarks Robert tongue-in-cheek, immediately debunking the idea that this will be the familiar *Unplugged* arrangement. Jimmy straps on the cherry red Gibson and picks out the welcoming chords of 'Thank You', a tentative run through delivered in the arrangement employed on last year's *Fate Of Nations* tour. Jimmy switches to the Gibson '58 prior to his ex-partner uttering the words "and if I say to you tomorrow" right next to him. You have to go back twenty-two years for the last time these words were spoken on stage within the vicinity of the pair. 'What Is And What Should Never Be' is much welcomed if slightly flawed with Jimmy particularly hesitant on the solo. It warms up towards the end as Jimmy scrubs across the strings for that familiar stereo panned *Zep II* trademark.

For the next song Jimmy settles into a chair and straps on an Andy Manson three-necked guitar. Robert introduces Nigel Eaton on hurdy-gurdy, James Sutherland on bodhran percussion and Porl Thompson on acoustic guitar and welcomes to the far left of the stage an Indian vocalist Najma Akhtar... who will duet with him on 'Battle Of Evermore'. It's a joy to hear Jimmy picking out the melody against the whirring hurdy-gurdy and the interplay between Robert and Najma is very effective. Towards the close they add a new coda reminiscent of 'Achilles'. Never an easy number to project live, this arrangement is the first fruits of the ambitious extended Plant Page alliance. And it work supremely well.

"From here to Batley is not that far," jokes Robert, referring to the cabaret circuit. The same line-up (minus Najma) stays on for 'Gallows Pole'. Long rumoured to be part of the new set, Jimmy strums over the 12- and 6-string Ovation double neck, Charlie provides a steadfast bass anchor to the intricate arrangement, Porl handles the banjo parts and Michael Lee storms in as the pace builds. This is the first display from the drummer that again confirms his ability to bring just the right amount of dynamics to the rhythm section, striking his drums in a very Bonham-like manner that adds to the whole atmosphere. As the song speeds to a climax Robert really lets go, losing himself in the 'Keep a swinging' repeat refrain before it all dramatically stops.

"We'll be back in a while," announces Robert, signalling the end of part one. As the lights go up we excitedly exchange views. Everybody has been knocked out with the last two numbers and are similarly agreed that the opening pair of *Zep II* standards had been merely a warm up. But of course we really haven't seen anything yet.

After the break Jimmy and Robert reappear with Charlie and Michael. Charlie stands beside a huge double bass as the principal pair settle down on seats at the centre of the stage. "Perhaps this is how we should have done this song originally all those years ago," announces Robert as Jimmy picks out on acoustic guitar the intro of 'Rain Song'. Robert comes in with the first verse and then the orchestra majestically glides in to replace the Mellotron parts of the studio version. This is quite breathtaking. Robert sings the lyrics beautifully and Jimmy plays perfect fingerstyle in all the right places. As the song beefs up Michael comes in with suitably dynamic tom-tom injections (early on in the song he'd used brushes like Bonham). It's left to Jimmy to close pro-

UNLEDDED REHEARSAL, LONDON STUDIOS: AUGUST 24, 1994

ceedings with the descending scales that he carries off perfectly.

From one emotional moment to another. Jimmy returns to the Gibson and picks out another familiar intro, this time to 'Since I've Been Loving You' and it's played with all the intensity of 1971. This is a real crystallisation of the power of the Plant/Page alliance, aided subtlety by the string orchestra. On the chorus they strut forward over the mic à la *The Song Remains* movie version. Plant is brilliant here, breaking into a fully fledged mid-Seventies pose with mike in hand and Jimmy's solo is a crescendo of notes, the like of which we haven't heard for many a long year. This is Led Zeppelin in all but name and the spirit is alive and kicking, compellingly so.

Next Robert offers stage right to the arrival of the Egyptian string and drum section led by Hossam Ramzy who is handed the mike to personally introduce the boys in the band. He develops an instant rapport with the audience as he runs through the team sheet and inspires much amusement when he gets in a plug for his brother's Indian restaurant. "I think we should dedicate this to the original drummer with four sticks," says Robert to rapturous cheers. An ambitious arrangement of 'Four Sticks' follows

Good Evening...

Let's get, er,

plugged in then

ROBERT PLANT

THE FIRST SIGHTING...

with Michael tearing along with two sticks in each hand - a lovely tribute. Robert interprets every nuance and phrase of the original lyric in a slightly lower register while Jimmy plays the riff on acoustic guitar and it all speeds up to a compelling climax as the three sections (European strings band/ Egyptian strings) compete for authority.

Robert asks Jimmy to introduce the next number and as ever he greets the audience humbly before handing over to the Egyptian section for a lengthy intro. This is shades of Bombay orchestra '72, a little unsettled in tempo early on but unravelling successfully enough by the second verse. If 'Friends' appeared just a trifle laboured, the next number wipes out any minor misgivings completely. Robert duly delivers a lengthy and revealing speech regarding this new alliance and their desire to look back and revisit some past glories. And they don't come any more glorious than 'Kashmir'.

The 'Pride Of Led Zeppelin' is radically reworked for the Nineties opening with Robert singing the first verse in a slow tempo accompanied by Jimmy on the Trans Performance Gibson, creating a phased gizmo effect on the pedals. This merges into the Hossam percussion of the East and then on into the familiar and invigoratingly performed riff and they're off on that mystic road again. What makes this exercise so fulfilling is the interplay between band and orchestra - on numerous occasions Jimmy and Robert halt the band performance and glance over to the Egyptian players who take it all into a different time zone. The finger cymbal player merrily jigs around to the riff much to Jimmy's amusement. As we get to the fade and the "Let me take you there"

PORL THOMPSON AND NAJMA AKHTAR, *UNLEDDED* FILMING: AUGUST 25, 1994

refrains, the whole thing speeds up into a truly memorable climax which sees Jimmy playing a rumbling 'Achilles'-like riff off against Michael Lee's stop-start drumming. In turn they pass the riff over to the Moroccan brass and string players, formulating a call and response sequence that threatens to take the roof off. If the TV cameras have got the right angles this will look sensational on screen

With 'Kashmir' successfully climbed they leave the stage together, smiling and waving as they go. That appears to be the end, particularly when the background blues music strikes up again, but minutes later they appear from behind the black curtain and make their way on stage again. Jimmy straps on the Ovation double neck, Robert makes another little speech: "This was written on the side of a Welsh mountain in a cottage about half an hour before the young lady furiously taking pictures in front of me was conceived (a reference to Page's daughter Scarlet in the front row). Was I there? Possibly!" laughs the man, with Jimmy grinning behind. "See we're happy again!" - a memorable statement which the entire audience would certainly endorse.

A lovely laid back arrangement of 'That's The Way' follows with Michael Lee adding a new drum accompaniment and Porl taking up the banjo. Robert picks up the tambourine and strikes up that classic pose − a pose I'd long since give up ever seeing again. Jimmy meanwhile rocks back and forth as he strums out the chords to a song last performed live by the pair nigh on twenty years ago.

Smiles, handshakes, cheers, waves, goodbye and it's all over. "Thanks for coming along - hope to see you tomorrow," says the man from MTV. The crowd filters out still starstruck. And incredibly there's more to come tomorrow...

DATELINE: FRIDAY AUGUST 26

Festival Pier 5 p.m. Here we go again. The waiting this time out takes place in an orderly queue along the Thames. It's a markedly more relaxed atmosphere amongst us - many are here for the second night and we know what to expect. Over at the London Studios the demand for entry seems to have heightened considerably with many more red ticketed guests in line. Lining up towards the door is tense with more than a little confusion of who is eligible to go in and who is not. Once inside studio 2 it's evident there are far more in attendance tonight, with many

ALBUM FLYER

IN STORES

jimmy page robert plant

NO QUARTER

NOVEMBER 8th

1. **WHAT IS**
   (Robert/Jimmy/Michael/Charlie/Ed)
2. **THANK YOU**
   (Robert/Jimmy/Michael/Charlie)
3. **BATTLE OF EVERMORE**
   (Robert/Jimmy/Michael/Charlie/Paul/Nigel/Jim/Nashma)
4. **GALLOWS POLE**
   (same minus Nashma)

----

bring on orchestra

----

5. **RAIN SONG**
   (Robert/Jimmy/Michael/Charlie/Ed plus Western Strings)
6. **SINCE I HAVE BEEN LOVING YOU**
   (same)
7. **FOUR STICKS**
   (Robert/Jimmy/Michael/Charlie/Ed/Western Orchestra/Egyptian Strings/Moroccan Drummers)
8. **FRIENDS**
   (same)
9. **KASHMIR**
   (same plus brass)

--ENCORE--

10. **THATS THE WAY**
    (Robert/Jimmy/Michael/Charlie/Porl)
11. **WONDERFUL ONE (loop)**
    (Robert/Jimmy)

THE PROPOSED SET LIST FOR FRIDAY, AUGUST 26, 1994

NO QUARTER
JIMMY PAGE AND ROBERT PLANT
UNLEDDED
(Fontana 526 362 2)

No Quarter (the Unledded tag has been somewhat played down in the packaging) is a lengthy, 14-track CD clocking in at over 79 minutes - a mere three minutes less than *Physical Graffitti*. The actual sleeve design I find disappointing. A low

key shot from Corris Slate that offers a rather windswept portrait of the ageing dynamic duo. The CD booklet itself is sparse on detail and the discographer in me again bemoans the lack of sleeve notes. If ever an album's evolution was worth explaining then it was this one. It strikes me that the official press release notes produced for the MTV premieres would have fitted in very well here. An enigmatic

photo of a bizarrely painted hand maintains the mystery of sleeve images of old. The nod to the original credit for 'Bron Y Aur' (they've reverted to that spelling again) first deployed on the *Led Zep III* inner sleeve is a nice touch and one that vividly illustrates (as I'd hoped when I undertook The Making Of *Led Zeppelin III* feature back in the early summer) their allegiance to the original unplugged concept

from 24 years back.

The sequencing differs from the MTV broadcast, skitting around from Wales, London and Morocco rather haphazardly. I would have preferred to see it retain the more cohesive flow of the film with all the Moroccan tracks particularly, in one block.

From Morocco, 'Yallah' retains plenty of atmosphere enhanced with an echoed spoken intro and a very live-in-the-marketplace feel.

'Wah Wah' has a quaint charm but does lose some of its impact when stripped of the visual scope of the film, while the previously unused 'City Don't Cry' emerges as a plaintive croon with a strong Gnaoua presence. While these excursions are admirably executed and remain a worthy record of their travels, the latter two songs do come over as a little too ethnic to broaden their appeal with repeated plays.

standing around the doorways at each corner of the studio. The Indian warm-up music is Robert's choice. Once the big door is shut and the red light goes on it's also evident that those assembled are a lot more relaxed tonight and in the mood to enjoy every moment of this last night of filming.

This ambience transcends itself to the players and after a polite intro Jimmy and Robert stride up and take the stand. Looking well at ease Robert throws a nutmeg to the intended set list by switching into 'What Is And What Should Never Be' and then 'Thank You'. The opening number is marred slightly by some feedback but 'Thank You' is spot on and inspires the first spontaneous cheer of the evening when Jimmy turns his back towards Michael and spits out a fluid Gibson solo.

The set list for the rest of the proceedings is similar to the previous night. 'The Battle Of Evermore' is perfection - a modern day mantra that puts any previous, precarious incarnations well into the shade. During a break following a false start for 'Gallows Pole' Robert sings the opening line to 'When The Levee Breaks' explaining that "This was one we did to eight people including two sheep in Wales last week". 'Gallows' duly follows and is again heightened by some intensive Plant scat singing at the close.

Back on stage with the orchestra 'Rain Song' is performed with much subtlety if not quite the fluency of the previous night. "This is one of everybody's favourites" is the signal for them to take it up a gear for another startling delivery of 'Since I've Been Loving You' with a solo that prompts another spontaneous burst of applause from the appreciative audience.

Another enjoyable factor tonight is the relaxed on stage banter between Robert and the audience. The intimacy of the studio allows for a clear rapport, inspiring heckles along the lines of "Tell us a joke Jimmy"; "He doesn't know any," replies Robert. Another bit of light-hearted banter revolves around Robert's comment on his own between-song raps on various bootlegs. "Have you heard some of the talking on the bootlegs – crap isn' t it?" he says. "Especially last night," shouts out some wag. "Oh wait till I tell Jimmy that!" says Robert moving over to where Jimmy is tuning up.

The Moroccan roll of 'Four Sticks' and 'Friends' bursts forth with the latter infinitely better than Thursday's version, and Messrs Plant and Page then deliver a new revamped version of 'Kashmir'. This really is awesome, a mesmerising performance complete with retro "Woman talkin to ya!" adlib from Plant during the drawn out section and an improvised final five minutes which reincarnates the spirit of Led Zeppelin with dazzling accuracy as they improvise dangerously around the speeded-up finale. It brings to mind the crazed unpredictability of middle period Zep live epics such as 'Dazed' and 'No Quarter' - and all the while Plant undercuts it with the pleading charm of the lyric and the Egyptian section bring it on home. Truly this is the pride of Plant and Page.

A standing ovation is nothing less that they deserve. Back they stride for the new look 'That's The Way'... and off they go again as the lights go up. Some people think it's all over... but a welcome announcement to return to our seats signals the arrival of Jimmy and Robert who take their seats at the front of the stage. Jimmy dons the Ovation double neck. A tape loop recreating the absent Moroccan musician due to play on this number revolves

PERFORMING 'SINCE I'VE BEEN LOVING YOU', *UNLEDDED* FILMING: AUGUST 25, 1994

Have you heard some of the talking on the bootlegs – crap isn' t it?
ROBERT PLANT
Especially last night!
AUDIENCE MEMBER

'Wonderful One' is still... well... wonderful. No other word for it. This version is an alternate recording from that which appeared in the film with Robert committing an affectingly sensitive vocal over Jimmy's equally sensitive strumming.

From the mountains, 'No Quarter' fascinates with its phased reverb and modal tunings while 'Nobody's Fault But Mine' stomps and grinds to a knockabout climax (listen carefully for the off mic "Thank you very much"- comment at the end). I'd love to hear 'Levee Breaks' and 'Gallows' from the same session and hopefully along the way we will. From London there are some truly outstanding moments: 'Thank You' delights in its sheer familiarity, 'Friends' via its dramatic intro, 'Since I've Been Loving You' as a classic blow and 'The Battle Of Evermore' with its ethereal feel and Najma's searing vocal

That leaves the final four numbers: 'That's The Way', 'Gallows Pole', 'Four Sticks' and 'Kashmir'. Here the sequencing is really spot on as one classic dovetails magnificently into another. This part of the album really does capture the excitement so evident on screen. And as a bonus 'That's The Way' appears as the previously unheard treat. Led by Jimmy's swaying Ovation double neck, Robert offers an evocative trip through the memory bank in an arrangement enhanced by Michael Lee's subtle drum part and Porl's lilting banjo. It's a performance that again reflects Page's 'same picture within a different frame' ethic.

The travelogue nature of proceedings on the *No Quarter* CD may skip uncomfortably across the continents at times but the journey is ultimately a fulfiling one.

I find myself treating it like a favourite radio station - dipping in and out with repeated pleasure every time. Because here on Radio Unledded via the World Service you're never too far away from a solid gold classic.

THE FILMING SCHEDULE

REHEARSING 'WONDERFUL ONE', LONDON STUDIOS: AUGUST 24, 1994

around the studio. It is the premier of the new Plant/Page composition 'Wonderful One'. The loop has a repetitive percussive feel similar to the opening of 'Come Into My Life' from *Fate Of Nations*, and the song itself develops mournfully as Jimmy drifts over the strings. Plant sings poetic couplings in the 'All My Love' vein as the gentle love song washes over.

The exercise is repeated when they run through the number again for the benefit of the camera angles. 'Wonderful One' is the first newly premiered live Plant/Page composition since they ushered in 'Hot Dog' and 'In The Evening' at Copenhagen and Knebworth.

It seems to be all over... until an MTV official consults with the outside Manor Mobile Studio and realises there needs to be more, so back they stride again. "We're gonna do one number again and then one we didn't think we were gonna do, so here goes," announces Robert before they swing onto 'That's The Way' with Jimmy weaving some beautiful descant chording around those familiar lyrics.

Finally, and this time it really is finally, with help from Porl on guitar and the hurdy-gurdy man, Robert leads them through a welcome 'Nobody's Fault But Mine' ("Another one we did in Wales to eight people including two sheep"). However this is not the heavyweight blues stomping *Presence* arrangement but a swinging, rootsy, semi-acoustic run through with Jimmy on the Ovation double-neck. In fact this arrangement has far more in common with the Blind Willie Johnson original than any other version I've heard them attempt and it all flows to a satisfying climax. There s a great moment for the cameras as they make their way from the stage, Jimmy and Robert cuddling together, both smiling gleefully. It's a moment that crystallises the spirit of the whole event.

For Robert it's back to the Midlands to follow the fortunes of Wolverhampton Wanderers. A relaxed looking James Patrick emerges with chauffeur happy to pose and sign autographs .

What was most striking about the MTV filming was the integrity that Robert and Jimmy brought to the whole affair. Sidestepping the hyperbole of a fully fledged Led Zeppelin reunion, Jimmy and Robert managed to recreate the key ingredients of the Zep ethic by cleverly reinventing the catalogue. In recycling those original songs for Nineties consumption the pair have brought a respect to this project that has been sorely lacking in the mega tour reunions of their Seventies peers.

It also goes to prove what dividends lengthy rehearsals can provide. The chemistry of this re-alliance was more than plain to see and it put into perspective once and for all the shortcomings of the ill-prepared Atlantic 1988 reunion.

You can expect it all to come flowing back within days - but given a responsible period of preparation and the affinity these long term musicians and friends have for each other becomes very evident.

Finally, in employing the extra trappings of the orchestra and Egyptian players this MTV project has proved to be a case of Page and Plant completing a previously unfinished picture. The experimentation on certain numbers is what would probably have emerged had there been an *Eighties Tour Part One*.

This was always the beauty of Led Zeppelin - never a vehicle for mere rock music. Time and again they transcended the genre. Now 14 years on in the hands of two of the main components the group's legacy has been reborn.

And they have ultimately proved that they really were the very best. Page and Plant... Plant and Page... which ever way it lines up the chemistry remains.

With the MTV film in the can, the next logical move was to take the show out on the road, and manager Bill Curbishley drew up an ambitious itinerary that would commence in America early in 1995.

The pair decided to extend the formula used for the MTV shows, employing the Egyptian string and percussion ensemble led by Hossam Ramzy and dubbed The Egyptian Pharaohs. Under the direction of Ed Shearmur they enlisted the assistance of local orchestras in each area they performed, thus enabling them to repeat the successful formula used for the *Unledded* filming which allowed fresh interpretations of the Zeppelin catalogue.

Just prior to the tour opening in February, Page and Plant reunited with John Paul Jones and Jason Bonham for an appearance at New York's Waldorf hotel to accept Led Zeppelin's induction into the Rock'n'Roll Hall Of Fame. Jonesy's comment – "Thanks for my friends for remembering my phone number" – during his speech was a curt acknowledgement of his displeasure at being ignored.

Rehearsals for the Page Plant tour took place in London, and a preview of what was in store occurred when the pair did a live link up for the American TV Awards, performing 'Black Dog'.

In early April I was lucky enough to catch their two day stint at the Meadowlands Arena in America. The second night where they strolled on to the stage and moved into 'Thank You' remains a defining memory. Further shows I attended in Paris, Glasgow, Sheffield, St Austell, Poole, Birmingham and London proved conclusively that despite their advancing years the duo's ability to recreate the power and grace of Zeppelin was without question.

REFERENCES: **TIGHT BUT LOOSE 12**

PAGE & PLANT:13
WORLD TOUR OVERVIEW 1995/6

It was a glorious period as long time fans and those too young to have seen Zep in their prime revelled in what was all in name the Zeppelin reunion we had all hoped for. By the tour's end it was evident that Jimmy Page was playing better than at any time during the previous fifteen years. Indeed for a project that began as a request to strum a few Zep tunes unledded style for MTV's acoustic showcase, when played live night after night this reappraisal of the Zeppelin catalogue developed into a fully ledded experience - a trend that would continue when they returned to the live action in 1998.

The *TBL* coverage of the tour was extensive. *Issue 11* included a gig by gig summary aided by the input of many first hand views. For the next issue I was able to reflect on the entire 115 dates coming up with the best 53 peformances that might form a definitive retrospective view of this long awaited comeback. In keeping with the imaginary *Led Zeppelin Live* chronological live album chapter explored in *A Celebration*, I've reproduced the entire text of the Page Plant World tour overview providing a clear focus on one of their most prolific periods of the post Zep era.

PAGE AND PLANT PERFORMING 'IN THE EVENING' AT MADISON SQUARE GARDEN OCTOBER 27 1995

The evolution of Led Zeppelin continues...

The Page Plant 1995/6 world tour finally came to an end on March 1, 1996, with the 115th date of a tour that spanned 370 days. The entire trek covered five continents and 19 countries and included nearly 2,000 individual song performances.

After a 15 year hiatus it was at last an opportunity for fans old and new to witness first hand the musical chemistry that Jimmy Page and Robert Plant still maintain. A chemistry that was at the forefront of their achievements within Led Zeppelin

It was a unanimous success - not least because of the unorthodox stance the pair took in approaching their back catalogue. Never a mere exercise in nostalgia, in reinterpreting the likes of 'Kashmir' and 'In The Evening', the clever deployment of the Egyptian Pharaohs worked superbly well. Similarly, bringing local orchestras under the direction of Ed Shearmur in each location to embellish performances of 'Since I've Been Loving', 'Going To California', 'Babe I'm Gonna Leave You' etc, added a fresh dimension. It was a master touch that kept the momentum flowing throughout the year long excursion.

Some admissions and conclusions: Firstly the controversy. Should they have included Jones? And should they have billed it as Led Zeppelin?

Jones' absence remains a disappointment. Many will feel he should have at least been offered the opportunity to participate and should certainly have been informed first hand of their plans.

As for the name, well by the tour's end they were openly projecting it on the billboards ("Playing the legendary songs of Led

notable additions to the set list.

They were back in the US in the fall, kicking off with three dates in Mexico. This leg of the tour saw them reach new levels of intensity with a series of near flawless gigs on the West Coast. The US tour ended with a memorable two night stint at the old Zep stamping ground Madison Square Garden in New York.

Second guitarist Porl Thompson opted out of the line-up at this point and Jimmy took on all the guitar chores thereafter. Following four massive stadium dates in South America, Page and Plant holidayed in Hawaii, then undertook ten shows in Japan including six nights at the Budokan.

This run of shows saw them change the set list nightly, pulling out debut performances for the Zep standards 'The Rain Song' and 'Tea For One'. The final leg took in five shows in Australia. They arrived on February 22, almost 22 years to the day of the commencement of Zeppelin's only Australian visit. The final date took place at Flinders Park, Melbourne, on March 1.

Great moments along the away? So many really: Page's nightly off the cuff riffing before 'Black Dog', those unpredictable medley's during 'Calling To You' and 'Whole Lotta Love', the theremin battle during 'Shake My Tree', that stirring intro to 'In The Evening' with Plant in all his Arabic vocal glory, Porl's soloing in 'Song Remains The Same', Michael Lee's drumming throughout - a key ingrediant to the success of the whole project, the joyous crowd participation in 'Hey Hey What Can I Do', the 'Stairway' tease in 'Babe I'm Gonna Leave You', the interchanging set lists in Japan.

There were a few irritants: The rigid nature of the set lists dur-

ONE OF THE MANY TOUR BOOTLEGS - SAN JOSE: MAY 20, 1995

ON TOUR, USA: 1995

Zeppelin" as the Australian ads proclaimed). The heavy swing towards the Zep catalogue also made it something of a Zeppelin concert in all but name.

By not using the name they did avoid all the hype that would have gone with it and in avoiding the fully-fledged reunion many felt they upheld the integrity of the group.

Whatever name it went under, when Page and Plant took flight on something like the middle section of 'Whole Lotta Love', well it wasn't to hard to detect where the essence of all that had come from. The thrill of the two frontmen redefining the original Zep premise to go ever onward was undeniable.

The tour kicked off in Pensacola on February 26. The first part of the tour took in 27 dates running into April. Early set list surprises included a version of The Cure's 'Lullaby' and the Coverdale Page track 'Shake My Tree'. After a nine day break they undertook a further 27 dates in Europe including eight outdoor festival appearances. The UK dates included an acclaimed performance in the veterans slot on the Sunday line up at Glastonbury and two more intimate venue dates at St Austell and Poole. 'The Battle Of Evermore' and 'Going To California' were

ing the UK tour, Plant's general reticence to adopt his familiar mic in hand poses until the encores - his customary stances and movements that were so prominent in Zep but noticeably absent during his solo years, replaced by a sometimes stilted stage presence as he stayed glued to the mic.

Finally it all comes down to the music - and many hours of this tour has made it onto unofficial recordings. There have surely been few tours that have been so extensively chronicled. The advent of the mini DAT recorder has opened up the floodgates for good quality audience recordings.

In a move inspired by The Grateful Dead's relaxed laissez-faire gig taping policy (that certainly would not have happened under the iron rule of Peter Grant), during the US first leg the duo allowed fans to tape their gigs in special taper sections behind the mixing desk. By making shows widely available on tape the hope was that this would alleviate the need for fans to invest in bootleg CDs. It didn't stop something like 80 bootleg CD titles surfacing from the tour, including no less than three 20-CD box sets (the UK chronicle *Get Rid Of The Smoke* and two Japanese tour sets *Ten Days* and *Live Legend*) plus a stock of privately circulated audience shot videos.

DREAM FOUR-CD COMPILATION

With so many tapes at our disposal, there is ample scope to take a retrospective view of the tour. Having listened to hours of material drawn from the many tapes of the tour, I have compiled an imaginary four-CD compilation that takes in all the major developments along the way. It includes the one-off gems slotted in, the stand-out performances, the offbeat sequences and all the historic moments building into a true overview of the entire tour. It features 53 extracts drawn from 26 different locations spread over 28 shows; nearly five hours of musical Page and Plant highlights that capture the often barely believable events that thousands of fans were privileged to enjoy during those 370 days.

So this is Page and Plant on tour together at last in 1995 and 1996. Proving conclusively that the evolution of Led Zeppelin continues...

CD1: US TOUR FIRST LEG

Intro: Tales of Bron - Robin Williamson poem
'Immigrant Song' intro/'The Wanton Song'
Thompson Bowling Arena, Knoxville, Tenessee, March 3 1995
The previous date in Atlanta had seen the amalgamation of 'Immigrant Song' into 'Wanton Song' as the set opener. On that occasion they had some trouble sorting out the ending (it was after all the first live airing of 'Wanton Song' in 20 years!). In Knoxville it all came together with Page leading the way with some dexterous runs. The atmospheric opening introduction poem that proceeded became a familiar opening ritual to a major-

'Song Remains The Same' which effectively took over the 'Achilles' slot the next night.

Watching the video shot from the show, it's clear they were enjoying reliving this crucial Zep track - the pair could be seen clustered together in a classic pose during the "Aha... Aha" refrain.

At times the February 28 delivery of 'Achilles Last Stand' recreated the spirit of Led Zeppelin better than any other single performance on the tour. Maybe that's why they decided to drop it. Perhaps they both felt it was just a little too close to what went before...

'House Of The Rising Son'/'Good Times Bad Times'
UNO Lakefront Arena, New Orleans, Louisanna, March 11 1995
From the moment Plant casually walked up to the mic and oozed into the traditional local blues standard 'House Of The Rising Sun', this second night in New Orleans was destined to be special.

They then switched straight into 'Good Times Bad Times', the only performance of the rarely played *Led Zep I* opener. And it was a joy to hear them rumble through the familiar stops and starts of the track with Michael Lee on drums proving his worth.

'Lullaby'
UNO Lakefront Arena New Orleans Louisanna March 11 1995
When the first set lists were posted on the Internet many presumed this was a new song and listed it as 'Spiderman'. In actual fact it was a revivial from Porl Thompson's Cure days. It worked as an offbeat interlude amongst the Zep numbers with Plant

ON TOUR, USA: 1995

BOOTLEG OF LANDOVER: MARCH 23, 1995

ity of the US first leg and some European dates. The choice of the little known Incredible String Band album extract recalled Plant's fondness for this Sixties outfit, and by the time Robin Williamson had got to the line "There is the flavoured haunt of pleasure, no haunt or threat or malediction, but sweet of music strikes the air" the fans knew what was coming next as the silhouettes on stage burst into life.

'Wanton Song' went on to become the favoured set opener, clocking over 80 performances during the tour.

'Achilles Last Stand'
The Omni, Atlanta, Georgia, February 28 1995
'Achilles' was always a prime contender for reworking on this tour so it was no real surprise when it turned up in the set lists of the two opening dates in Pensacola and Atlanta. More baffling was the fact it was never played again. On the evidence of the passion they brought to this performance there appears no logical reason why. It was a more than competent display that kicked along with all the verve of the best Zep deliveries circa 1977. Robert introduced it as "One of the first songs Jimmy and I wrote relating to travel" - a similar spiel would be given over to introducing 'The

immersed in the lyric and Page cutting fine precise lines against Porl's rhythm work. 'Lullaby' survived in the set until the early part of the European dates before being deleted.

'The Song Remains The Same'
UNO Lakefront Arena, New Orleans, Lousinna, March 11 1995
"There's a...."
At the beginning of this mid-period Zep classic, Plant twice taunted the crowd with the opening line from the well known Rolf Harris cover. Instead Page led them into a powerful rendition of the *Houses Of The Holy* opener. This was a definite highlight of the US leg with Page and Porl Thompson trading licks most effectively, with the latter's speed on the Gibson jumbo guitar really pushing the song along. Plant reached the high notes with ease as it led it into a glorious finale. "Can you feel it?" asked the singer afterwards. Absolutely.

'Tangerine'/'Hey Hey What Can I Do'
US Air Arena, Landover, Washington, March 23 1995
Two superb performances lined up back to back during this show. 'Tangerine' made its only appearance on this leg performed in a

I can see Lionel's wages

going out of the window...

it's not like working for

The Searchers and...

it's not like working for

The Shadows.

ROBERT PLANT

full band arrangement. The crowd reaction as Page hit the familiar notes was nothing less than euphoric. Porl played some suitably laid back electric parts against Page's Ovation acoustic strumming. A nostalgic first outing for the *Zep III* standard that was last performed live twenty years back at Earl's Court.

The underrated *Zep III* leftover (and subsequent US B side to 'Immigrant Song') 'Hey Hey What Can I Do' was another revelation with the crowd egarly joining in the chorus. Videos from the tour of this track show Page beaming with pride and duck walking along the stage.

'Boogie Chillun' sequence

Skydome Arena, Toronto, March 27 1995

"One night I was laying down"... The John Lee Hooker standard was an integral part of the 'Whole Lotta Love' medley in the Zeppelin era. This was its only appearance on the tour, emerging during the 'Calling To You' medley. The way it developed out of a lengthy Page solo was invigorating and for those in attendance a rare revival for another part of the Zep live canon.

'Calling To You' including 'Break On Through'/ 'As Long As I Have You'/ 'Dazed And Confused' inserts

Brendan Byrne Arena, Meadowlands, East Rutherford, New Jersey, April 6 1995

'Calling To You' had previously been a highlight of Plant's *Fate Of Nations* tour. With Jimmy on board it quickly developed into an extended piece that included a compelling guitar battle with Porl, a seminal riff exercise and then into an anything-could-happen medley sequence in the grand Zep tradition. This night in Meadowlands was exceptional for the inclusion of Garnett Mimms 'As Long As I Have You', a staple of the first two Zeppelin American tours but not performed by Page or Plant since. It followed the now customary delivery of The Doors' 'Break On Through' and then merged with a few lines from 'Dazed And Confused'. Another memorable sequence.

'Shake My Tree'

Great Western Forum, Inglewood, Los Angeles, California, May 17 1995

On the face of it this was a rather bizarre choice for inclusion on the tour. A highlight of the 1993 *Coverdale Page* album, it says much of Plant's compatibility with Page at the time that he agreed to sing the Coverdale lyrics, albeit in a slightly amended form. 'Shake' was actually a great riff exercise which allegedly was first conceived during the Zep *In Through The Out Door* sessions. On stage it gave Plant the chance to pull out the old "Suck it!" refrain at appropriate moments and for Page to weave those weird sounds from the theremin.

'Kashmir'

Great Western Forum, Inglewood Los Angeles, California, May 17 1995

When Page and Plant breezed back into the Forum some 17 years after the night of *Listen To This Eddie*, a tradition of spontaneity was upheld. During 'Kashmir' they were joined by guest violinist Lili Hayden who brought a impulsive virtuoso feel to the end section as she pitted her talents against the Egyptian Pharaohs. "Ladies and gentlemen Lili Hayden appears at the Viper Room in Hollywood every Sunday night," Plant informed the audience at the close.

CD2: EUROPE / UK

'Dancing Days'/'Down By The Seaside' sequence

Omnisports, Bercy, Paris, June 6 1995

Page was on blistering form on the opening night of the European trek, in turn inspiring Robert to lift his performance to new heights. Two selections form the Bercy date: 'Dancing Days' had been included in the set in an all electric arrangement early on the US tour and then in an alternate arrangement with the Egyptians from mid May. It's the latter version that Plant introduced in both French and English on this opening night in Europe. A wonderfully relaxed affair with the shrill Egyptian violins merging with Jimmy's powerful riffing.

'Down By The Seaside' was a regular insert into the 'Calling To You' medley. It was presented in the new slower arrangement Plant had used to record the version with Tori Amos that appeared on the then just released *Encomium* tribute album. Plant's vocal delivery in Paris was sheer perfection, adding all the original nuances ("Yes she will, yes she will") to a song that was enjoying renewed recognition during this period.

'In The Evening'

Glastonbury Festival, June 25 1995

Into the open air for a memorable performance at the Glastonbury Festival. Their appearance in the veterans slot earned them a healthy respect from the vast crowd present and the thousands watching the live Channel 4 coverage. This latter day Zep standard had already established itself as one of the tour's favourites. In the early evening sun it shone as brightly as ever, capturing that dramatic intro with Plant's vocals echoing across the fields, Page manically string-bending over the Stratocaster and the Pharaohs dancing with delight behind them.

'The Crunge' sequence

SECC Arena, Glasgow, July 12 1995

It was evident on the Europe tour how much more relaxed the pair had become since the tensions during the early part of the US tour. This lighter mood spilled over into moments such as this occasion in Glasgow. When the double neck guitar needed tuning before 'The Song Remains The Same', Jimmy was left with no instrument. This inspired Plant to fill the void by leading Michael and Charlie through a spontaneous version of 'The Crunge'. The ad-libbed lyrics found Plant humourously sniping at Jimmy's guitar tech Lionel: "I can see Lionel's wages going out of the window... it's not like working for The Searchers and it's not like working for The Shadows...".

'Since I've Been Loving You'

Sheffield Arena, Sheffield, July 13 1995

Ten years on from *Live Aid* another special night. Sheffield was an outstanding show, made all the more impressive by a remarkable delivery of 'Since I've Been Loving You'. On the spur of the moment Plant began inserting verses from the then unplayed *Presence* Zep track 'Tea For One'. It created a unique hybrid delivery of two of their most notable custom blues compositions.

'Whole Lotta Love'

St Austell Coliseum, Carylon Ba,y St Austell, July 15 1995

A rare medley-less delivery of 'Whole Lotta Love' was a surprise set opener for this date at, as it was billed "The entertainment centre of the west". A throwback to the version Zeppelin first employed back in 1970, this new 1995 version really packed a punch with Page exhorting the classic riff from his new sparkle red Transperformer Gibson guitar.

'Blue Jean Bop'/'Black Dog'

St. Austell Coliseum, July 15 1995

The intimate confines of the St Austell Coliseum found them in playful mood on a hot Saturday night. From the early US dates it became a nightly ritual for Page to warm up 'Black Dog' with a random run of teasing riffs including moments from the likes of 'In My Time of Dying' and 'Out On The Tiles'.

On this occasion it went one step further as Plant kicked them into an ad-hoc delivery of Gene Vincent's 'Blue Jean Bop' that collapsed playfully under Michael Lee's attempt to bring in the proper 'Black Dog' riff. This prompted a smiling Page to apologise for the breakdown on mic. A fully fledged 'Black Dog' followed - another tour highlight as Plant tossed away his inibitions, ripped the mike off the stand and rocked out in a manner reminiscent of the golden age.

'Egyptian Intro'/'Celebration Day'

The Point, Dublin, July 20 1995

Robin Williamson's Tales Of Bron poem had by now been replaced by an Egyptian music intro tape that began serenely and

ON TOUR, USA: 1995

We're gonna try some

different things tonight.

That was the first different

thing. I don't think we've

played that for 17... 18...

20... 27,000 years!

ROBERT PLANT

then built up the drama, usually accompanied by the arrival of a silhouetted Page dancing along to the tempo. As an opener for this Dublin date they pulled out a fast and furious rendition of the *Zep III* rocker 'Celebration Day' (rarely played on the early US tour) indicating this might be a night of surprises.

'Custard Pie'
The Point, Dublin, July 20 1995
...And surprises there were. 'Custard Pie' - never performed live by Zeppelin - was wheeled out in an arrangement similar to the one Jimmy played on the *Outrider* tour. Page lashed out wah-wah runs in between the muscular drive of Michael Lee's drumming, and Plant threw in a spirited harmonica solo and at the close Page inserted a riff from 'The Ocean'. It's revival prompted Plant to inform the crowd afterwards "We're gonna try some different things tonight. That was the first different thing. I don't think we've played that for 17... 18... 20... 27,000 years!"

'The Battle Of Evermore'
NEC, Birmingham, July 23 1995
This esoteric version of 'The Battle Of Evermore' was a highlight of the MTV *Unledded* filming and finally made its presence felt live again during the night of surprises in Dublin. It was retained for the Birmingham and London gigs. This gave Plant the opportunity to duet with Najma Akhtar who added a suitably exotic edge to the familiar *Zep IV* song. The pair's closing "Ah ah ha" refrain smouldered above Page's triple-neck guitar.

'Candy Store Rock' sequence
Wembley Arena, London, July 26 1995
A final UK soundbite incorporating Plant's acknowledgement of Peter Grant's presence ("And a special thank you Bill Curbishley and Mr Peter Grant who is with us tonight"), leading into the pairs playful skit around 'Candy Store Rock' preceding the encore of 'Black Dog'. It signalled the end of the 1995 UK tour.

CD3: US SECOND LEG /SOUTH AMERICA

'Heartbreaker'/'Rock And Roll'
El Palacio De Los Deportes Arena, Mexico City, Sept 24 1995
The US fall tour opened with two riotous nights in Mexico City. The enthusiasm for being back on the road again was obvious as these two segments demonstrated.

An encore barrage of two classic rockers – 'Heartbreaker' played in full for the first time on the tour (later versions omitted the final verse when segueing into 'Ramble On' or 'What Is') and 'Rock And Roll' - making a long awaited entry into the set. The bootleg video that surfaced from the show captured the sheer enjoyment of both band and audience.

'Bring It On Home'/'What Is And What Should Never Be'
Fiddlers Green Amphitheatre, Denver, Colorado,
September 30 1995
They really began to cook on this part of the tour. This Denver show witnessed the elevation of 'Bring It On Home' into the set

AT GLASTONBURY: JUNE 25, 1995

'Thank You'/'Going To California'
(Wembley Arena, London, July 26 1995)
From its introduction at the beginning of the MTV filming and its frequent inclusion on the tour 'Thank You' had developed into something of a signature tune for the whole Page Plant reunion. There were many great deliveries of the song along the way (Meadowlands, San Jose and Paris to name but three), but there was something almost spiritual on the final night of the UK tour. Perhaps it was the presence of Peter Grant, or the knowledge that they would not be performing it again for some time. Whatever it was, the commitment of both Page and Plant on this outing was more than evident. Page lurched magnificently into the solo as Plant passionately ad-libbed the final lines, echoing out the final "I wanna thank you..." A mesmerising performance.

'Going To California' was another new addition to the final part of the UK leg. A delicate rendering made all the more so with the aid of a subtle orchestral string backing.

opener slot where it paved the way for a welcomed *Zep II* throwback 'What Is And What Should Never Be'. This had been tried in a somewhat shaky manner at the MTV filming. They now felt confident to push it back to the forefront of their live show.

'That's The Way'/ 'Friends'
Shoreline Amphitheatre, Mountain View, California,
October 7 1995
The US fall tour now hit a real peak with shows at Irvine (October 3) Boise (October 9) and Salt Lake City (October 10) taking them to a new level of consistency. In between there was a memorable Saturday night at the Shoreline from which this pair from *Zep III* emerged. Plant's singing and phrasing was significantly poignant during this version of 'That's The Way', played in the now familiar MTV filming semi-electric version. 'Friends' came complete with the atmospheric Pharaohs finale with Page raising the tempo for the songs climax.

'Whole Lotta Love' medley including 'The Ocean'/ 'How Many More Times'/'We're Gonna Groove'/'Break On Through'/'Dazed And Confused' inserts
Shoreline Amphitheatre, October 7 1995
By now 'Whole Lotta Love' was firmly established as the vehicle for all manner of medley fun. This 21-minute marathon packed it all in: the Knebworth '79 revamped riffing, Plant's "Na na na na na na" 'Ocean' chorus, Page's flashy theremin battle and subsequent Zeppelin re-incarnated riffing, and then the real fun started.

"I give you all I got to give... rings, pearls and all."

Charlie rolled out that evocative bass line and there was 'How Many More Time' being played live for the first time since the Zep US shows in 1975. This than led into 'We're Gonna Groove' on its first live outing for some 26 years. The more familiar 'Break On Through'/'Dazed' inserts completed the medley, though not before Page had ripped into a scintillating wah-wah run. One of the greatest performances of the entire tour.

'Over The Hills And Far Away'
United Center Chicago, Illinois, October 13 1995
Yet another first. 'Over The Hills' performed live for the first time since August 11, 1979. Perhaps not quite in the LA '77 class but still very welcome. The confidence of Plant's voice was highlighted by his decision to sing the chorus in the high register, something he never attempted in the post-1972 Zep era.

'Ramble On'/'Laride'/Nigel Eaton solo/'Gallows Pole'
Madison Square Garden, New York, October 27 1995

a warm welcome to Mr Jimmy Page," was Robert's enthusiastic introduction to 'No Quarter'. By this time the track had developed into an improvised Page-led opus far removed from the simple MTV *Unledded* delivery. At the beginning Page employed the same chord sequence he used to open his 'White Summer' solos in the Zep era. Not the easiest of live pieces to deliver and sometimes not the always best received, they kept with it, turning in 102 performances.

CD4: SOUTH AMERICA/JAPAN/AUSTRALIA

'Babe I'm Gonna Leave You'
Rio De Janeiro, Brazil, January 27 1996
Another later tour highlight, the *Zep I* vintage 'Babe' had been rehearsed as far back as the MTV filming (it was dropped from the first night filming at the last minute) and it was always planned to perform it with the orchestral backing. It finally made its debut in Mexico on September 29. This new wide screen arrangement included a newly added spiralling solo section which garnered a huge response from the massive Rio crowd. Their biggest cheer was held for the finale when Page closed the song using the opening chords to 'Stairway To Heaven' - a tactic first employed when Robert performed the song with Fairport Convention at the Cropredy Festival in 1992.

'Nobody's Fault But Mine'
Budokan Hall, Tokyo, Japan, February 6 1996
'When The Levee Breaks'

UK TOUR: JULY, 1995

> *It's a great pleasure to bring you a man who hasn't played in your city before. Please give a warm welcome to Mr Jimmy Page.*
> ROBERT PLANT

The Garden was always going to be special and they did not disappoint. 'Ramble On' had been a consistent part of the set but this incarnation was the last to benefit from Porl Thompson's duel lead guitar part - he was to leave the band soon after this show. The arrangement did lose a little when Page later attempted it on his own. It shined brightly for this final time as a guitar duet on this night with Plant lifting the song with his "Come on children... come on children" refrain. Nigel Eaton's hurdy gurdy solo, appearing under its grand title 'Laride', was altered slightly for the fall leg and now merged directly into 'Gallows Pole'. The latter did suffer a little from over exposure, being the only song to be played on every single date. This version featured a speeded-up finale with Page demonstrating his understanding of the folk tradition.

'No Quarter'
Apoteose Square, Rio De Janeiro, Brazil, January 27 1996
To the vast open air arena of Rock in Rio. "It's a great pleasure to bring you a man who hasn't played in your city before. Please give

Budokan Hall, Tokyo, Japan, February 8 1996
Two performances of the similarly styled semi-acoustic blues workouts that were initially performed for the MTV filming at Corris Slate in Wales. These tracks were rotated at random to precede Nigel Eaton's solo on the tour. Perfect for Plant's classic blues vocalisms, 'Nobody's Fault' looped along with a pleasing bounce. "That was a song from a preacher in 1929... his name was John Paul Jones... whoops... Blind Willie McTell," was Plant's caustic comment at the close. 'Levee' was played in the Corris Slate arrangement - harsh and grinding in a semi acoustic stomp - sensibly there was no attempt to replicate Bonham's master drum sound of the original.

'The Rain Song'
Budokan Hall, Tokyo, Japan, February 8 1996
This third Budokan night was plagued with false starts and technical trouble, prompting Plant to call it the rehearsal night. However, there was a certain charm to be derived from some of

'"WE'RE HAPPY AGAIN"

Thanks for a great response and a great night. It will be a long time before we hear this noise again... so give it to us again!

ROBERT PLANT

their failings. This live premier of 'The Rain Song' was one such example. Jimmy completely lost his way on the intro and, spurred on by Plant, then drifted off into an instrumental solo before they got it all back on course. Always a highlight of the MTV filming, this long awaited live delivery was every bit as arresting, aided by the orchestra.

The final solo from Page was played out with breathtaking intensity. "I don't know if you could spot all the mistakes there... but it'll sound great on bootleg and this is the place to get it," was Plant's comment at the end.

'Yallah'
Budokan Hall, Tokyo, Japan, February 13 1996
Plant's made for MTV new song 'Yallah' (or 'The Truth Explodes' as it was retiled for the MTV *Unledded* video) had something of a chequered history along the tour. It was discarded fairly early on in the US and was played infrequently in Europe. In Japan it enjoyed something of a renaissance despite the problems with the backing tape loop that caused the total abandonment of the Feb 8 version. This attempt a few days later was more successful with Page underscoring the loop and orchestral support with a blazing riff feast.

'Ten Years Gone'
Castle Hall, Osaka, Japan, February 15 1996
"This is a song for the happy people of Osaka," was Plant's low key introduction to another slice of Page Plant history. They had begun rehearsing the *Physical Graffiti* classic 'Ten Years Gone' during their Budokan stint and now it was served up in all its glory with Page back on the Telecaster for perhaps the most emotionally charged performance of the tour. Peerlessly performed with Page stringbending the notes in customary fashion. "I'm never gonna leave you," Plants final pleas prompted memories of the latter era of Zeppelin. This outstanding performance that recalled the spirit of 1977 and 1979, was revived for one night only. Like 'Achilles' maybe they felt it was just too precious to repeat it again.

'Tangerine'
Century Hall, Nagoya, Japan, February 17 1996
A similarly misty eyed revival, with the opening chord accompanied by an excited "Oh Jimmy!" squeal from one of the audience. Earlier in the tour it had been performed in a full band version.

For the Japanese dates it was back in an arrangement similar to when Zep played it in Japan back in 1971. Simple, bleak and profound.

'Tea For One'
Century Hall, Nagoya, Japan, February 17 1996
'Tea For One', the *Presence* closing track had been hinted at as far back as the hybrid 'Since I've Been Loving You' performance in Sheffield. Eventually for this leg of the tour they worked on a complete version. They took a little time to get it right (again the Feb 8 show being something of a test run), but by the time they got to Nagoya it had developed into a uniquely relaxed affair.

Rarely on the tour did they sound so laid back and at ease as on this delivery of a previously unplayed song. Page cut in with some stirring blues runs against the soaring strings of the orchestra. It was only performed on six occasions but 'Tea For One' emerged as the musical discovery of the tour, Page bringing a new maturity to a no longer under exposed part of the Zep catalogue.

'The Song Remains The Same'
Entertainment Center, Sydney, Australia, February 25 1996
So to Australia for the home straight. The departure of Porl Thompson left Page taking on all the chores of this track alone. It may have stunted his stage movements a little but it only enhanced the quality of his playing. This version breezed along with all the aural assault of the New Orleans version of a year back. It may have been the 114th show, but the pair's total application was still very apparent.

'Four Sticks'/'Wonderful One'
Flinders Park, Melbourne, Australia, March 1 1996
Two selections from the last night of the world tour - both initial inspirations from the very first night of filming for MTV. 'Four Sticks' may have been a familiar part of the set but it still retained its original spark, creating a fresh nostalgia of its own - not for the 1971 studio album version but for the more recent golden evenings of August 1994. The clap-along speeded up finale was still a delight 108 performances on. Not bad for a song played live only once in the previous 25 years.

'Wonderful One' had returned to the set during the Japanese leg in a more substantial orchestral arrangement. Initially tried on the US first leg it was dropped due to problems co-ordinating the backing tape loop. With the aid of strings it flowed far more effectively. A very pretty melody with lyrically couplings reminiscent of some mid-Seventies Plant writings

This version was a played as an encore on the night after which Plant told the crowd: "Thanks for a great response and a great night. It will be a long time before we hear this noise again... so give it to us again!"

'Jam sequence'
Flinders Park, Melbourne, Australia, March 1 1996
Another short soundbite - performed prior to 'Black Dog'. As was customary, Page staggered out some appropriate riffs to warm up before 'Black Dog' but on this occasion was joined by Charlie and Michael and then Plant leading them through a fast grunge like rock'n'roll piece with nondescript "Oh baby" lyrics. Allegedly this jam was built around one of the unreleased tracks they recorded in rehearsals for the MTV filming.

'Rock And Roll'
Flinders Park, Melbourne, March 1 1996
The final date, the 115th gig. A chaotic encore of 'Rock And Roll' featuring bass tec Richard Davis (introduced by Plant as Garth Brooks: "Take it away Garth, eye thank yew") on guitar, Michael Lee dressed in a rabbit suit and Charlie dressed as an elephant. "We've got to go back to kindergarden. Bye bye... see you next time." Plant's final statement from the world tour.

It brings to an end nearly five hours of material that accurately chronicles the long awaited reunion of Page with Plant - the evolution of Led Zeppelin as it unfolded from February 1995 through to March 1996.

In 1997 I requested an interview with John Paul Jones through his manager Richard Chadwick. The timing proved perfect – John was about to begin recording his *Zooma* solo album that would propel him back into the spotlight as a fully fledged solo artist. He was more than happy to oblige. Rather like the Peter Grant interview, I saw this as an opportunity to present a complete career overview. Our meeting was to prove very illuminating. John was extremely forthcoming on all levels – happy to discuss his pre-Zep career, the trails and tribulations of life in and out of Zeppelin, his thoughts on his being ignored by Page and Plant for *Unledded* and his plans for the future. Our conversation spread over three hours and it was evident John was very keen to put the record straight on several issues. The resulting text was published in *TBL 13*.

Like the Peter Grant interview, it stands as the longest question and answer John Paul Jones feature ever published. Since then John has re-established his career with the *Zooma* and *The Thunderthief* albums and accompanying tours.

Prior to that artistic rebirth, this interview found the once unassuming quiet man of Zeppelin finally having his say.

REFERENCES: **TIGHT BUT LOOSE 13**

THE JOHN PAUL JONES
INTERVIEW:14

I first heard John Paul Jones voice on the radio back in late 1973. He had agreed to do a rare interview for Radio One's *Rockspeak* programme to explain his involvement with Madeline Bell's new album *Comin' Atcha*. In between the failing medium-wave frequency, JPJ's soft spoken tones wafted out of the radio as he discussed the recording of Ms Bell's album and a few Zeppelin topics.

Two things struck me on that first hearing. How on earth did this softly spoken chap fit in with all the off-stage craziness that surrounded Led Zeppelin? And this rarely heard voice certainly offered an intelligent perspective of the group that was quite distinct from the more high profile, interview-friendly Plant and (to a lesser degree) Page. His viewpoint was an important one but, in the long tradition of bass players, rarely heard.

Sitting in front of John Paul Jones in a very comfortable tea room in Holland Park nigh on 25 years later, not much has changed. He still speaks in that soft spoken clipped English accent, sometimes drifting into third person phrasing to illustrate a point. His perspective on what happened to him between 1968 and 1980 is still intelligently and perceptively presented. And that's the purpose of this meeting: to hear the gospel according to John Paul Jones.

For too long JPJ has been the silent voice of Led Zeppelin. Now is the time to put that right. In the light of the *BBC Sessions* album release, John has decided to be the main spokesman of the group in their dealing with the media. A number of interviews have been lined up, and an Internet on-line Q & A session arranged.

My own request for an interview actually occurred before it became apparent that he would be more loquacious than ever before when answering questions about his former group. It was back in September that I first decided to approach his management re a full scale interview for TBL. Just prior to that, Chris Charlesworth from Omnibus had bumped into Jonesy at a party following the unveiling of the Jimi Hendrix English Heritage plaque on Brook Street in London's Mayfair. Chris told me that John had been most complimentary about my *Concert File* book - describing it as one of the very best ever written on the group.

Faxes and phone calls went to and fro throughout October - and the response was positive. John would be happy to do an interview as soon as his schedule would allow. Come November and the impending BBC release, I was keen to get things moving. Thus it was a big relief when JPJ's manager called me to relay a date and time for the interview to take place: Wednesday, November 12, 3.30pm.

"Was the interview to be based around the BBC session?" I enquired. "John's quite happy to talk about whatever you like," was the most welcome reply.

You have to go back a long way (possibly as far back as a 1977 interview in *Guitar* magazine) for the last real major Q&A interview with John. In the intervening years he has rarely opened up (or been asked to divulge) about the Zeppelin years. It was something I was very keen to redress. I spent the preceding week putting together a list of suitable questions.

Wednesday, November 12, a mild, early, winter afternoon. Armed with the trusty *TBL* notebook and dictaphone I arrive at the comfortable basement office from which this seasoned musician conducts his business affairs. He looks... well typically Jonesyish. For his 50 plus years he is wearing remarkably well. A pile of freshly delivered BBC CD's sit on his desk awaiting his autograph for US promotion purposes. Wearing a pair of cords and well-cut woolen bomber jacket, his hair is around the length of the mid-Seventies period Zeppelin.

We walk the short distance across Holland Park to a classy tea-room tucked away from the main road. Nobody recognises him as we walk along - but then again, nobody ever did. Above us, perhaps symbolically, a promotional airships hovers in the air. "Now there's an omen," he grins.

It's around then that I have a minor fit of pre-match nerves. How is he going to fare with all these questions about his past? His treatment of the press can be curt at best. I have a momentary flashback to the *Melody Maker* poll awards in 1979; JPJ sporting a *Rock Against Journalism* badge and dismissing a junior reporters'

I knew Jimmy well from the session scene of course. He was a very respected name. So I rang him up. He was just about to go up to Birmingham to see Robert.

JOHN PAUL JONES

CONCERT FOR KAMPUCHEA: DECEMBER 29, 1979

plea to the question "Any quotes?" "Quotes?" he replied, "Oh Eric quotes, haven't seen him!"

Luckily there's to be no such confrontation this afternoon. Seated before a pot of tea in a secluded corner of the tea-room, John proves to be an illuminating interviewee, just as I had hoped. We sat discussing countless topics from the Zeppelin era and beyond for the best part of three hours. John was often very keen to emphasis a point, sometimes slipping into third person. Mostly he was bright and upbeat - once or twice stony-faced and intensely serious. "Well it's all out now!" was his good humoured final parting as I left him at the office signing the BBC CD's.

So what follows is the complete transcript of this major *TBL* interview, part of which was previewed in the January 1998 issue of *Record Collector*. This is John Paul Jones talking lucidly and authoritatively on the way it was for him to be part of what those BBC ads so rightly put as "the group that continues to be the world's biggest rock band".

DL: During your stint as a session musician, were you asked to join other groups before Zeppelin came along?

JPJ: No. I was viewed as a session man really primarily, and a very in-demand one. I'd been in groups before the sessions started, notably with Tony Meehan. After a few years of non-stop sessions it got too much. I was making a fortune but I wasn't enjoying it

any more. It was my wife Mo who noticed an item in *Disc* saying that Jimmy was forming a new band out of the old Yardbirds. She prompted me to phone him up. It was the chance to do something different at last.

DL: So it was more a case of you approaching Jimmy, rather than being asked to join?

JPJ: Yes. I knew him well from the session scene of course. He was a very respected name. So I rang him up. He was just about to go up to Birmingham to see Robert. He told me he had already been turned down by Terry Reid. He came back and said Robert was fantastic and had suggested a drummer. That was John Bonham, who was at the time with Tim Rose. Peter Grant had to persuade him to give up his £40 a week job to come and join us! From the first rehearsals it was obvious we could do something with this line-up. It seemed to come together very quickly from making that call to Page and then being on the first tour finishing The Yardbirds' outstanding Scandinavian dates.

DL: What memories do you have of the first Led Zeppelin album sessions?

JPJ: The first album was really our live act of the time. It was what we'd been doing on stage up to that point. It didn't take a lot of preparation. We had those Willie Dixon blues things; and 'How Many More Times' and 'Dazed And Confused' had arisen out of The Yardbirds' last days. My contributions were 'Good Times Bad Times' and 'Your Time Is Gonna Come'.

DL: That latter number featured organ. What is always the intention for you to play keyboards as well as bass?

JPJ: Yes it was. I remember at an early rehearsal at Jimmy's place there was a Honer organ and we did a couple of things using that. One was 'Tribute To Burt Burns' (later to be released as 'Baby Come On Home' on *Boxed Set 2*) and I recall we also rehearsed 'Chest Fever by The Band from *Big Pink* - though we never took that further. I had some bass pedals made at the time so it was quite easy to take the organ on the road and work it with the group.

DL: The breakthrough for Zeppelin in America seemed to occur very quickly. What do you think the turning point was as far as the UK was concerned?

JPJ: America wasn't entirely instant. We did have to work really hard to make a name for ourselves. During the first 12 months of the band we seemed to be on tour in America constantly. We also did a lot of radio promotion. FM radio was just beginning to have a huge influence - they weren't afraid to play longer tracks or even whole albums. We went around a lot of radio stations to plug the record. We would turn up at little shacks that doubled as radio stations in some very odd places. You have to remember that we also suffered from some terrible press early on in America. All that stuff about us being a hyped band - that didn't help us early on. When people saw us live though they realised that we were actually trying to make some very good music.

In the UK it took a while for us to register and we were playing lots of club dates. Then the album began to get noticed. As for turning points, I seem to recall a great night at Birmingham Town Hall. This would have been just after our album came out here. The Albert Hall was another good one. The UK was slower mainly because we had so little press coverage. What also helped, of course, was the early BBC radio appearances

DL: What do remember about the Danish TV recording?

JPJ: It was all a bit strange. We had a good giggle when we set up surrounded by all these people sitting on the floor wondering what we were about. Later on we had all that trouble in Copenhagen with the Countess. Bit of a mad woman really. Odd things did keep happening to us in that part of Europe.

DL: How important was Peter Grant to the overall success of Zeppelin?

JPJ: Absolutely vital. He left the music completely up to us. He made all the decisions on when and where we would tour and took care of all the business side. It was great to have so much artistic freedom. He was crucial to the band and as we all know, virtually rewrote the rule book on group management. It was very sad when he died. I couldn't get to the funeral as I was in America but Mo went. He really made so many things possible for us.

DL: Why do you think the BBC sessions were so important to the band?

Later on we had all that trouble in Copenhagen with the Countess. Bit of a mad woman really.

JOHN PAUL JONES

BACKSTAGE LA FORUM: SEPTEMBER 4, 1970

JPJ: Well we were very young and cocky at the time, very sure of ourselves. I don't think too many bands were doing the sort of improvising we were doing and the BBC, particularly the *In Concert* live recordings, allowed us the scope to do that on the radio. This was in the days of restricted needle time so we were determined to make the best of every BBC radio opportunity.

DL: Are you happy with the sound on the recently released BBC sessions album?

JPJ: It's something that I did worry about when I knew we were going to release the tapes, but Jimmy has really done a great job on it. There were certain limitations with the sound at the BBC studios at the time so when listening to the sessions now you have to take that into consideration. Overall though it's an excellent job. The first version we got was on cassette from a DAT tape. That wasn't that good but by the time it got to mastering on CD all the early flaws had been ironed out. Brilliant.

DL: Were you aware of the many bootlegs that exist of these sessions?

JPJ: Yes I'm aware of some of them - I get sent them now and again. I must say the packaging has certainly come a long way.

DL: Do you remember recording the session for the Alexis Korner show which was subsequently wiped by the BBC?

JPJ: I can't really - they all seem to blur a little. We recorded different shows in different studios like Maida Vale and the Playhouse Theatre. I know we would have been very pleased to do anything that Alexis was associated with.

DL: What's your opinion on the two previously unreleased tracks on the album 'The Girl I Love' and the cover of Eddie Cochran's 'Something Else'?

We were very proficient musicians and it was a joy to get involved in those improvisations. Mind you, later on they did begin to stretch to ridiculous proportions!

JOHN PAUL JONES

BACKSTAGE CIRCA '69

JPJ: 'Something Else' was a fun thing that I recall we did as an encore in the live set at that time. It gave me the chance to bang around on piano. As for 'Girl I Love', that sounds like one of those jam type numbers we often made up as we were going along.

DL: The Playhouse Theatre 1969 live version of 'You Shook Me' has a lengthy organ solo - is that a stand-out performance for you?

JPJ: What's good about the BBC CD set is that we are able to illustrate how we varied every track. There are two versions of that song and I think the Playhouse version is almost double in length to the first BBC version we cut. As I said earlier that's one of the key elements about our approach. We were very proficient musicians and it was a joy to get involved in those improvisations. Mind you, later on they did begin to stretch to ridiculous proportions! With something like 'No Quarter' it was a test each night to see how it would work out. Nothing was pre-planned about the solos - we took some chances and sometimes we'd get a bit lost. But when that improvisation really worked it was very satisfying.

DL: The 1971 live version of 'Stairway To Heaven' is a very tentative arrangement. Was it a difficult number to play live initially?

JPJ: It was like that with a lot of new numbers, and there were certainly a lot of different moods to that number. You had to concentrate to get it right with every change. At the time we didn't know it was going to turn into something of a monster - we just played it as part of our new album. We certainly felt it was one of our best compositions up to that point.

DL: Did you have much input in compiling the BBC set?

JPJ: I'm still one third of the surviving group so I'm very keen to be involved in releases such as this. Jimmy did the actual compiling but I have my say on the track listing, artwork etc.

DL: How would you like the new BBC set to be perceived?

JPJ: It's an excellent opportunity to hear the band in the making. It was an early stage in our career. That first session captures us just after coming back from America and we were pretty hot. It's good to compare that feel to some of the later stuff. It also once again shows just how good John Bonham was - and how vital to our sound. The thing about John was that he was much more than a mere drummer who kept time.

He was a true musician with an incredible feel for the music. He was a big Tamla Motown fan and he seemed to bring a lot of influences into his drumming. He never played the basic drum patterns the same and that's what made it such an exciting band to be a part of. As a rhythm section it was everything I could have wanted and more.

DL: Now that the BBC album has been released - would you be happy to see more archive tapes released - perhaps a chronological live album box set or even a Beatles type anthology with accompanying visual footage?

JPJ: If it sounds good, then yes, I would be happy with that. I don't know how much live stuff there is left though I would think Jimmy knows what's there. I'm pretty sure there's scope to do it. As for a video - if it's a good representation of the group then that's fine. *The Song Remains The Same* movie did not turn out as we would have liked, so it would be nice if something more representative was out there. It was good to present some of that stuff in the recent 'Whole Lotta Love' promo clip. The only thing is I don't really want to spend too much time digging up the past - I've got plenty of current music to do.

DL: Can you think of many unreleased Zeppelin tracks that might be lining the archive?

JPJ: Hardly anything if anything at all. We weren't the sort of group to hoard tracks. If something didn't get used on one album it tended to be carried over to the next album.

DL: There was a lot of unrest at Zeppelin gigs in America around 1970 and 1971 with the police making their presence felt. How did you cope with that being on stage?

JPJ: It was around the time of student unrest in America and obviously the police didn't help. Then we would get some people turning up and trying to claim the gig as a free show. It became a bit of a two way fight. From our standpoint it was like saying "Hey, we're up here as well - just listen and enjoy it". Robert was always making gestures for calm. I think we then realised we'd be better off without the police and got rid of them and brought in our own security.

PERFORMING 'GOING TO CALIFORNIA', EARL'S COURT: 1975

DL: Getting back to the music, 'Black Dog' is obviously your riff, how did that come about?

JPJ: I recall Page and I listening to *Electric Mud* at the time by Muddy Waters. One track is a long rambling riff and I really liked the idea of writing something like that - a riff that would be like a linear journey. The idea came on a train coming back from Page's Pangbourne house. From the first run-through at the Grange we knew it was a good one.

DL: On the third and fourth albums you began using mandolin. Had you played the instrument prior to that?

JPJ: No, I just started learning it from scratch. I brought a ropey old copy of *Teach Yourself Bluegrass Mandolin*, and that was it. Buying mandolins has been a hobby ever since that period.

DL: 'No Quarter' was an ambitious arrangement, how do you look back on it now?

JPJ: It just came about sitting around the piano. Using various effects. I knew instantly it was a very durable piece and something we could take on the road and expand.

DL: It turned into something of a marathon.

JPJ: Yes, I suppose too long in the end, as some things were. It was fun. I used to use it to challenge myself musically. I was getting a bit blasé, but something like that tested you. Sometimes it worked but on other occasions it didn't. But it was worth taking a chance because when it was good it was so fulfilling.

DL: You even threw in a version of 'Nutrocker' on the '77 tour.

JPJ: I put it in spontaneously one night and they all said I should keep it in, but it got a bit tiresome.

DL: With Zeppelin you used many different instruments including the Mellotron. How difficult was it to play?

JPJ: The trouble with the Mellotron was that it would not stay in tune. Everybody used to moan about it and say it works for The Moody Blues - but they had the guy who invented it working with them and I didn't! In the end it had to go. Later with Zeppelin I used the GX1 Dream Machine keyboard synth. Along with Stevie Wonder, I was one of the first to use this. It was excellent for the time because it could do everything on one unit that three keyboards had done before. I got some great sounds out of it - things like 'In The Evening' and 'All My Love'. They came out of experimenting with it in the studio.

DL: What about that three-necked guitar that you began using on Zeppelin's 1977 US tour?

JPJ: That came about after the guitar tech Andy Manson came to see us live and saw how many guitar changes I was going through. He told me he could build a guitar that would incorpo-

rate mandolin, six and 12-string acoustic. I also had a bass pedal unit. It worked well on 'Ten Years Gone' though it took a while to set it all up.

DL: Was 'In The Light' another of your ideas?

JPJ: 'In The Light' had that drone on which I think Page and I came up with - he might have used the bow. I had a VCS 3 synth, it was attempting to get a sort of Indian sound. The challenge was trying to get an ethnic sound out of a synthesiser. It was similar with 'Kashmir' - we did the strings with an English orchestra in Olympic Studios. I'd worked out all the parts beforehand rather like I would have done for one of the Sixties sessions.

DL: Did you ever feel some of your ideas went unaccredited within the band's song-writing credits?

JPJ: Looking back now there were some major contributions that seemed to get lost in the final credits. 'Achilles Last Stand' is one - that bass line that I created with the Alembic eight-string was an integral part of the song. I think John suffered like that as well. Lots of things came out of jams.

I came up with a lot of arrangement ideas such as 'Friends' on the third album. What one put into the track wasn't always reflected in the credits. It probably didn't seem worth shouting about at the time. A more democratic four way credit might have been a better idea on some things.

DL: Tell me about the time you told Peter Grant that you wanted to leave the group to become choirmaster at Winchester Cathedral?

JPJ: The choirmaster thing was a tongue-in-cheek joke I made to some journalist who made more of it than it was. It is true, how-

FILMING AT SHEPPERTON STUDIOS: AUGUST, 1974

ever, that I did consider leaving after our American tour in 1973. I'd just had enough of touring and I did go to Peter and tell him I wanted out unless things were changed. There was a lot of pressure on my family what with being away so long. Funnily enough things changed pretty quickly after I'd seen him. We didn't tour in the school holidays as much and there was more notice given for when we were touring. Things had to change and they did, so it quickly blew over. I trusted Peter to put it right.

DL: How do you look back on the experience of making The Song Remains movie?

JPJ: It was a massive compromise. We never knew what was happening. When we first had the idea, it was a relatively simple one - to film some shows and then release it as a film. Little did we know how difficult it would all become. There's that claim about how I wouldn't wear the same stage clothes over the filming nights. It's not true - what happened was is that I'd ask if we were filming tonight, but be told that nothing was going to be filmed so I'd think, "Not to worry, I'll save the shirt I wore the previous night for the next filming". Then what would happen is that I'd get on-stage and see the cameras all ready to roll, nobody seemed to know what was going on. It was frustrating.

DL: You then re-shot some of the live footage at Shepperton.

JPJ: Ah yes... the trouble with that was that the office rang me up and asked if I needed anything for the Shepperton shoot. I replied, "Well how about six inches of hair for starters!" I'd just had it cut short! We had to re-shoot the scenes because there were gaps in

The office rang me up and asked if I needed anything for the Shepperton shoot. I replied, "Well how about six inches of hair for starters!" I'd just had it cut short!

JOHN PAUL JONES

BACKSTAGE AT THE LYCEUM: OCTOBER 12, 1969

The main memory of that album is pushing Robert around in the wheelchair from beer stand to beer stand!

JOHN PAUL JONES

the footage so I had to use a wig which caused some laughs. Then there were the fantasy sequences. Somebody said, "You've got to do a fantasy sequence" and I thought "What?" Actually, my idea was to use an old film, *Doctor Sin*, which had all these horseman crossing the marshes and have me added in at the end. Turns out the film is owned by Disney, so I had to do all the riding myself which was hilarious really as I can't ride that well.

DL: Presence was recorded incredibly quickly, and had little keyboard input. Can you recall why that was?

JPJ: We rented these houses in Malibu and it became apparent that Robert and I seemed to keep a different time sequence to Jimmy. We just couldn't find him. I wanted to put up this huge banner across the street saying "Today's the first day of rehearsals". Myself and my then roadie Brian Condliffe drove into SIR Studios every night and waited and waited until finally we were all in attendance, by which time it was around two in the morning. I learned all about baseball during that period as the World Series was on and there was not much else to do but watch it. There just wasn't a lot of continuous rehearsal and it was easy to lose interest. When we eventually started recording in Munich I just sort of went along with it all. Jimmy did work really hard then and it came together quickly - possibly because the studio time was limited. The main memory of that album is pushing Robert around in the wheelchair from beer stand to beer stand! We had a laugh I suppose, but I didn't enjoy the sessions really. I just tagged along with that one. The one good thing about that period was that I'd started using the Alembic 8 string which I felt really added to our sound.

DL: You then made your singing debut on the 1977 tour. Were you happy about that?

JPJ: They got me to sing on 'Battle Of Evermore'. I'll never know how I agreed to that! I suppose Jimmy and Bonzo weren't going to do it so it was left to me - that happened quite a lot - "Oh Jonesy will do it". We got through it, but it was all part of the acoustic set which we all agreed should be a part of our live show again.

DL: By the time of that 1977 US tour, the whole Zeppelin operation had become huge. How did you cope personally with all the offstage goings on?

JPJ: If it was fun you joined in, if it wasn't you didn't. I was often in another part of the hotel I guess. But that sort of stuff got a bit tedious after a while. Things were getting a little crazy with Richard Cole and the likes of John Bindon. He was actually a nice bloke in the daytime, but at night just went crazy. I just avoided it because I disliked all that violence stuff. I know Robert never

liked it and Jimmy was not around much on that tour. In fact, Robert and I used to go out walking a lot to try and get a day-time existence. Every band was doing the drugs thing at the time - we didn't really worry much about it - but by then it was getting a bit out of control.

DL: How do you view the Oakland incident?

JPJ: Well I remember there being a lot of running around with security before the show - screaming and shouting - but that happened a lot at the time, so I didn't take much notice. In fact, I seem to remember the Oakland show was a good gig. I actually had all the family over and was due to travel to Oregon the next day. I'd rented a motor home and I had it parked outside the hotel. We heard the Police were on the way and they were swarming around the lobby. So me and my family went down this service elevator out the back, through the kitchen and into this motor home - which I'd never driven - pulled out of the hotel, onto the freeway and away from the trouble.

DL: Then the news came of Robert's tragedy?

JPJ: Well I just couldn't believe it. I was up in Oregon. Somewhere in Oregon I called in to New Orleans - I was going to stay with Tommy Hullat from Concerts West. It was quite a time for him, what with the Zeppelin tour being cancelled, and then Elvis died a couple of weeks later and he had to sort that out too. Anyway, Robert had gone home with Bonzo and I drove on to Seattle. It was a very strange time. We just knew we had to give him time.

DL: What did you do during the lay-off?

JPJ: I had just got a farm in Sussex so I did a bit of farming - and generally caught up with my family life. It was a case of cooling out and just taking stock. We'd been working hard for so long. We needed some breathing space. Getting back together at Clearwell was a bit odd. I didn't really feel comfortable. I remember asking "Why are we doing this?" We were not in good shape mentally or health wise.

DL: Did that become frustrating?

JPJ: It did, but it wasn't easy to do much about. Perhaps nobody was strong enough to stop it - including our manager who wasn't that well himself anyway. In the end it was like "Let's get through this and get back on stage". If I was a little down Robert would try to cheer me up, if he was down I'd do the same and pull ourselves through. Around that time I did get closer to Robert. It's not that we didn't have a laugh at Clearwell, it just wasn't going anywhere.

DL: It was around then you acquired the GX1.

JPJ: I was one of the first to get one - I think it was Stevie Wonder and myself. It certainly added to the sound. It was much easier to sit down and play at one keyboard. The sound that one could get out of the machine was at the time very inspiring.

DL: What about that telephone that sat on top of it at Knebworth and the Over Europe shows?

JPJ: I just put it on in rehearsal and it looked good and we kept it. It always ended up in the flight case - it was just one of our in jokes.

DL: Of all the Zeppelin albums, In Through The Out Door is the one that carries your influence more than most. Why do think that was?

JPJ: Because for much of the time at those Polar sessions only Robert and I were turning up. There were two distinct camps by then, and we were in the relatively clean one. We'd turn up first, Bonzo would turn up later and Page might turn up a couple of days later. The thing is when that situation occurs you either sit around waiting or get down to some playing. So that's what we did in the studio. I'd got this huge machine installed and I wasn't going to sit and just look at it. That's where 'All My Love' came out and things like that. I know Jimmy has said that song wasn't right for Zeppelin but the same could be said for 'Down By The Seaside' so I don't agree with that at all. The thing is Robert and I spent much of the time drinking pints of Pimms and waiting around for it to happen. So we made it happen. I think there's some excellent stuff on the album. I worked really hard to get 'In The Evening' and 'Carouselambra' right. It was a transitional period. It was a chance to see what else we could do. The next album would have been even more interesting had we followed that direction.

DL: During the latter period of Zeppelin's career the band suffered a major backlash in the wake of the punk revolution. How did you view all that?

JPJ: I must say I didn't like punk at first. It just sounded loud and horrible. Actually, at the time, the stuff I did like was the 2-Tone bands such as The Specials, Selector and The Beat. That was kind of punky - I didn't like The Sex Pistols initially, though I did begin to appreciate it later. For us it was a case of just carrying on regardless. I would say that that sort of stuff did get us writing numbers with that kind of energy. Punk did remind us of the way we had sounded early on - all brash and confident - as you can now hear on the BBC set. In the wake of the punk thing we began recording tracks like 'Wearing And Tearing', which we did in Abba's studio in Stockholm. We could still turn our hand to that high energy stuff and have great fun in the process.

DL: Were you apprehensive about returning to live performances in the UK by playing at Knebworth?

JPJ: Only in so far that it was going to be a very big gig and you had to do your best. I remember the sound initially was ropey, but then I found they didn't have the bass on for the first three numbers which was a little disturbing. It was after a long lay-off and Robert was getting back into it. That was around the time he started using harmoniser effects on his voice, which I can't say I was in favour of really. That seemed to change the vocal delivery too much. Overall though it was great to be back doing it as a band again and we really hoped it would now go on from there.

DL: How would you describe the band's state of mind when it came to undertaking the Over Europe tour in 1980?

JPJ: The state of mind was this: let's sharpen up, cut the waffle out, take a note of what's going and re-invent ourselves. Actually re-invent is too stronger a word. It was like, let's take it to the next stage. It was a way of getting back to the people and I really enjoyed

about something. I had to go in and say hold it and tell them what happened. It was such a shock.

DL: Where do you think Zeppelin might have headed had you not have been forced to disband after John Bonham's death? Was there a feeling that the best days of the group might have been behind you by that time?

JPJ: For all the lay-offs that we had endured I know there was a feeling that we still had much to offer. If anybody within the band felt otherwise it wasn't really apparent. We did have a job getting Robert to tour America again after all his personal tragedies, but after our Europe tour in 1980 he agreed, and it was all set up. As far as I'm concerned we just needed to get back to America, get on the road and then get into the studio. I still felt that we had a lot to offer. I certainly felt no desire to do anything outside of the group. I think we were still up for it. We were keen to make our mark on the Eighties as we had done in the Seventies. But it was not to be.

DL: After John died, was there any way you could have continued - or was it immediately apparent that without Bonzo there could be no Zeppelin?

JPJ: There was no way he could be replaced then. We knew it was going to be the end.

DL: What was it like for you personally after John died - it must have seemed very odd not being in a group after all those years?

JPJ: At first the main emotion for me was anger. It seemed such a waste. There was also a feeling of mortality - after all it could have happened to anyone of us. It was a difficult period. I was supposed to be managed by Peter still, but during those first couple of years it was hard to get hold of him. He wasn't coping very well at all. It

USA TOUR: 1977

THE 1985 SOUNDTRACK ALBUM

PERFORMING 'TRAMPLED UNDERFOOT', EARL'S COURT: 1975

the European tour. I know we spent much of it trying to persuade Robert to go to America which he finally agreed to. We were battling on. Looking back on that period it did seem Robert and I were holding it together, while the others were dealing with other matters. The thing was it seemed to be such a shame to let it go down the toilet. You know... it was what we did. Nobody ever wanted to say it was over. We certainly didn't want to throw that away.

DL: So you were ready to take on America again?

JPJ: It was all very positive. Peter played it clever in making sure we were going back in different stages and not taking on a 30-date tour straight off. It was positive right up to when Benji and I found John. We were at Page's house in Windsor. We got up and went to look for Bonzo. Jimmy had a guest suite at his house so we went to stir him. It was just so tragic. I remember after we found him I came out and Jimmy and Robert were in the front room laughing

was a frustrating time.

DL: Did you consider joining another band?

JPJ: No, that was never an idea. I mean, how do you follow being in Led Zeppelin?

DL: Did you have much input into the compiling of the Coda album?

JPJ: Yes. In fact, it was my title. It seemed to close the book on that chapter. We had a bit of a job finding enough tracks - there was also talk of a live album, but that came to nothing.

DL: Your first substantial work in the Eighties was the Scream For Help soundtrack.

JPJ: It was a horrible film - a bit of a disaster all round really. There was a couple of good tracks - the one that Jimmy played on called 'Crackback' was good fun to record.

DL: What was it like performing at Live Aid and the Atlantic reunions?

It was a bit unsettling seeing someone else play my bass and organ parts to say the least. Calling it 'No Quarter' was also pretty baffling.

JOHN PAUL JONES

STAND-UP BASS FOR 'BRON YR AUR STOMP', EARL'S COURT: 1975

JPJ: At *Live Aid* it was great when we got there. I forced myself onto it really. I guess that was the beginning of not being asked to do these things... I wasn't asked, but I knew Robert was doing it and then somehow Jimmy got involved. It looked as though it was going to be a Zeppelin event so I didn't really want to miss out on that. But when we got up there - well it was fantastic. It was like we'd never been away. Very exciting.

DL: You had that get-together in Bath in early 1986. Did you feel that a proper reunion might be on the cards?

JPJ: I suggested after *Live Aid* that it might be nice to have a bit of a blow again. It was obvious after *Live Aid* that the demand for the band was as great as ever. I felt we should do something. So we started to feel our way back in at Bath. The first day was alright, I don't know if Jimmy was quite into it, but it was good. I had all sorts of ideas for it. In fact, I've still got some tapes from the Bath session somewhere.

Then Tony Thompson was involved in that accident. What I recall is Robert and I getting drunk in the hotel and Robert questioning what we were doing. He was saying nobody wants to hear that old stuff again and I said, "Everybody is waiting for it to happen". It just fell apart from then - I suppose it came down to Robert wanting to pursue his solo career at the expense of anything else.

DL: And Atlantic '88?

JPJ: Great in rehearsal, particularly with Jason. He was really into it and had listened to all the arrangements on the live bootlegs. On the night I remember coming off thinking it had been OK. But the sound was terrible on the TV. As I said, the rehearsal the day before was really good. Again, perhaps something could have come out of that but we never took it any further.

DL: Wasn't there another effort to reform around the time of the Remasters releases?

JPJ: Yes, I'd forgotten about that. There was a meeting at Trinifold to discuss it all. Robert wasn't keen on using Jason. I remember Jimmy and I coming away from the meeting and going to Tower Records in Piccadilly and buying a video of Faith No More because he was the drummer who had been mentioned. Once again it did look as though something might occur, but once again, for whatever reason it did not.

DL: Then Jimmy teamed up with David Coverdale.

JPJ: Well I could see where Jimmy was coming from on that because he wanted to work and Robert was stalling. Jimmy was playing well. I'd seen him in the Firm I think at Hammersmith and he was on good form then. He wanted to play and he wanted to play Zeppelin numbers live, so David Coverdale who is a good singer in that style, seemed be an alternative.

DL: You were obviously very surprised when Robert and Jimmy teamed up for the Unledded project and subsequent world tour?

JPJ: The surprise was in not being told - and hearing it from other sources. There had been talk of an *Unplugged* project after we had all attended the *Q* Awards. It was being mooted that Robert had been asked to do something. I was asked if I'd be interested and well, I have plenty of acoustic instruments, so obviously I was interested. I also remember Robert coming down to my place when he played Glastonbury. He'd just had a baby and was showing us the pictures - but nothing was said then. Then there was that story in *The Sunday Times* at the beginning of the year. The next thing I know is that they are working together for the *Unledded* MTV film. It would have been nice to have been told about it. I first learned of it from our accountant − it was like "Oh didn't you know they're working on an MTV *Unplugged*?"

I was on tour in Hamburg with Diamanda Galas when I switched on the TV and saw a bit of the film. It was a bit unsettling seeing someone else play my bass and organ parts to say the least. Calling it 'No Quarter' was also pretty baffling. I remember at the time being asked for my comments on 'No Quarter' by a journalist at a press conference for Diamanda. He was obviously referring to the *Unledded* project. I curtly replied that I considered it to be one of the best compositions I'd written, which shut him up. I was answering that sort of question constantly, and it did hurt to have to deal with it. It was a great shame, particularly after all we'd been through together. As for the tour - well I felt that Evolution Of

Led Zeppelin slogan on the adverts was a bit too close for comfort.

DL: What was the Hall Of Fame reunion like?

JPJ: A proud occasion, but a difficult one. I was determined to do it though. I remember doing the soundcheck on my own - no sign of the others so not much had changed in that department! There was a bit of fuss about Jason playing from some quarters yet again. As for the acceptance speech, well I did have that line ready. I just thought I couldn't go up without doing something. It was funny because Robert's sniping at Herman's Hermits didn't really get the required response - Herman had sold a lot of albums in the US. I credited Peter Grant because it was pretty stupid he wasn't there. After we'd finished that jam with Neil Young I saw Neil prod Robert and shout "Don't forget his phone number again!" which was very funny looking back. There was an interview planned afterwards but that was cancelled because I think they felt I might have more to say.

DL: And then you picked up the American Music Award in LA.

JPJ: I just happened to be in LA on business so it was good to be able to pick the award up in person. I think the original plan had been for us all to have been at their London rehearsal which I wasn't really into. It was good to see Tom Jones again and be there in person for what was another great honour.

DL: To bring the story up to date, you have been working on a solo album. Is it nearing completion?

JPJ: I'm recording it at my home studio and it's coming along nicely and should be ready next summer. It's an instrumental album and mainly blues and rock based. It also incorporates computerised processing over a live rhythm section. I'm really

tour: somebody shouted-out "The song remains the same", and typical of her she shouted back "No it doesn't motherfucker!"

DL: Do you listen to much new music?

JPJ: Well one of my daughters is looking to open a club and it would be drum and bass dominated - and that stuff I really like - its one of the few things that sounds really fresh. My daughter gets all these great jungle tapes from DJ's. It's not something I'd like to get involved in myself but I can certainly see the appeal. Of the new bands I do think that Radiohead are very good.

DL: A last few Zeppelin questions - what are your personal favourite Zeppelin tracks?

JPJ: 'Kashmir', 'The Ocean', 'Over The Hills And Far Away', 'When The Levee Breaks', 'In My Time Of Dying'... it tends to be the ones where the dynamics of the band were at full strength.

DL: And favourite Zeppelin albums?

JPJ: Definitely *Physical Graffiti*... the fourth album. It's funny that once they were done we hardly ever listened to them much, so I sometimes have a job remembering which songs were on which album.

DL: What about the various books?

JPJ: Well the Richard Cole one and *Hammer Of The Gods* just lack so much humour - they come over as so miserable, which wasn't the way it was most of the time. I must say the amount of detail in *The Concert File* book is quite striking. It reminds me of how hard we worked, particularly in the early years.

DL: Absolutely finally, why do you think the appeal of Led Zeppelin has proved so durable?

JPJ: Nobody has been able to touch what we did. It still sounds

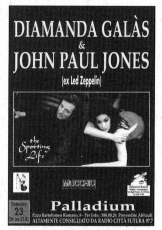

> *Somebody shouted-out "The song remains the same", and typical of her (Diamanda) she shouted back "No it doesn't motherfucker!"*
>
> JOHN PAUL JONES

LIVE ON THE DIAMANDA TOUR: 1994

pleased with it. I'm using 10-string and four-string bass plus steel guitar - that's something that came out of working on the Diamanda Galas project. I enjoy that sound very much.

DL: Have you any plans to tour following its release?

JPJ: Yes very much so, probably as a three-piece. I'll be using a drummer and stick bass player and computerised effects. This obviously helps when I'm doing the steel guitar parts etc. I'm really looking forward to getting out there.

DL: Would your set incorporate any Zeppelin numbers?

JPJ: I might do one or two perhaps, as an encore for a laugh. But it will be mainly new material. I'd like to take it all around Europe and Japan and the US. Some of the Diamanda gigs were really good and I've really got the touring bug again. I thought what we were doing with Diamanda was exceptional. In a way it was an extension of what Zeppelin did - all that call and response stuff. In fact I must tell you something that happened in Chicago on their

fresh. It might be a bit dated by the actual sound. We didn't have the benefit of the Nineties recording techniques but it all sounds so exciting still. There's a lot of conviction to it. We were very committed, very professional and always wanted to put on a good show. We came along at a time when bands would just amble on and play. A Zeppelin show was designed to hit hard from the start – you know, the first three numbers non-stop... blam! We thought about that presentation constantly. It was a dynamic show. I have so many great memories from our touring days. Playing at The Boston Tea Party for four hours with a 45 minute set... The Royal Albert Hall... Earl's Court... and the LA Forum – which was fantastic every time we went back. Zeppelin at its worst was still pretty much better than most bands could ever be... And at its best it was stunning. I'm immensely proud to have been part of it.

Many thanks to Richard Chadwick for making this interview possible.

To accompany the release of their *Walking Into Clarksdale* album, Page and Plant undertook a second world tour in 1998. In contrast to the extravagant presentation of the *Unledded 95/96* campaign, this time they went out in a stripped down four-piece plus keyboards line up. The formula enabled the pair to attack the Zeppelin numbers with the power and sonic bombast of old. Whilst initially they were keen to promote the *Clarksdale* album, the quota of Zeppelin songs increased as the tour wore on. The album itself sold only moderately. Far from the expected riff fest, it was curiously understated affair, rich in composition and texture, although in retrospect lacking in diversity

The tour kicked off in Eastern Europe and from the start they were really on fire. It was a trend that would continue in America in the summer and a round of festival dates in August which included a bill topping appearance at the Reading Festival. However the sterility of the set lists on their fall European tour hinted at Plant's growing disenchantment. This all came to a head at their final performance on an Amnesty International bill at the Bercy Paris.

"I began to feel intimidated committing myself to large parts of touring," he confessed soon after. "All the big time trappings – it became exasperating and too demanding on my calender. I mean I like 'Heart-breaker'… but I don't want to sing it for ever."

Rather than continue the tour into Japan and Australia, much to Page's annoyance Plant opted out and went back to his Midlands roots to re-evalute his career. This Page and Plant reunion was at an end.

The combination of TV appearances and high profile gigs on the *Walking Into Everywhere* tour provided huge scope for coverage in the pages of *TBL*. What follows is an extensive personal tour watch diary of events chronicled as I attended them and as they unfolded during 1998.

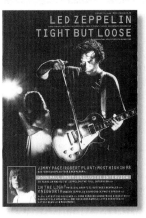

REFERENCE: **TIGHT BUT LOOSE 13 & 14**

15 : PAGE & PLANT – WALKING INTO EVERYWHERE 1998

PERFORMING 'RAMBLE ON', SHEPHERDS BUSH EMPIRE: MARCH 25, 1998

PART ONE

THURSDAY MARCH 5, 1998
Bostanci Centre, Istanbul

This is a moment that crystallizes yet another rejuvenation. It happens towards the end of 'Thank You' which is being performed in a slightly different arrangement to last time. As they come out of the final verse Robert, as is customary, picks up the tambourine and stands in that classic pose. Jimmy swings around with the Gibson, low slung as ever and they're both primed for the finale... Robert glances at the guitarist expecting the solo to hit in, Jimmy for his part hesitates for about three seconds. Robert is momentarily knocked off guard and then it happens. Page takes a few steps towards Michael Lee and crunch! He scrubs those strings like there is no tomorrow... like it just might be the final solo ever. Robert gives a knowing grin, picks up the flow and checks in for the final pleadings. "You're my heart and soul, I still love you so, I wanna thank you, oh oh oh ooh."

The song grinds to a halt and there's the singer shaded by the golden spotlight soaking up the applause - and to his left the guitarist happy and smiling, knowing the joy he has brought to the audience.

And Istanbul surrenders. Just as in the past, Mannheim has surrendered... Sydney has surrendered... Los Angeles has surrendered... Wembley has surrendered... Sheffield has surrendered... You name the location - their music has touched every culture and country they've come into contact with.

Surrendered to the sheer power and glory that these two musicians have been championing for nigh on thirty years. From the earliest days of Led Zeppelin through to this latest and long awaited new incarnation. And right now it still feels and looks so utterly convincing. Dancing Days are here again? Too true they are.

Yes it's been a long time. To be precise, it's been 949 days since I'd last heard that final cry of 'Thank You' ring out aloud. Back then it was in Wembley Arena in July 1995 - the final night of the *Unledded* UK tour. Since then they've gone through some changes... and we have to. Back in January though, the wheels began to roll again with the announcement of an eight-date East European tour.

After considering and discarding various options, Istanbul seemed the best, the seventh night of a tour on which initial reports were enthusiastic, albeit not without some reservations. Like many others I was a little disappointed that the set list structure was very much along the lines of the '95/6 jaunt. On closer inspection there are nine songs performed that I have yet to see Page and Plant play live. I'd been lucky enough to receive an audience video of the Budapest show so I had a good idea of the set list and stage set up. 'Burning Up' and 'Walking Into Clarksdale'? Bring them on...

In the afternoon a press conference is held at the Merit Antique Hotel. The Turkish press are afforded a playback of the album as they await the arrival of the pair. Around 3pm Jimmy and Robert saunter in, apologising for being late and for the next forty-five minutes fend off many inane questions. One of the first is "Where is John Paul Jones?" Understandably this irritates them. "Believe it or not that's not the first time we've been asked that question," replies Plant. Jimmy only becomes interested when someone asks about the Puff Daddy 'Kashmir' project. "We set up a studio satellite link with LA and it sounded really good." At one point, Plant takes a few pictures of the assembled with his own camera.

The venue itself is situated a few miles over the city in the Asian area of Bostanci. And outside there are lengthy queues and much scurrying around. It holds around 4,000 and already there are a number of fans huddled around the front. The audience are a mixture of young Turks grateful for any kind of rock event in their vicinity and older looking fans weaned on *Zep IV*. There's also quite a strong young female presence.

We endure the half hour support act progressive rock (ie what Marillion would sound like if they'd been born in Turkey) which actually goes down well with the locals. There's the usual milling around the stage from the roadies - and it does begin to get very exiting when Jimmy's theremin is tested - and when the guitar tech straps on the Gibson for testing. Finally Robert arrives to

whip the microphone off its stand and strut in regal pose seconds into the opening number 'Wanton Song'.

I get a mental flashback to the sense of awe at the opening of previous Zeppelin events - notably Cologne in 1980. Because this is another rejuvenation.

As they stomp through the opening number it's immediately apparent how much more focused this 1998 set-up is. This is Page and Plant functioning in a four-piece rock band again and boy does it rock. And they look good too. I'd had reservations about Plant's earlier appearance in the tour with the baggy pants, but tonight he looks every inch the veteran star frontman. Long sleeved pattern shirt and leather pants tucked into boots; Page with black T-shirt, perhaps a little paunchier, but hey, this lot have a combined age of 104! It could and maybe should look faintly ridiculous. But somehow it just doesn't. It just looks like it should do - two superb musicians performing with an enthusiasm that simply defies the years.

They don't need to justify being up there. The crowd reaction does that as they leap up and down in time to Robert's pogoing. The opening salvo of 'Wanton Song', 'Bring It On Home', 'Heartbreaker' (first time I've seen that played live since August 4, 1979) is immensely exciting. It's Plant who catches the eye: in 1995 he was often content to hug the mic stand and recoil from those old poses, perhaps rendering them redundant with age. Not tonight. He's up there agile as ever and strutting, mike in hand, with supreme confidence. Jimmy shares that confidence, playing with a fluency that we could only have dreamed of a few years back. It may not be note-perfect and there are a couple of early fluffs but nothing that blows the momentum. The PA sound is also a revelation - crystal clear to enhance the quality of Plant's vocals.

"Good evening Istanbul. Tonight we'd like to do some new songs, some old songs and some hot songs."

'Ramble On' inspires more pogoing down the front - and is still a great tune. There's a switch of guitar (a new addition to the guitar army: a PRS model with tremelo arm) for the new 'Walking Into Clarksdale'; another delight with its rockabilly guitar and deft change of tempo. Here Page lays back and shoots out the first real solo evoking memories of The Yardbirds' latter days with its fluttering style.

The stage lay-out and lighting is much changed from 1995. Gone is the big cloth backdrop. The stage rig relies on the lighting alone to shadow it. The lighting itself is really impressive with clever use of solo spotlights supplemented by on-stage spots that are often used to illuminate the crowd; simple but effective. From our vantage point up on the terracing by the left hand side of the stage it provides many visual flashbacks as the silhouetted figures wallow in the light.

The next number brings a great cheer from the crowd but it seems controversial: the familiar electric keyboard motif of 'No Quarter' played à la Zeppelin circa 1973. In the light of John Paul's absence, opinions might have been divided on the merit of including this but they pull it off very well. Jimmy's solo is very spirit of MSG '73 and his grin seems to confirm his pleasure at dishing that one out again.

The acoustic interlude follows with Plant on a stool and Page sitting down with the acoustic. Keyboard player Phil Andrews supplies the mandolin. 'Going To California' garners a huge audience response and is followed by a wonderfully nostalgic 'Tangerine' (first time I've heard it played live since May 25 1975), Plant off the stool, dragging the mic around. Thankfully Robert avoids the "In olden days" spiel for 'Gallows Pole', opting for the tale of how the song travelled up the Mississippi Delta to the UK. It sounds fresher in a more simplified arrangement than during the '95 tour and both are well animated for the speeded up finale.

It's back to the full force for 'Burning Up' from the new album. Page excels here as he churns out the smouldering riffs that lead the song, and Michael Lee is also impressive, underpinning it all with a solid time honoured tom-tom fills. Only Plant suffers a little - sometimes straining on the chorus although he is supplemented later by what appears to be some sampled backing vocals, as on the album. 'Babe I'm Gonna Leave You' follows and is a real highlight. Faultlessly delivered with all the required dynamics and a

THE *WALKING INTO CLARKSDALE* ALBUM

WANTON SONG
BRING IT ON HOME
HEARTBREAKER
RAMBLE ON
CLARKSDALE
NO QUARTER
CALIFORNIA
TANGERINE
GALLOWS POLE
MOST HIGH
BABE I'M GONNA LEAVE
HOW MANY MORE TIMES
BURNING UP - DIST BASS
WHOLE LOTTA LOVE

BLACK DOG
ROCK & ROLL
THANK YOU

EASTERN EUROPE SET LIST

EASTERN EUROPE TICKET STUBS

This is the last night of the

tour... so let's have some fun.

ROBERT PLANT

twist in the arrangement that allows Page to turn in a very bluesy 'Since I've Been Loving You' type solo.

"Do you like jazz?" asks Plant as they play the Coltrane-like intro of 'How Many More Times'. Now this is really something. They haven't played this in full since 1975 and the audience soak it up, the younger element probably familiar with the song from the recent BBC set. Page wields the violin bow for the eerie middle section before it drifts into 'In The Light' (à la the' Calling To You'/'Whole Lotta Love' medleys of last time out). There's a great moment when they cluster together in 'Achilles'-like tandem before the pressure's back on for the up-tempo ending which again raises the crowd to a frenzy.

"This is our new single, and it's one of my favourite new numbers," announces Plant over the looping Arabic intro to 'Most High'. This is already becoming something of a '98 tour signature tune, Page's revolving guitar riff kick starting them into an infectious trek through some proven ground. It's a track that carries all the pomp and extravagance of past Arabic adventures and the crowd immediately clue in on its infectiousness.

"Thank you for your hospitality in your country - we've got to say goodnight." Page keeps the sparkle Transperformance Gibson on to fire out the riff of 'Whole Lotta Love' whose over-familiarity could easily grate on me but it never fails to have us pumping the air with its barnstorming riff which in turn leads to the Knebworth revamp section "1234 da da da dadadum". Then Page stalks over to the theremin for a final bout of showmanship. Lights up, handshakes, hugs and farewells. Then they are gone.

It starts, a slow rumble first then building to a crescendo: "Zeppelin... Zeppelin... Zeppelin... Zeppelin". The repeated cry goes up. It's along time since I've heard this sort of eager reception.

They return for a beautifully restrained 'Thank You', performed in a new arrangement that finds Page hanging on to every solo. Then there's that great moment of hesitancy before he scrubs out the final run. More exits left, more chanting and then it's welcome to 'Rock And Roll'. ("This is how we say... Oh no not again..."). Page has saved up some energy for this, duck walking across the stage, pausing for a couple of mini-jumps (at least four inches off the ground!) while Robert milks the crowd for the "Lonely lonely" parts. In fact there's one great final visual image: Robert down on one knee, then jumping up and grabbing the mic in a pose that's identical to the Neal Preston photo to be found on page 104 of Cross & Flannigan's *Heaven And Hell*.

"Istanbul Goodnight!"

FRIDAY MARCH 6 1998
Bostanci Centre, Istanbul

Outside a very wet and miserable Bostanci Centre it's evident that there are many more in attendance than the previous night. It's also a younger age group overall and things get a little bit scary when around 8.30 the whole place is plunged into darkness. Heavy pushing and shoving results in a few fans being carried out for medical assistance.

The lights come back on partially. An announcement from the stage informs us that the area has been hit by a power cut and the PA is being powered by an emergency generator (shades of Copenhagen '79). Thankfully the lighting improves and the support act kick off around 9.30. By the time the stage is cleared ready for Page and Plant the arena is packed to overflowing with little room for manoeuvre. I'd say at least 2,000 more are in tonight. Around 10.15 PM the lights go down and we're off again. Page retains the black T-shirt garb; Plant has switched to the dark with white trim T-shirt he'd worn on earlier dates, with the leather trousers.

The show runs very much to last night's structure. If anything Robert's performance is even more impressive. During 'Heartbreaker' he does one classic shimmy across the stage that ignites the crowd into a huge roar. "This is the last night of the tour... so let's have some fun."

On 'Burning Up' he hits the notes perfectly, sparring with Page's trademark licks and riffs. Tonight's crowd offer up most response to 'No Quarter', 'Babe I'm Gonna Leave You' (especially the final 'Stairway' tease) and 'How Many More Times' ("Do you like jazz... liars!"). Robert throws in a quite breathtaking

accapella verse from 'In My Time Of Dying' before the 'In The Light' insert.

'Most High' is also enthusiastically received, spurring Plant to raise the tempo as they hit the finale. Prior to delivering the new single, Plant had welcomed over various record company people who had come here for the weekend. During 'Whole Lotta Love' Jimmy does a quick guitar change mid-song from the red sparkle Trans Gibson to the light brown model.

"We'll try and see you in the summer when we'll play outside and the tickets will be cheaper," explains Robert as they reappear for the encores of 'Thank You' and 'Rock And Roll'. "I guess this is why we've been doing this for 30 years," is Robert's comment as he surveys the adulation. It's obviously a moving moment for him as he hauls up Ross Halfin on stage to photograph the crowd, perhaps for his own picture album.

The usual bows and waves... and the 1998 Eastern European Tour is over.

WEDNESDAY MARCH 11 1998

There have been rumours of a special Page Plant launch gig for the album happening in London for some time. They did attempt to book the Shepherds Bush Empire back in January. Locations in Islington and Kilburn have also been checked out in recent weeks. An early morning fax from the PP PR office confirms that on March 25 they will be playing a special gig at a London venue.

Tickets will be made available on a first come first served basis from 8am on Saturday at the Virgin Megastore in London - limited to just two per person. The London Forum (formerly known as the Town And Country Club where Plant played in the late '80's/ early '90's) is named as the venue - but this is quickly retracted by midday when it becomes official that the gig will now take place at the popular Shepherds Bush Empire.

Jimmy and Robert announce the fact during an excellent early afternoon live interview on the alternative rock London radio station XFM. For me this kick-starts a hive of *TBL* activity as I speedily mail out a stop gap Newsletter Extra and inform many others by phone. It soon becomes apparent that to ensure entry it's going to mean an early morning trip to London to buy tickets. Fellow *TBL* crew member Gary Foy and I plan our strategy. Only 1,000 tickets are going to be sold and as the news spreads it's evident that many fans are making a big effort to get in line.

WEDNESDAY MARCH 25 1998
Shepherds Bush Empire, London

There's no doubt that this particular show at Shepherds Bush Empire has spurred a huge wave of interest and the demand for tickets is staggering. They are recording a *Top Of The Pops* segment at Elstree tomorrow night, and a live appearance on Friday on the popular Channel 4 show *TFI Friday*.

The gig itself is being used by Mercury to launch the new album, with over 800 tickets being made available for European press and media. In the delightfully named Moon On The Green on a grey March afternoon, it's very apparent that this is a very hot ticket. Touts are selling tickets for up to £200. There's a real buzz in the air, this one really does feel like an event.

The excitement mounts as the lights go down inside the theatre, the spotlights flashing on the assembled and the Egyptian music signifying the Page Plant return to London. From my view I can clearly see Jimmy with Gibson strapped on in the darkness at the far side of the stage waiting for the cue and for Robert to fly on as they hit the intro of 'Wanton Song'. And fly on he does, dressed in identical garb to the Istanbul second night, black leather trousers tucked in the boots, dark rimmed T-shirt. 'Bring It On Home', 'Heartbreaker' and 'Ramble On' follow in quick fire succession. Plant may not be quite as immediately vibrant as he was in Istanbul, pacing himself maybe for what's to come. Page, though, is already lighting up the stage, seemingly lost in the noise of his own creating.

"Well the old devils are back," laughs Plant. 'Walking To Clarksdale', featuring Page on the new PRS guitar with McCarty neck follows, complete with that supercharged tempo change and then it's into 'No Quarter'. Here Page drifts through the solo, eyes closed, leaning back.

ISTANBUL: MARCH 5, 1998

So far so good. Then an early magic moment occurs when Page plays a couple of heavily reverbed chords, and those in the know can tell what's coming: the world premiere of a new ballad 'When I Was A Child'. This is masterful as Plant unfolds the reflective tale with ease.

It's always a real privilege to witness a piece of Page Plant history unfolding and that's how it feels as they delicately offer up this new one. There's a great moment right at the close as Robert goes into the final lines "When I was... when I was a..." stepping back from the mic each time as Jimmy's final chords echo around the theatre.

Robert continues a running banter with our own resident *TBL* barrack boy, responding to a shout of "California" as they take to the chairs with "No it's Birkhamstead actually!" They deliver a wonderfully melodic 'Tangerine', causing instant Earl's Court retro lump in the throat for this particular viewer. An urgent stomp through 'Gallows Pole' follows.

From there on in they can really do no wrong. 'Babe I'm Gonna Leave You' enjoys its first UK live airing by the pair for some 29 years. 'Burning Up' is dominated by Page scrubbing out that repeated riff and 'How Many More Times' is just outstanding. I have a perfect view of Page leaning back and stepping on the wah-wah for the intro.

The violin bow episode is greeted by huge cheering and the moment it all speeds up lets Michael Lee prove his worth yet again. 'Most High' is next as we hit the home straight. A cocksure 'Whole Lotta Love' signals the end of the main proceedings.

Then they're back on and it's another premiere, an incessant drum track booms out and then Page holds down the most delightfully grunge like wah-wah for 'House Of Love'. This one really swings live with Plant screeching out the chorus line "It's just a little too much", and Page hitting those descending chords. A 'Sick Again' for the millennium. "So this is the alternative to Radio Two," laughs Robert. "It's been great, thank you!"

They're back on again and Page begins pumping out some fast urgent lines. For one minute I thought this was going to swing into 'Sons Of Freedom' from the new album, instead it heads into a blistering rendering of 'Crossroads' performed in a similar arrangement to the Cream version. Finally we get an emotional 'Thank You' which has Page again taking on the solo in his own time and Plant commenting at the close "Just some silly old buggers singing some love songs!" 'Rock And Roll' then inspires the best reaction from a London crowd I've heard since... well you name it... They take a bow and exit right.

THURSDAY MARCH 26 1998
Top Of The Pops, Elstree
A dull and wet Elstree at 7pm on a Thursday for the special recording of Page and Plant on BBC's *Top Of The Pops*. That's right, *Top Of The Pops*, the programme on which Led Zeppelin stoutly refused to appear, yet which nevertheless featured 'Whole Lotta Love' (in a big band rock version) as its theme tune of throughout the Seventies and beyond.

They are filming tonight for what will be an exclusive live performance insert in the coming weeks of their new single 'Most High'. Radio One gave out a phone number to call for tickets. The regular *Top Of The Pops* has already been filmed earlier in the evening, and we wait to gain access to the studio.

After nearly three hours of waiting we are led into the small studio. A small stage set up with a cut down Page amp run (one Fender amp, two cabs and oddly, the theremin set up) features a large Jimmy Page Robert Plant logo on the actual floor which will no doubt be captured by the overhead camera.

A pair of warm up announcers relay instructions. "We want you to make the most amazing noise possible when they come on." To get us in the mood, the studio version of 'Rock And Roll' is played. The rent-a-crowd behind me push forward, giving me a splendid vantage point right in front of Jimmy. Last night was close, but hey, how much closer can you get?

'Rock And Roll' fades and on they walk, Robert wearing the long sleeve shirt he had on at the first Istanbul concert, Jimmy his first noticeable change of clothes on the tour - pin stripe trousers and a nice dark silk shirt sensibly worn outside the strides. They move forward, shaking out stretched hands at the front. I had wondered if they were going to do a mime playback to 'Most High'. From the moment Jimmy slugs out the opening chords I know I couldn't have been more wrong. This is most definitely live and we are most definitely high!

From Istanbul via Shepherds Bush to Elstree. 'Most High' has travelled a bit in the last few weeks and now, here at 10.10 on a Thursday evening, not far off the *East Enders* set, it sounds a very British experience despite the ethnic feel. To the left Phil Andrews adds the oriental keyboard solo as Jimmy turns to Michael Lee to add some rough-shod rhythm.

It's all over too soon, and what we want is a little bit more. Robert looks over to Jimmy and nods. "Here's a new one from our latest tablet of stone," laughs Robert. The backing drum track of 'House Of Love' duly rolls out but hold it – Jimmy has a problem. He waves his arms. "No hold it - I can't see my cue!" It would seem

Just some silly old buggers

singing some love songs!

ROBERT PLANT

the cameramen leaping in and out of them has covered the cue sheet that rolls on one of the monitors. Second take and they're off. This is turning into a great live number with Robert's "It's just a little too much' refrain' incessantly hitting home.

More milling around on stage ensures... will they or won't they? They will! Jimmy goes off to change his sweat soaked shirt. He returns wearing an Abbey Road T-shirt. Meantime, Robert enjoys some banter with the crowd. "Wolves for the cup," shouts one wag. "You don't mean that!" he laughs. "Where's Pans People?" (the all girl dance troupe the programme featured years back) is another cry that inspires a laugh on stage.

Jimmy reappears and Robert explains the origins of the next number. "OK here's one that was written even before we were born." A compact run through 'Crossroads' follows. At the close Jimmy holds the Gibson aloft, and even before he has had time to finish the song a member of the audience jumps on stage to shake his hand, to be followed (a little foolishly) by a handful of others who hug Robert and add to the on-stage chaos. Fearing "Zeppelin stars in stage riot at *Top Of The Pops*" headlines assorted roadies disperse the crowd and Jimmy and Robert lead off. It would seem the mini invasion has curtailed anything else they might have been planning.

"Well that was absolutely fucking brilliant!" shouts the announcer back on stage. Are they doing anymore... hold on, no, that's if for tonight. Thanks for coming!"

FRIDAY MARCH 27 1998
TFI Friday, London

And so it goes on. This week really is turning into one of, if not the most, memorable Zeppelin related since Earl's Court and today it's Friday so it must be *TFI Friday*, the immensely popular music show hosted by the incredulous Chris Evans and scripted by big Zep fan Danny Baker. Page and Plant were announced for the show a couple of weeks back.

A studio announcer runs us through proceedings and gets the rules out of the way. We've got to keep smiling and dancing throughout whichever band is on. "I know a lot of you are here to see one special act," says the man to a huge cheer. Before long it's ready to roll, red light on and cue the music.

Chris Evans is giving the programme run down... he's already making a big thing of Page and Plant being on - and as he's doing that, it all starts happening down the front. Tim, Charlie and Michael are in position, Jimmy climbs up to the stage and straps on the Gibson. Robert hugs the mike waiting for the cue. Jimmy retains the pin stripe trousers and reverts to the black T-shirt; Robert has a similar T-shirt on to Wednesday, but opts for the baggier trousers similar to those worn early on the Eastern Europe dates. "They sold 100 million albums... second only to The Beatles and Woolworths! They raised rock on high, they juggled both Led and Zeppelin... and they're here now, and now with 'Rock And Roll' here are Jimmy Page and Robert Plant!"

A nd it bloody well is - right in front of our eyes. How close can it get! Bedlam follows as we rock it up with them, Jimmy looking supremely confident as he struts around; Robert mike off within a minute - all the old poses. It's absolutely glorious.

Three and half sweat soaked minutes later and they finish to rapturous cheers. "Led Zeppelin!" proclaims Evans. "Led Zeppelin's 'Rock And Roll' by Mr Jimmy Page and Mr Robert Plant!"

The rest of the show follows - we nod along to The Smiles and Divine Comedy, cheer to a montage of Gary Lineker's goals that are shown during his interview and get well excited every time Evans mentions Page and Plant – every time he does, the riff of 'Whole Lotta Love' is played, inspiring mass air guitar movements from Evans and those in the bar. After an interview with *Full Monty* star Paul Barber (who says he's a fan) it's time to welcome Page and Plant for their interview. We see them walk along the gantry into the bar. The interview is excellent. Plant has a Wolves scarf tied around his wrist and comments dryly that "Old men do it better!" in reply to Evan's question on how they keep it up. Evans brings in Steve from Manchester, a fan who had rung into to his radio show in the morning. (The popular Virgin Radio show had turned into a 45-minute spontaneous Zeppelin showcase.) He

asks about the chronological live album. "Yeah it could happen in the future," replies Page. Jimmy is really good-humoured throughout the interview, reflecting the fun they seem to be having. Chris manages to get their names mixed up in his own excitement (Robert Page and Jimmy Plant) and asks a question faxed by Jeremy Clarkson: "Is it true you once cancelled a tour due to the hose pipe ban," gets a hoot of laughter from Plant. "That's a good one!" Plant also does his own Midlands accent describing how the Wolves fans comment to him, "Alright Planty, still doing a bit then!"

Down on stage the cameras have been moved allowing us the ultimate vantage position right under Plant's monitor. How close can you get! (again). Evans introduces the finale, "Page and Plant playing the new single 'Most High'." Charlie and Michael kick into a riff as the boys climb down the stairs and up on to the stage.

Our signature tune kicks in yet again, Page's guitar sound pure and clear as he strikes the strings just feet away is just awe inspiring. Robert meanwhile wheels the mike stand around, narrowly avoiding the top of our heads. On the solo oriental part Jimmy crunges out the most amazing riffs, leading where the oriental part usually leads. And then the finale - with Plant extending the lyrics (rolling up on the monitor in front of us incidentally) and it's over. Huge cheers, big smiles. They've done it once again.

Even some of the younger fans here for The Divine Comedy picked up on the vibe. It feels so good to be part of it, knowing that a UK audience of four million are about to see it on the small screen themselves.

Outside Riverside Studios, Robert emerges to applause and walks along with his five-year-old son Jesse. Eventually he climbs into his gold 500s Mercedes, pausing to make a call on his mobile, and drives off with Jesse in the back, bound for the Midlands and a Sunday rendezvous at Molineux for Wolves against Portsmouth. Jimmy is in an upstairs hospitality room behind Cedric's Cafe. A swelling crowd of well wishers, press photographers and autograph hunters await. Eventually he strolls out looking very relaxed happy to sign for all and sundry, posing with a small child and parents. Then he's driven off in a blacked-out car.

PART TWO

August was going to be a busy month. Page and Plant had already been confirmed as headliners for the Friday, August 28, Reading bill with additional European festival dates lined up alongside a date at Dublin's The Point two days before Reading.

WEDNESDAY AUGUST 26 1998
Dublin, The Point

It's pretty hectic down the front but stimulating to say the least as they leap into the set with abandon. No major changes early on, the initial highlights being a very fluent 'No Quarter and the standout moment of the set 'Shining In The Light'. This for me has entered the category that might loosely be dubbed "The new Zeppelin canon". It's the sort of thing that would have lit up the 1981 Zeppelin album had it been written then. And they perform it tonight with such spark, Plant with mic off and Jimmy skipping around towards the speeded-up finale.

'Heart In Your Hand' also shines tonight despite its low key nature. It's sung intensely by Plant as if he is living every aching word. 'Babe' is its usual dynamic self and 'How Many More Times' swaggers along with an extended 'In The Light' middle section. 'Most High' is just that and there's a no nonsense finale leaden with the classics that are 'Whole Lotta Love', 'Black Dog' and 'Rock And Roll'.

"Maybe we'll see you at one of those weddings," is one of Plant's final comments to the crowd - a reference to the informal live appearance they had made three weeks earlier in Co. Kerry at lighting designer Tom Kenny's wedding.

Witnessing this show it's apparent that there is now a real consistency of performance. Some 46 gigs along the way, this Page Plant tour has reached a real peak. In the current edition of *Mojo*, Matt Snow remarked that Page and Plant might well be the most exiting live rock band on the planet right now. Tonight in Dublin that statement can be uttered with absolute conviction.

On the way out I see a guy who had been proclaiming The Edge as his hero earlier. "You were right!" he shouts, "Jimmy Page is the one!"

FRIDAY AUGUST 28 1998
Reading Festival
Luckily the weather is favourable, not over sunny but no sign of rain. So anticipation is high as we mingle with the crowd underneath the giant stage. An American fan nearby is telling how effective they were when he caught up with the show in Philadelphia in the summer. "When did you last see them?" he asks... "Er, two days ago actually," is my unintended conceited reply. Underneath the stars, the familiar Egyptian music booms out, they stride on and with no messing we are into 'Wanton Song'. Adorned in familiar dark attire they look fit and eager to fulfil their bill topping status.

"We're in the presence of legends!" is one excited teenagers repeated cry behind me. By the time they've romped into 'Heartbreaker' one thing clearly strikes me. This is a clear case of men against boys. I mean, really. For all the good intentions of the others on the bill, the experience and sheer power that these old veterans convey is startling. It makes for a great couple of hours. Sadly 'Shining In The Light' is dropped in favour of 'Burning Up' though it's good to hear that again. The video screens to the left and right of the stage convey some great images, causing a shiver down the spine and clear memories of Knebworth when the violin bow appears to the left of me, high and mighty on the big screen. A 'Babe I'm Gonna Leave You' that touches the nerve ends and a

sure fire 'How Many More Times' with a regal sounding 'What Is' insert, 'Whole Lotta Love' and encores of 'Black Dog' and 'Rock And Roll' are duly delivered in stadium filling soundscape mode. The reception across the darkness confirms that this has been a very shrewd decision. Reading rocked and it was great to be there to witness it.

And to top it all Wolves have taken the points at Watford as Plant remarks "It's 2-0 down at Vicarage Road."

PRE-UK TOUR AUTUMN SUMMARY
There's absolutely no let up as we move into the autumn. The rumour machine has been in overdrive with news of secret warm-up dates slated for Brighton, Wolverhampton Civic Hall, Oxford... you name it.

In amongst all the rumours there are plans for P&P to do some sort of show to tie in with a new sponsorship deal with Molson beer in Canada.

FRIDAY OCTOBER 30 1998
University of London, London
"Tomorrow it's Barnsley at home," Robert Plant.

Some days are very special in the Zep related scheme of things, and this is definitely one of them. Aside from the events that will unfold in London tonight - at home in the morning I take a call from John Paul Jones, interviewing him for Record Collector.

The gig itself is at the University Of London Union. The audience is made up of about 300 Canadians who have scooped a prize to see Page and Plant in London, courtesy of Molson Beer.

SHEPHERDS BUSH EMPIRE: MARCH 25, 1998

The remaining 200 are made up of various record company staff and invited guests.

The hall is situated deep inside the University building, it consists of a main stage and an open plan hall that would accommodate only the first front block of Wembley Arena.

Down the front there are a few Canadians milling around. Few of them seem to be hard core fans and they are pretty laid back about it, though the presence of the English contingent soon ups the enthusiasm. In a year when I've enjoyed some very close associations in front of Page and Plant, this is an incredibly exciting way to round it all off. The place reminds me of the set-up at Leicester University when Plant played a warm up there back in January '88. I consider that night one of the best evenings of live music I've ever witnessed. Tonight could be similar.

There's a short pre-announcement from one of the University staff... and then, with no fanfare or Egyptian music, on they walk. "Welcome to the party," says Robert as he adjusts the mic. Plant is in a light blue and white striped long sleeved shirt worn outside, Page in black, and it's straight into 'Wanton Song'. It was like seeing them at the local youth club. They might have performed slicker shows along the way but for sheer in-your-face out-an-out live experience this really was special. The fact that they get lost a little half way through 'Heartbreaker' matters little - this is spontaneous rock'n'roll, warts and all.

Watching Jimmy ring every last note out of the 'No Quarter' solo inspires simultaneous "Best since Earl's Court" exclamations from Phil T and myself. 'When The World Was Young' is a stand out. From the first moment I heard it on the album this one

You...'. Wrong. Come in 'Misty Mountain Hop', played for the first time since the opening night in the US back in May. A quick tune up from Jimmy and 'Trampled Underfoot', its first complete airing by Page and Plant since Hammersmith in 1988. And there's new life in the old dog as Plant immediately takes up the challenge - throwing in a classic clenched fist shape each time the riff rolls around. A glorious noise to behold.

And if that wasn't enough here comes an epic speech: "This is a new song, well not new, it's just that we've never done it before and it's incredibly old and there are bits of it we're not liking that much yet... so we'll see what happens!"

Very soon I can trace out that revolving riff that lit up the opening track on side four of *Physical Graffiti* all those years ago. Robert's opening line confirms it − "I received the message from my brother 'cross the water he sat laughing as he wrote the end's in sight."

A piece of Zeppelin history unfolds as Page and Plant perform the first ever a live version of 'Night Flight'. Always one of my all time faves, I've waited nigh on 24 years to hear them play it on stage. Bedlam ensures. 'Rock And Roll' follows in a blur and they're off. Not before Robert has reminded us that tomorrow is match day. "Thank you very much... it's Barnsley at home tomorrow."

TUESDAY NOVEMBER 3 1998
Manchester, Evening News Arena
"It's just another day... this one's for the budgies," Robert Plant.

After the intimacy of the ULU it's quite a shock to be in the cavernous surrounds of the Evening News Arena, but it's a smart

THE FINAL SHOW, AMNESTY INTERNATIONAL, BERCY PARIS: DECEMBER 10, 1998

begged for live performance and like all their great live deliveries they adapt it by adding various delightful twists and turns. Plant's repeated "Wohoa" refrains before the chorus (not unlike the vocal "aha-ah" effect on 'Achilles') and Jimmy's extended solo puts this track right up there with the best musical moments of the whole Page Plant reformation. The way the solo swells up and then levitates, spiralling upwards and out in a manner that was only hinted at on the album is simply awe inspiring.

Other notable moments: 'Going To California' with it's '32-20 Blues' insert, an intense 'Heart In Your Hand', 'Babe I'm Gonna Leave You' which has Plant nearly missing a cue and a strange incident when part of the lighting rig drops next to Charlie, much to Plant's amusement. There's also a stomping 'How Many More Times' with 'Boom Boom' insert. When they march off stage you get the feeling that there may be some set list surprises on the way.

And surprises there certainly were. When Phil Andrews takes to the keyboard when they come back on I was expecting 'Thank

place. Transglobal Underground have just finished their set and it's down the front for what is becoming a familiar ritual.

Plant stomps on in black short sleeve shirt, Page back to the black sweat shirt. The sound is well up to scratch - the real revelation tonight is Robert who seems in a very good mood and very talkative. In fact he's in one of those great spieling moods that were such a part of Zeppelin, and even unfolds a strange tale of supporting budgerigars in Manchester years back. "Back in the Sixties Jimmy played here with The Yardbirds, and somebody was telling me in the hotel today that they saw me at the Princes Domino social club in between performing budgerigars and female impersonators. Not much has changed. We've still got the female impersonators - and the budgerigars we'll play with later!"

He will return to the budgie theme again during the gig, rather like the *Badgeholders* in LA 1977. Plant's jovial mood ups the enjoyment level considerably - it's a shame he doesn't come out with this sort of banter more often. I also spot a new mic technique during the solos in 'Clarksdale', nonchalantly throwing it over his back and swaying around the stage.

"This is a song we intended to write in 1968," is Plant's slightly cryptic intro to 'When The World Was Young'. Page takes the Gibson cherry red and in my enthusiasm for this piece I manage to bash the guy next to me on the head.

Things are a bit calmer for 'California' ("I don't know if it was a leaning to budgerigars that made us write this next song – one thing's for sure – it's been played in Manchester before"), and 'Tangerine' and after the well-received 'Gallows', they play 'Heart In Your Hand'. Plant's phrasing reminds me of the late great Frank Sinatra at times and Jimmy's strung out lines eerily echo across the stage.

There are some minor set list variations. During the "Oh baby" finale of 'Babe I'm Gonna Leave You', Plant wanders into lyrics from 'If I Were A Carpenter', the 'Stairway' tease receives a rapturous applause. 'How Many More' times leads into the excellent 'That's The Way' with Jimmy strumming the sort of minor key changes that used to light up the likes of 'Woodstock' and 'San Francisco' way back.

Another Plant observation: "You may wonder why we still do this? Well we really kick ass up here, there are journalists who will no doubt use that as a headline." (Which the Manchester *Evening News* duly roll out the next day.)

Then it's a grand welcome back for the mad March anthem 'Most High' which once again confirms its more than successful transition from studio mediocrity to on stage rouser. A compact 'Whole Lotta Love' which finds Page deploying minimum use of the theremin takes us out.

They're back on soon enough, "Thanks a lot folks... it's just another day." Disappointingly there's no 'Night Flight' or 'Trampled' or 'Misty' tonight but there is a great return for 'Thank You', sung with the now expected conviction. "Here's one for the budgies!" 'Rock And Roll' closes proceedings and Plant's predominantly good mood continues to his final stage action, signing off with an enthusiastic "Suck it!" after Michael's extended flurry.

THURSDAY NOVEMBER 5 1998
Wembley Arena

The London crowd has its drawbacks - there's always a bit of the 'go on then entertain me' attitude. Tonight's crowd are pretty receptive but down the front there's little of the friendliness of Dublin or good natured banter of Manchester. The set is something of a disappointment for those expecting any real deviation. Robert also lacks the rapport that he seemed keen to develop in Manchester.

There is, however, one reflective comment early on when he tells the audience, "Well it's been a long time since the performing pigs and the high wire all for 15 shillings. But it's still happening here." It was back in 1971 when Zep performed here supported by various circus acts.

Overall, the performance is acceptable if not exceptional. 'Clarksdale' finds Plant adopting his swinging mic technique. 'Heart In Your Hand' is again superbly performed with Page's final chord ringing out across the arena. "It's been a long time since the performing pigs and highwires," states Plant in a rare moment of reflection. The insert for 'How Many More Times' is a piercing 'Season Of The Witch'. The encores line up as 'Black Dog' and 'Rock And Roll'. By their standards it's an average night - although most of those in attendance will not have noticed that. Perhaps that's one disadvantage of seeing a few shows close together.

FRIDAY NOVEMBER 6 1998
Wembley Arena

For a Wembley crowd the atmosphere is excellent, the Egyptian intro being greeted with a huge roar. And there they are. Page, no surprise in black; Plant back to the black short sleeved shirt.

From the opening blast you can feel that they are up for this one, Plant's mood perhaps evident from the tying of a Wolves scarf next to the amp. To add to our delight there are also several set list variations, the first of which is a superbly applied take on 'What Is And What Should Never Be' occupying the space normally reserved for 'Ramble On'.

The absolute stand-out performance comes with 'When The World Was Young', which is perhaps the best musical moment of this whole 1998 adventure. The reason is simple. Jimmy Page approaches the solo with all the on-the-brink fluency of the '77 'Over The Hills'. It's much extended from its studio counterpart as the man scratches out new plains of abstract beauty from the cherry red Gibson.

There he is strutting around with such unforced passion and joy, turning to Robert for the final chorus in a scene reminiscent of the classic 'Achilles' pose of old. From there, 'California' and 'Tangerine' both enjoy a huge reception, as does the crowd pleasing stomp of 'Gallows Pole'.

There's also a very welcome return for the powerful 'When I Was A Child', a highlight of Shepherds Bush which again finds Plant in superb voice, meandering away from the mic to deliver the final lines. The good times keep on coming. 'If I Were A Carpenter' is back in the break of 'Babe', 'Most High' rocks furiously with Plant offering one of those great raised key vocal effects for the verse, "Where are the words of the king who moves the stars and the sun".

'Down By The Seaside' enjoys another revival in 'How Many...' and after 'Whole Lotta Love' they're back for the first encore, a spirited 'Misty Mountain Hop' quickly followed by the re-scheduling of 'Ramble On'. Finally, it's a second encore and in a fitting finale it's a most welcomed reprise of 'Night Flight', perhaps baffling some of the audience, but those in the know heeding its significance. Then it's 'Rock And Roll', then Plant takes up the Wolves scarf off the amp and they're gone. The 1998 UK tour is over.

THE ULU INVITE

WALKING INTO EVERYWHERE
GIG BREAKDOWN

Europe First Leg	**11** shows	December 7 1997	to	March 30 1998
US First Leg	**34** shows	May 19 1998	to	July 19 1998
Europe Second Leg	**5** shows	August 6 1998	to	August 28 1998
US Second Leg	**17** shows	September 5 1998	to	October 2 1998
Europe 3rd Leg	**22** shows	October 30 1998	to	December 10 1998
Total	**89** shows	*(Note: US list includes 2 Canadian shows)*		

NUMBER OF GIGS PER COUNTRY

Austria **1**	Belgium **1**	Bulgaria **1**	Canada **2**	Croatia **2**	Czech Republic **2**
Eire **2**	France **8**	Germany **5**	Hungary **1**	Italy **1**	Liechtenstein **1**
Poland **1**	Rumania **1**	Switzerland **1**	Turkey **2**	UK **8**	USA **49**

Note: List includes concert appearances only. TV appearances not included.

NUMBER OF TIMES SONG PERFORMED

88 Rock And Roll	**87** Babe I'm Gonna…	**87** Gallows Pole
86 Most High	**86** Wanton Song	**86** Heartbreaker
86 How Many…	**86** No Quarter	**86** Walking Into…
83 Going To C'fornia	**81** Tangerine	**81** Ramble On
77 Whole Lotta Love	**68** Heart In Your Hand	**66** Bring It on Home
48 Thank You	**39** When The World…	**29** Shining In The Light
20 What Is And…	**19** Black Dog	**17** Burning Up
10 When I Was A Child	**6** Misty Mountain Hop	**5** Celebration Day
5 Crossroads	**4** Night Flight	**3** Trampled Underfoot
1 House Of Love	**1** In The Evening	**1** I've Got A Woman
1 Baby Please Don't Go	**1** I'm Goin' Down	**1** Mystery Train
1 Unidentified Blues…	**1** Move It	**1** Over The Hills…

SONGS DRAWN FROM

Led Zeppelin I **2**	Led Zeppelin II **6**	Led Zeppelin III **3**
Fourth Album **4**	Houses Of The Holy **1**	Physical Graffit **3**
Presence **0**	In Through The Out Door **1**	Walking Into Clarksdale **8**
Others **6**		

Note: List includes full songs only performed – does not include inserts into How Many More Times.

Many thanks to Paul Sheppard for this information.

WALKING INTO EVERYWHERE TOUR OVERVIEW

In line with the overview of the *Unledded* tour featured in *TBL 12*, I compiled a similar round up for the 1998 tour. It again singles out the best individual song performances for an imaginary CD compilation.

The 1998 *Walking Into Everywhere* Page & Plant tour finally wound up in Paris on December 10. It ended a nigh on year long jaunt that had seen them perform 89 gigs in 18 countries. The stripped down four-piece line up made for a much punchier show than that experienced on the 1995/6 *No Quarter/Unledded* tour.

Back then the embellishment of the Egyptian Ensemble created a different texture to the song arrangements, very successful in their own way but sometimes watering down the sheer fire power of old. For the *Walking Into Everywhere* tour Jimmy and Robert made a conscious effort to get back to basics. In going out as a four piece with occasional input from Phil Andrews, the focus was a direct throwback to the formula that worked so well in Zeppelin. From the first few dates in Eastern Europe, it was evident that these were going to be very powerful and intense on stage performances. It was a trend that continued throughout the next few months.

When we left the tour in *TBL13*, Page & Plant were about to embark on the first leg of the US tour which opened in Pensocola on May 19. Some 34 dates were played, mainly one stop arena shows with Lili Hayden as support. The set list for this leg stayed much in line with the Eastern European tour, the only variations being the addition of the excellent 'Shining In The Light', 'Heart In Your Hand' (alternated with 'When I Was A Child'), and the occasional appearance of 'Black Dog' as an encore. There were reports of soundcheck run-throughs for 'Sons Of Freedom' and 'Tea For One', though neither song made it in to the shows.

'How Many More Times' remained the main vehicle for mid-song improvising with fragments of the following appearing at random during this part of the tour: 'Down By The Seaside'/'I Can't Quit You Baby'/'Killing Floor'/'Mystery Train'/'Season Of The Witch'/'What Is And What Should Never Be'/'That's The Way'/'Morning Dew'/'Nobody's Fault But Mine'/'In My Time Of Dying'/'We're Gonna Groove'/'For What It's Worth'/'In The Light'/'Spoonful' and 'For Your Life'.

The main gripe of the whole tour surrounded the unchanging nature of the set list. There was little of the off-the-cuff spontaneity of some of the '95/96 nights, and little was left to chance as they stuck rigidly to the standard set list formula. This was acceptable for the average fan who only went to one show, but displeasing for the keener fans who took in a series of gigs and voiced their feelings on the internet. It remains a mystery why they can shake up the set list nightly over the space of ten shows back in Japan in 1996 but offer little variation over a whole tour.

Looking back to the Zeppelin latter era there is a parallel to be drawn from 1973 onwards the Zeppelin set was rarely prone to change. I guess the attraction then was how the songs were stretched and elongated as the mood took them. It also remains a disappointment that 'Blue Train', the generally accepted highlight of the *Walking Into Clarksdale* album, was never performed live.

The album itself proved to be a short lived success in the US, entering the top ten but - even with the aid of the tour - quickly disappearing from the *Billboard* chart, failing to cross over and gather many new converts. Overall there was not quite the same fervour of interest in 1998 compared to the 1995 visit.

The novelty of the *Unledded* reunion had worn off and while the tour grossed a handsome income (around £15m by the year's end), there were plenty of reports of some venues failing to sell out, a trend also apparent during some of the Europe dates in the fall.

Despite the sterility of the set list, the quality of the performances remained consistent, earning them some very favourable press reviews and generally enthusiastic response from those who witnessed it. At this stage of the tour Jimmy and Robert, although enduring the very hot American summer climate, seemed to be enjoying themselves as much as ever, Jimmy in particular raising his standard to a point where it was no real surprise at the consistency of his performance.

READING FESTIVAL: AUGUST 28, 1998

We might have had some misgivings about his abilities in '95. Not so in 1998 where he was in his element night after night. The US tour wound up with an intense performance at the Jones Beach Theatre on Long Island - according to Page, one of their very best shows.

After a short break they were back on the road in August for European festival dates in Liechtenstein, a very wet Bizarre Festival in Cologne (later aired in full on the on the German WDR TV station) and the Friday bill topping appearance at the Reading Festival. For the condensed festival sets they performed a truncated 'How Many More Times' that segued into 'Whole Lotta Love'. They also played two dates in Dublin, the first a non-public performance on August 6 at the Drumquinna Hotel, County Kerry, for the wedding reception of their lighting tech Tom Kenny. This produced an off the wall set list that read 'I've Got A Woman'/'Crossroads'/unidentified blues/'Baby Please Don't Go'/'Rock And Roll'/'Mystery Train'.

On August 26 they played a superb show at The Point Dublin. Ex-Zepp publicist BP Fallon was in attendance, reviewing the show for the *Sunday Independent*. He commented: "Hell I was nervous. In my heart I didn't want the gig to be good. I wanted it to be brilliant. And it was. Absolutely outstandingly roof liftingly brilliant."

On September 5 they kicked off the second leg of the US tour in Vancouver. This leg took a further 17 dates, winding up in Memphis on October 2. For this segment, 'Shining In the Light' was replaced by another *Clarksdale* favourite 'When The World Was Young'. 'What Is And What Should Never Be' and 'Celebration Day' were occasional set list additions. The delivery of 'Going To California' was enhanced by an insert from Robert Johnson's '32 20 Blues'.

There were some great performances during this period, in particular the September 21 San Diego show where 'Trampled Underfoot' was the surprise insertion in 'How Many More Times'. The New Orleans show on October 1 was recorded for broadcast by Westwood One.

A little under a month later the UK leg of the tour kicked off with the special Molson gig at the tiny ULU in London. This proved to be an extraordinary occasion with encores providing some long awaited surprises. 'Misty Mountain Hop', 'Trampled Underfoot' and a premiere for 'Night Flight' elevated this gig to classic status.

1998 TOUR BOOTLEGS -
LAS VEGAS: SEPTEMBER 23 AND
NEW ORLEANS: OCTOBER 1

With support from Transglobal Underground, Glasgow and Manchester followed and then it was Wembley Arena where the second show on November 6 provided another tour high. It's worth noting that they came in for some justified criticism for playing so few UK shows (particularly when compared to Europe), Birmingham being a notable omission.

Finally the tour took in a further 17 dates in Europe, officially ending at the Frankfurt Festhalle on December 3. 'Night Flight', 'Misty Mountain Hop' and 'Trampled Underfoot' were periodically employed as encores. Inserts into 'How Many More Times' included 'Fever' (Efert/Frankfurt), and a first time out since Frankfurt 1980 for 'Money' (Gent/Belgium). The version of 'Whole Lotta Love' performed at the Frankfurt show included a short burst of 'Train Kept A Rollin''.

At short notice they were then added to the bill of the Amnesty International benefit gig at the Bercy in Paris. Here they performed a 37-minute mini set ('Most High'/'Ramble On'/'When The World Was Young'/'Babe I'm Gonna Leave You'/'Gallows Pole'/'Rock And Roll') preceding Radiohead's headlining appearance. This spurred Radiohead's manager to comment "Blimey now I know we've made it - we had Led Zeppelin as a support act!"

1998 DREAM 3-CD COMPILATION

So ended another chapter in their history. The *Walking Into Everywhere* tour proved to be a huge success. It saw them put the real power back into their music and bring the evolution of Led Zeppelin full circle, recalling the spark and chemistry of where it all began for Jimmy Page and Robert Plant over thirty years ago.

There's more than enough reason therefore to store the memories permanently. To that end what follows is an imaginary 3-CD compilation of the best moments of the second Page & Plant tour. You may recall I attempted a similar exercise in *TBL 12*. The criteria is as before: to compile in chronological order from the various sources available a series of hypothetical 70-minute CDs that offer a balanced overview of the tour, taking in the best performances of all principal songs aired along the way, plus a selection of off the cuff inserts that lit up 'How Many More Times'.

This is *The Evolution of Led Zeppelin Vol 2*, perhaps the concluding episode in the recent post *Unledded* Page and Plant alliance.

CD1

'Move It'/'Over The Hills And Far Away'
Cafe De Paris, December 7, 1997
It all started with this low key appearance at the Senior Tennis Tournament aftershow charity bash. "Please absolutely no photographs," warned Pat Cash during his introduction. "There are three all time great singer songwriters. McCartney & Lennon, Jagger & Richard, but in my opinion the best of them all... Robert Plant and Jimmy Page. Welcome!"

From the moment Plant squealed out the line "Let me tell yer baby it's called rock'n' roll" during their cover of Cliff's 'Move It', it was evident they had lost none of their ability to slip effortlessly into that timeless vintage rock'n'roll mode that had lit up so many moments of their past.

A relaxed stroll through 'Over The Hills And Far Away' followed - surprisingly a number they would not return to for the tour. Rehearsals were booked - and Eastern Europe beckoned.

'In The Evening'
Dom Sportova Zagreb, February 21, 1998
A staple part of the 1995/6 tour, 'In The Evening' was employed just once in 1998 - the opening night in Zagreb. Minus the Egyptian influence, it returned to the more basic structure used for the Zeppelin outings. For some reason they decided to drop it from the set thereafter, alleviating this delivery to rare one off '98 status.

'Wanton Song'/'Bring It On Home'/'Heartbreaker'/'Ramble On'
Winter Palace Of Sports Sofia, March 2, 1998
Their ability to gel as a basic four-piece was a striking factor of the

first few nights of the tour. The direct approach added more fuel to the already proven power of the opening salvo of numbers. There may have been little variation throughout the tour in the opening structure of the set, but the sheer conviction with which it was expressed, particularly in 'Heartbreaker', was indication that they meant business. Sofia surrendered.

'Thank You'
Bostanci Centre Istanbul March 5 1998
A memorable stop off in Istanbul continued the momentum. 'Thank You' was to be a familiar and consistent part of the *Walking* tour. Performed in a slightly differing arrangement with Page hanging on to every solo and that great moment of hesitancy before he scrubbed out the final run.

'In My Time of Dying'/'In The Light' ('How Many More Times Insert')
Bostanci Centre Istanbul March 6 1998
Early indication that the middle section of 'How Many More Times' would be employed for all manner of improvised fun. On the second night in Istanbul Robert drifted into the *Physical Graffiti* blockbuster, by my reckoning for the first time with Jimmy since the 'Rip It Up' delivery in LA on June 25 1977. Superbly sung in semi acappella style, it then drifted into 'In The Light'. Another part of Zeppelin's heritage restored

'Walking Into Clarksdale'/'House of Love'/'Crossroads'
Shepherds Bush Empire, March 25, 1998
This London showcase will be remembered as one of the very best nights of the post Zep era. Having honed the show in Eastern Europe they were really on fire. Despite the fact that the album was still a month off release, the title track was generously received (by the way - listen for my excited "whooh!" captured right after Robert's introduction on the official CD single). The encores provided a couple of rarities. The only in-concert performance of 'House Of Love' led by Michael Lee's incessant drum track and a speedy trek through the rarely played 'Crossroads'.

'We're Gonna Groove' ('HMMT' insert)/'Most High'
La Cigale Paris, March 30, 1998
Five days later in Paris they reproduced their London form in similar intimate surroundings. The old 1970 stager 'We're Gonna Groove' was affectionately plucked from the Zep juke box, highlighted by a scintillating Page solo. 'Most High', meanwhile, was already staking its claim as the tour signature tune. "In a desperate attempt to win new friends and influence people below the ages of 90 we have a new single that relates to our friends in the East," was Robert's tongue-in-cheek introduction.

'Morning Dew' ('HMMT' insert)
Coliseum, Jacksonville, May 23, 1998
'Mystery Train' ('HMMT' insert)
Civic Center, Birmingham, Alabama, June 1, 1998
A pair of one off impromptu inserts to 'How Many More Times'. In Jacksonville, Plant fondly recalled the old Tim Rose tune 'Morning Dew', later to feature on his *Dreamland* album. In Birmingham, Alabama, it was an authentic run through Elvis' 'Mystery Train', a number they performed in similar impromptu style on the last ever Zeppelin US gig in Oakland on July 24, 1977.

CD2

'No Quarter'
Civic Center, Birmingham, Alabama, June 1, 1998
Performing the Jonesy showpiece in a classic Zeppelin arrangement was always going to be controversial choice. Sacred ground or not, it worked very well indeed with Jimmy recreating the spirit of 73/5 with a consistently inventive solo - this hot summer night being one example of many fine performances.

'Black Dog'
Gund Arena Cleveland July 3 1998
Recalled to duty as an encore favourite, 'Black Dog' began appear-

ing in the set during the summer tour. No frills and complete with the 'Out On The Tiles' intro, it raised the temp in required style. Plant's closing comment "What a good night and it's only Friday night," must have been appropriate music to the ears of those Zep Fest '98 attendees in the audience.

'Killing Floor' (HMMT Insert)
MCI Centre, Washington, July 7, 1998
For this particular improvisation, it sounded as though Plant was about to move it into the familiar 'In The Light'. Instead he approached the mic and uttered the words, "I could have quit you baby long time ago" - the signal for them to move into a slow and brooding 'Killing Floor' à la *Zep II*.

'Down By The Seaside'/'For What It's Worth' ('HMMT' insert)
Continental Airlines Arena, East Rutherford, NJ, July 18, 1998
Another enjoyable improvisation as the 'How Many More Times' middle segment drifted through a laid back 'Down By The Seaside' and Buffalo Springfield's 'For What It's Worth', a Plant fave since the days of 'Blueberry Hill'.

'Shining In The Light'/'How Many More Times'/ 'Spoonful'/'Whole Lotta Love'
Bizarre Festival, Cologne, August 23, 1998
A great night out in the rain-soaked fields of Cologne as seen on the German TV coverage. 'Shining In The Light' had developed during the US tour as one of the outstanding new songs. Live, it combined a cool spaciousness and straight ahead drive with Page at the centre spraying out melodic Gibson runs.

The end result – a song worthy of the description "New Zeppelin". For their condensed festival performances 'How Many More Times' was merged into 'Whole Lotta Love', amalgamating the aggression of both pieces into a memorable seamless form. In Cologne it was effectively bridged by the insertion of the blues standard 'Spoonful'.

'Tangerine'/'Heart In Your Hand'
The Point, Dublin, August 26, 1998
Two suitably emotional moments from a suitably emotional return to Dublin's fair city. 'Tangerine' had become a nostalgic part of the semi-acoustic interlude. Driven by Page's jangling double neck Ovation work and Phil Andrews mandolin solo, Plant was on peak form as he recreated the sound of *Zep III*.

The unfamiliarity of 'Heart In Your Hand' may have unfairly inspired a mass rush to the bars and rest rooms. Those that stuck it out were rewarded with one of the most intensive live Plant performances of recent years.

'Burning Up'/'Gallows Pole'
Reading Festival, August 28, 1998
It was a case of men against boys, simple as that. To demonstrate that fact Page revved up the riffs to churn out the turbo driven 'Burning Up' for its final appearance of the tour... and Reading rocked. The familiar swing of 'Gallows Pole' inspired mass audience participation amongst the thousands. As the young guy next to me put it, "Legends, we are in the presence of legends".

'Going To California'
Shoreline Amphitheatre Mountain View, Cal, September 12, 1998
Around this part of the tour Robert began inserting various ad-libs into the song; the "Gone to Chicago" parts of 'Levee Breaks' and later in Europe Robert Johnson's '32-20 Blues'. When the song came back to its lyrical home on this night, it began with Robert ad-libbing the old gospel tune 'Jesus On The Main Line'. A calming acoustic interlude.

'Trampled Underfoot' ('HMMT' insert)
Cox Arena, San Diego, September 21, 1998
Another outstanding show with Page at his improvisational best. No surprise then that they used this platform to bring back 'Trampled Underfoot' inside 'How Many More Times'. It burned slowly at first as Plant moaned out the opening lyric "Greasy slick down body" then settling into a funky mid-tempo. Just before it all

evaporated back to the 'How Many Times' theme Plant threw in some lines in from The Isley's 'It's Your Thing' - just as he had done years back on the BBC 1969 *In Concert* version of 'Communication Breakdown'.

CD3

'I Can't Quit You Baby' (HMMT Insert)/'Celebration Day'
Lakefront, New Orleans, October 1, 1998
The slow blues insert of 'I Can't Quit You Baby' enjoyed periodical recall during the tour, reviving memories of where it all started in Buxton. The nostalgic Zeppelin rocker 'Celebration Day' was briefly recalled to action during the fall US visit - for this Lakefront Westwood broadcast it added suitably retro excitement to the encores.

'Misty Mountain Hop'/'Trampled Underfoot'/'Night Flight'
ULU, London, October 30, 1998
No real explanation necessary here. 'Misty Mountain' back for the first time since the first US date in May, 1998, a complete 'Trampled Underfoot' performed by Page & Plant for the first time in full since the epic Hammersmith jam in April 1988, and 'Night Flight' which was never played live before, it's only known previous performance being that 1973 Zeppelin soundcheck run through. Quite simply history in the making.

'Babe I'm Gonna Leave You'/'That's The Way' ('HMMT' Insert)
Evening News Arena, Manchester, November 3, 1998
'Babe I'm Gonna Leave You' became a pivotal almost ever-present part of the *Walking* tour. This expansive delivery in Manchester was in keeping with Plant's upbeat mood. He added extra dynamic to the piece by inserting brief lines from 'If I Were A Carpenter' during the "Oh baby Oh baby" refrain. Equally effective was a cool drift through the backwaters of *Zep III*, side 2 - 'That's The Way' with Page adding the required structural grace with some pleasing minor chord work.

'What Is And What Should Never Be'/'When The World Was Young'/'When I Was A Child'
Wembley Arena, London, November 6, 1998
Three of the finest moments in London. 'What Is And What Should Never Be' was back in the set on the second night just as it had been way back in the days of pigs and plates at the Empire Pool. Then there was 'When The World Was Young' - a stand out performance deceptively subdued then bursting into life with Page turning in some of his finest guitar playing of the year. Plant's performance on the delicate 'When I Was A Child' was also exemplary. A *Clarksdale* highlight from earlier in the tour, it possessed a calming atmosphere all of its own.

'Money' ('HHMT' Insert)
Exhibition Centre, Gent, December 1, 1998
Another pleasing one off - the old Barrett Strong standard known in Zep circles for the 1980 Frankfurt performance dusted down as another variant in 'How Many More Times'.

'Fever' ('HMMT' Insert) 'Whole Lotta Love'/'Train Kept A Rollin'
Festhalle, Frankfurt, December 3, 1998
Talking of Frankfurt – their return to the Festhalle on the last scheduled night of the tour also heralded some insert fun. 'Fever' was a surprising addition to the shows in Messehalle and this Frankfurt stop off, while the final 1998 performance of 'Whole Lotta Love' included 'Train Kept A Rollin', another 1980 Zep throwback.

'Rock And Roll'
Bercy, Paris, December 10, 1998
And finally, the last word from the condensed mini-set performed in Paris for the Amnesty benefit. And could it be anything else, the track that enjoyed more performances than any other on the tour, the expected finale delivered with admirable gusto some '88 performances on.

Following the publication of his extensive interview in *Tight But Loose*, John Paul Jones forged ahead in establishing his solo career. The all instrumental *Zooma* album was issued in 1999 followed by his first ever solo tour, taking in dates in America, Europe and Japan. Further touring took place in 2000 to be followed by the writing and recording of a second solo set, *The Thunderthief*. This album saw him taking on vocals alongside his familiar multi-instrumentalist role.

John's willingness to provide first hand details of all his solo projects to *TBL* has provided an invaluable platform for the magazine to chronicle and mirror his intentions. The various *TBL* interviews conducted around the release of both the *Zooma* and *Thunderthief* albums reproduced for this book clarify the artistic resurgence of the no longer forgotten ex-Zep bassman.

REFERENCES: **TIGHT BUT LOOSE 14**

JOHN PAUL JONES, FROM ZOOMA TO THE THUNDERTHIEF : 16

A 35-year gap between solo releases is lengthy by any standards. John Paul Jones, though, was occupied elsewhere during the years that have separated his 1964 debut single 'Baja' and the release this month of his first solo album *Zooma*. There was a 12-year stint as bassist and keyboard player in the most successful rock band of all time for starters, not to mention countless session/arranging credits from the Sixties and more than 20 years producing and arranging on projects since Zeppelin called it a day.

He may have been less high-profile than the other ex-Zep members in recent years but he has been far from idle. After the working with The Mission, R.E.M. and The Butthole Surfers, John Paul Jones has finally returned to his solo career. His ambitious new album *Zooma* is a firm reminder of just how important a role he played in shaping the sound of Led Zeppelin.

The nine-track all-instrumental set may not find itself alongside The Chemical Brothers in the upper reaches of the album chart but it will bring renewed attention to a consummate and often underrated musician.

And it's that self-styled consummate musician who greets me in a plush Holland Park hotel on a hot late June Friday afternoon. Last time we met at this location some 18 months back it was to undertake the lengthy interview that appeared in *TBL 13*. This time we have something very new to talk about. "I guess we can pick up where we left off last time," is his encouraging opening line.

The man looks very well indeed - shirt worn outside his light trousers (à la Noel or Liam), hair cut short in a style that suits him and plush loafers with no socks. He's in the middle of a round of promotional interviews for the album, for which an outside PR company has been employed. Seeing my notes, the efficient PR aide Susie comments "Looks like you're well prepared" and goes off to arrange tuna sandwiches for the hungry ex-Zeppelin bassist.

Our conversation is lucid and informal. It's more than obvious that the release of his long awaited new album finds the man in a contented state of mind. His enthusiasm for his music and the process of music making is most apparent throughout our conversation.

DL: How long did the album take to record?

JPJ: The actual recording of the initial tracks were done in about a month with Pete Thomas, but I've really made the album twice. I demoed it all first with drum machines and tapes to give me an idea of how it was all going to fit together. Then I did all the overdubs and the mixing. On and off it did stretch out to around two years. It wasn't something I wanted to rush. I don't think the next one will take as long. I wasn't sure how it was going to sound in the beginning as I only had a few ideas down. Then slowly I began to think through the direction it was going to take.

The first thing I worked on was 'Zooma', the title track. Then I went back through a couple of tapes and re discovered 'B Fingers'. That was a track I'd written around the time of the Diamanda Galas album. I tried it out with Pete and discovered neither of us could play it. That's typical of me - write something and then discover nobody can play it! We eventually did manage to get it down but we couldn't play it for any length of time. It was a good riff so we began to learn it and it came out well.

DL: Do you have a library of work in progress tapes that you refer back to?

JPJ: I do have a few things. I've got loads of odd tapes but I don't often go back and listen to them. Generally if I listen to something work in progress it tends to inspire other ideas.

DL: Were all tracks written as instrumentals?

JPJ: Yes that was the whole idea. I don't sing and I didn't really want to join a band and get a singer in and go that way. I simply wasn't interested in coming up with song based rock.

DL: How did you choose the musicians for the album?

JPJ: Pete Thomas was on Diamanda's album. I knew he was a really conscientious drummer and he also does what I ask of him. Basically I always say that from the waist up drummers can do what they like. But from the feet down they're mine. I know exactly how the bass drum interlocks and I know exactly what I want to hear. It makes a lot of difference to how effective a riff or pattern is so I write up parts for the drums in that way. The fills, cymbals and all that, well they can do what they like. So first of all I did the tracks at home with Pete. Then I burnt a CD ROM of the sessions and took it over to America and recorded Paul Leary of The Butthole Surfers who I worked with in the past and Trey Gunn from King Crimson, plus Denny Fongeiser on a couple of cuts. He plays a big African hand drum called a djembe. I came across him when I was producing Heart. The djembe is not as heavy as a normal drum sound but not as light as congas. It was perfect for a track like 'The Smile Of Your Shadow'.

DL: You also used the London Symphony Orchestra on the track 'Snake Eyes'.

JPJ: I'm used to arranging orchestras but it was real indulgence to orchestrate one of my own compositions. It was great because I didn't have to ask anyone what they wanted which usually happens on sessions. I was paying for the session so as I could do anything I cared to do. It was real fun to have that freedom. We recorded the LSO in Air Studios. It's a big room there and it sounded fantastic.

DL: It's an ambitious arrangement.

JPJ: Yes, well it's a compositional thing really. When you are composing, composers talk of problems and solutions. Simply put, the composition problem is how do you start the piece and another is how you finish it. So on that track I wanted to use strings and when it came to deciding how the ending would turn out it was a question of "Do we fade the orchestra down for the finish?" I thought, no wait a minute, wouldn't it be good if we faded the track but keep the strings going bringing them right up in the mix. It gave the whole piece a quite different texture. That element of surprise and variation in composition is very important. To me that's what it's all about.

DL: Was most of the album was recorded at your home studio?

JPJ: That's right. I feel much more comfortable doing it that way and you don't have to worry about the clock ticking away. The studio has excellent equipment which I've built up over the years - better that most of the studios I've worked in. The overdubs were done in various locations - Paul Leary and I recorded in Willie Nelson's studio in Austin. As I said previously, I burnt a CD at home took it to the States and loaded up their computer and Paul

recorded the solo in one take. Then I recorded Trey Gunn in Los Angeles using the same method.

DL: The album has definite Zeppelin trademarks within the arrangements - was that something you were aware of when you were recording?

JPJ: It's not something I consciously think about but I guess it still comes through. It's the way I play. Diamanda Galas once told me that having worked with me she felt a lot of the Zeppelin riffs had John Paul Jones trademarks. I mean I have been influenced by the overall Zeppelin sound myself. Having been in the band that long, it's hard not to have been but. I've always had that groove to my playing even before Zeppelin.

DL: 'B Fingers' recalls to mind the bass riffs of 'Black Dog' and sounds like it was cut very live.

JPJ: Yes, some of the tracks we did with a live rhythm section. That's a track I'm looking forward very much to playing live. I've just got some new amps I'm trying out and the sound just sounds huge. It fills out the whole stage. You only need the drums to compensate the sound. I recorded 'B Fingers' as an intense jazzy party rocker. I had this feeling that it would be great if we made the track feel like it was being performed in bar some-where. So I looked up some samples and added on a babble of voices at the end. You have all this going on and suddenly it's finished and everybody keeps on talking and nobody really cares what they're hearing. Again it was a compositional thing.

DL: It's interesting how you deploy the bass guitar as the lead instrument.

JPJ: Talking about the bass as a lead instrument makes it sound pretty dull. In reality it's a very workable concept and that is the intention with the album. I've always loved riff-led things and the ten and twelve string basses really fill out all those riffs so there's not much room for anything else. Even on the bridge section of 'Zooma' it sounds like a whole pile of overdubs, but in fact all I do is hit the bass pedal - it's still the one instrument but with a different effect. I also use electric mandola to re enforce the melody line of the riff. The weird noises are from Kyma, my computer designed system.

For 'Smile Of Your Shadow' I played the 12-string bass and by taking off all the distortion made it sound quite acoustic. I just played it like a 12-string guitar. I also added a lap steel guitar played in the style of a pedal steel guitar. I guess that more than compensates for any lack of conventional electric guitar. I've still got the Andy Manson three-necked guitar I used on stage with Zeppelin. It's possible I may bring that out again.

DL: How did you go about getting a new record deal?

JPJ: I've had enough of dealing with the big record labels and to be honest there wasn't much interest in some of the initial approaches that were made to one or two of the big labels. My manager also handles Robert Fripp and he told me about the Discipline Global Mobile set up. So I asked him what the deal was with his label. Turns out it's pretty unusual. Fripp believes that there should be no contract and that all artists should own the copyrights and masters. Robert hates the music industry and believes it should be musician-led. So I looked into it a bit more and found out it had good distribution and good mail order and I thought, "Well I could go with this lot", and it'd be good to be part of something ethical and worthwhile. It might help them in continuing their policy of exposing less commercial music.

DL: Where do you think the album sits in the current marketplace?

JPJ: Not a bloody clue! I can't really think like that. I obviously want people to hear it and I want people to buy it. All that stuff about I'm only making music for myself... well, why bother to record it - you could just sit at home and play.

I think a lot of Zeppelin fans will like it. It wouldn't be alien to them even though there are no vocals. I'm sure that people who were excited by Zeppelin will find excitement in this stuff. I've always liked playing Zeppelin for the same reason I like playing these tracks. It's exciting stuff. The bass and drums interact well. It's cooking. There's that intensity about it. This is how I play rock and roll.

If I wanted to be commercial I'd have got a singer and gone with whatever's commercial today. But I don't need to do that. This is rock under my own terms. It will also be something that I

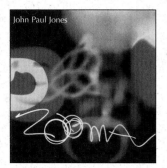

***ZOOMA*, THE ALBUM**

ZOOMA PHOTO SHOOT: SUMMER 1999

I'm sure that people who were excited by Zeppelin will find excitement in this stuff. I've always liked playing Zeppelin for the same reason I like playing these tracks. It's exciting stuff. The bass and drums interact well. It's cooking. There's that intensity about it. This is how I play rock and roll.

JOHN PAUL JONES

will enjoy going out to perform. It's going to be really exciting on stage because of the way the material can be adapted live.

DL: You'll soon be taking to the road again - have you missed the buzz of playing live in recent years?

JPJ: That's basically what the album's for. An excuse to go out on tour again. The Diamanda tour really got me going again. It's a little bit scary but I'm really looking forward to it.

DL: Can you tell me which musicians you'll be touring with?

JPJ: I was looking to use Trey Gunn who plays on the album but he's tied up with King Crimson. Robert Fripp recommended I contact Nick Beggs (ex- Kajagoogoo and Ellis Beggs and Howard). So I called him up and said 'do you fancy being a part of this' and he was most enthusiastic. So he came down and we tried some stuff and it worked out really well. In fact, on stage something like 'Goose' from the album can work well because when I'm playing lap steel Nick can still play the bass end and then when I'm playing bass he play the top end. So that should work well. As for the drummer – it's not quite finalised yet but it looks like Geoff Dugmore will be joining us. He's done loads of sessions and was in The Europeans.

DL: Which Zeppelin songs would you consider playing live?

JPJ: Now that would be telling! The short answer is not many of them. Maybe a couple of them. I don't have a singer but there are some possibilities I'm looking at. What I won't be doing is playing a load of Zeppelin songs and then a couple of mine. If anyone wants to know what the live show is going to be like they need to listen to the album because that's what I'll be playing. The whole album.

DL: When are we likely to see you play live in the UK?

JPJ: I'm looking to start in the US in October for about three weeks visiting the major cities. Then it'll be Europe and the UK in late November. I'm looking to play the sort of place where you can see the audience. On stage they'll be a bit of sitting and a bit of standing. As I said, I'm eagerly looking forward to it. The plan is then to go out again next year, going a bit more in depth and possibly taking in Japan

DL: Will the demands of touring and the new album prevent you being involved in one-off production projects in the future?

JPJ: If it was an interesting offer I'd consider it. Particularly arrangements because they're quicker. I don't want to do too much production to be honest because it takes up two or three months of your life. You can also get into a situation whereby the A&R guy who set it up gets fired by the time of release and it all falls by the wayside which is what happened with The Butthole Surfers. So it can be a bit disheartening.

DL: You recently picked up an award for sales of Zeppelin's fourth album with Jimmy Page in New York, how did that come about?

JPJ: They informed us we'd got this Diamond award for the fourth album. It turned out we'd actually got four - somebody had counted it up wrongly which is a shame because we could have picked them all up in one go. I'm not really one for the award ceremonies. It's obviously nice to be recognised and quite flattering. I was over in New York and I managed to tie it in with some other things.

DL: Are there any plans for future Led Zeppelin releases?

JPJ: Not as such. Although in time there probably will be. There's been some talk of another 'best of' compilation. The record company are always keen. They say it'll bring new people to the music but there's then the danger of people saying "If this is the best I don't need to listen to the rest" and it doesn't draw attention to the catalogue. So I don't know about that. We always hated 'best of' albums in Zeppelin. Peter Grant never wanted them. If we find some other stuff though, something really interesting, that would be different. Jimmy's always on the look out for anything that might prove worthy. People bring tapes to his attention. If it's something like that then I'm all for it and I'd be pleased to hear it myself.

DL: Would you still consider working with Jimmy Page and Robert Plant again if the right opportunity arose in the future?

JPJ: I don't think so. I've moved on. I can't see myself playing Zeppelin stuff for the rest of my life. It was great and I love it but it's a case of leaving it at that. I think the moment's passed.

DL: Since the demise of Zeppelin, which project has given you most satisfaction?

JPJ: Well this album is easily the most satisfying thing I've done

I can't see myself playing Zeppelin stuff for the rest of my life. It was great and I love it but it's a case of leaving it at that. I think the moment's passed.

JOHN PAUL JONES

in recent years. I also like some of the classical things I've been involved with. The piece I did for Red Byrd called 'Amores Pasados' springs to mind. Overall though, this album has been great fun to do and has really got me fired up again.

DL: What albums have you been listening to recently?

JPJ: I buy a lot of albums and try to listen to what's going on. I quite liked the Dark Star record. I've got the Limp Biscuit album. That's a bit too hip hop for me. I've got the new Red Hot Chilli Peppers' album. Actually they wanted me to do an arrangement on that, but I couldn't do it and they ended up using a string machine which is a shame as I'd have liked to work with them. I've got The Chemical Brothers and Underworld's on in the car. I also listen to lots of bluegrass, the *Buena Vista Social Club*. Lots of Cuban stuff. I like to keep in touch with all music. Like with the drum and bass - my daughter supplies tapes of that stuff. There's a tongue in cheek thing on the album called 'Bass And Drums' which is exactly what it says.

DL: What do you consider your favourite album of all time?

JPJ: Oh that's so difficult I guess Miles Davis' *Sketches Of Spain*. It's too difficult! I mean, there's loads of jazz albums that I could choose from alone. I listen to so much variation of music from classical to rock and back.

DL: What about favourite Zeppelin albums?

JPJ: Well I still have great affection for the first album. There was so much enthusiasm in our playing. *Physical Graffiti* is the other real landmark. We had time to stretch out then and really investigate the different aspects of our sound. It's actually very hard for me to separate between the albums. We were good on quality con-

Led Zeppelin's
Legendary Bass & Keyboardist

John Paul Jones
in Concert

レッド・ツェッペリンのベーシスト
ジョン・ポール・ジョーンズが
キャリアの集大成となる
初のソロ・アルバム『ズーマ』を携え
日本上陸！

TOKYO
12.10 Fri. 7:00pm 渋谷公会堂
S席¥7,000 A席¥6,000 (税込)
主催: InterFM 後援: bayfm「パワー・ロック・トゥディ」
お問い合わせ: ウドー音楽事務所
Tel.03(3402)5999 http://www.udo.co.jp/
チケットは、下(K青山チケットエージェンシー 03(3401)9999
ウドー横浜 045(664)6969 チケットぴあ 03(5237)9999 にて発売。

協力: 株式会社ボニーキャニオン
招聘: ウドー音楽事務所
企画運営: ウドークリエイティブアーティスツ

ZOOMA OVER JAPAN, 1999

trol and anything that didn't come up to scratch was thrown out. I think that's very apparent to anyone who picks up on the Zeppelin catalogue.

DL: What's your memories of Earl's Court?

JPJ: One thing I remember about that time is that my home Steinway piano was going to be renovated by Steinway. I'd brought it in about 1970. So what we thought we could do was as it was leaving home we could take it to Earl's Court. So it was on stage with me for those shows. So my solo in 'No Quarter' was played on my real Steinway from home. I remember hearing the bootlegs later and it was pleasing to find out how good the piano sounded at Earl's Court. After that I remember that it went into Steinways' from Earl's Court.

Actually there's a funny story connected with the Yamaha piano I used after that. We were in Shepperton rehearsing and I had this Yamaha GP 70 and it was this miserable little black thing on legs. So we were looking at it thinking "that doesn't look too good" and one of the scene builders came over and said "I could knock you something up that would look great", so he built us a complete white concert grand outer case which folded flat into a flight case. So what we did is we pushed the Yamaha inside it so it looked like a grand piano but it actually wasn't anything of the sort!!

DL: What about Knebworth memories?

JPJ: Well aside from the bass not being on for three numbers - three instruments on stage and I'm not one of them! The vibe though was amazing flying in over the crowd in the helicopter. It was a real event - our last one as it turned out.

DL: Did you feel towards the end of Zeppelin there was still the inclination to move forward musically?

JPJ: Yes, definitely. The day before John died we were rehearsing and the morale was very high. It was all going to start for us again. We'd gone through a down period and we'd turned a corner after the European tour where we stripped it all down. It was still hard and rocking. I had loads of ideas and so did Page.

DL: Do you still draw influence from your partnership with John Bonham?

JPJ: Yes, for sure. That's the way I liked to hear a rock and roll rhythm section and that's what I want the drums to be doing. To be interacting with the bass and John did that better than anyone I've ever worked with. So that influence is always going to be there. There are times when I'm recording that I stop and think, "Well that's how John and I would have approached this". The difficulty of doing a solo album was how to successfully draw from all the many influences I have and still make the album sound coherent. I didn't want it to sound like... here's a bluegrass track, here's a jazz track, here's a blues track.

Then it would not have flowed as I'd liked. The whole point with *Zooma* is that there is influence but it all turns into something else. I know it's sacrilege to say it but the one good thing about vinyl was that it was on two sides. With CD once you get up to an hour it gets too much. If it doesn't fit on to one side of a C90 cassette then it needs editing! Getting back to the point, the whole deal with *Zooma* is that there is influence and then it turns into something else.

That's what I've always said about Zeppelin. We all had different musical influences but it turned into something that was uniquely Zeppelin when we got together to play. I wanted to retain that. I liked the way we did things in Zeppelin and I used that as a role model. Knowing that it was possible to have a fairly wide range of influences but still come out with an album that was cohesive and made sense. I do tend to think of it as a complete album rather than as just a bunch of tracks. Having got this one out of the way I'm already thinking of ideas for a second solo record, so I view *Zooma* very much as a new beginning. Playing this album live is also going to be really exciting for me.

DL: Two final questions, how would you like Zeppelin to be remembered in years to come?

JPJ: I suppose as the greatest band of all time!

DL: And how would you like Zooma to be viewed?

JPJ: (long pause) That's not easy to answer... I guess for people to discover that *Zooma* is what I'm all about. I just hope they get to hear it! That's all I want really.

John Paul Jones takes *TBL* readers track-by-track through *Zooma*

'Zooma'

JPJ: The opening's a bit like desert island discs! Originally the track was written on a beach when I was producing a band called Elephant Ride. It was actually written on Zuma Beach - same name but spelt differently. I couldn't work out how it was going to start so I went for one of my customary walks and suddenly heard all these seagulls. When I wrote it I imagined walking on the beach. I could just see something appearing on the horizon. It just developed from there. The bass leads it all in. In the bridge section it sounds like a whole host of overdubs but all I do is hit the pedal. It's still the one instrument with different effects. The mandola just re-enforces the melody line. All the weird noises come form the Kyma, my computer designed system.

TBL summary: Opens with sea and seagull effects before JPJ's rumbling 10-string bass kicks in. Mainly taken at mid-tempo pace before some additional abstract guitar parts. Unmelodic and tense in a 'Walter's Walk' style.

'Grind'

JPJ: It's a 12-string bass showcase which turns into an almost Duane Eddy type thing. It's a deep melody line that sounds rather like a big animal. Again recorded with electronics and effects.

TBL summary: On the surface a mid-tempo straight ahead rocker employing a repeated simple riff. However that's merely the foundation from which JPJ then layers on all manner of effects including some weird spoken word soundscapes.

'The Smile Of Your Shadow'

JPJ: I'm on 12-string bass and it sounds quite acoustic if you take out the distortion. It's played like a 12-string guitar. Then I added on lap steel guitar in the style of a pedal steel guitar and then there's a mandola solo. Quite a busy track.

TBL summary: Moody, laid back, mellow piece led by JPJ's wavering lap steel solo. Builds up with drums and some complex Spanish sounding guitar. Ends with a gentle coda.

'Goose'

JPJ: Another heavy one, though more mid-temp than 'Zooma' with some live processing and a lap steel solo at the end. Again another number that should work well on stage.

TBL summary: Fades in slowly then the incessant grinding bass riff kicks in. Listen for the very Bonham-like drum fill at around 1 minute 50. The bass riff never lets up and commands attention throughout.

'Bass'n'Drums'

JPJ: Which is literally just bass and drums. I play a four-string bass on this. It's quite short and a fun thing. It turned out just as I wanted it to.

TBL summary: A showcase for JPJ's jazz styled bass playing - the bass solo in the 'Lemon Song' is a reference point here. A sparse arrangement supplemented by some excellent drumming. Listen carefully for JPJ's laugh at the close of the track.

'B Fingers'

JPJ: I'm really pleased with this track. I wasn't sure how it was going to turn out. Live it should really fill out the whole stage. When it began to take shape I thought 'wouldn't it be great if we made it sound like we were playing in a bar', so it all stops and all the people just keep on talking. So that's why there's all those voices talking at the close.

TBL summary: Opens with incredibly overbusy 'Black Dog' type riffing aided by some forceful drumming from Pete Thomas. From there the pace never lets up as they drive through an inventive, live-sounding abstract off-beat arrangement. Reminded me in places of a faster paced 'Who's To Blame' from *Death Wish 2*. Ends with that curious babble of foreign sounding voices.

'Snake Eyes'

JPJ: I wanted to use a proper orchestra on it and it was a case of 'wouldn't it be good if...'. It was great fun orchestrating my own composition. It was a compositional decision to fade the track down and bring the strings soaring in. It makes the whole arrangement quite different from what's normally accepted.

TBL summary: A churning bass led intro reminiscent of 'For Your Life' sets the scene for an initially dark, menacing arrangement. Some Doors-like organ lightens the feel before the addition of the LSO conducted by Jones alters the direction of the piece yet again. Builds to a climax when the orchestra is brought to the fore, launching into an impressive symphonic finale. You can just

That's what I've always said about Zeppelin. We all had different musical influences but it turned into something that was uniquely Zeppelin when we got together to play.

JOHN PAUL JONES

imagine Page entering the fray at this point a la 'I'm Gonna Crawl'!

'Nosumi Blues'

JPJ: It's a blues that starts off with me on lap steel and then just goes into a mid- temp steel blues type of thing. No frills really, just a laid back blues sound.

***TBL* summary:** Something of a 'Nobody's Fault But Mine' feel to the intro before moving into a 'Travelling Riverside' tempo. Basically a blues, led by Jonesy's lap steel guitar. Couldn't help thinking this might have worked better with vocals - indeed one wonders what Robert Plant might have brought to the proceedings.

'Tidal'

JPJ: It's an intensive number. Fast and intense, and a little bit scary. One of the more immediate numbers on the album. Again a good example of how I like to play in a rock style.

***TBL* summary:** Superb closing track. Opens with a barrage of 10-string bass riffs that vividly recall latter period Zeppelin with a very Bonham/Jones like rhythm pattern. Proof perhaps that Page wasn't the only riffmaster in Zeppelin. Subsequently peaks with a 'Carousalambra' sounding manic synth solo and then ends abruptly. Could easily have been an *Out Door* period backing track outtake if we didn't know otherwise.

Zooma: The verdict

One less than obvious parallel that eventually became apparent to me was how at times the album resembles the instrumental moments of Page's *Outrider* album - in the way that Jimmy also brought a distinct Zeppelin feel to the instrumentals on that set - i.e. 'Writes Of Winter', 'Liquid Mercury' and 'Emerald Eyes'. Whilst references from the past abound, *Zooma* is a very contemporary sounding set that draws on the varying production skills John Paul Jones has honed over the years. Its release will do much to re affirm JPJ's standing as an integral part of the greatest rock band of all time. It's also a much overdue reminder of the man's musical warmth and intelligence.

THUNDER AND FREEDOM

THE THUNDERTHIEF, THE ALBUM

After a 35-year gap between solo releases, John Paul Jones has taken a mere 28 months to come up with a successor to his debut solo set *Zooma*. In that time he has performed nearly 80 live gigs across three tours, the most recent a US support slot to King Crimson. For the erstwhile Zep bassist there's been none of the three or four year gaps between albums that dogged the later Zep period. His remarkable work rate is a testament to the sheer enthusiasm John has displayed in establishing a new lease of life in his role as a professional musician.

Now comes *The Thunderthief*, 46 and a half minutes of new JPJ music recorded at his home studio, accompanied by his touring band of Terl Bryant and Nick Beggs. As one would expect, rather than create a *Zooma 2*, John has experimented with differing ideas and moods – the end result being an album that sees him expanding on his proven multi-instrumentalist role and broadening his scope as a writer and singer of his own songs.

I caught up with John in between a hectic schedule early in 2002 as he prepared for the Manchester Mine Aid charity show. We began by discussing how long the album had taken to come to fruition.

REFERENCE: **TIGHT BUT LOOSE 16**

MINE AID BENEFIT, MANCHESTER: JANUARY 27, 2002

JPJ: I suppose I've been working on it on-and-off for about 18 months in between a few breaks. As usual I recorded it twice - first I demoed it all and then Terl and Nick came in and we started laying it down properly. The actual recording was about three or four weeks. It was all recorded at my home studio, which I've really got used to now. It was good to use Nick and Terl because we have really got used to each other now we've done quite a few gigs.

DL: *So how do you think this album differs from Zooma?*

JPJ: I wanted to move on from *Zooma*. Initially something like 'Leafy Meadows' does have the same feel to *Zooma* - it has the bass riff and the main structure but I wanted to move on and add more texture to the sound of this album. On a lot of tracks there are counter melodies going on and all sorts of interesting things so it quickly developed into more than *Zooma Part 2*.

This time John has boldly taken on all the album's vocal duties. Never by his own admission a strong singer, we know him best only for singing Sandy Denny's part on the '77 Zep live version of 'Battle Of Evermore'. He also did some of the vocal parts on his 1985 *Scream For Help* soundtrack.

JPJ: With the singing I just felt it was time to step forward - singing gives the whole thing more identity to my work which I feel is needed. It adds something to it all and it becomes much more than just a bass and keyboardist up on stage and it's definitely the direction I'm taking.

I think it's worked out fine and being my hardest critic I have to be satisfied it's up to standard. Writing lyrics is also a new challenge and I'm relishing that part of it as well. I did use Peter for two of the tracks. [Peter is Peter Blegvad who has worked with The Golden Palaminos amongst others.]

I met him through my wife being a friend of his wife. I'd heard some of his work and knew he'd be interesting so he came over and we began collaborating on the 'Thunderthief' track and then 'Ice Fishing'. Knowing he was also a cartoonist it seemed logical to ask him to come up with the cover - I think it's a really striking image and fits in with the album's mood.

Having lived with the album for the past couple of weeks, I'm keen to get JPJ's impression on the making of the album so we began discussing each of the tracks as they line-up on the album. Beginning with the opener 'Leafy Meadows' which I felt did hark back to the structure of *Zooma*.

JPJ: You could say 'Leafy Meadows' is something of a link-track to *Zooma*. It's how I originally set out to make the album before it changed direction. It was nice to have the label boss Robert Fripp come in and play on this. I actually wanted him to do a little more but he was on tour at the time. The solo really is excellent.

DL: *The title track struck me as a very wide-screen with shades of Leonard Bernstein's West Side Story.*

JPJ: Yes, it has got a really good sound on it. This is the first time I've engineered an album on my own and it gave me the freedom to play with all sorts of different mike set ups etc. The vocal is filtered to add to the atmosphere. I must say I'm also very pleased with the drum sound from Terl - we took a lot of care to get that right.'

DL: *'Hoediddle' has a really strong guitar sound on the intro, which was not all it appears.*

JPJ: It's actually the electric mandolin on the intro. We've been doing this live and it works really well. There's a bit of a mountain feel early on - like travelling in the Himalayas. Then there's a Celtic feel. There's a bit of bluegrass in there too. I like the idea of merging all these influences into one piece."

DL: *Do I hear echoes of the type of arrangements you came up with for R.E.M.'s Automatic For The People album on the next track 'Ice Fishing At Night'?*

JPJ: Possibly. I did think about using an orchestra here but we kept it simple and the vocals turned out as I'd hoped. I'm a strict critic of my own work so they had to get by me first! I'm pleased with this. The piano is again well recorded.

DL: *So who's 'Daphne'?*

JPJ: The title comes from a really beautiful boat I saw called Daphne. There's a bit of a cocktail party going on in the middle. I play the old Fender Jazz bass on this and I also used my old Wallace amp I've had since the Sixties session days. We distorted the sound like I used to in Zep.

DL: *'Angry Angry' is a real departure from anything you've cut as a solo artist - is there a message in the lyric?*

JPJ: Not in the first person, no, though I do get angry! It started out as just the riff. My American publicist put me in touch with Adam Bomb and I went to see him play at the Borderline.

I immediately asked him to come over and put a solo down. It fitted in perfectly. I'd looped the riff and a drum machine on the computer and he played over it. Then I had to come up with a lyric. It is not necessarily first person. Everyone knows someone who does nothing but moan so I came up with the angry theme. It matched the urgency of it".

DL: *The mood changes for the next track 'Down To The River To Pray' - the traditional tune recently brought to prominence by Alison Krauss on the Oh Brother Where Art Thou soundtrack.*

JPJ: This features my new triple-neck mandolin which Andy

MINE AID BENEFIT, MANCHESTER: JANUARY 27, 2002

Manson built for me. Zeppelin always had a folk side and this has elements of how we brought that in. Then there's 'Shibuya Bop' - Shibuya is a place in Tokyo where young people gather - I was there on tour and it just had a great energy about it. I'd heard a techno track out there with a real claustrophobic feel and I wanted to bring that to the track. I use the Koto I first got when we were in Japan in '72. I also play the Hammond organ, which I used in Zep.

DL: *The final track, 'Freedom Song', is another departure from what we might expect - an almost Jethro Tull lament with some very direct lyrics.*

JPJ: It's a sort of protest song. At least it's me using the song as a protest to modern living. It's great to play something like a

---

Crimson tour '01
That's the way

With *The Thunderthief* completed, JPJ took to the road in a support slot to labelmates King Crimson on a 26-date US tour. The compact 65 minute set is well captured on a CDR recording from the November 15 Universal Theatre show in Los Angeles.

The grinding bass sound of 'Zooma' moves onto *Thuderthief*

opener 'Leafy Meadows'. Following a sublime 'Shadow Of Your Smile' comes the standout moment, John's vocal take of 'That's The Way'. "Contrary to expectations we are going to travel back in time a bit," is his introduction. The mandolin arrangement is right out of any concert hall Zep visited circa '71/2 and the vocal has an engaging feel of its own comparable perhaps in style to Nick Drake. It's a brave

and successful re-creation of the past that still sounds entirely in the present.

'Steel Away' has a definite 'Since I've Been Loving You' vibe in its construction while the new 'Freedom Song' is a quirky but successful departure. The home straight mixes the brand new ('Hoediddle') with the less new ('Tidal') and finally the legendary ('Black Dog').

ZOOMA LIVE, SHEPHERDS BUSH EMPIRE: NOVEMBER 22, 1999

There's no attempt to sing

it like Robert – and I'm not

about to attempt the

'Immigrant Song'!

JOHN PAUL JONES

ukulele - we did this on the Crimson tour and when the audience saw the instrument they must have wondered what was coming! It is slightly folksy again and lyrically it's a common experience for us all - just wanting to be free and changing your environment.
DL: You did air some of the new album on your recent support slot to King Crimson's US tour. So how did that go down?
JPJ: It's been really great - Detroit was fantastic on the Crimson tour and LA was too. The Crimson crowd seem to take it all in and obviously there was some of my own audience now. The reception I get on tour is really inspiring, particularly in the US. I'm begin-

ning to see familiar faces out there and it's good to know people want to come and see the show again.
DL: Are there plans to take The Thunderthief on the road in a full set?
JPJ: Yes, I really want to do it but it's a case of getting the right venues. I hate it when musicians say touring is my hobby - it's a bit more than that as there are people to be paid and my set-up is pretty elaborate. So yes I'm sure it will happen and I'm looking forward to playing the new material live.
DL: Despite your past reticence to taking on the vocal chores, you've now gone the whole hog by performing the celebrated Zep 3 Plant opus 'That's The Way' on stage.
JPJ: I wanted to have more than one number where I sang and we were doing 'Freedom Song' and I just thought it would be appropriate. I've always liked the track, in fact I was doing a bit of a tease of 'That's The Way' in my live version of 'Going To California' on the Zooma tour. There's no attempt to sing it like Robert – and I'm not about to attempt the 'Immigrant Song'! It was great to do though and the audience seem to like it.
DL: The mandolin arrangement is very Zep like and could be from any night on the road in 1971/2.
JPJ: Yes it could be, though I'd like to think I play the mandolin far better now than I did back then, so it's hopefully an improvement."
DL: So you have no problems reviving the Zeppelin numbers?
JPJ: I'm comfortable with that but I don't want to overdo it. It's not a Zeppelin revival show. I know people love to hear the old numbers and it's great to do things like 'Levee'.
DL: Did I detect a 'Since I've Been Loving' feel to the live blues workout 'Steel Away'?
JPJ: It's just a blues variation - as we didn't use keyboards for the support slot to Crimson we decided to do basic things like that.
DL: Have you ever thought of doing your latter period Zep epic 'Carousalambra' on stage?
JPJ: That would certainly be a challenge, but there are no plans and I do want to present my new music as a priority – anyway I sold the GX1 to Keith Emerson years ago!
DL: Are many instruments you use on stage ones that have survived from the Zep days?
JPJ: I'm a bit reticent to take some of them out now and that includes the Fender jazz bass and the three-necked triple from Zeppelin. I got Andy Manson to build a new one as the original is a bit precious. I have a vast collection of instruments but I'm not a collector - instruments are for playing, in fact I brought a ukulele for £50 off the internet just last week. I'm also getting Andy to build a baritone ukulele. Thinking about it, the thing about our stage set-up that gets the most attention are two old flight cases stencilled with 'JP Jones Led Zeppelin'.

I get people coming up taking photographs of those and local stage hands seem to get a particular thrill when humping those about which is mildly amusing!
DL: The shadow of the Zeppelin looms ever large. The most recent 'Zep to reform' rumour surrounded Paul McCartney's request for you to join together for the September 11 benefit concert in New York last October. So what was the story there?
JPJ: I was in the car and heard a radio report about it and thought 'well I don't know too much about this'. I did tell my manager I was available but in actual fact nobody was ever asked to do it - it was purely speculation.'
DL: The other big Zep talk has been the possibility of further

---

The Thunderthief: The album

Less Zooma 2…
More ever onward
The easy route would have been to replicate the winning formula of *Zooma*. But John Paul Jones has far too much musical creativity to take the easy route and *The Thunderthief* presents a variety of twists and turns. That said, the opener 'Leafy Meadows' does pick

up where *Zooma* left off - rich growling bass lines over which Robert Fripp adds the customary abstract soloing on which he has built his reputation.
The title track comes over very wide-screen and cinematic, not unlike something Leonard Bernstein might have come up with. Elsewhere the shadow of the Zeppelin seeps though, confirmation again of his vital contribution to

the band. The stark and tender 'Ice Fishing At Night' benefits from an impressive piano arrangement reminiscent of the live keyboard improvisations Jones often deployed on stage with Zep. The version of the traditional 'Down To The River To Pray' is a mandolin led instrumental in the classic 'Going To California' romantic Zep tradition during which any moment you expect Robert Plant to enter pro-

ceedings.
Page himself would be impressed with the meandering guitar work and electric mandolin that lights up 'Hoediddle'.
Aside from the Zep connotations, the album also carries something of a modern day prog-rock feel - both the inventive 'Daphne' and the oriental 'Shibuya Bop' contain echoes of the synth and keyboard mayhem similar to the likes of Emerson and

Wakeman in their pomp.
The major departure from *Zooma* is John's decision to sing and compose his own lyrics. His vocal delivery is a curiously engaging mix somewhere between Nick Drake and Robert Wyatt. He stamps his own wry wit on both 'Angry Angry' and 'Freedom Song'. The former, an unexpected and perhaps slightly out of place Jilted John-meets-Blur punk-stomper, has

Zeppelin archive releases, notably a possible DVD release. What do you know about that?

JPJ: We have had talks and meetings and we did all come in for a viewing of the Albert Hall film - it looked good, parts of it very good but some of it's a bit dark. As usual with us, though, it takes an age for anything to finally get the seal of approval. We always were slow at making decisions but something will probably surface. Really, Page takes care of all that. He seems to know where everything's located - he was always the band's archivist. I think I've told you before, there really isn't much studio stuff to work with because we tended to finish only what we were totally satisfied with.

DL: It also occurs to me there's potential for a John Paul Jones box set anthology covering your early Sixties work through Zep, the many post Zep collaborations and now.

JPJ: It's not something I've ever thought about. I'm too busy producing new material to look back too much. Maybe when I've got another album under my belt I can put out a 'greatest hits' though you probably need to have hits in the first place to do that!

DL: So what about a collaboration album using guest vocalists and musicians like Jools Holland?

JPJ: Again not keen really - it becomes less your album than those that are on it so I can't see the point of that, especially as I'm just building up something of a solo career myself with the writing and singing aspect.

DL: Are there other artists you would be keen to work with?

JPJ: Yes a few - I'd liked to have used Robert Fripp on more of the album. Danny Barnes is another and Alison Krauss. I'd liked to have her do some fiddle parts on 'Down To the River To Pray' as she did on the *Oh Brother* soundtrack.

DL: What's been on your play list lately?

JPJ: Lets have a look... Radiohead's *Kid A*, Ben Harper, The Strokes, Nine Inch Nails, Tricky, Gillian Welch... the usual bluegrass things. As you know I like to keep up with as many new releases so I can hear the production qualities.

DL: What is your fave album of all time?

JPJ: Still Miles Davis' *Sketches Of Spain*.

DL: What was the first record the young JPJ purchased?

JPJ: It was Jerry Lee Lewis' 'Great Balls Of Fire' bought from the record shop off Eltham High street.

DL: If you could have been any other musician who would it have been?

JPJ: I'd say Charlie Mingus, though not for his personal life... purely as a musician.

DL: What's planned for the future?

JPJ: I'm already logging ideas for the third album. I want to build on the two albums – there will be more lyrics and more vocals and in much the way Zep did I want to continue to combine various styles and moods and retain an overall identity. I'm also looking to tour with *The Thunderthief*.

What's been really pleasing about this album is that I really didn't want to repeat myself too much. After recording and living with it so long I very rarely play my stuff at home. However recently I had to put on a track to check something out from the new album and ended up playing through the whole album and at the end of it I thought 'this is bloody good!'.

MINE AID BENEFIT, MANCHESTER: JANUARY 27, 2002

We always were slow at making decisions but something will probably surface. Really, Page takes care of all that. He seems to know where everything's located – he was always the band's archivist.

JOHN PAUL JONES

lyrics that could be aimed at certain former band mates. The latter is a quaint folksy lament sounding not unlike *Aqualung*-era Ian Anderson.

And that's *The Thunderthief*. As with everything John Paul Jones applies himself to, it's never less than interesting and always deserving of attention.

Underground Rising
Zooma tour '99:
Doing the Shibuya Bop
Back in December 1999 John brought the *Zooma* tour to Japan. The three dates included two nights in Nagoya and a final stop off in Tokyo for a date at the Shibuya Public Hall. This visit would later inspire *The Thunderthief* track 'Shibuya Bop'. This two CDR set captures one of the best *Zooma*

tour nights. Highlights include a stirring three track opening trio of *Zooma* songs: the title track, 'Goose', and 'Grind'.

These are followed by a simple but effective arrangement of 'No Quarter', a recall to arms for the *Scream For Help* soundtrack extracts 'Spaghetti Junction' and 'Crackback'.

There's also the instrumental showcase JPJ performed with the

triple neck guitar, a memorable highlight for me personally at the 1999 Shepherds Bush gig a few weeks before. The enthusiastic Japanese audience are finally treated to a two-song Zep finale of 'Trampled Underfoot' and 'Black Dog'.

All in all this a superb unofficial souvenir of the debut JPJ tour.

As the Nineties unfolded, *TBL* was well placed to chronicle the undulating fortunes of Jimmy Page's career. From the initial optimism of Coverdale Page, through the excitement of the Page Plant liaison and on into the collaboration with The Black Crowes, the story has taken more than one unexpected turn along the way. This chapter mines the *TBL* coverage of the man to provide an overview of Page's movements during the past decade. There's also a sequel to the original Page chapter in the first *Celebration* book which spotlights a further 12 examples of his work spanning the past twelve years. Each one a further illustration of…

The Master and his art

REFERENCE: **TIGHT BUT LOOSE 8 TO 16**

17 : JIMMY PAGE IN THE 1990'S

BACKSTAGE AT THE BUDOKAN, TOKYO, COVERDALE PAGE JAPANESE TOUR: DECEMBER, 1993

For Jimmy Page the Eighties had been an uneven and often frustrating decade. Facing up to life without Zeppelin, he drifted from project to project. Tentative studio sessions in '81 with Yes bassist Chris Squire and drummer Alan White never got beyond a few demos. His commission to produce the *Death Wish 2* soundtrack did provide renewed studio focus and the 1983 ARMS tour in the presence of Beck and Clapton ignited his passion for playing live again. The subsequent collaboration with Paul Rodgers in the short lived group The Firm proved to be an unfulfilling

JIMMY BACKSTAGE AT KNEBWORTH: JUNE 30, 1990

mismatch with mediocre album sales and the lack of any Zeppelin material leading to half-full venues. A potentially fruitful liaison with Roy Harper never developed further than the low key *Whatever Happened To Jugula?* album. More promising was the *Outrider* solo album and tour, the first signs of the guitarist successfully reconciling his past with the present. This time the lure of his vast back catalogue proved irresistible and by presenting the *Outrider* tour as a career overview, it finally gave Page the opportunity to get back to what he really wanted to do - play the music of Led Zeppelin.

Jimmy Page entered the Nineties with his options firmly open. He had considered recruiting a new band of young players for a new recording venture but that idea went on ice when he took up Atlantic's offer of remastering the Zeppelin catalogue for a retrospective box set and 'best of' album. In May 1990, working with engineer George Marino, he painstakingly remastered the entire Zep catalogue - the result being the huge selling box set and *Remasters* albums. "I was very keen to do it," Page commented at the time, "because the CDs that had been issued were from such poor tapes. I worked wherever possible from the original master tapes. The essence of it all is in the resequencing of the tracks that gives it that same pictures with a different frame ethic. Sitting there listening to it all was like reliving ten years of my life."

The entire year was peppered with the call of his old band. In late April, he rejoined Plant and Jones to perform a Zeppelin set at the reception for Jason Bonham's wedding. In June he was back on stage at Knebworth for a nostalgic and memorable cameo with Plant's band at the Silver Clef concert, including a swaggering romp through the previously unplayed live Zep song 'Wearing And Tearing'. In August he made a couple of appearances with Aerosmith, reviving 'The Train Kept A Rollin'' at Donnington and a clutch of Yardbirds/Zep tunes at the Marquee.

In the autumn there was a round of promotional work to promote the *Remasters* albums. The most obvious question posed to him was whether all this activity would lead to a Led Zeppelin reunion? His reply backstage at Donnington was: "You'll, have to ask Robert that. I'd love to. I love playing that stuff. It's part of me and I love playing it."

In early 1991 meetings were held with Plant and Jones to discuss a reunion. Faith No More drummer Mike Bordin was earmarked for the hot seat at the back but much to Page's frustration Plant eventually vetoed the idea, opting to pursue his solo career.

When it was evident that Robert would not relent, Page shifted his thoughts to putting together a new band. He waded through scores of demos from singers but couldn't find anything that inspired him. Then, in a bizarre twist to the story, he linked up with ex-Deep Purple and Whitesnake singer David Coverdale. Plant and Coverdale had been involved in several press spats over the years, with Plant criticising Coverdale for aping his style. Even Page was bemused by Whitesnake guitarist Adrian Vandenberg using his trademark violin bow technique. "When I saw the video for that track ('In The Heat Of The Night') and the part where the guy starts playing with a bow, I actually fell around laughing. That's how silly it had become."

In what may have appeared as an act of sheer spite, Page defected to the Coverdale camp. It was more likely a marriage of convenience. "I got a call from my manager suggesting I meet with David Coverdale. So we had a meet to just see how it went socially. We thought we'd give it a couple of weeks - and if it didn't work out we'd shake hands - I just hoped it wasn't going to be me that couldn't pull it off." Conveniently, both artists were signed to the Geffen label whose A&R man John Kalodner instigated a meeting in March 1991 in New York. Page had been seen around the area jamming with local band The Reputations at the China Club and Les Paul at Fat Tuesday's club.

There was enough rapport from that initial meeting for them to decamp to Coverdale's Lake Tahoe home where the ideas started flowing. "The first day we wrote 'Absolution Blues' and it got better from there," he said. They next went to Barbados where they penned 'Barbados Blues', later to be retitled 'Pride And Joy', and a whole batch of other songs.

In May the pair appeared on stage at a Poison/Slaughter show in Reno. The encore jam included Zep's 'Rock And Roll'. Page also turned up at a club in Reno to jam with local band Solid Ground.

Within weeks they had began rehearsals that led to recording sessions commencing in Vancouver. They initially sought The Who's John Entwistle to play bass at the sessions but when he was unavailable they brought in former Montrose and Heart drummer Denny Carmassi and Bad English bassist Ricky Phillips.

The album's recording was somewhat fragmented due to personal reasons – Page's marriage was breaking down and Coverdale's mother died. In early 1992 Page attended the Hall of Fame induction of The Yardbirds in New York, joining an all star jam that included Neil Young and Keith Richards (he would return in 1995 with Plant and Jones to accept Zeppelin's induction). In March he joined Harry Connick Jnr on stage at Miami's Knights Center, jamming on a couple of blues numbers. Further sessions for the album took place in Miami and it was eventually mixed and completed at London's Abbey Road studio in the autumn. Page also took time to compile the second box set of Led Zeppelin studio recordings, bringing in Coverdale Page engineer Mike Fraser to mix the previously unreleased *Zep 1* outtake 'Baby Come On Home'.

Reflecting on the Coverdale Page album he said, "I wanted to present the best I could get out of myself. And there is no doubt that we coaxed the best out of each other. It's the best I've played since the days of Led Zeppelin."

The completed Coverdale Page album was issued on Geffen in

COVERDALE PAGE: 1993

March 1993. It was the most focused performance on an album by Page in years, his playing ranged from the nondescript *In Through The Out Door* leftover riffs of 'Shake My Tree' to the descending chord passages of 'Take Me For A Little While'. It was a remarkable performance, encompassing all the dynamics that lit up his best work. Coverdale's agile style made it easy for Page to weave his finely tooled riffs , a throwback to the days when hard rock meant just that.

Coverdale and Page undertook a round of promotional interviews and ambitious plans were unveiled for them to play a 45-date tour in the US. The optimism soon petered out, however, when the album soon faded from the charts and disappointing ticket sales led to the tour's cancellation. They did get to play a seven date Japanese tour in December but by then the short-lived collaboration was at an end. The inability of the pair's respective managements to agree on a future strategy was the root of the problem, as Page noted: "It's the powers that be, the relative managements involved. All I know is what is recommended to me at the end of the day. I was up for playing anywhere but there's nothing on the table after our Japanese dates." With the planned Coverdale Page tour unable to hold off the effects of a US recession, what was conceived by Geffen as an obvious money raking exercise now had less potential. The powers that be, as Page put it, obviously saw little commercial future in the project.

The gigs in Japan (with a band compromising Guy Pratt on bass, Brett Tuggle on keyboards and Danny Carmassi on drums) featured a cross section of Zeppelin and Whitesnake tracks plus material from their album. Although appearing somewhat overweight, Page's performances were encouraging. He was clearly rejuvenated, hammering out old Zeppelin numbers such as 'Kashmir' and 'In My Time Of Dying'.

There had been rumours that Page would next undertake a solo project with Killing Joke's Jaz Coleman and the Cairo Orchestra but that came to nothing. With the Coverdale link looking less likely to progress, Page received a surprise call from Plant who had received an offer from MTV to appear on their *Unplugged* series. He felt to do justice to the Zeppelin material in this setting it would require the vital ingredient of his old partner.

On route to rehearse with Coverdale for the Japanese tour, Page met with Plant in Boston in late '93 and agreed to renew their partnership for the MTV show, later to be dubbed *Unledded*.

By the early spring of the following year Page and Plant were back rehearsing together. In April they appeared on stage together at the Alexis Korner benefit show in Buxton. The MTV

I wanted to present the best I could get out of myself. And there is no doubt that we coaxed the best out of each other. It's the best I've played since the days of Led Zeppelin.

JIMMY PAGE

THE UNLIKELY TOP 3 HIT

project gave them ample scope to reinterpret the Zeppelin catalogue with the assistance of an Egyptian ensemble and English orchestra. Two special shows in late August at the London Studios provided the bulk of the material for the show. They also recorded additional songs in Marrakesh and Wales.

The resulting album and MTV special, aired in October 1994 was the catalyst for the pair to head back on the road. Between February 1995 to March 1996 they played a total of 116 gigs across America, Europe and Japan. Ex-Cure man Porl Thompson assisted Jimmy as second guitarist on a bulk of the dates.

Following the tour they took a break and Page's personal life became more stable. He settled down with a new partner, Jimena, whom he had met in Brazil, and she gave birth to a daughter, Zofia, in the spring of 1997. Around the same time the first fruits of new Page and Plant studio endeavours were issued on the benefit album for ailing guitarist Ranier Ptacek, *The Inner Flame*. Ptacek had worked with Plant on the *Fate Of Nations* album sessions. Their cover version of Ranier's 'Rude World' with its trip hop rhythm and phased guitar effects hinted at the left field approach they would pursue in the future.

That autumn Page and Plant went into London's Abbey Road to work on their first studio collaboration for 17 years, employing as engineer grunge master Steve Albini whose past credits included The Pixies, Nirvana and PJ Harvey. The resulting album, *Walking Into Clarksdale*, was issued in the spring of 1998.

Rather than embellishing the material with the trademark riffs, Page fleshed them out with subtle fills, creating several unexpected twists in the process: the invigorating tempo change on the title track, echoing tremolo arm reverb on the opening of 'When I Was A Child', and a jangling Byrds-like run on 'Blue Train'.

"We wanted it to be a performance album," said Jimmy. "Every note that was played was in its place to mean something. There were no embellishments just for the sake of it. So it is a minimalistic record."

Asked about the lack of solos and riffs Page replied: "There's less solos? Depends what you call a solo. There is loads of guitar on every song. I guess it depends whether you think of a song as being an excuse to play a solo at some point, or as a journey which you just travel on the guitar."

It was evident from the texture of the record that Page had forfeited the widescreen riffing of the *Coverdale Page* album, Plant's influence leading him to a more ethereal and measured feel. Anyone looking for the more brutish elements of Led Zeppelin would be disappointed, and this may have been responsible for the mediocre sales the album clocked up.

In 1997 Page also took time out to compile the well received Led Zeppelin *BBC Sessions* set and began initial work on restoring the Zeppelin visual archive, the first results being the 'Whole Lotta Love' promo film made to accompany the belated release of the track as a single in the UK. Another extracurricular activity saw him forge an unlikely liaison with US rapper Puff Daddy, aka Sean Combs. The pair worked in separate studios in London and New York via a satellite link to produce 'Come With Me', basically a re write of 'Kashmir' that was used for the *Godzilla* soundtrack.

There's less solos? Depends what you call a solo… I guess it depends whether you think of a song as being an excuse to play a solo at some point, or as a journey which you just travel on the guitar.

JIMMY PAGE

JIMMY PAGE 1993

It provided Page and Puff with a worldwide smash single

Jimmy promoted the 'Come With Me' remake on the May 9, 1998, edition of *Saturday Night Live*. The track was later deployed as a link for the BBC's TV coverage of the 2002 World Cup. While on their *Walking Into Everywhere* tour in 1998 Page and Plant recorded a version of 'Gonna Shoot You Right Down (Boom Boom)' in Detroit for inclusion on an all star album for the late blues man Jimmy Rogers.

That second Page Plant tour took them across Eastern Europe, America and Central Europe. The stripped down five-piece line-up of Page, Plant, Michael Lee on drums, Charlie Jones on bass and keyboard player Phil Andrews was in stark contrast to the *Unledded* tour. Page, taking on all the guitar chores, was back to his absolute best, consistently turning in focused, incendiary performances. Although certain songs from the *Clarksdale* album were showcased in the set, as the tour progressed there was an increased emphasis on the Zep songs which made it seem like they were on a mission to uphold the Zep legacy. This suited the audiences and Page but Plant became less enthusiastic, and plans for the tour to continue to Japan and Australia in early 1999 were scuttled when Robert quit on the eve of the trip.

Page was left to pick up the pieces. He did record some backing tracks with drummer Michael Lee for a planned new Page Plant album in the hope it would prompt Plant to return to put vocals on. It never happened. "I presented scenario after scenario to Robert," Page said later. "We were supposed to get together last May to do some writing but he cancelled at the last minute. Then it was August and nothing happened so he's out on his own now."

Page ploughed on, determined to keep playing. In June he performed 'Dazed And Confused' at a charity show for the Kosovo crisis appeal in London's Whitehall with bassist Guy Pratt and Michael Lee. He then found salvation in the company of The Black Crowes after linking up with the erstwhile retro rockers for a charity gig at London's Cafe De Paris.

Page was asked to spearhead the gig that would benefit Scream (Supporting children through re-education and music) and the ABC Action for Brazil's children trust. Photographer Ross Halfin suggested Page ask The Black Crowes, who were in town to play with Aerosmith, to join him. Ironically Jimmy had been introduced to the Crowes by Plant and had attended their 1995 Albert Hall show. He also jammed with them soon after at a gig at the Zenith club Paris.

On a memorable June night, Page and the Crowes performed 'Shake Your Money Maker', 'In My Time of Dying', 'Whole Lotta Love' and a version of Fleetwood Mac's 'Oh Well'. Aerosmith's Steven Tyler and Joe Perry joined them for 'The Train Kept A Rollin' and 'You Shook Me'.

Following the success of the London show Page was asked by the Crowes' management if he'd like to extend the liaison for six US shows - three in New York, one in Worcester and two in Los Angeles - and he jumped at the chance.

As a prelude to the October dates, Jimmy also took part in the Net Aid benefit show at New York's Giants Stadium where he was joined by Puff Daddy for 'Come With Me'. He also performed an instrumental 'Dazed And Confused', a further new work-in-progress instrumental dubbed 'Domino' plus Zep's 'In My Time Of Dying' and 'Whole Lotta Love' with Rich and Chris Robinson from the Crowes.

For the US shows Page and The Black Crowes would perform a set that featured predominantly Zeppelin numbers, and this gave Page the opportunity to revive rarely played gems such as 'Ten Years Gone' and 'Your Time Is Gonna Come'. The additional guitar input from Crowes Audley Freed and Rich Robinson allowed them to reproduce the complex, multi-tracked studio arrangements in a live setting. As Page acknowledged, "When we did 'Ten Years Gone' it was the first time I'd ever heard all the guitar parts from the record played live. It was like being in guitar heaven. The whole thing went like a locomotive. The Crowes really groove. You can hear that in their own music. And when they applied that groove to Led Zeppelin material it was really cool. We had a great time. It was an unforgettable experience for me."

A resulting live album from the tour titled *Live At The Greek/ Excess All Areas* was initially made available via the Internet in early 2000. Offered by *Musicmaker.com* as a pioneering digital music compilation, the deal was that the 19 tracks recorded over two shows on October 18 and 19 the previous year could be customised or downloaded by the purchaser in any track order they requested. Interest in this controversial move was high and it quickly became the largest selling custom CD and paid on line download in the history of the Internet up to that point.

At a press conference in New York in February to launch the Internet release, Page noted, "The whole thing about this is choice. It was an uncomplicated thing for us. We did not have to go messing about with record companies. It's wonderful to be at the forefront of this."

Bypassing traditional retail channels did cause some industry debate and eventually the album was officially released as a standard CD via TVT Records in America and SPV in Europe. In the wake of the overpopulated dotcom boom, *Musicmaker* eventually went into receivership.

The live album accurately captured Page's enthusiasm for a collaboration which allowed him to further explore his illustrious past. Whilst there was no doubting Page's prowess, the project had its limitations. It was an entertaining stopgap and as a gig a guaranteed good night out, but the novelty did wear with repeated listening.

On the back of the success of the album, Page and the Crowes returned to the road in America in the summer of 2000 for a further eleven shows, kicking off on June 24 in Chicago. However continued back problems forced Page to pull out of a round of dates with The Who in the late summer and a planned 13-date late

WITH THE BLACK CROWES: 1999

I presented scenario after scenario to Robert. We were supposed to get together last May to do some writing but he cancelled at the last minute.

JIMMY PAGE

TOUR BOOTLEG. NOTE THE CYNICAL NOD TO HIS EX-PARTNER

ABC SAMBA PARTY, CAFE ROYAL, LONDON: DECEMBER 2, 2002

autumn European tour, thus signalling the end of his association with the band.

Page then underwent a series of physiotherapy sessions and with little chance of playing live he and his wife Jimena concentrated on setting up of the ABC charity dedicated to assisting underprivileged children in Brazil. Page actively promoted the charity by attending a variety of functions.

Page and Plant were reunited in June 2001 for a one-off performance celebrating the Sun Records label at the Montreux Festival. Their mainly rockabilly set including a rare delivery of Zep's 'Candy Store Rock' and the Sonny Burgess track 'My Bucket's Got A Hole In It' which the pair also recorded at Abbey Road studios for inclusion on the album *Good Rockin' Tonight/ A Tribute To Sun Records*.

While he was happy working with Plant on these collaborations he still hankered after a more permanent reunion. Stating his intentions in an interview with *Classic Rock* he said: "I love playing Led Zeppelin music. For me they were one of the best bands ever and they made some of the best music ever, and we should be out there playing it."

The divisions between the respective Page and Plant camps was in evidence at the high profile series of Teenage Charity gigs held on February 2002 at the Royal Albert Hall, the first ever occasion when both artists performed separately on the same bill. Plant opted for a low key set with his Strange Sensation line-up and Jimmy turned back the years with a spirited delivery of 'Dazed And Confused', backed, somewhat bizarrely, by Paul Weller's band.

A month later he was back on stage with the students of Epsom college when he and Jimena were invited along to see the work pupils of the college had done on behalf of the Task Brazil charity. Jimmy attended a master class, answered questions, signed autographs and jammed with the school band on four numbers, including a version of Dylan's 'Subterranean Homesick Blues'.

Jimmy spent the rest of the year compiling the *Zeppelin DVD* and live album projects. Working with director Dick Carruthers, he waded through the entire Zeppelin sound and visual archive, producing a five-and-a-half-hour double DVD compilation and the triple live CD, *How The West Was Won*, with assistance from sound engineer Kevin Shirley. This was drawn from material recorded in Long Beach and Los Angeles on Zeppelin's 1972 tour.

At the end of the long haul to bring it all to fruition a delighted Page commented: "I always had faith in the creative value of this project. I genuinely believe it deserves a fanfare of trumpets when it's released - it's five hours of favourite moments from start to finish of Led Zeppelin live."

In the wake of all this activity the inevitable 'Zeppelin to reform' rumours went into overdrive – with the Foo Fighters David Grohl cited as a potential replacement drummer. This time Page was quick to refute the idea. In an interview with Nick Kent he said: "I started to hear this rumour when I was in the studio putting together the DVDs and CD and I immediately thought that the most ridiculous thing we could do is to put out a live album and then tour on the strength of something we did 30 years ago. Nobody in the band had even discussed it."

With the burden of this long postponed Zeppelin project finally lifted, as he approaches his 60th birthday Jimmy Page deserves a well-earned rest. At the time of writing his next step is undecided. Collaborations with Pearl Jam's Eddie Vedder and his old Yardbirds partner Jeff Beck have been touted. He could easily take on a similar role to the veteran Carlos Santana, using his playing and influence as a platform to work alongside renowned musicians of varying styles.

At the back of his mind, though, there must linger a nagging urge to try and persuade his former band mates to have one last final live Led Zeppelin blow out.

Clearly he has projects he has yet to fully investigate. "I do have a project in mind that's going to be incredible," he told journalist Mick Wall back in 2000. "I can't really say what it is but it's the sort of thing that people are going to say 'Thank God - I've always wanted him to do that. I've already got material that I've written. I did a new number, 'Domino', at *Net Aid*. It's an instrumental in its earliest stages. I know what it's going to be once I can get my claws into it. But I've got loads of things like that... really good ideas of what I want to do. Great rhythmic things."

On the evidence of the depth and passion he has brought to his playing throughout the last decade, Jimmy Page still has the desire to expand the barriers of his undoubted virtuosity. He remains the eternal keeper of the Zep flame... and the quintessential rock guitar hero.

THE MASTER AND HIS ART 2
A summary of the key Jimmy Page performances spanning the years 1993 to 2002:

1: OVER NOW
COVERDALE PAGE (1993), from the album Coverdale Page
A highlight of the riff leaded return to active service. All the Page trademarks are present: the monolithic grinding tempo, the angular orchestrated riffing, the deceptive time signatures, the snarling wah-wah effects. A most welcome virtual tour de force of the Page guitar armoury.

2: TAKE ME FOR A LITTLE WHILE
COVERDALE PAGE (1993), from the album Coverdale Page
A return to the delicate electric strumming style of 'Ten Years Gone', this has a beautifully descending chord passage overdubbed via a six-string bass. Coverdale drives in the reflective chorus before Page dominates with a superbly structured solo. A triumph of emotion over technique.

3: WONDERFUL ONE
JIMMY PAGE ROBERT PLANT (1994), from the album Jimmy Page Robert Plant No Quarter - Unledded
Composed against a repeated tape loop, this first new Page/Plant studio song for 14 years features Page strumming mournfully on an Ovation double neck guitar. The shimmering melodic lift that he brings to the piece provides a ripple of pleasure every time it comes around.

4: KASHMIR
JIMMY PAGE ROBERT PLANT (1994), from the album Jimmy Page Robert Plant No Quarter - Unledded
From the subtle intro wherein Jimmy glides over the Transperformance through to the dynamic rumbling riffs of the finale, this is a masterful repositioning of the pride of Led Zeppelin, and in turn the pride of Page and Plant. During the previous decade, it was almost unthinkable that he could stamp authority on his past work as effectively as this epic performance.

5: GUITAR SOLO/WHOLE LOTTA LOVE MEDLEY
JIMMY PAGE ROBERT PLANT (1995), from a live performance recorded at Irvine Meadows Amphitheatre California, October 3, 1995
Page's proven record as a studio architect is well recognised but the sense of showmanship he can bring to his playing on stage is often is less documented. His relief at finally being in the company of the singer and songs he works with best gave rise to some

WITH THE BLACK CROWES: 1999

stunning performances on the *Unledded* tour. That showmanship is vividly personified by the extended guitar solo he undertook within the 'Calling To You' and 'Whole Lotta Love' medley on the '95 tour. This night in Irvine Meadows is as good an example as any. Page spits out the riff, shooting out feedback into the night air and then on into a devastatingly brutal riff phrase that is archetypal Page. It's a shame he never took this idea back into the studio with Plant as there is definitely the framework of an epic piece here.

6: BURNING UP
JIMMY PAGE ROBERT PLANT (1998), from the album Walking Into Clarksdale
Page as the unimpeachable riff master was a role he underplayed on the *Clarksdale* album with one notable exception. When they began the first sessions for the album Page brought in 'Burning Up' a growling bombastic blast of guitar fire that duly ignited Plant into a ferocious vocal performance.

7: BLUE TRAIN (1998)
JIMMY PAGE ROBERT PLANT (1998), from the album Walking Into Clarksdale
The other side of the coin. For sheer understated melancholy beauty this may be Page's best recorded moment of the Nineties. He periodically injects the necessary Zeppelinish dynamics to the sullen Plant narrative, then slides into a beautifully plangent Byrds-like jangling guitar solo constructed in a way that is just unmistakably Jimmy Page. In doing so, he succeeds in stripping the guitar to its rawest most emotional form.

8: COME WITH ME
PUFF DADDY FEATURING JIMMY PAGE (1998)
From the Godzilla soundtrack
An unlikely merger with the noted rapper, this remake of 'Kashmir' married the familiar beguiling crunch of the past with the rhythmic hip hop of the present. The Daddy's incessant pleadings against Page's monster riffing builds the tension all the way. His legacy may have been sealed in another era but this massive hit was proof of Page's enduring contemporary appeal. More respect to the man with the Gibson Les Paul...

9: DOMINO
JIMMY PAGE (1999), from a live performance recorded at Net Aid, Giants Stadium, New York, October 9, 1999

A work-in-progress instrumental premiered for the *Net Aid* show, this saw Page introduce yet another part of the armoury, a strange shaped Ovation double neck.

A step on the old wah-wah brings the necessary hard edged grind to Michael Lee's Bo Diddley beat before the trademark symmetrical riffing kicks in. Even in its bare boned format, 'Domino' hinted strongly at the scope for new Page music.

10: THE LEMON SONG/KILLING FLOOR
JIMMY PAGE AND THE BLACK CROWES (1999)
From the album Jimmy Page And The Black Crowes Live At The Greek/Excess All Areas
One of the more interesting Zep retreads played live with the Crowes, this basic blues run through Chester Burnett's old stager is performed faithful to the arrangement on *Led Zeppelin II*, with Page appropriately layering on some vintage speed runs right out of that golden era.

11: SHAPES OF THINGS
JIMMY PAGE AND THE BLACK CROWES (1999)
From the album Jimmy Page And The Black Crowes Live At The Greek/Excess All Areas
Of equal vintage was this re-run through one of The Yardbirds' best moments. In a subtle nod to his ex-guitar partner in crime, the arrangement deployed here has more in common with The Jeff Beck Group delivery of the song from their *Truth* album. Page takes hold of both the smooth woman tone solo and the more fiery Beck inspired kamikaze run that follows.

12: DAZED AND CONFUSED
JIMMY PAGE (2002), from a live performance recorded at the Royal Albert Hall, London, February 9, 2002
Fittingly for a decade dominated by his old band, a final backwards nod to one of his most celebrated creations. Faced with a guest appearance at the Teenage charity shows and with no liaison with Plant on the cards, Jimmy took it on himself to brave a version of 'Dazed And Confused' with Paul Weller's backing band.

Despite the lack of rehearsal, his sheer charisma more than won the day - this compact, close to *Led Zep I*, delivery saw Page wield the violin bow and then push the framework of the song to the limit just as he had done over twenty years ago at the same venue.

It was a night for the veteran guitarist to strip the years away. A thrilling re assurance of the master... and his art.

"Outside my window, strange things come every night and day,
It's strange, so very very strange..."

Robert Plant sang these opening lines from Donovan's 'Season Of The Witch' directly in front of me as he moved centre stage in the tiny Boardwalk club in Sheffield on the night of September 25, 1999. It was the first time I'd seen Robert's band Priory Of Brion and – as the song implied – it was very, very strange to see him in a small club venue again. It was the start of yet another fascinating journey that would bring Plant into closer proximity to his audience than at any time in the previous two decades.

The repertoire he performed was a virtual music history lesson of the late Sixties and along the way it drew attention to the many influences Robert took on board to shape his style in the Midlands before Zep took off. Ultimately his work with the Priory would provide the foundation for further developments within Strange Sensation, the band that would support the recording of his first solo record in nine years.

This chapter traces the development of Robert Plant's post Page/Plant career drawing on material and interviews documented at the time in *TBL* issues *14*, *15* and *16*. From the Priory to *Dreamland* this is yet another twist to the story...

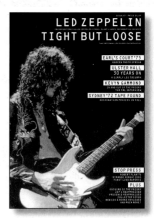

REFERENCE: **TIGHT BUT LOOSE 14, 15 & 16**

18 : ROBERT PLANT – FROM THE PRIORY TO DREAMLAND

Poppy House Promotions
presents

The Priory of Brian

*Obscurities from the
summer of love and beyond*
**Friday 23rd July........doors open 8.30pm
at the Three Tuns, Bishop's Castle**
with special guest Peter Keeley
Tickets : £6.00 in advance only from The Poppy House 20 Market Square,
Bishop's Castle 01588 638443 or £7.50 on the door (if there's any left!!!)

**HOME-MADE FLYER, CREATED ON
PLANT'S COMPUTER**

ROBERT PLANT AND STRANGE SENSATION: 2002

On December 10, 1998, Robert Plant and Jimmy Page took the to stage at the Bercy Omnisports Arena in Paris. They were a late addition to a special Amnesty Charity show which featured performances from the likes of Bruce Springsteen, Tracy Chapman, Radiohead and Peter Gabriel. It was the final date of a year long tour that had commenced the previous February in Eastern Europe. But for Robert Plant it was one gig too many. Tiring of the endless hotel to gig to hotel to gig treadmill, he was mapping out a very different agenda that would not include Jimmy. Their 27-minute six-song mini set would prove to be the last in this format.

"Coming away from that Amnesty gig I thought it was too far off," said Robert later. "Everything had become remote. I felt I was too far away from everybody. I'd been marooned in hotels in the middle of nowhere knowing there's something happening back in England. I thought 'I've only got one life. I'm in the wrong spot'."

Page and Plant had intended to continue their tour into Japan and Australia in early 1999, but over Christmas Plant decided enough was enough. "I'd just had enough. There was a spring coming and I thought how many springs can you see now. I needed to lose the game for a while."

On January 21, to the dismay of Page and manager Bill Curbishley, Robert informed them that he would not be undertaking the Japan-Australia leg of the tour. He wanted to take time out from his collaboration with Page, thus signalling the end of the renewed partnership that had dominated the past five years.

Plant retreated to his Worcestershire home, had his hair cut in a swept back shorter style and chilled out. In late January he recorded a version of Moby Grape's Skip Spence song 'Little Hands' for release on the Skip Spence tribute album more *More Oar*. It was a definite pointer to where he was heading musically.

In the early summer he began rehearsing with Kevyn Gammond, his long time friend and neighbour with whom he played in the Band Of Joy, along with local musicians Andy Edwards on drums, Paul Timothy on keyboards and guitar and Paul Wetton on bass. Plant had previously performed with Gammond and Edwards in an ad-hoc line up at the annual party for his local tennis club in Bewdley in late 1997.

Robert saw this as his next logical move. "It seemed a lot of bands were a pastiche of the golden era of the Sixties with that jingle jangle sound. I said to Kevyn we used to do that... let's do it again. He said he knew some great guys at the collage who were teaching and did a lot of mixing and dance music and had played in bhangra bands in Birmingham. So we had a rehearsal in a barn and it was thrilling."

Their repertoire was a mixture of songs that took Robert's fancy before the advent of Zeppelin. They centred around the West Coast late Sixties sound of Moby Grape, Love, Jefferson Airplane, The Youngbloods and Buffalo Springfield. Some had even been part of the Band Of Joy's set list. "These songs are the cornerstone to a period of my life. I've been touched and moved by these songs. They've got such depth and I've sung them forever in the shower. I've always wanted to sing them so I'm singing them now. I'm on holiday and that's what I want to be," he told a local reporter at the time.

In a move that mirrored his back to the roots approach in the immediate post Zep period with the pick up R&B band The Honeydrippers, Plant began by playing a series of low key club dates. The first was on Friday July 23 at the Three Tuns at Bishop's Castle, advertised with a poster designed by Robert on his home computer.

The set included their interpretations of Love's 'House Is Not A Motel', 'Bummer In the Summer' and '7 And 7 Is', The Youngbloods' 'Darkness Darkness', a psychobilly arrangement of Cliff's Richards' 'Move It', 'No Regrets' by The Walker Brothers, 'Gloria' by Them and Billy Fury's 'Wondrous Place'.

Dubbing the line up "Priory Of Brion featuring founder members of The Band Of Joy", they turned up at choice locations such as the Queen Mary Ballroom at Dudley Zoo, in a tent at the Ashby Del La Zouch Folk Festival and in the Central Station nightclub in Wrexham. The name was adapted from the secret Knights Templars society called Priory Of Zion. "I changed it slightly, remembering in the film *The Life Of Brian* how reverential people can be over nothing. And I thought after the career I've had - all that 'we are not worthy shit', well, that name was spot on."

Commenting on his position with Page, Plant said: "This year I've turned down a couple of things that have affected my situation with Jimmy. We were asked to headline the revived Woodstock Festival and then Neil Young asked us to play the Bridge benefit in San Francisco. I told my manager I couldn't just have four days rehearsal and start playing Led Zeppelin songs again. There was a bit of an outcry and they said, 'Well you just do what you want and then let us know when you feel like coming back'."

This new band provided fans with a rare closeness to the

IN THE TENT, ASHBY DEL LA ZOUCH: OCTOBER 31, 1999

singer and as word spread the Priory Of Brion built up an ardent following. On December 18 they performed at the Zodiac Club in Oxford supported by Tim Rose. Plant brought Rose on stage to join him in a duet of 'Morning Dew', originally a hit for Rose in 1967. Robert's delight at having established an alternative outlet to perform was obvious. He told *Folk Roots* magazine: "With the Priory the music doesn't have any reference to time or style. And I don't think I've ever sung better. I couldn't have sung these songs like this before. I can let my voice swoop and soar and dip and glide and hit those Arabic quarter notes in a way I couldn't do on something like 'Heartbreaker'."

After holidaying in India, in the new millennium Plant regrouped with the Priory for more dates, including appearances in Stoke, Cambridge and Northampton. Now sufficiently confident to announce dates upfront and happy for his name to be tagged on, Plant took the band across Europe for a series of festival dates in the summer. In the UK they played well received sets at Glastonbury, the Cambridge Folk Festival and the annual Fairport Convention bash at Cropredy. In Europe they played the Nice Jazz Festival, supporting the Count Basie Orchestra and Billy Cobham. In between Robert reunited briefly with Jimmy to record the Sonny Burgess track 'My Bucket's Got Hole In It' for the Sun Records tribute album (and in July 2001 he again reunited with Page for a rockabilly set at the Sun Records tribute night at the Montreux Festival).

In September the Priory booked time at Mono Valley Studios in Monmouth, cutting versions of 'Morning Dew, 'Evil Woman' - a track he performed live in the Sixties with The Band of Joy - and Elmer Gantry's 'Flames'.

These songs are the cornerstone to a period of my life. I've been touched and moved by these songs. They've got such depth and I've sung them forever in the shower. I've always wanted to sing them so I'm singing them now. I'm on holiday and that's what I want to be.

ROBERT PLANT

DREAMLAND, THE ALBUM

The recordings were more for Plant's own reference than for release on an album. "I don't want to play the game because the process is too time consuming," he said. "The whole process of the Priory is that I have nothing to prove other than I can still sing really well. So to do it on any level where I would want to see results beyond that would defeat the object."

It was this lack of firm direction, however, that would ultimately signal the end of the project. After a further round of UK gigs they flew to Greece for a four day stint. Three Christmas dates followed in Crewe, Derby and Wolverhampton. Perhaps significantly, on that final home date Plant finally relented and performed Zep's 'Thank You' as a final encore. After over 70 shows in the space of 18 months The Priory Of Brion experience was over. Management pressure to record a new solo album led Robert to close this chapter of his career, but he would compromise by covering these late Sixties songs but employing a group of more high profile musicians with which to present them.

Robert entered 2001 with a series of outstanding Scandinavian dates to fulfill. Rather than return with the Priory line up he formed Strange Sensation – an entirely new band featuring long term Page/Plant band member Charlie Jones on bass; ex-Jah Wobble and Sinead O' Connor guitarist Justin Adams; John Baggott on keyboards (known for his work with Massive Attack); and drummer Clive Deamer, whose previous credits included Portishead. Also back in the fold was Porl Thompson, the ex-Cure guitarist who had toured with Plant and Page on the *Unledded* tour in 1995. The deployment of these better known musicians suggested that a return to full time music was imminent.

> *There are probably three or four thousand albums in my house that could fuel another Dreamland but maybe I'll write an album next time.*
>
> ROBERT PLANT

PRIORY OF BRION, GLOUCESTER: 1999

The new line up made their debut in Denmark in April. An altogether more serious affair, the new band took on more elaborate arrangements of Priory Of Brion staples such as 'Season Of The Witch', 'Morning Dew' and 'A House Is Not A Motel', and the set also included a smattering of Zeppelin numbers, amongst them 'Four Sticks', 'In The Light' and 'Whole Lotta Love'. Plant took the band to America for six late spring dates and after more summer festival dates they began recording at Rak Studios.

The resulting album with the Strange Sensation line up was titled *Dreamland* and issued in June 2002. It was an eclectic collection with Plant on peak form vocally, turning in pleasing renditions of 'Morning Dew', Tim Buckley's 'Song To The Siren' and Dylan's 'One More Cup Of Coffee'. 'Win My Train Fair Home (If I Ever Get Lucky)' was a moody swirl through Arthur Crudup's original. An ambitious take on 'Hey Joe', the traditional tune Plant

played live back in the Band Of Joy and made famous by Jimi Hendrix, took on in a very left field arrangement. Four original songs credited as group compositions were in line with the retro feel: 'Red Dress' was built around a Bo Diddley beat while 'Dirt In A Hole' had the edgy west coast feel of Arthur Lee's Love. These songs represented Plant's first songwriting for four years. He had been reluctant to even add lyrics to 'Life Begins Again', a collaboration with the Afro Celt System that surfaced in early 2002 on their album *Future In Time Vol 3*.

Dreamland carried a similar organic quality to that of his last proper solo album *Fate Of Nations*, released in 1993. Even back then Plant was making music in his own rootsy taste with echoes of the blues tripping into the West Coast on his own 'Promised Land' or the now significant cover of Tim Hardin's 'If I Were A Carpenter'. *Dreamland* carried on that tradition and was well received critically on both sides of the Atlantic. His vocal performance on the album led to two nominations in the annual Grammy awards, but the low key nature of the project was never going to stack up mega sales and without the draw of his former partner it sold only moderately.

At the time of its release Robert reflected on the course leading up to the album's completion. "The Priory did create the right environment for this to happen. My ability and vocal cords are in good shape, but I haven't felt substantially relevant as a lyricist for a long time. These are the songs I've always loved and I don't see them as covers because I was around when they were being written. So I thought I'm dry as a bone lyrically, but these songs are

STRANGE SENSATION, DENMARK: 2001

still vibrant. There are probably three or four thousand albums in my house that could fuel another *Dreamland* but maybe I'll write an album next time."

The band supported the release of the album with a series of UK and US gigs with ex-Cast guitarist Skin replacing the departing Porl Thompson. A series of special guest support slots to The Who took him back to large arenas such as Madison Square Garden - which could be viewed as a quiet victory for his management. The band also appeared on VH1's high profile *Storytellers* series. Alongside material from *Dreamland* and the Zeppelin covers, Plant took the opportunity to revive some of his own past solo highlights including 'Ship Of Fools' and 'Tall Cool One'.

In the autumn the band undertook a successful 13-date UK trek finishing at London's Hammersmith Apollo. That day Plant combined an afternoon playback of the then work-in-progress

---

LIFE IN THE PRIORY
Guitarist Kevyn Gammond

"There was no agenda with the Priory. If we wanted to do a gig we did it. We didn't need to play the media game. We had no real knowledge of our next destination until it shaped up. Musically it was a constant challenge.

"One night it might be brilliant - another we might not be as satisfied. We were always testing ourselves. But Robert was singing so well. It got to the stage in something like 'Song To The Siren' where I'd just stop and let him go on his own. Just leave the voice there... that was a real joy to be a part of.

"I know people would really love to see Robert up there with Jimmy, but the thing is, in the Priory we were just so passionate about what we did. In the first two or three numbers we might get people

shouting for 'Black Dog' but it soon settled down. What was so good about the Priory was that we just followed our instincts.

"We didn't have to worry about breaking America or any marketing plans. We were lucky enough to take these songs into places they hadn't been done before in those arrangements, songs like 'Darkness Darkness' and 'A House Is Not A Motel'.

"It gave us a real freedom to recreate in a modern setting the songs Robert and I have loved for thirty years."
Keyvn Gammond, 2001

LIFE IN THE PRIORY
Drummer Andy Edwards

"I'd played the tennis club gig in Bewdley with Robert a year before, but the first proper gig was at Bishop's Castle and I was really nervous. It would have been terrible had we let him down... but it was great. We'd go to Robert's house and he'd pull out all these crazy vinyl LPs - everything from Ray Charles to Lets Active and Moby

Zep DVD with the an excellent evening show in the capital. From London the tour moved to Scandinavia and ended in St Petersburg and Moscow where 'Rock And Roll' was performed for the first time since 1998.

Closer to home Plant became patron of Kevyn Gammond's Kidderminster College fronted label MAS, donating an excellent studio version of The Priory Of Brion's version of 'Curse The Evil Woman' for the label's launch CD compilation.

He also put in a couple of studio cameo roles, adding harmonica to the track 'The Lord Is My Shotgun' for Primal Scream's *Evil Heat* album and adding vocals to the track 'Let The Boogie Woogie Roll' for Jools Holland's *Small World Big Band Vol 2* set. He was also awarded a lifetime achievement in the Midlander Of The Year media awards staged in Birmingham.

Despite a fresh round of Zep reunion rumours, Plant resumed working with Strange Sensation in 2003.On December 31, 2002 BBC 2 aired their annual Jools Holland *New Years Eve* show which saw Robert performing with Solomon Burke and Tom Jones. In early January he travelled to Timbuktu to appear with Justin Adams at the *Festival In The Desert* in Essakane, Mali, perfoming a unique version of 'Whole Lotta Love'. Back in the UK he undertook a round of promotional appearances to support the release of the single 'Last Time I Saw Her'/'Song To The Siren'. This included TV slots on BBC3's *Re-Covered* and BBC2's *Live Floor Show*. These dates saw the addition of Billy Fuller on bass replacing the departing Charlie Jones to join Goldfrapp. Plant's first proper gig of the year with Strange Sensation took them to Norway for an appearance at the *Ole Blues Festival* in Bergen.

In the summer of 2003 Plant and Strange Sensation were busy on the European festival circuit, and further studio recording with this line-up was also on the cards. Commenting on his work in Strange Sensation Plant said: "There's an energy about this music and a style that is worth pursuing and pushing a bit more. There's a musical empathy here I haven't felt for a long time."

Following the high profile release of Led Zeppelin's long awaited DVD and live album, Robert turned his attention to compiling his own solo retrospective anthology due for release in the fall of 2003. Away from music, Robert was delighted that Wolverhampton Wanderers FC, of whom he is a lifelong supporter, won promotion to the Premiership in May 2003.

Four years on from his curtailment of the Page/Plant collaboration, Robert has carved out another rich musical tapestry. Essentially looking back to look forward, he has succeeded in pleasing himself as well as his audience.

Vocally he is singing as well as ever, and is ambitious to test his vocal control with a variety of material, be it inspired versions of songs he grew up with in the Sixties, experimental recordings

STILL DREAMING, DENMARK: 2001

in the desert or new music drawing on influences as diverse as The Electric Prunes and The Flaming Lips.

"I never want to be stereotyped as being relevant to one era or one type of music," is how he summarised his continuing motivation recently. "The gift's the gift... and you can keep it to yourself or you can go out into the world and use it."

There's an energy about this music and a style that is worth pursuing and pushing a bit more. There's a musical empathy here I haven't felt for a long time.

ROBERT PLANT

Grape to Jeff Buckley. He's such an enthusiast of all sorts of music, and we'd make a list of the songs and then rehearse them. It was a simple process really.

"But the thing with the Priory is that it was a really unique band. I don't think there has ever been a major artist who has ducked out of the music business and just done it on his terms. It was almost like being in a teenage band again. We

would solve every problem between ourselves. How we got to the gigs, the flight cases, the guitar leads, who we took on the crew. All the things normally a record company would look after.

"It was so real. It's like the young Zep on the *DVD*. There you see a brilliant band playing brilliant songs - not even dressed up or anything.

"So when we started to gig, people loved seeing Robert in that set-

ting and it started to run. It's also worth noting that for perhaps the first time this was a band that created its message by word of the Internet. Fans were looking on the *Tight But Loose* site to see what we were doing next, reading the set lists and seeing where we were developing. Initially it was like that. Everybody was a part of that. Even when it got a little bigger, it was still us running it. The band ran under

its own rules. Things like 'Darkness Darkness' and 'As Long As I Have You' had a life of their own when we developed them onstage. We were coming up with all sorts of jamming and experimentation.

"It wasn't just Robert Plant's play-thing. That was the frustration for us in the end. There was always management murmurs from above to get Robert to work with a bigger thing. You know 'Like why isn't he

working with Jimmy or Jeff Beck?' That did put us under pressure as it went on. We wanted to move it to another level but it was difficult. Robert had a lot of responsibility in keeping it together.

"We knew we were a good band and doing interesting things. There was a lot going on. It's a shame there wasn't enough faith in it for us to take it to America and beyond.

"I'm really glad we have some-

MOTEL
LAZY ME
BUMMER
BLUEBIRD
MORNING DEW
CARPENTER
DARKNESS
FLAMES
AS LONG AS I
HEY JOE
EVIL WOMAN
GROOVE
GLORIA
BABY PLEASE DONT GOO

No Regrets
Season
SIREN / TROUBLE

PRIORY SET LIST, WRITTEN BY THE SINGER

The gift's the gift… and you can keep it to yourself or you can go out into the world and use it.

ROBERT PLANT

LIVE WITH STRANGE SENSATION: 2002

thing left to show for it because something like the Priory recording of 'Evil Woman' shows we were right out there, and Kevyn was really right out there. I think what Robert went on to do with Strange Sensation was built on what we did. I saw their VH1 TV recording and they were excellent.

"I remember looking at Robert's hair in front of me at the last gig in Wolverhampton and thinking I won't ever have this view again, so it was sad to be moving on.

"It was all a fantastic experience and I learnt so much from it. He is one of the great singers... he can sing anything. His voice is unique. Working with him was unique."
Andy Edwards, 2003

CREATING STRANGE SENSATIONS
Guitarist Justin Adams

"What we want to do is to present Robert's heritage in a way that combines elements of his past with the present. It provides us with an opportunity to bring an unpredictable edge every night.

"We can go off on different directions and then it all it all meets somewhere in the middle. It's a real challenge because we don't want to come over as a mere tribute band. Something like 'Four Sticks' has been great to do.

"When we first set out to do that I could relate to what Page and Bonham were doing with the rhythm and I could hear in my head what was going on and what I might add to it.

"Then the real challenge was to do something that really fitted in. The way we take on the intro has added a fresh edge. It's again down to how we add our identity to things like that. With the Zeppelin tracks Robert has a similar approach to the way Bob Dylan re-invents his songs. They always come out freshly inspired."
Justin Adams, 2002

Interviews by Dave Lewis for
Tight But Loose.

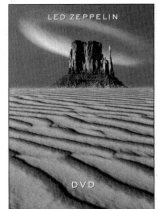

In August 1981 a film director visited the Swan Song offices on the day I was delivering the latest issue of *TBL*. We got talking and he asked me if I'd like to view some of Led Zeppelin's video tape archive to which he had access. A couple of weeks later I was invited back, and sitting alone in the Swan Song interview room I experienced a kind of blissed-out ecstasy, viewing over seven hours of Zeppelin's performances from Earls Court, Seattle and Knebworth on video tape on the old U-matic video format. Even in their unmixed state, it was evident that these performances could be used to produce some sort of official release. Over the years I carried with me vivid memories of that exclusive playback, clear in the knowledge that they deserved to be seen by the legion of Zeppelin fans.

Now, after two decades of rumours, delays and counter rumour, the deed has been done. I'm holding in my hand *Led Zeppelin DVD* – a two DVD set containing over five hours of digitally restored footage. Looking at the distinctive Arizona desert emblazoned cover, it's hard to believe I can actually access and be transported back to the Royal Albert Hall, Madison Square Garden, Earl's Court and Knebworth at the flick of a switch. And if that wasn't enough, there is also a triple live CD set *How The West Was Won* – an accompanying release that once and for all officially captures the real-deal of Zep live.

The furore behind all this activity in the summer of 2003 enabled Led Zeppelin's profile to rise to levels reminiscent of their Seventies peak. It was a truly exhilarating time to be a Led Zeppelin fan. As Jimmy Page himself summarised recently: "People always come up to me and say 'I grew up listening to Led Zeppelin. It's the soundtrack to my life.' Well I grew up with it to too. They are still my favourite band."

The extraordinary sales of the DVD and live set would indicate that Page's last statement also rings true for thousands upon thousands of admirers across the globe. This final chapter chronicles the long running saga of these historic releases.

THE LED ZEPPELIN DVD & : 19
HOW THE WEST WAS WON

Tuesday November 2, 1976. BBC 2. *Old Grey Whistle Test.* 11.30.pm. Across the TV screen in crystal clear colour there is Robert Plant, hair flowing, bare chested, howling out the opening lines of 'Black Dog'.

This is a pivotal moment. I'm witnessing moving images of Led Zeppelin on TV for the first time, courtesy of an exclusive *Whistle Test* preview of the soon to be premiered *Song Remains The Same* movie. This is the band that have shied away from TV aside from a few tentative moves into the medium early in their career. As Peter Grant would comment at the time: "TV just doesn't capture the magic of Zeppelin."

Fast forward 27 years later. I'm ensconced in the viewing room of Metropolis Productions watching similar footage of 'Black Dog' - this time courtesy of an exclusive playback of the soon to be premiered *Led Zeppelin DVD*. It's the same viewing room that the three ex-members have sat in at various times over the past few months assessing their illustrious past.

Much has happened in the intervening years, not least the enhancement of both sound and picture quality of TV video reproduction. Peter Grant's assumption that Zep and the small screen were incompatible can be re-assessed in the era of Digital Versitile Disc, 5.1 surround sound and PCM stereo, all of which are able to recreate the live magic of Led Zeppelin in your own living room.

But it's taken a long, long time to come to fruition. As the co-director of the *Zeppelin DVD* Dick Carruthers explained to me at the playback: "This was a search for buried treasure. Once Jimmy and I had located the masters from the archive we were faced with the huge task to make it all presentable."

They more than succeeded.
The genesis of Page and the group's desire to be presented on film on their own terms stretches right back to the night of January 9, 1970, when Grant commissioned noted film director Peter Whitehead, whose previous credits included The Rolling Stones and Pink Floyd, to shoot the band's prestigious gig at London's Royal Albert Hall. The plan was to use the footage for an intended Zeppelin documentary to be sold to BBCTV and other worldwide networks. On the night the gig was also professionally recorded on Pye Record's mobile unit. Further filming was planned on their next American tour. The gig was filmed on 16mm by two hand held cameras, but when the band looked at the original rushes they decided some of it was too darkly lit. Ultimately the project was shelved and the film was left to languish in their archive.

In 1973 another attempt was made. Grant enlisted film direc-

REUNITED AT THE NEW YORK PREMIERE: MAY 27, 2003

tor Joe Massot to shoot the final weeks of their hugely successful US tour, specifically three gigs at Madison Square Garden. This footage eventually made up the bulk of their feature film *The Song Remains The Same*, released three years later. In 1974, after a dispute with Massot, production duties for the film were handed over to Australian Peter Clifton. In order to assess his suitability for the job he was given access to the 1970 Albert Hall footage and asked to put together a showreel cut of 'Whole Lotta Love'.

As the demand to see Zeppelin increased, by 1975 they were playing huge arenas. When they played five sold out dates at the 17,000 capacity Earl's Court in London, to ensure fans could benefit from the best possible presentation they erected a giant Eidophor screen above the stage - the first time this device was ever used. The Earl's Court gigs were duly videotaped via three to four close cameras and beamed above the band as the action happened. The shows were also recorded professionally.

After the gigs, the masters were tucked away in their archive. The big screen presentation was used periodically on the 1977 US tour, notably at their Seattle Kingdome show, and again the tapes were retained by Page and Grant.

The huge scale of what would be their final two UK shows at Knebworth in August 1979 dictated the deployment of an impressively large back screen projection - a stunning visual effect that did much to enhance the grand scale of the shows.

The two gigs were filmed by a 16-strong multi-camera unit and professionally recorded. The fact that the band were asked to wear identical clothing for both gigs to aid continuity in any subsequent editing was a clear indication that the footage might be officially released.

People always come up to me and say 'I grew up listening to Led Zeppelin. It's the soundtrack to my life.' Well I grew up with it to too. They are still my favourite band.

JIMMY PAGE

SAN DIEGO: JUNE 23, 1972

ROYAL ALBERT HALL: JANUARY 9, 1970

The Albert Hall film was all

mute so we had to match the

relevant visuals with the

audio. All the film was

cleaned up frame by frame

as it had a lot of scratches

on it.

DICK CARRUTHERS, CO-DIRECTOR

The demise of the band following John Bonham's death in September 1980 put paid to any such plans. In 1990 Page did allow MTV access to some of the Seattle and Knebworth footage to promote the *Remasters* releases and the accompanying promo videos for the project. The Aubrey Powell directed 'Travelling Riverside Blues' and 'Over The Hills And Far Away' were compiled using footage from these sources.

In January 1990, BBC2 screened one of the few surviving TV appearances of Zeppelin, the March 1969 half-hour showcase aired originally on the Danish TV network, the confusing titled Danmarks Radio.

During the Nineties it became increasingly apparent that there was scope for a Zeppelin visual and audio history. Page had long harboured a plan to produce a chronological live album set from the tape sources they had logged, and tentative steps towards this were taken in 1976 when Jimmy had one of the first computerised mixing desks installed at his home studio in Plumpton.

He revisited the idea in 1977 and again in 1981 when Atlantic asked for a posthumous album that would eventually emerge as the outtake set *Coda*. For whatever reason, he could not get the others to agree and nothing happened.

In the Nineties the idea was again mooted but Page's indignant comment in early 2000 seemed to put paid to such a project ever seeing the light of day.

"I've always wanted to put out a chronological live album of Zeppelin stuff," he said. "There's some incredibly good stuff but I can't get the others to agree, so I've stopped trying."

Luckily for all concerned they finally reconciled their differences and all agreed something should be done with both their visual and audio archive.

A concerted effort to assess the extent of their visual archive was undertaken in 1997 when directors Nick Ryle and John Mayes employed a variety of clips including the aforementioned Albert Hall, Earls Court, Seattle and Knebworth sources for a promo video to support the release of 'Whole Lotta Love' as a UK single.

Significantly, in 1999 the band secured the rights and masters of the Royal Albert Hall from sources close to director Peter Whitehead. An initial screening of the footage in the presence of all three ex-members offered ample proof that the film had both historical and artistic merit.

It was also evident to Page that the development of the DVD format, with its enhanced sound capabilities, offered at last a real worthy medium to presenting the best possible sound and visual package. The initial idea was to present the Albert Hall show as a concert DVD in its own right but this idea was quickly vetoed when they realised the full extent of their unreleased material.

In early 2002 Page enlisted the assistance of director Dick Carruthers to begin the long trawl to a proper official document. Carutthers CV included work with The Rolling Stones, Oasis and The Who, with whom Page and Plant now shared manager Bill Curbishley. He had been impresssed by Carruthers' direction of the DVD for The Who's Teenage Charity Royal Albert Hall gig in 2001 and suggested a meeting with Page, after which the task began.

The first job was to search out every master visual and audio in their archives. Various UK archive storage vaults were trawled and a full inventory compiled. They then began the painstaking task of matching visuals with the equivalent audio masters and digitally cleaning them up. Page brought in sound engineer Kevin Shirley, with whom he had previously worked on the *Live At The Greek/Black Crowes* album, to supervise the sound.

WINNING THE WEST IN 1972

"Led Zeppelin The Forgotten Giants?" was the headline that jumped out of *Melody Maker* in late June 1972. It contained Roy Hollingworth's remarkable report from New York where Led Zeppelin had just performed two shows at the Nassau Coliseum. He witnessed a three-and-a-half hour marathon show that included four encores and heard first hand the disappoint-

ment the group were feeling at being ignored in the press. In a moment of rare irritation John Paul Jones commented: "Here we are slaving away constantly getting incredible reactions and nobody back home cares."

Hollingworth's description of the Nassau show remains one of the most evocative of their entire career. "The noise cajunked and beefed outwards, filling each corner

of the circular space aged Nassau Coliseum. 16,000 people didn't know whether they were coming or going. Led Zeppelin had been off stage four times and four times an unnatural din had brought them back for more. It was one of the most amazing concerts I'd seen from any band at any time. Nothing had gone missing. It had been the complete act. There had been power, climax after climax, beauty, funk,

rock, boogie, totally freaked passages and such constant snarling energy that on this evening Led Zep could have provided enough human electricity to light half of America. Does anybody really know how big Led Zeppelin are?"

Such descriptions had me pining to see them again on stage. I'd have to wait another six months before they returned to London to invade Ally Pally - but boy how I would

have given anything to hear a tape of that night back in June 1972, or any from that tour for that matter. Who would have thought that 31 years on, this period would inspire a belated live album set that would top the US charts instantly.

But that's exactly what happened following the release of *How The West Was Won* on May 26, 2003.

Before we get to that, it's worth reflecting on Zep's frame of mind at

EARL'S COURT: 1975

MADISON SQUARE GARDEN: 1973

During the search Page came across the multi-tracks for 1972 performances at Long Beach and Los Angeles. It was these tapes that would eventually emerge as the accompanying live CD set *How The West Was Won.*

Part of the restoration process involved having the tapes baked at 55 degrees for three weeks to ensure they did not crumble when played back. There was also the problem of locating a video machine that would play back the old two inch masters.

They began with restoring the Albert Hall film. "The Albert Hall film was all mute so we had to match the relevant visuals with the audio," explained Carruthers. "All the film was cleaned up frame by frame as it had a lot of scratches on it. There was an added complication when we found some of the tracks had long gaps in where the film reels had run out, so we had those to fill as well."

The bulk of the Royal Albert Hall performance filmed on January 9, 1970, takes up all of the first DVD. This is a vintage 102-minute portrayal of the band without the visual flash that would unfold in later years. Amid the denim, plimsolls and long hippie hair are some devastating performances and the 5.1 surround sound is awe inspiring, with Bonham's straight from the wrist drumming sweeping across the speakers. Watch him clatter around the kit on the opener 'We're Gonna Groove' and it's immediately apparent how vital he was to the band and how irreplaceable he remains.

'Dazed And Confused' can be viewed at its most dark and dynamic with none of the hamming up of later years as Page reaches for the violin bow and attacks it straight off with THAT sequence that sends shivers every time. 'Whole Lotta Love' is offered in the relatively compact 45 rpm format that saw them ensconced in the top five of the American singles chart that very week back in 1970.

Elsewhere we see them as unpretentious good time rock-'n'rollers, romping through a remarkable back-to-back Eddie Cochran tribute that takes in 'C'mon Everybody' and 'Something Else'. Page plays the rare Gibson 'Black Beauty' guitar that was stolen a few months later.

The second DVD opens with a ferocious 'Immigrant Song' sourced from the 1972 LA gig as featured on the accompanying *How The West Was Won* CD cut to silent super-8 cine film of the band shot by a roadie on the side of the stage in the bright open air at their appearance at the Sydney Showground on February 27 1972 during their only Australian visit. It's the perfect linking track. Two years on from those auspicious Albert Hall beginnings Zeppelin were conquering the world.

A year later American audiences were more keen to see and hear Led Zeppelin than any other artist on the planet. They had elevated from being a mere rock group into a US institution and the following footage, taken from the filming that resulted in the *Song Remains* movie, is now ample proof.

"Jimmy was very keen to look at the outtakes from their Madison Square Garden footage used for the *Song Remains* movie," said Carruthers. "We received the Garden footage all spooled direct from Warners film archive in Burbank. It was all over the place. We had to re-join the footage to identify it all. We knew what we were looking for performances of 'Over The Hills And Far Away', 'Misty Mountain Hop', 'The Ocean' and 'Thank You'. 'Over The Hills' and 'Thank You' were just too incomplete but we were pleased with 'Misty' and 'The Ocean'. Jimmy also wanted to recut 'Black Dog' and 'Since I've Been Loving You' as we had great audio of that. It took us over six weeks alone to do the four Madison Square performances."

Jimmy also wanted to recut 'Black Dog' and 'Since I've Been Loving You' as we had great audio of that. It took us over six weeks alone to do the four Madison Square performances.

DICK CARRUTHERS, CO-DIRECTOR

the time. As Plant told Hollingworth: "Something has really clicked here. The spirit within the band is fantastic. They'd never believe how good it is here a back home. They'd just never believe what happened tonight."

Zeppelin's US tour of that June took in a compact 19 dates. It was all but ignored in the press (bar that *Melody Maker* feature) and vastly overshadowed by the Rolling

Stones' comeback US tour that kicked off at the same time.

As Bonzo reflected a couple of months later to the *NME's* Roy Carr: "It's the Stones this, the Stones that... it made us feel we were slogging our guts out and for all the notice we were getting we might as well been playing in Ceylon. Kids in England didn't even know we were playing the States."

The lack of press coverage would

inspire Grant to hire a proper PR firm for the next US tour, and with Danny Goldberg on board it would be a very different story in 11 months time.

Despite the low key coverage, the tour found Zeppelin on fire musically.

Fresh from the trip to Australia and a break back in England, and fuelled by the progress they made on their fifth album during the

spring, the momentum within the band was at a new high.

Their eagerness to present the new material resulted in them premiering five songs from their fifth album *Houses Of The Holy* which would not be released for another ten months.

With the acoustic set still intact, the shows consistently ran to three hours and over. This tour also allowed them to showcase material

from their six month old watershed fourth album.

On June 19 they played a remarkable show at the Seattle Coliseum. One of their longest ever sets saw them preview 'The Ocean', 'Back Country Woman' (prepared for *Houses* but eventually issued on *Physical Graffiti*), 'Over The Hills And Far Away' plus 'Dancing Days'.

The latter was actually performed twice - as they revived it as

2003 PROMOTIONAL BLIMP

The care and restoration that went into those clips pays massive dividends. The 1973 extracts are now vivid reminders of the way the band swept all competition aside as they blazed across the US that summer, with a cocksure arrogance and onstage showmanship evident in every shot. From Bonzo's hammerings in 'Black Dog' through the jaunty version of 'Misty Mountain Hop', a familiar but no less impressive recut of 'Since I've Been Loving You' and a truly astounding delivery of 'The Ocean' that is one of the stand out moments of the whole package - happy, smiling, gelling and just chilling out on an encore groove. This is Zeppelin in all its unchained, unabashed, carnal glory.

The programme now cuts to Earl's Court two years later via a striking image of a young Zep fan holding aloft a bootleg scarf with the words Led Zepplin (sic). In stark contrast to the exuberance of the Garden in '73 we see Jones, Page and Plant relaxed and front of stage for the acoustic 'Going To California', all shot in crystal clear video. Subsequent intimate performances of 'That's The Way' and 'Bron Yr Aur Stomp' are the absolute epitome of the light and shade that set them apart from their peers.

The Earls Court 1975 footage survived on two-inch videotape. The challenge here was to overcome the limited camera angles - most of it was shot close up to the stage and there was no luxury of multi-camera tapes. What they found they had was the original footage as it was deployed on to the screens above the stage. The close proximity to the band only enhances the stark clarity of these images.

At Earl's Court we see Zeppelin in all their celestial elegance. The thrill of seeing this, the most revered previously unseen

PERFORMING 'BRON YR AUR STOMP', SAN DIEGO: JUNE 23, 1972

footage of any band anywhere, is just electrifying. Marvel at the permanently out on the edge delivery of 'In My Time Of Dying', the chronically rampant 'Trampled Underfoot' and the emotion packed 'Stairway To Heaven'. The latter is a key highlight, bringing renewed dignity to the once much maligned anthem, capturing Page in a thrillingly gratuitous flourish of twelve-string histrionics.

The two Knebworth gigs presented another challenge. This time they did have the luxury of multi-camera video tapes from the 16 cameras that were used - but Carruthers was keen not to oversimplify the spirit of the event with editing trickery. "There is a textual variation in how we presented the Knebworth sequence and made it look like film as opposed to video," he said. "It gave it a slightly refreshed look. I think it adds to the narrative structure we were aiming for. It's some of the most absorbing footage we had."

The Knebworth sequence is an absolute revelation: brilliantly

edited and with subtle cine film juxtaposed within the main footage. By selecting the very best of the performances from the first date on August 4, Page and Carruthers have rewritten history. Far from looking the tired old dinosaurs the press would label them, 'Achilles Last Stand', 'In The Evening' and 'Kashmir' offer vivid reminders of the band's still impressive majesty. They may have been a tad rusty from all the lay offs but the spirit was more than willing. Further evidence is supplied by the stunning romp through 'Rock And Roll' and the grand finale - the revamped arrangement of 'Whole Lotta Love' with its extending barrage of riffs repeatedly honed by Page, Jones and Bonham. "Thanks for eleven years," is Plant's final farewell. 'You'll Never Walk Alone' sung by the multitudes brings the journey to an end.

Watching Led Zeppelin leave the Knebworth stage evokes more than a tinge of regret, not least because the rapport and chemistry we see on that stage indicated that they still had new places to travel.

Alongside the main programme are a variety of additional extras and menus. On Disc 1 we see the band in its early incarnation. All black and white posing and thrashing blues rock on the mimed promo for 'Communication Breakdown' shot for a Swedish TV station. Similarly we see the intense black and white live TV Byen Dansh TV performance from the same era. The advent of colour brings new life to Page's psychedelically painted Telecaster and Plant's hippie clothing for a compact delivery of 'Dazed And Confused', Zep's contribution to the *Supershow* feature film that showcased a variety of blues artists shot in a disused warehouse in Staines in March 1969. Finally we are treated to the bizarre setting of Zep as the guests that spoilt the party on *Tous En Scene*, a French variety show that illustrates why Peter Grant was right to decide enough was enough when it came to Zeppelin on the small screen. Not before they have baffled the audience with another blitzkrieg that takes in a frantic 'Communication Breakdown' and part of 'Dazed And Confused'.

On Disc 2 the extras include a 1970 New York press conference where a bearded Page and Plant hold court and answer questions surrounding their elevation to being 'bigger than The Beatles'. Black and white Australian news footage shows a panoramic view of them blasting through 'Rock And Roll' and a period piece press reception where a young Germaine Greer eyes the young black country boys and Bonzo offers some articulate observations on their fourth album.

In an interview for the *Old Grey Whistle Test* in January 1975 we hear Robert Plant's comments to Bob Harris backstage in Brussels when asked about playing in England again. "What we want to do in England if we can find the right venue and I think we possibly can, is turn it into something of an event and go to town on it in true style," is a hint of the glory of Earl's Court to come. The 1990 promos for 'Travelling Riverside Blues' and 'Over The Hills And Far Away' with montage footage culled from Danish TV, Seattle, Knebworth etc can now be viewed as mouth-watering tasters for their archive - now finally served up to full potential on this DVD.

The menus are another treat. As Dick Carruthers told me: "The main features are the real focus - then you have all these extras that you may not notice until you've played the discs and menus a few times."

Click in the right place and there's the band arriving in Iceland in 1970 followed by an eerie segment featuring Page

---

a final encore. A week later they were on their favoured West Coast stamping ground for dates in San Diego, Berkeley, the Los Angeles Forum and Long Beach Arena.

It's the latter two dates that Page has rediscovered in their tape archive to assemble the 3-CD set, appropriately titled *How The West Was Won*.

The results are utterly startling.

Both dates are well familiar to

Zep bootleg collectors. The LA date has long been held in high esteem via an excellent audience recording released on CD under the title B*urn Like A Candle*. Long Beach has surfaced via a lesser quality tape issued on Cobra Standard's *Wild Beach Party*.

The existence of full official tapes has been hinted by soundboard snippets from that date that have seeped out on bootlegs, namely

'What Is And What Should Never Be', 'Dancing Days' and 'Moby Dick'.

That summer found Zeppelin in absolute prime form. "1972 was a particularly great year for us. We were right on top of what we were up to," reflected Plant in the promotion for the new set.

Now thanks to some sterling work from Page and engineer Kevin Shirley, the full throttle power of

that era can be replayed time and time again. Page has cleverly edited both nights to present a full Zeppelin concert.

This is the official live album we've always craved. From the drone noise as they walk on stage through to a breathless 'Bring It On Home', this one has it all.

Great previews from *Houses* in 'Over The Hills And Far Away', 'Dancing Days' and 'The Ocean', a

PERFORMING 'ACHILLES LAST STAND', KNEBWORTH: AUGUST 4, 1979

REUNITED AT THE LONDON PREMIERE,
EMPIRE, LEICESTER SQUARE: MAY 15, 2003

to do justice to the personalities and the canon of work, without ever losing the essence and integrity of the source material. Jimmy has applied, as only he can, his structural and sequencing knowledge of the band to present something lasting and special."

To support the release all three ex-members attended the Leicester Square London premiere on May 15. Prior to the screening they took to the stage for a short introduction - the standing ovation they received was as deafening as Bonzo's opening snare shots on that introduction to 'We're Gonna Groove'. It was an emotional night for both the band and its guest audience. As John Paul Jones noted: "For me it was so great to see so much of Bonzo. It reminded me how much Led Zeppelin revolved around him. Sitting there watching him on the big screen at the premiere I really missed him. As people cheered at the end of his drum solo I joined in - it was like 'Play some more'. Everything on stage revolved around him. Whenever we started to improvise or change direction musically, you'd see everyone move towards the drums."

Plant was equally moved. He told Nick Coleman of the *Independent*: "Seeing Bonzo 40 foot high and across the screen doing his magnificent thing in front of all these people while sitting next to John's son Jason well... it was too much."

On May 27, Page, Plant and Jones and the Bonham family attended the New York premiere at Loew's 34th Street Theatre. They also made a joint appearance on the NBC Today talk show.

The extraordinary sales of both the DVD and accompanying *How The West Was Won* album was reminiscent of Zeppelin's chart domination in the Seventies. The live album entered at number one on the *Billboard* chart, shifting 150,000 its first week. In the UK it registered at number 5. The *DVD* quickly became the biggest selling music DVD ever, topping the DVD charts in America, the UK, Australia, Canada, France, Norway and Sweden. In the US alone it shifted 120,000 copies.

During the many promotional interviews they undertook, the most-asked question was the inevitable: would all this renewed activity now lead to a full blown reunion? Page was slightly optimistic in his reply: "None of us have actually discussed reforming. If we got back in a room and played a Zeppelin number and there were smiles behind our eyes then maybe it could be possible. Until that happens, it's hypothetical. I wouldn't discount it. I just don't know."

John Paul Jones had this to say: "One quarter of Led Zeppelin is gone. It wasn't just a drummer. It couldn't ever be the same."

Robert Plant, always the most reticent when such talk emerges, perhaps summed it all up by stating: "I don't know if it could work in this century. You're talking about a lot of years later. I'm sure it would be evocative for people in the crowd but I don't know if we could do it properly. If anything the DVD really opens and closes the issue because it's so explicit of what it was all about. It's the epitaph of Led Zeppelin – stunning, a lot of energy, a rollercoaster ride, four guys melding in this great fusion of music... and it's gone."

Gone but not forgotten. Now, at the flick of the DVD scanner, we can relive so many magic moments from their history. And every time he comes into view or supplies that integral percussive groove to it all, John Bonham's presence is a constant reminder of why it can never really ever be the same.

Reunion? Who really needs it now? The DVD is a reunion in itself - and it confirms without question that they are, were and always will be the best.

Fact.

wielding the violin bow on stage in Reykjavik. We see fascinating cine film shot by the roadies in a car travelling to the Ulster Hall show in Belfast 1971 - culminating in the four of them crossing the road to go into the pub. There's atmospheric footage backstage in Madison Square Garden with Page looking every inch the quintessential English rock star.

Click the intro of the Knebworth menu to view some nostalgic cine film shot by *TBL* reader Andy Banks and first brought to Page's attention via the Knebworth feature in *TBL 14*. Then there's proof of Page's amnesty with the bootleggers in the epic version of 'The Song Remains The Same' from LA on June 21, 1977, direct from the *Listen To This Eddie* bootleg synched to some powerful 1977 tour cine film images, including a great side on shot view of them slaying across the stage in Birmingham Alabama. The audio prompt menu also has some atmospheric 1975 US tour cine film form Seattle matched to the version of 'The Crunge' segment during 'Whole Lotta Love' from Earls Court May 25, 1975.

The only omission seems to be a complete lack of acknowledgement to Peter Grant. Aside from a couple of shots in the wings he is rarely seen - a menu of footage of the towering fifth Zep would have paid appropriate dues to the man who led them to so much worldwide success. From the main features it would have been good to see Jones showcased fully on a version of 'No Quarter', but really this is mere nitpicking.

Five and a half hours of footage is an embarrassment of riches. It may have been a very long time coming but as Zeppelin fans old and new soaked up this monumental outpouring, the massive sales and positive feedback was a clear indication that Page and Carruthers had exceeded all expectations. "I knew I had a huge responsibility in doing this," concludes Carruthers. "I had

If anything the DVD really opens and closes the issue because it's so explicit of what it was all about. It's the epitaph of Led Zeppelin – stunning, a lot of energy, a rollercoaster ride, four guys melding in this great fusion of music... and it's gone.

ROBERT PLANT

---

wonderfully relaxed acoustic set, a sprawling 'Dazed' with off the cuff inserts of 'Walter's Walk' and 'The Crunge', Bonzo's craft on 'Moby Dick' and a revved up 'Whole Lotta Love' medley that tips its hat to John Lee Hooker, Elvis and Ricky Nelson. Individually they are bursting with creativity.

Plant's vocals would never again match the high register range he propels here, Page is off on a tan-

gent at every turn of the way and Jones and Bonzo are locked together in familiar tight but loose fashion. The whole affair is superbly mixed with just the right amount of crunch and bluster.

The last word goes to Jimmy Page, the creator of all this outpouring of material: "Playing the West Coast was always fantastic. Each member of the band was playing at their best during those

1972 performances.

"And when the four of us were playing like that, we combined to make it a fifth element. That was the magic – the intangible."

APPENDIX 1: CHRONOLOGY, 1991 TO 2003 *COMPILED BY GARY FOY & DAVE LEWIS*

1991

January 8, 9 & 10 Robert Plant plays The Town & Country Club, London. All three shows rescheduled from November 1990.

January Roberts's two gigs at the Rock In Rio Festival on January 20 & 24 are cancelled along with dates in Alegne, Brazil, San Porto, Brazil and Caracas, Venezuela due to a recurring throat problem.

January 18 John Paul appears on stage at the Queen Elizabeth Hall with vocal renaissance group Red Byrd. The group perform Jones composition "Amores Pasodas". John plays lute, harpsichord and vihuela.

March Jimmy jams with Les Paul at Fat Tuesdays in New York for the guitarist's birthday.

March 23 Jimmy jams with local band The Reputations at the China Club in New York.

March Whilst in New York Jimmy and David Coverdale hold the first tentative meeting to discuss a the possibility of working together.

May In a interview in *The Music Paper* John Paul reveals he has been producing an album for his daughter Jacinda (aged 23) at Peter Gabriel's Real World Studios. He also talks about his recent production work for La Furu Del Baus and Red Byrd.

May Jimmy stays at Coverdale's home on Lake Tahoe in Nevada where they begin writing material together.

May 12 Jimmy along with Coverdale join US rock group Poison on stage at Lawlor Events Centre, Reno for a encore jam of 'Rock'n'Roll', 'The Rover' and 'Stairway To Heaven'.

May 18 Robert attends the wedding of his daughter Carman to his bassist Charlie Jones at St Peters Church, Upper Arley near Kidderminster. The reception for 400 guests is held at Robert's Shatterford home.

May 29 Jimmy jams with local band Solid Ground at the Christa Bay Club, Reno, Nevada.

October Robert appears at the Market Tavern, Kidderminster along with Jason Bonham and local bands The Ripps and Billy & The Bowel Movements for a benefit concert in aid of the family of the late Darren Norwood, former percussionist with local band Kernal Klark.

November Page and Coverdale begin recording at Little Mountain Studios in Vancouver.

November Page and Coverdale appear at the Yale Club, Vancouver, jamming on several numbers including 'Dazed And Confused'.

December 7 Jimmy joins Long John Baldry in a club in Vancouver for a thirty minute blues jam.

1992

January 15 Jimmy attends *The Rock and Roll Hall Of Fame* induction of The Yardbirds at the Waldorf-Astoria Hotel and joins in with Jeff Beck, Neil Young, Keith Richards, Mitch Mitchell, Noel Redding, Robbie Robertson and John Fogerty for an all-star jam of the Hendrix classic, 'All Along The Watchtower'.

January Robert jams several times with ex-Move guitarist Trevor Burton during his weekly residency at the upstairs bar of the Adam and Eve pub in Birmingham.

March 14 Page joins Harry Connick Jnr on stage at the Knights Centre, Miami, jamming on a couple of blues numbers.

April 20 Robert joins the remaining members of Queen at the *Freddie Mercury Tribute* concert at Wembley Stadium. He performs the Queen numbers, 'Innuendo' and 'Crazy Little Thing Called Love' and includes snippets of 'Kashmir' and 'Thank You' and also appears on stage at the end for the grand finale of 'We Are The Champions'.

May 8 John Paul attends the premiere of his new composition 'Macanda', at a night of World Music billed as "Electrifying Exotica" at The Southbank in London.

May 22/23 The first ever UK Led Zeppelin Convention takes place at The Royal National Hotel, London.

August 11 Robert joins Fairport Convention at their warm-up gig at The Mill Theatre, Banbury, performing 'Girl From The North Country', 'Babe I'm Gonna Leave You', 'In The Evening' and 'Ramble On'.

August 14 Again Robert joins the Fairport's, this time at their annual Cropredy Festival performing the same four numbers.

September 12 Brian Eno's *Nerve Net* album is released, featuring John Paul on several tracks.

October 5 REM's *Automatic For The People* is released, a multi-platinum album that features four tracks with string arrangements by John Paul. All four numbers, 'Drive', 'Sidewinder Sleeps Tonite', 'Everyone Hurts' and 'Night Swimming', are released as singles over the next eight months and are all hits themselves.

October Page and Coverdale complete their album at Abbey Road. Page also mixes the unreleased Led Zeppelin track 'Baby Come On Home' for release on the forthcoming *Boxed Set 2*.

November 18 Jimmy, Robert and John Paul, along with Jason Bonham representing his father, are presented with a *Q* magazine Merit Award for Led Zeppelin at the Park Lane Hotel in London.

1993

March 15 *Coverdale/Page* album released, reaching number 4 in the UK chart.

March 29 The John Paul Jones produced album by The Butthole Surfers, Independent Worm Saloon, is released.

April 26 Robert releases his first single in nearly three years, '29 Palms', which peaks at 21 in the UK charts.

April 28 Robert records an appearance for *Top Of The Pops* performing '29 Palms'. Later in the evening he and his band attend the official launch party for *Fate Of Nations* at Commonwealth House London.

April 29 Robert's *Top Of The Pops* performance of 29 Palms is aired

May 1 Robert appears in front of 160,000 at the Piazza San Giovanni in Rome, performing 29 Palms and Whole Lotta Love. The event is also shown live on Italian TV.

May 6 Robert joins UK rockers Def Leppard on stage at The Forum in Copenhagen, Denmark for encore jam of 'Rock And Roll', 'Black Dog' and 'Whole Lotta Love'.

May 12 Robert records a second appearance for the BBC's *Top Of The Pops*, again performing '29 Palm's. On the set of *TOTP* Robert also records an interview with Claire Sturgess for Radio One's *Friday Rock Show*.

May 13 Roberts's second *Top Of The Pops* performance is broadcast

May 14 Robert plays a secret gig at The Kings Head, Fulham under the pseudonym *Fate Of Nations*.

May 18 Robert records a guest spot on the BBC 2 show *Later With Jools*, performing 'Calling To You', 'If I Were A Carpenter' and 'I Believe'.

May 20 Robert plays a second gig at the Kings Head Fulham, this time billed as the Band Of Joy. Nigel Kennedy guests on Calling To You and You Shook Me.

May 21 Robert's *Friday Rock Show* interview is aired on Radio One and the *Jools Holland* appearance is broadcast on BBC 2.

May 22 Robert is featured on Radio One's *Johnnie Walker* show in the afternoon, chatting and performing an acoustic set with Francis Dunnery and Kevin Scott McMicheal featuring the numbers, 'I Believe', 'If I Were A Carpenter', '805', 'Bluebird' and 'Whole Lotta Love'.

May 26 Robert plays the Slavia Hall, Prague.

May 27 Robert plays the Petofi Hall, Budapest.

May 29 Robert plays the Ernst Happel Stadium, Vienna, Austria. (Festival appearance)

May 30 Robert plays the Rock AM Ring. Nurburgring, Germany (Festival appearance).

May 31 Robert releases *Fate Of Nations*, his seventh album, reaching number 6 in the UK charts. In June Robert begins a tour of Europe in the support slot for American rocker Lenny Kravitz.

June 2 Robert plays the Mannheim MaiMarchkethalle, Germany.

June 3 Robert plays the Munich Olypiahalle, Germany.

June 4 Robert plays the Cologne Sporthalle, Germany.

June 6 Robert plays the Berlin Deutchlandhalle, Germany.

June 7 Robert plays the Hamburg Sporthalle, Germany.

June 9 Robert plays the Essen Grudahalle, Germany.

June 11 Robert plays the Patinoire De Malley, Lausanne, Switzerland.

June 12 Robert plays the Palatrussardi, Milan, Italy.

June 13 Robert appears on Italian TV show *Videomusic Roxy Bar*, filmed in Bologne, performing an acoustic set along with Francis Dunnery and Kevin Scott McMichael. The set list includes 'Hoochie Coochie Man', '29 Palms', 'Thank You', 'I Believe', 'Whole Lotta Love', 'Boogie Chillin'', and 'Going To California'. Robert is introduced as Robert Palmer!

June 14 Robert plays the Le Summun Grenoble, France.

June 15 Robert plays the Zenith Omega Toulon, France.

June 16 Robert plays the La Patinoire Meriadex Bordeaux, France.

June 18 Robert plays the Sports Palace Barcelona, Spain.

June 19 Robert plays the Sports Palace.Madrid, Spain.

June 22 Robert plays the Palais De Bercey. Paris, France.

June 23 Robert spends two days in Bude, Cornwall filming a video for the forthcoming single 'I Believe'.

June 25 Robert plays the Glastonbury Festival, England.

June 26 Midtfyns Festival, Denmark.

June 27 Robert Plant plays the *Park Pop Festival*, Den Haag, Holland.

June 28 Coverdale/Page release their first UK single, 'Take Me For A Little While', which reaches 29 in the charts. On the same day, Robert releases his second single off *Fate Of Nations*, 'I Believe', reaching 64 in the charts.

July 1 Robert plays the Roskilde Festival, Denmark.

July 2 Robert plays the Montreux Jazz Festival, Switzerland.

July 3 Robert plays the Pistoia Blues Festival, Piazza Del Duomo, Pistoia, Italy.

July 6 Robert plays the Rheims, Parc Des Expostions, France.

July 7 Robert plays the Frankfurt, Festhalle, Germany. Robert jams with Lenny Kravitz on 'Celebration Day' during Kravitz's set.

July 9 Robert plays the La Coruna, Estadio Raizor, Spain (festival appearance).

July 11 Robert plays Frauenfeld, Out On The Green, Switzerland (festival appearance).
The European Tour finishes with two excellent UK shows.

July 14 Robert plays the Birmingham NEC.

July 16 Robert plays the Brixton Academy, London. Chris Robinson of The Black Crowes jams on 'You Shook Me'.

August 14 Robert appears at the Fairport Convention annual Cropredy festival, this time accompanied by Charlie Jones and new band member Innis Sibun. Along with the Fairports, they perform Misty Mountain Hop', 'Ramble On', Thank You', '29 Palms', 'If I Were A Carpenter', 'Girl From The North Country', 'Jesus On The Main Line', Babe I'm Gonna Leave You' and Whole Lotta Love'.

August 23 'Calling To You' released as a UK single

August 28 Robert and Francis Dunnery appear on Italian TV show, Italian Democratic Party TV Show, performing '29 Palms', 'I Believe', Hoochie Coochie Man' and 'Whole Lotta Love'.

September John Paul teams up with Lenny Kravitz to play bass on Lenny's hit 'Are You Gonna Go My Way' for the USA MTV Awards show.

September Coverdale/Page announce a 45-date US tour to commence on October 15 in Miami. The tour is subsequently cancelled amid rumours of poor ticket sales.

September 10 Robert appears on the David Letterman show performing '29 Palms' from the CBS studios in New York.

September 15 & 17 Robert plays the Sunrise Music Theatre, Miami.

September 18 Robert plays the Civic Auditorium, Jacksonville.

September 19 Robert plays the Fox Theatre, Atlanta.

September 21 Robert plays the Pelham Oak Mountain Amphitheatre, Birmingham, Alabama.

September 22 Robert plays the Mud Island Amphitheatre, Memphis.

September 24 Robert plays the Starwood Amphitheatre, Nashville.

September 25 Robert plays the Nutter Centre, Dayton.

September 26 Robert plays the Louisville Gardens, Louisville.

September 27 Led Zeppelin *Boxed Set 2* released alongside the ten CD set *Complete Studio Recordings*.

September 28 Robert plays the Memorial Hall, Kansas.

September 30 Robert plays the McNichols Arena, Denver.

October 1 Robert plays the Salt Air Hall, Salt Lake City.

October 3 Robert plays the Schnitzer Auditorium, Portland.

October 4 Robert plays the Paramount Theatre, Seattle.

October 5 Robert plays the Paramount Theatre, Seattle.

October 7 Robert plays the Orpheum Theatre, Vancouver.

October 8 Robert plays the Hult Centre, Eugene.

October 10 Robert plays the Shoreline Amphitheatre, Mountain View.

October 11 Robert plays the Cal Expo Theatre, Sacramento.

October 12 Robert plays The Pavilion, Concord.

October 13 Robert appears on the *Jay Leno Show* filmed at Burbank Studios, California, performing '29 Palms' and 'Tall Cool One'.

October 14 Robert plays the Ballys Event Centre, Las Vegas.

October 15 Robert plays the County Bowl, Santa Barbara.

October 16 Open Air Theatre, San Diego (cancelled).

October 18 Coverdale/Page release their second single in the UK, 'Take A Look At Yourself', which charts at number 42.

October 18 Robert plays the Universal Amphitheatre, Los Angeles.

October 19 Robert plays the Mesa Amphitheatre, Cosa Mesa.

October 25 Robert plays the Municipal Auditorium, Lubbock.

October 26 Robert plays the Frank Erwin Centre, Austin.

October 28 Robert plays the Convention Centre, Dallas.

October 29 Robert plays the Woodlands Pavilion, Houston.

October 30 Robert plays the Lakefront Arena, New Orleans.

November 1 Robert plays the Civic Centre Music Hall, Oklahoma City.

November 3 Robert plays the Aire Crown Theatre, Chicago. Blues harp player James Cotton jams on 'Look Over Yonder', 'Sweet Home Chicago' and 'Gamblers Blues' Cotton was support to Zeppelin on the Texas Pop Festival in 1969.

November 5 & 6 Robert plays the Fox Theatre, Detroit.

November 8 Robert plays the Northrop Auditorium, Minneapolis.

November 9 Robert plays the Mecca Auditorium, Milwaukee.

November 11 Robert plays the A.J. Palumbo Centre, Pittsburgh.
November 12 Robert plays the Veterans Memorial Auditorium, Columbus.
November 14 Robert plays the Savage Hall, Toledo.
November 15 Robert plays the Public Hall, Cleveland.
November 17 Robert plays the Sheas Theatre, Buffalo.
November 18 Robert plays the Landmark Theatre, Syracuse.
November 20 & 21 Robert plays the Orpheum Theatre, Boston. It's at these Boston gigs that Jimmy Page meets Robert to discuss a proposed MTV *Unplugged* show.
November 23 Robert plays the The Forum, Montreal, Canada.
November 24 Robert plays the Varsity Arena, Toronto, Canada.
November 26 & 27 Robert plays the Tower Theatre, Philadelphia.
November 28 Patriot Centre, Mason University, Fairfax (cancelled).
November 30 & December 1 Robert plays the Paramount Theatre, New York City.
December 6 Robert plays the Konserthuset, Stockholm, Sweden.
December 7 Sentrum, Oslo, Sweden (cancelled).
December 9 Robert plays the Grosse Friheit, Hamburg, Germany.
December 10 Robert plays the E-Werk, Cologne, Germany.
December 12 Robert plays The Depot, Frankfurt, Germany.
December 13 Robert plays The Zenith, Paris, France.
December 15 Robert plays the Terminal 1, Munich, Germany.
December 16 Robert plays the Palasesto, Milan, Spain.
December 17 Robert plays the Volkshaus, Zurich, Switzerland.
December 19 Robert plays the La Luna, Brussels, Belgium.
December 20 Robert plays the Paradisco, Amsterdam, Holland.
December 20 Robert releases his fourth single off *Fate Of Nations*, 'If I Was A Carpenter', reaching 63 in the charts.
December 22 Robert plays the Civic Hall, Wolverhampton, England.
December 23 Robert plays the Brixton Academy, London, England. With the cancelled USA tour behind them, Coverdale/Page embark on a seven-night tour of Japan. These would be their only official live shows.
December 14 & 15 Coverdale/Page play The Nippon Budokan, Tokyo.
December 17 & 18 Coverdale/Page play the Yoyogi Olympic Pool, Tokyo
December 20 & 21 Coverdale/Page play the Castle Hall, Osaka.
December 22 Coverdale/Page play the Nagoya Gym, Nagoya.

1994

After a two-week break Robert and the band finally get to play South America including some festival dates.
January 15 Robert plays the Hollywood Rock Festival, San Paulo.
January 17 Robert plays the Velez Sarsfield, Buenos Aires.
January 19 Robert plays the Veledrome, Santiago.
January 22 Robert plays the Hollywood Rock Festival, Rio de Janeiro.
January 25 Robert plays Caracas.
January 28 & 29 Robert plays the National Auditorium, Mexico.

These are the final gigs that Robert performs with this line up.
February 28 The Soundtrack to *Wayne's World 2*, the hit comedy movie featuring Robert and his band's version of 'Louie Louie', is released.
March Robert and Jimmy stage initial reheasals at the Depot Kings Cross London.
April 17 Robert and Jimmy appear at the Alexis Korner Tribute Concert in Buxton, England. Numbers played include 'Baby Please Don't Go', 'I Can't Quit You Baby' and 'Train Kept a Rollin''.
July At the end of the month Jimmy and Robert have a week of rehearsals at CTS Studios in Wembley with the new band plus an Egyptian orchestra and an English String orchestra.
July Atlantic relaunch the Zeppelin catalogue on remastered CDs.
August 9 First day of filming finds Robert and Jimmy set up in a ancient Moroccan courtyard in Marrakesh with four Moroccan Gnaoui musicians. They perform two new numbers, 'City Don't Cry' and 'Wah Wah'.
August 10 Next day finds Robert and Jimmy in the J'ma El Fna Square in the centre of Marrakesh. As the sun set they perform 'Yallah' and Wah-Wah' to a drum loop to amazed on lookers.
August 12 Having flown back the day before Robert and Jimmy attend the Cropredy Festival in Banbury, Oxfordshire, but do not play.
August 12-16 John Paul Jones performs with Heart at the Backstage, Seattle.
August 16 More filming for *Unplugged*, this time at Dolgoth, on a mountainside in Wales. They perform a new acoustic version of 'No Quarter'.
August 17 Charlie Jones, Michael Lee, Porl Thompson, Nigel Eaton and Jim Sutherland join Robert and Jimmy at the Corris Slate Quarry in Bron-Yr-Aur, Wales, where there perform 'Gallows Pole', 'Nobody's Fault But Mine' and 'When The Levee Breaks'.
August 24,25 & 26 Studio 2, London TV Studios. A night of rehearsal is followed by two nights of filming for the MTV *Unplugged* show.
September The whole of this month is taken up mixing the TV show and soundtrack album, mostly in CBS Studios, Whitfield Street London.
September 30 Robert and Jimmy conduct interviews with the press at a coffee house around the corner from Whitfield Studios.
October 11 Robert and Jimmy attend the New York preview of *Unledded* at The Beacon Theatre in New York. A similar preview is held at The Planet Hollywood Cinema in Shaftsbury Avenue, London on the same night.
October 12 *Unledded* is broadcast on MTV in the USA.
October 15 Robert and Jimmy attend a press conference at the Cirque d'Hiver in Paris, France.
October 17 *Unledded* is broadcast on MTV in Europe. As *Unledded* is shown around the world, this month John Paul Jones begins a short European tour with avant-garde diva, Diamanda Galas, dates include:
October 19 John Paul & Diamanda Galas play the Grosse Freiheit, Hamburg, Germany.
October 20 John Paul & Diamanda Galas play Metrol, Berlin, Germany.
October 31 John Paul & Diamanda Galas play the Shepherds Bush Empire, London England.
November 1 Jimmy and Robert begin rehearsals for the forthcoming world tour at London Studios.
November 7 *No Quarter*, the new Page and Plant album taken from the *Unledded* shows is released in the UK.
November 8 Jimmy & Robert record appearance for the Jools Holland's *Later With...*show, recorded at the BBC TV Centre, London. Numbers performed are 'Gallows Pole', 'Wonderful One' and 'Four Sticks'.
November 8 *No Quarter*, the new Page and Plant album is released in the USA.
November 10 Jimmy & Robert appear on the Japanese entertainment show *The News Station*, TV Asahi, Japan. The pair are interviewed and perform a shortened acoustic version of 'Stairway To Heaven'.
November 14 *No Quarter* is released in Europe, reaching number 7 in the UK charts.
November 16 Robert and Jimmy appear on 3MMM FM Radio in Sydney, Australia. They are interviewed and perform 'No Quarter'.
November 16 Later in the day the pair appear on *The Andrew Denton TV Show* from Sydney, and perform 'Black Dog' complete with didgeridoo player and a version of Rolf Harris' 'Sun Arise'.
November 19 The *Jools Holland Show* is aired on BBC 2.
November 20 Robert and Jimmy appear on Buenos Aires Radio in Argentina. There are interviewed and also perform 'I Can't Quit You Baby' and 'Dazed and Confused'. Whilst Jimmy and Robert criss-cross the world on an endless promotional tour John Paul continues to tour with Diamanda, spending a month in the USA.
November 10 John Paul & Diamanda Galas play the Irving Plaza, New York City.
November 13 John Paul & Diamanda Galas play the Irvine Auditorium, Philadelphia.
November 15 John Paul & Diamanda Galas play the The Michigan Theatre, Ann Arbor.
November 17 John Paul & Diamanda Galas play the The Vic, Chicago.
November 18 John Paul & Diamanda Galas play the Barrymore Theatre, Madison.
November 20 John Paul & Diamanda Galas play the Lied Centre, Lincoln.
November 22 John Paul & Diamanda Galas play the Mershon Auditorium, Columbus.
November 24 John Paul & Diamanda Galas play the The Phoenix, Toronto, Canada.
November 26 John Paul & Diamanda Galas play the Lincoln Theatre, Washington.
November 30 John Paul & Diamanda Galas play the Paramount Theatre, Austin.
December 2 John Paul & Diamanda Galas play the Grady Gammage Auditorium, Tampa.
December 4 John Paul & Diamanda Galas play the Wadsworth Theatre, Los Angeles.
December 6 John Paul & Diamanda Galas play The Filmore, San Francisco.
December 8 John Paul & Diamanda Galas play the Art Museum, Portland.
December 10 John Paul & Diamanda Galas play The Moore, Seattle.
December 12 John Paul & Diamanda Galas play The Commodore Ballroom, Vancouver, Canada.
December 5 Page & Plant's 'Gallows Pole' is released as a single in the UK, reaching number 35 in the charts.

Throughout December and January Robert and Jimmy continue to rehearse at The Depot, New Kings Cross, London for the forthcoming world tour.

1995

January 12 Led Zeppelin are inducted into *The Rock and Roll Hall of Fame*, at The Waldorf-Astoria Hotel in New York. Robert, Jimmy and John Paul, along with Jason and Zoë Bonham, attend to accept the award. Afterwards the three remaining Zep's jam with Aerosmith's Steve Tyler and Joe Perry and also Neil Young. Numbers performed include 'Train Kept A Rollin'', 'Bring It On Home', 'Baby Please Don't Go' and, with Young, 'When The Levee Breaks'.
January John Paul spends January producing new band Elephant Ride in Shangri La Studios, Zuma Beach California. Whilst here John began putting ideas together for his own solo album. The first track was written here and would emerge, after a change of spelling, as the title track, 'Zooma'.
January 30 Led Zeppelin are awarded the *International Artist Award* from The American Music Awards. John Paul receives the award at the ceremony in Los Angeles and Robert and Jimmy are seen on a "live link" from London performing a new version of 'Black Dog'. The so-called live link was actually recorded five days earlier at The Depot in London where the pair were busy rehearsing for the world tour.
February 4 Jimmy jams with The Black Crowes at The Zenith Club, Paris on 'Shake Your Money Maker'.

After a couple of days dress rehearsals the *Page & Plant World Tour* kicks off with much media attention.
February 26 Page & Plant play the Civic Arena, Pensacola, FL.
February 28 & March 1 Page & Plant play the Omni, Atlanta, GA.
March 3 Page & Plant play the Thompson-Boling Centre, Knoxville, TN.
March 4 Page & Plant play the Pyramid, Memphis, TN.
March 6 Page & Plant play the Miami Arena, Miami, FL.
March 7 Page & Plant play the Orlando Arena, Orlando, FL.
March 10 & 11 Page & Plant play the UNO Lakefront Arena, New Orleans, LA.
March 13 Page & Plant play the Frank Erwin Centre, Austin, TX.
March 14 Page & Plant play the Summit, Houston, TX.
March 16 Page & Plant play the Barton Coliseum, Little Rock, AR.
March 18 Page & Plant play the Reunion Arena, Dallas, TX.
March 20 Page & Plant play the Rupp Arena, Lexington, KY.
March 22 & 23 Page & Plant play the US Air Arena, Washington, DC.
March 25 Page & Plant play the Civic Arena, Pittsburgh, PA.
March 27 Page & Plant play the Sky Tent, Toronto, Canada.
March 28 Page & Plant play the Gund Arena, Cleveland, OH.
March 31 Page & Plant play The Palace, Auburn Hills, MI. An attempt on Page's life is foiled when a 23-year-old fan who rushes towards the stage and gets within 50 yards of him is overpowered. He claims that demons surrounding Page drove him to it, leading to the predictable "Satanic Curse" stories appear in the press.
April Release of the Led Zeppelin tribute album *Encomium*.
April 1 Page & Plant play The Palace, Auburn Hills, MI.
April 3 Release of the video Jimmy Page Robert Plant *Unledded No Quarter* via Universal.
April 3 & 4 Page & Plant play The Spectrum, Philadelphia, PA.
April 6 & 7 Page & Plant play the Meadowlands Arena, East Rutherford, NJ.
April 9 & 10 Page & Plant play the Boston Garden, Boston, MA.
April 25 Page & Plant play the Riverfront Coliseum, Cincinnati, OH.
April 26 Page & Plant play the Market Square Arena, Indianapolis, IN.
April 28 & 29 Page & Plant play the Rosemont Horizon, Rosemont, Chicago IL.
May 1 Page & Plant play the Bradley Arena, Milwaukee, WI.
May 2 Page & Plant play the Target Centre, Minneapolis, MN.
May 5 Page & Plant play the Kemper Arena, Kansas City, MO.
May 6 Page & Plant play the Kiel Centre, St. Louis, MO.
May 8 Page & Plant play the McNichols Arena, Denver, CO.
May 10 Page & Plant play the America West Arena, Phoenix, AZ.
May 12 Page & Plant play the MGM Grand, Las Vegas, NV.
May 13 Page & Plant play the Sports Arena, San Diego, CA..
May 16 & 17 Page & Plant play the Forum, Los Angeles, CA.
May 19 Page & Plant play the Oakland Coliseum, Oakland, CA.
May 20 Page & Plant play the San Jose Arena, San Jose, CA. After the show on a flight to Portland Page is arrested for smoking on the plane.
May 23 Page & Plant play the Coliseum, Portland, OR.
May 24 Page & Plant play the Tacoma Dome, Washington.
May 26 Page & Plant play the PNE, Vancouver, Canada.
May 27 Page & Plant play The

Gorge, Washington.

After a week's rest the Page & Plant tour rolls into Europe, which includes eight festival dates.

June 6 Page & Plant play the Palais Omnisports, Bercy, Paris, France.

June 7 Page & Plant play the Tony Garnier Halle, Lyon, France.

June 9 Page & Plant play the Marseilles Dome, Marseilles, France.

June 10 Sonaria Festival, Milan, Italy. Festival in which Page & Plant are second on the bill to The Cure.

June 12 Page & Plant play the Palais De Sports, Toulouse, France.

June 15 Page & Plant play the Ahoy, Rotterdam, Netherlands.

June 16 Page & Plant play the Forest National, Brussels, Belgium.

June 18 Lunenburg Festival, Germany. Page & Plant are second on the bill behind Elton John and before Sheryl Crow.

June 24 Page & Plant plays the Schwalmstadt Festival, Germany.

June 25 Page & Plant plays the Glastonbury Festival, England, third on the bill behind Simple Minds and The Cure. Some of the set is broadcast live on Channel 4 TV and the BBC broadcast some more of set on Radio One that evening.

June 28 Page & Plant play the Navel Museum, Stockholm, Sweden.

June 29 Page & Plant play the Roskilde Festival, Denmark.

July 2 Page & Plant play the Olympic Stadium, Munich, Germany. Second on the bill to Elton John.

July 5 Page & Plant play the Madrid Sports Palace, Madrid, Spain.

July 6 Page & Plant play the Barcelona Sports Palace, Barcelona, Spain.

July 8 Page & Plant play the Out in the Green Festival, Switzerland.

July 9 Page & Plant play the Belfort Festival, Eurokenes, Metz, France.

July 12 Page & Plant play the S.E.C.C, Glasgow, Scotland.

July 13 Page & Plant play the Sheffield Arena, Sheffield England.

July 15 Page & Plant play the Cornwall Coliseum, St Austell, England.

July 16 Page & Plant play the Poole Arts Centre, Poole, England.

July 19 & 20 Page & Plant play The Point, Dublin, Ireland. On the second night Najma Akhtar appears to sing her parts for The Battle Of Evermore, for the first time on the tour.

July 22 & 23 Page & Plant play the NEC, Birmingham, England.

July 25 & 26 Page & Plant play London's Wembley Arena, England.

Peter Grant attends the final European gig and Robert name checks him after 'Kashmir'.

Page & Plant take a two month break before the Second leg of the USA tour begins.

September 23 & 24 Page & Plant play the Palacio de los Deportes, Mexico City.

September 27 Page & Plant play the Pan Am Centre Las Cruces NM..

September 29 Page & Plant play the Tingley Coliseum, Albuquerque NM.

September 30 Page & Plant play the Fiddlers Green, Denver, CO.

October 2 & 3 Page & Plant play the Irvine Meadows Amphitheatre, Irvine CA.

October 6 Page & Plant play the Cal Expo Amphitheatre Sacramento CA.

October 7 Page & Plant play the Shoreline Amphitheatre, Mountain View, CA.

October 9 Page & Plant play the BSU Pavilion, Boise, ID.

October 10 Page & Plant play the Delta Centre, Salt Lake City, UT.

October 12 Page & Plant play the Hilton Coliseum, Ames, IA.

October 13 Page & Plant play the United Centre, Chicago, IL.

October 15 Page & Plant play the Palace of Auburn Hills, Detroit, MI.

October 16 Page & Plant play the Gund Arena, Cleveland, OH.

October 18 Page & Plant play The Forum, Montreal, Canada.

October 19 Page & Plant play the Buffalo Memorial Auditorium, NY.

October 21 Page & Plant play the Civic Centre, Hartford, CT.

October 23 Page & Plant play the Fleet Centre, Boston, MA.

October 24 Page & Plant play The Spectrum, Philadelphia, PA.

October 26 & 27 Page & Plant play Madison Square Garden NY.

November 23 Zeppelin manager Peter Grant dies of a heart attack.

December 4 Peter Grant's funeral held at St Peter and St Paul's Church Hellingly, East Sussex.

1996

January 20 Page & Plant play the Pacaembu Stadium, Sao Paulo, Brazil.

January 23 Page & Plant play the Estadio Sausalito, Vîa del Mar, Chile.

January 25 Page & Plant play the Buenos Aires, Argentina.

January 27 Page & Plant play the Apoteose Square, Rio, Brazil.

After the South American leg Page and Plant holiday in Hawaii, before continuing into Japan and Australia.

February 5, 6, 8, 9, 12 & 13 Page & Plant play the Budokan Hall, Tokyo, Japan.

February 15 Page & Plant play the Castle Hall, Osaka, Japan.

February 17 Page & Plant play the Century Hall, Nagoya, Japan.

February 19 Page & Plant play the Castle Hall, Osaka, Japan.

February 20 Page & Plant play the Marine Messe, Fukuoka, Japan.

February 24 & 25 Page & Plant play the Sydney Entertainment Centre, Sydney, Australia.

February 27 Page & Plant play Brisbane, Australia

February 29 & March 1 Page & Plant play Melbourne, Australia

March A proposed gig in Bombay is cancelled, despite the gig appearing on official merchandise.

August Jimmy and his girlfriend holiday in Lencois, Brazil.

August 9 Robert attends Fairport's annual Cropredy Festival in Banbury, Oxfordshire but doesn't play.

August During this month Robert jams with local blues band Texas Line in a small club in Bobbington in the Midlands and also plays in a charity soccer match in aid of a hospice in Bridnorth.

September 26 Jimmy attends The Yardbirds gig at The 100 Club in London along with Jeff Beck, but neither play.

September 27 A joint press release from Page, Plant and Jones is

issued, denying rumours that Led Zeppelin were to reform and play a show at Knebworth as a tribute to Peter Grant.

November Robert and Jimmy spend a month rehearsing new material for a new album.

November 30 Robert and Jimmy are presented with a *Lifetime Achievement Award*, in Mumbai, India. They receive the award on Channel V music awards show and also mime to 'Rock And Roll', with Queen's Roger Taylor on drums and Remo Ferandez, a local bassist.

1997

March Jimmy Page begins initially assessment of the Zeppelin visual archive, the first result of which is the video to accompany the release of 'Whole Lotta love' as a single.

March Page and Plant record 'Rude World', a tribute to Rainer Ptacek, to be included on the album *Inner Flame*. When the longtime friend of Plant needed to raise money for cancer treatment, Plant co-produced this benefit CD.

April Jimmy begins remastering the tapes of Led Zeppelin's BBC sessions with engineer Jon Astley, working at Astley's home studio, The Pink Room, in Twickenham with the original BBC tapes.

May 29 Jimmy, Robert and John Paul attend the Ivor Norvello awards at the Grosvenor Hotel, London, where they are presented with a *Lifetime Achievement Award* by Atlantic co-founder Ahmet Etegun.

July 8 Release of the Rainer Ptacek album *The Inner Flame*. Sadly Ranier loses his battle with brain cancer in November.

August and September Robert and Jimmy record tracks in Abbey Road Studios for their new album, working with engineer Steve Albini..

September 1 Led Zeppelin's first ever UK single, 'Whole Lotta Love', is released, reaching number 21. It spearheads a promotional campaign for the Zeppelin catalogue on CD.

November 1 Robert appears at a charity gig in his local Tennis Club in Bewdley with Kevyn Gammond.

November 24 Led Zeppelin's BBC Sessions is released, reaching 23 in the charts.

December 7 Robert and Jimmy appear at the Café de Paris, London at a charity function organized by Pat Cash, the tennis pro. They play with Charlie Jones and Michael Lee and perform 'Ramble On', 'Move It', 'Over The Hills And Far Away', 'Thank You' and 'Crossroads'. All proceeds go to the children's charities *Goal and War Child*.

1998

January 3 Robert appears on the classical radio station Classic FM and is interviewed by Sally Peterson on her *Secret Fan* show.

February Jimmy films his parts for the Puff Daddy video to accompany the single 'Come With Me' at Pinewood Studios in England.

February Page and Plant play a series of Eastern European dates.

February 21 Page & Plant play the Dom Sportova, Croatia.

February 23 Page & Plant play the

Sports Hall, Budapest, Hungary.

February 25 Page & Plant play the Sparta Prague Sports Hall, Prague, Czechoslovakia.

February 26 Page & Plant play the Spodek Hall, Katowice, Poland.

March 1 Page & Plant play the Sala Palatului, Bucharest, Romania.

March 2 Page & Plant play the Winter Sports Palace, Sofia, Bulgaria.

March 5 & 6 Page & Plant play the Bostanci Centre, Istanbul, Turkey.

March 25 Page & Plant play the Shepherds Bush Empire, London.

March 26 At the BBC Studios in Elstree, Robert and Jimmy record a performance for the BBC show *Top Of The Pops*, performing the new single, 'Most High', 'House Of Love' and a cover of the Robert Johnson number 'Crossroads'.

March 27 More TV, at the Riverside Studios in Hammersmith, London for the prestigious Channel 4 show, *TFI Friday* hosted by Chris Evans. They open with 'Rock'n'Roll' and after an interview close the show with 'Most High'. The show is aired that night.

March 30 Page & Plant play the La Cigale, Paris, France'

March 31 Robert and Jimmy appear on the French TV show *Nulle Part Ailleurs*, recorded in Paris. Numbers performed are 'Most High', 'When I Was A Child', 'Ramble On' and 'Rock'n'Roll'.

April 6 'Most High', the first single from Page and Plant's new album, is released, reaching number 26 in the charts.

April 20 *Walking Into Clarksdale*, the second Page and Plant album is released, reaching number 3 in the charts.

May 5 Robert and Jimmy record an appearance on the BBC 2 show *Later With Jools* at the BBC TV Studios in White City, London, performing 'The Wanton Song', 'Shining In The Light' and 'Burning Up' and are interviewed by the host Jools Holland.

May 8 The *Later With Jools* show is aired.

May 9 Jimmy appears on the American TV show *Saturday Night Live* with Puff Daddy performing Come With Me'.

Page & Plant begin their North American Tour,

May 19 Page & Plant play the Civic Centre Pensacola, FL.

May 20 Page & Plant play the Ice Palace, Tampa, FL.

May 22 Page & Plant play the Civic Centre, Miami, FL.

May 23 Page & Plant play the Coliseum, Jacksonville, FL.

May 26 Page & Plant play the Coliseum, Charlotte, NC.

May 29 Page & Plant the Lakewood Amphitheatre, Atlanta, GA.

May 30 Page & Plant play The Coliseum, Tupelo, MS.

June 1 Page & Plant play the Civic Centre, Birmingham, AL.

June 2 Page & Plant play the Nashville Arena, Nashville, TN.

June 4 Page & Plant play the Myriad, Oklahoma City, OK.

June 6 Page & Plant play the Kemper Arena, Kansas City, MO.

June 7 Page & Plant play the Kiel Centre, St. Louis, MO.

June 9 Page & Plant play the Market Square Arena, Indianapolis, IN.

June 10 Page & Plant play the Bradley Centre, Milwaukee, WI.

June 12 Page & Plant play the Target, Minneapolis, MN.

June 13 Page & Plant play the Fargo dome, Fargo, ND.

June 15 & 16 Page & Plant play the United Centre, Chicago, IL.

June 16 'Shining In The Light' is released as the second single from *Walking Into Clarksdale*.

June 26 & 27 Page & Plant play The Palace, Detroit, MI.

June 27 Whilst in Detroit Page & Plant go into a studio and record their parts of 'Gonna Shoot You Right Down', for inclusion on the forthcoming Jimmy Rodgers tribute album.

June 29 Page & Plant play the Van Andel Arena, Grand Rapids, MI.

July 1 Page & Plant play the Civic Arena, Pittsburgh, PA.

July 3 Page & Plant play the Gund Arena, Cleveland, OH.

July 4 Page & Plant play the Molson Amphitheatre, Toronto, ONT.

July 7 Page & Plant play the MCI Centre, Washington, D.C.

July 8 Page & Plant play the Virginia Beach Amphitheatre, Virginia Beach, VA.

July 10 Page & Plant play the Corestates Arena, Philadelphia, PA.

July 11 Page & Plant play the Pepsi Arena, Albany, NY.

July 13 Page & Plant play the Fleet Centre, Boston, MA.

July 14 Page & Plant play the Great Woods, Boston, MA.

July 16 Page & Plant play Madison Square Garden, New York City, NY.

July 18 Page & Plant play the Brendan Byrne Arena (Continental Arena), East Rutherford, NJ.

July 19 Page & Plant play the Jones Beach, Long Island, NY.

July 25 The soundtrack *Godzilla*, featuring the Page/Puff Daddy collaboration is released and reaches number 13 in the charts.

August 6 Page & Plant perform at The Drumquinna Hotel, County Kerry for the wedding reception of their lighting tech Tom Kenny. Numbers include 'I've Got A Woman', 'Crossroads', 'Baby Please Don't Go', 'Mystery Train' and 'Rock And Roll'.

August 8 'Come With Me', the Puff Daddy and Jimmy Page single, is released and charts at number 2 in the UK.

August 21 Page & Plant play the Vaduz Festival in Liechtenstein.

August 23 Page & Plant play the Bizarre Festival in Cologne.

August 26 Page & Plant play The Point in Dublin, Ireland.

August 28 Page & Plant play the Reading Festival, Berkshire, England.

August & September John Paul Jones records his new album at The Malt House, London.

Page & Plant begin the second leg of their North American tour.

September 5 Page & Plant play the General Motors Place Vancouver, BC, Canada.

September 6 Page & Plant play The Gorge, Washington.

September 8 Page & Plant play The Rose Garden Portland, OR.

September 9 Page & Plant play the

Idaho Center Boise, ID.
September 11 Page & Plant play the Concord Pavillion Concord, CA.
September 12 Page & Plant play the Shoreline Amphitheatre San Francisco, CA.
September 15 Page & Plant play the UTE Center Salt Lake City.
September 16 Page & Plant play Red Rocks, Denver, CO.
September 18 Page & Plant play the Irvine Meadows Irvine, CA.
September 19 Page & Plant play the Hollywood Bowl Los Angeles, CA.
September 21 Page & Plant play the Cox Arena San Diego, CA.
September 23 Page & Plant play the MGM Las Vegas, NV.
September 24 Page & Plant play the America West Phoenix, AZ.
September 26 Page & Plant play The Alamo Dome San Antonio, TX.
September 27 Page & Plant play the Reunion Arena Dallas, TX.
September 30 Page & Plant play The Cynthia Woods Mitchell Pavillion at the Woodlands, Houston, TX.
October 1 Page & Plant play the UNO Lakefront. New Orleans, LO.
October 2 Page & Plant play the Pyramid, Memphis, TN.
October 30 Page & Plant play the University of London Union, England.
November 2 Page & Plant play the SECC Glasgow, Scotland.
November 3 Page & Plant play the Manchester Evening News Arena, England.
November 5 & 6 Page & Plant play the Wembley Arena London.
November 9 Page & Plant play the Liberte Arena Rennes, France.
November 10 Page & Plant play the Bercy, Paris, France.
November 12 Page & Plant play the Dom Sportova, Zagreb, Croatia,
November 13 Page & Plant play the Stadthalle, Vienna, Austria.
November 16 Page & Plant play the Messehalle, Erfurt, Germany.
November 17 Page & Plant play the Sparta Prague Sports Hall, Prague, Czech Republic.
November 19 Page & Plant play the Forum Milan, Italy.
November 20 Page & Plant play the Hallenstadion, Zurich, Switzerland.
November 23 Page & Plant play the Olympiahalle, Munich, Germany.
November 25 Page & Plant play the Zenith, Montpellier, France.
November 26 Page & Plant play the Patinoire, Bordeaux, France.
November 28 Page & Plant play the Zenith, Toulon, France.
November 29 Page & Plant play the Halle du Tony Garnier, Lyon, France.
December 1 Page & Plant play the Exhibition Hall, Gent, Belgium.
December 2 Page & Plant play the Oberhausen Arena Germany.
December 3 Page & Plant play the Festhalle, Frankfurt, Germany.
December 10 Page and Plant are a late addition to the all-star *Amnesty International Concert* in Paris at the Bercy Omni-sport Arena, performing a 37-minute, six song set. On the 50th Anniversary of the Universal Declaration of Human Rights, this concert also features Bruce Springsteen, Peter Gabriel, Youssou N'Dour, Tracy Chapman and Radiohead.

1999

January 13 Robert informs manager Bill Curbishley and Jimmy Page he will not be undertaking the planned Japan and Australia tour.
January Robert records 'Little Hands', a Skip Spence number, for inclusion on a Skip Spence tribute album. The track is recorded at a Bristol studio with Charlie Jones and Phil Andrews helping.
February 25 'Most High' wins a Grammy in the Best Hard Rock Performance category.
March 15 Jimmy attends the *Rock And Roll Hall Of Fame* ceremony at New York's Waldof Astoria.
March 16 At a ceremony at The Roseland Ballroom, New York, Ahmet Ertegun presents Jimmy and John Paul with a 'Diamond Award' honouring sales of over 20 million units for *Led Zeppelin IV*. (A 'Diamond Award' is for 10 million sales)
May Jimmy and drummer Michael Lee record backing tracks for a planned second Page and Plant album.
June 16 Jimmy appears on stage at music industry black tie dinner in aid of UNICEF Kosovo appeal benefit at the Banqueting Halls in Whitehall. Jimmy, with Michael Lee on drums and Guy Pratt on bass, performs an instrumental 'Dazed And Confused'. The evening raises £100,000.

Jimmy books a week at Nomis Studios from June 21 for rehearsals with The Black Crowes for a forthcoming charity gig.
June 27 Jimmy appears at the Café De Paris in aid of two charities, S.C.R.E.A.M and ABC. Following sets from Roger Taylor and The Stereophonics, Jimmy appears with The Black Crowes and performs 'Shake Your Money Maker', 'Sloppy Drunk', 'Woke Up This Morning', 'In My Time Of Dying', 'Oh Well' and 'Whole Lotta Love'. After a short break Jimmy returns with Michael Lee on drums and Guy Pratt on bass to perform 'Dazed And Confused', and are then joined by Aerosmith's Steve Tyler and Joe Perry to run through 'Train Kept A Rollin' and 'Heartbreaker' before The Crowe's Chris and Rich Robinson return for a finale of 'You Shook Me'.
July 6 *More Oar*, the Skip Spence tribute album is released in the US only. Robert is featured on the track 'Little Hands'.
July Having decided to curtail his partnership with Jimmy, Robert enlists the help of Kevyn Gammond, his old friend and former band member of The Band Of Joy, and along with three other local musicians forms Priory Of Brion.
July 23 POB play The Three Tons, Bishop's Castle, Shropshire.
July 25 Gibson Guitars honour Elvis guitarist Scotty Moore with his own signature guitar that Jimmy presents to him at a private function at Air Studios in Hampstead. Other guests include Albert Lee, Gary Moore, Jeff Beck, Steve Howe and Jack Bruce.
August John Paul spends a week in Japan on a promotional tour for his forthcoming album.
August 25 POB play The Walls, Welsh Walls, Oswestry, Shropshire.
August 26 POB play The Jazz & Roots Club, Butter Market, Shrewsbury.
August 28 POB play Olbury Wells School, Bridgnorth Folk Festival.
September 4 John Paul appears on Tom Robinson's BBC Radio 2 programme.
September 10 POB play The Kings Hotel, Newport, Gwent.
September John Paul appears on the Channel 4 *Big Breakfast* show UK TV show.
September 14 John Paul releases *Zooma*, his first solo album.
September 25 POB play the Boardwalk, Sheffield.
September 26 An episode of *Mr Rock N Roll*, a Channel 4 series about rock managers, features an hour-long look at Peter Grant. Notable by their absence are Jimmy and Robert.
October 2 & 3 John Paul plays Roisin Dubh, Galway.
October 4 John Paul plays Limelight, Belfast.
October 5 John Paul plays HQ, Dublin.
October 8 John Paul plays Crossing Border Festival, Hague, Holland.
October 9 POB play Ludlow Assembly Rooms, Ludlow.
October 9 While Robert is in Ludlow playing to a few hundred, over in Giants Stadium, New York. Jimmy appears on the *Net Aid* concert, firstly as a guest of Puff Daddy to perform 'Come With Me' and then on his own with Michael Lee and Guy Pratt to perform a instrumental 'Dazed And Confused' and a new instrumental number, 'Domino'. He is then joined by the Robinson brothers for versions of 'In My Time Of Dying' and 'Whole Lotta Love'.
October 12, 13 & 16 Jimmy & The Black Crowes play the Roseland Ballroom, New York.
October 16 Jimmy & The Black Crowes play the Worcester Centrum, Boston. Joe Perry from Aerosmith jams on 'Oh Well' and 'You Shook Me'.
October 18 & 19 Jimmy & The Black Crowes play the Greek Theatre, Los Angeles.
October 12 John Paul plays Pearl St, Northampton, MA..
October 13 John Paul plays Toad's Place New Haven, MA.
October 15 John Paul plays Paradise Boston, MA.
October 16 John Paul plays Irving Plaza New York.
October 17 John Paul plays Theatre of Living Arts, Philadelphia, PA.
October 19 John Paul plays The Odeon, Cleveland, OH.
October 20 John Paul plays Park West, Chicago, IL
October 21 John Paul plays Cabooze, Minneapolis, MN.
October 23 John Paul plays Ogden Theatre, Denver, CO.
October 25 John Paul plays Showbox, Seattle, WA.
October 26 John Paul plays Crystal Ballroom, Portland, OR.
October 28 John Paul plays The Fillmore, San Francisco, CA.
October 29 John Paul plays House of Blues, Los Angeles, CA.
November 1 John Paul plays The Joint at the Hard Rock Hotel, Las Vegas, NE.

As John Paul finishes a tour of the USA and begins a tour of Europe; Robert continue to gig around the UK.
October 29 POB play Queen Marchy Ballroom, Dudley Zoo.
October 30 POB play Guildhall, Gloucester.
October 31 POB play The National Forest Folk Festival, Moira, Leicestershire.
November 7 John Paul plays Munich Incognito, Germany.
November 8 John Paul plays Frankfurt Batschkapp, Germany.
November 9 John Paul plays Cologne Prime Club, Germany.
November 11 John Paul plays Konzertfabrik, Pratteln-Z7, Switzerland
November 12 POB play Lichfield.
November 13 POB play The Red Lion Folk Club, Kings Heath, Birmingham.
November 13 John Paul plays Milan Alcatraz, Italy.
November 15 John Paul plays Brussels Botanique, Belgium.
November 16 John Paul plays Paris Le Bataclan, France.
November 18 John Paul plays The Garage, Glasgow, Scotland.
November 19 John Paul plays Wilfrun Hall, Wolverhampton, England.
November 20 John Paul plays Manchester Debating Hall.
November 22 John Paul plays Shepherds Bush Empire, London.
November 23 Early Days. *The Best Of Led Zeppelin Pt 1* is released.
November 26 POB play Oakengate Theatre, Telford.
November 27 POB play Central Station Nightclub, Wrexham.
December Led Zeppelin's film, *The Song Remains The Same*, is released on DVD.
December 7 John Paul plays Club Quattro, Nagoya
December 8 John Paul plays Club Quattro, Osaka
December 8 POB play Stourbridge Town Hall, Stourbridge, West Midlands.
December 10 John Paul plays Shibuya Kokaido, Tokyo.
December 17 POB play The Market Harborough Leisure Centre.
December 18 POB play The Zodiac, Oxford.
December 23 POB play Regis Hall, Cradley Heath, West Midlands.

2000

February Jimmy & The Black Crowes hold a press conference in New York to launch the Internet only release of *Live At The Greek*, the double live CD recorded at last year's Los Angeles shows.
February 8 POB play Sugarmill, Hanley, Stoke-on-Trent.
February 11 POB play The Beaufort Theatre, Ebbw Vale, Blaenau Gwent.
February 16 POB play Junction, Cambridge.
February 18 POB play The Fiddlers Night Club, Bedminster, Bristol.
February 29 *Live At The Greek*, the Jimmy Page and The Black Crowe internet only CD is made available on line.
March 9 John Paul plays House of Blues, Orlando, FL
March 10 John Paul plays Fubar, Fort Lauderdale, FL
March 11 John Paul plays Frankie's Patio, Tampa, FL
March 13 POB play The Shed, Silver End, Brierley Hill.
March 14 John Paul plays House of Blues, New Orleans.
March 15 John Paul plays Fitzgerald's, Houston, TX.
March 16 John Paul plays Caravan of Dreams, Fort Worth, TX.
March 17 POB play Bridgend Recreation Centre, Bridgend, Wales.
March 18 POB play Arts Centre, Aberystwyth, Wales.
March 18 John Paul plays La Zona Rosa, Austin, TX.
March 20 John Paul plays Roxy Theatre, Atlanta, GA.
March 21 John Paul plays 328 Performance Hall, Nashville.
March 22 John Paul plays Bogart's, Cincinnati.
March 22 POB play Ballroom, Nottingham.
March 24 John Paul plays Shank Hall, Milwaukee, WI.
March 25 John Paul plays Park West, Chicago, IL.
March 27 *Latter Days: The Best Of Led Zeppelin Vol 2* is released.
March 27 John Paul plays Rosebud, Pittsburgh, PA.
March 27 POB play Voodoo Room, Liverpool.
March 28 John Paul plays Irving Plaza, New York, NY.
March 29 John Paul is interviewed on US VH1.
March 29 John Paul plays Jaxx Nightclub, Springfield, VA.
March 30 John Paul plays Daytona's, Pasadena, Maryland.
March 31 Robert cancels a gig at the Concert Hall, Reading due to a throat infection.
March 31 John Paul makes a TV appearance in Toronto, Ontario.
April 1 John Paul plays Club Soda, Montreal, Quebec.
April 2 John Paul plays Guvernment, Toronto, Ontario.
April 3 POB play The Roadmender, Northampton.
April 7 POB play The Brewery Arts Centre, Kendal.
April 8 POB play The Dome, Whitley Bay.
April 20 While on holiday in Florida Robert makes a surprise appearance at the *Disney Theme Park* taking part in Q&A session held on the *Beauty And The Beast* stage.
April 27 POB play Ole Blues Festival, Bergen, Norway.
April 28 POB play Venue Maxime.
May 03 POB play Planet K nightclub, Manchester.
May 12 POB play Coal Exchange, Cardiff, Wales.
May 20 POB play The Cheese & Grain, Marchket Yard, Frome, Somerset.
May 25 Robert attends the opening of the new pyramid stage at Glastonbury with owner Michael Eavis.
May 26 POB play The Roses Theatre, Tewkesbury, Gloucestershire.
May 31 POB play Theatre Brycheineiog, Brecon, Powys, Wales.
June 2 POB play Castlegar Showground's, Galway, Ireland.
June 3 POB play Cork Munster Showground's, Ireland.
June 5 & 6 POB play HQ, Dublin, Ireland
June 21 POB play The Hexagon, Reading.
June 23 POB play The Acoustic

Tent, Glastonbury Festival.

In June Jimmy & The Black Crowes begin a tour of the USA.

June 24 Jimmy & The Black Crowes play New World Music Theatre, Chicago, IL.

June 25 POB play Folken, Stavanger, Norway.

June 26 Jimmy & The Black Crowes play The Palace of Auburn Hills, Detroit, MI.

June 26 POB play Rica Ishavshotel,Tromso, Norway.

June 28 POB play Rica Hell Hotel, Trondheim, Norway.

June 28 Jimmy & The Black Crowes play Coca-Cola Star Lake Theatre, Pittsburgh, OH.

June 29 Jimmy & The Black Crowes play Summerfest, Milwaukee, WI.

June 30 Jimmy & The Black Crowes play PNC Bank Arts Centre, Holmdel, NJ.

July 1 POB play Puistoblues, Jarvenpaa, Finland.

July 2 Jimmy & The Black Crowes play Tweeter Centre, Mansfield, Boston, MA.

July 4 Jimmy & The Black Crowes play Alltel Pavilion, Raleigh, VA.

July 6 Jimmy & The Black Crowes play Nissan Pavilion, Washington DC.

July 8 Jimmy & The Black Crowes play E Centre, Camden, NJ.

July 9 POB play Shrewsbury World Music Day, Shrewsbury Castle.

July 10 Jimmy & The Black Crowes play Jones Beach Amphitheatre, Wantaugh, NY.

July 11 Jimmy & The Black Crowes appear on *The Conan O'Brien* TV Show, New York. After this the band take a month's break.

July 12 POB play "Rhythm of the Lake", Como, Lombardi, Italy.

July 14 John Paul Jones plays Tor Di Valle, Rome, Italy.

July 14 POB play Piazza Duomo (Pistoia Blues Festival), Pistoia, Italy.

July 15 John Paul Jones plays Piazza Duomo (Pistoia Blues Festival), Pistoia, Italy.

July 15 POB play Festival Vilar de Mouros, Vilar de Mouros, Portugal.

July 22 POB play Nice Jazz Festival, France.

July 24 The Page & The Black Crowe's album *Live At The Greek*, is made available in shops. The new version has an extra track plus enhanced video footage. It reaches number 39 in the charts.

July 24 POB play Blue Balls Festival, Luzern, Switzerland.

July 30 POB play Cambridge Folk Festival.

August 6 POB play Dranouter Folk Festival, Belgium.

August Robert and Jimmy record a version of the Sonny Burgess track 'My Buckets Got A Hole In It' for a *Sun Records* tribute album.

August 11 POB headline the Friday night Cropredy 2000 Festival, Banbury, Oxon.

August 12 Jimmy & The Black Crowes play Mesa Del Sol, Albuquerque, NM.

August 13 Jimmy & The Black Crowes were due to play the Blockbuster Desert Sky, in Phoenix but are forced to cancel due to Jimmy's reoccurring back problem.

August 14 Jimmy & The Black Crowes appear on *The Jay Leno Show*, NBC Studios, Burbank, CA.

Jimmy's back problems continue to cause concern and his doctor orders him to rest for a month, cancelling the rest of their schedule tour which was to include US dates with The Who, a European Tour and a Far Eastern Tour.

August 19 Robert contributes a phone interview to a 30th Anniversary of Broadcasting celebration show hosted by Bob Harris on Radio 2.

August 20 Robert and The Priory book into the Mono Valley Studios in Monmouth, recording material that include 'Flames', 'Evil Woman' and 'Morning Dew'.

August 28 POB play Ross-on-Wye International Festival.

September 6 POB play The Charlotte, Leicester.

September 18 POB play Alcatraz Club, Milan, Italy.

September 20 POB play Enzimi Festival, Campo Lanciani (Tiburtina Railway Station), Rome, Italy.

September 21 POB play Molo Ichnusa, Cagliari, Sardinia.

September 23 POB play Vox Club, Nonantola (nr Modena), Italy.

September 24 POB play Piazza del Mercato (Marchket Place), Naples, Italy.

October 4 POB play The New Trinity Community Centre, Bristol.

October 18 POB play The Coliseum, Coventry.

October 19 POB play The Woughton Centre, Milton Keynes.

October 23 POB play De Melkweg, Amsterdam, Holland.

October 26 POB play Den Atelier, Luxembourg City, Luxembourg – Rescheduled.

October 27 POB play Ancienne Belgique, Brussels – Rescheduled.

October 29 POB play La Cigale, Paris, France – Rescheduled.

October 30 According to the latest RIAA figures, Zeppelin have now sold 100.5 million albums, placing them second behind The Beatles whose sales top 150 million.

November 12 POB play Ancienne Belgique, Brussels.

November 13 POB play Atelier, Luxembourg.

November 15 POB play La Cigale, Paris, France.

November 21 & 22 POB play Mylos Club, Thessaloniki, Greece.

November 24 & 25 POB play Rodon Club, Athens, Greece. Due to flu Robert then cancels five shows in Scandinavia but back to full fitness, Robert and The Priory play three gigs in the UK.

December 14 POB play Victoria Community Centre, Crewe.

December 17 POB play Darwin Suite, Assembly Rooms, Derby.

December 21 POB play Wulfrun Hall, Wolverhampton. This is the final Priory show.

2001

February Robert begins rehearsing with his new line up in Bath.

April 4 Jimmy attends a fund raising auction for the ABC Trust at The Tower Club, Fort Lauderdale. He does not perform.

April Robert commences a mini tour of Scandinavia with his new band Strange Sensation.

April 22 Robert & SS play the Train, Aarhus, Denmark.

April 23 Robert & SS play the Amager Bio, Copenhagen, Denmark.

April 26 Robert & SS play the KB (Kulturbolaget) Halle, Malmo, Sweden.

April 27 Robert & SS play the Trägården, Gothenburg, Sweden.

April 29 Robert & SS play the Cirkus, Stockholm, Sweden.

May 1 Robert & SS play the Ole Blues Festival, Bergen, Norway.

May 2 Robert & SS play the Folken, Stavanger, Norway.

After a short break Robert and SS have more rehearsals and then head to the USA for a short tour.

May 25 Robert & SS play the Orpheum Theatre, Boston, MA.

May 27 Robert & SS play the Electric Factory, Philadelphia, PA.

May 28 Robert & SS play the DAR Constitution Hall. Washington DC.

May 31 Robert & SS play the *Robin Hood Foundation Benefit Charity Gig*, New York

June 1 Robert & SS play Roseland Ballroom, New York, NY.

June 3 Robert & SS play the Massey Hall, Toronto, ON.

June 4 Robert & SS play the State Theatre, Detroit, MI.

June 6 Robert & SS play the Riviera Theatre, Chicago, IL

June 10 Jimmy attends Roy Harper's 50th Birthday gig at The Royal Albert Hall, London but does not perform.

Robert again returns to Europe for some selective gigs.

June 19 Robert & SS play the Gwardia Stadium, Warsaw, Poland (supporting Sting).

July 7 Robert and Jimmy play at the Stravinski Auditorium, Montreux. This show sees Robert back with Jimmy as part of the *Sun Records Special* along with Mike Watts on drums and Ian Jennings on double bass. The set includes 'Heart In Your Hand' (from *Walking Into Clarksdale*) and 'Candy Store Rock', the never performed *Presence* track.

July 11 Robert & SS play the Olympic Stadium, Athens, Greece (supporting Sting).

July 13 Robert & SS play the Haapsalu Firenight Festival, Estonia.

July 15 Oktyabrsky Concert hall, St Petersburg, Russia (cancelled).

July 18 Robert & SS play the Workshop, Pori Jazz Festival, Finland.

July 19 Robert & SS play the Kipsale Exhibition Hall, Riga, Latvia.

August 11 Robert & SS play the Nandrin Festival, Grand Chapiteau, Belgium.

August 12 Robert & SS play the Lokerse Feesten, Belgium.

August 14 Robert & SS play the La Foire Aux Vins de Colmar Festival, Colmar, France.

September 22 John Paul posts a message on his web site: "I am sending you the message that I wrote a couple of weeks ago, before the horrendous events in New York and Washington. I hope that it will not seem too frivolous or inconsequential in the shadow of such enormous suffering. My thoughts are with you. So it's finally finished! Done and dusted. Mastering, artwork, everything. I'm very pleased. I've even had a short break! The

album is called *The Thunderthief* which is the title of one of the four songs that I sing. John Paul Jones September 2001."

November Robert & SS spend a month in RAK Recording Studios, London, recording a new album.

November 8 Jimmy Page appears on the MTV-Europe awards show at Frankfurt's Festhalle. Playing a double-necked acoustic, Jimmy accompanies Fred Durst of Limp Bizkit and Wes Scantlin from the group Puddle Of Mudd for a version of 'Thank You'.

November John Paul's new album *The Thunderthief* goes on sale in Japan, a whole three months before anywhere else in the world. To promote it, John Paul supports King Crimson on their USA tour.

November 9 & 10 John Paul plays 328 Performance Hall, Nashville, TN.

November 13 John Paul makes an in-store personal appearance at the Guitar Centre San Francisco.

November 14 John Paul plays The Warfield Theatre, San Francisco, CA.

November 15 John Paul plays the Universal Amphitheatre, Los Angeles, CA.

November 16 John Paul plays the Web Theatre, Phoenix, AZ.

November 17 John Paul plays the House Of Blues, Las Vegas.

November 19 John Paul plays the Paramount Theatre, Denver, CO.

November 21 John Paul plays the Grand Ballroom at River Centre, Minneapolis, St Paul, MN.

November 23 John Paul plays the Barrymore Theatre, Madison, WI.

November 24 John Paul plays the Chicago Theatre, Chicago, IL.

November 25 John Paul plays The Pageant, St. Louis, MO.

November 26 John Paul plays the Murat Theatre, Indianapolis, IN.

November 27 John Paul plays The Madrid Theatre, Kansas City, MO.

November 29 John Paul plays the Promowest Pavilion, Columbus, OH.

November 30 John Paul plays the Lakewood Civic, Cleveland, OH.

December 1 John Paul plays the Royal Oak Theatre, Detroit, MI.

December 2 John Paul plays the Palace Theatre, Greensburg, PA.

December 4 John Paul plays the University of Buffalo, Centre for The Arts Buffalo, NY.

December 5 John Paul plays the Massey Hall, Toronto, Canada

December 6 John Paul plays the Place Des Arts, Montreal, Canada.

December 8 John Paul plays the Orpheus Theatre, Boston, MA.

December 9 John Paul plays the Palace Theatre, New Haven, CT.

December 11 John Paul plays the Tower Theatre, Philadelphia, PA.

December 12 John Paul plays the Lisner Auditorium, Washington DC.

December 13 John Paul plays the Beacon Theatre, New York, NY.

December 14 John Paul plays the Beacon Theatre, New York, NY.

2002

January 27 John Paul plays at the *Mine Aid Event* in Manchester along with Julie Felix, Roy Harper, Bill Wyman, Steve Harley, and others.

February 5 *The Thunderthief*, John Paul's new album is finally given a

world wide release.

February 5 Robert & SS play a warm-up gig at the Anson Rooms, Bristol University.

February 9 Robert & SS perform at The Royal Albert Hall, London as part of the all-star line up in aid of the *Children's Cancer Charity*. The show also features Jimmy performing 'Dazed And Confused' with Paul Weller's band.

March 4 Jimmy and his wife attend an ABC charity event at the Epsom College. The couple arrive early in the afternoon and stay until the end of the evening. Jimmy takes part in a question and answer session, an auction and watches a concert by the pupils, even getting up and playing four numbers with the student band. The whole event raised over £10,000.

March Jimmy begins work on the *Led Zeppelin DVD* and live album. Working with director Dick Carruthers and sound enginer Kevin Shirley, the project takes up the rest of the year.

March 9 John Paul is interviewed on the high profiled *Jonathan Ross* show on BBC Radio 2.

March 11 John Paul is interviewed on the *Nicky Campbell* show on BBC radio 5 Live.

March 13 John Paul is interviewed on the *Libby Purvis* show on BBC Radio 4.

March 15 John Paul is interviewed on the *Andrew Callin* show for BBC 6 radio.

April 12 John Paul supports Julie Felix at a free gig at London's Oxford Street Borders bookstore. The gig is in aid of *MAG* (Mines Advisory Group), the same charity he and Julie were involved with in January. JPJ plays mandolin, backing Julie for over an hour. He stays on to sign autographs.

May Jimmy Page receives a *Lifetime Achievement* award at Japan's MTV Music/Video awards in Tokyo. Robert performs three concerts in Portugal previewing numbers from the forthcoming studio album Dreamland.

May 22 Robert & SS play the Aula Magna, Lisbon, Portugal.

May 23 Robert & SS play the Aula Magna, Lisbon, Portugal.

May 25 Robert & SS play the Coliseum, Porto, Portugal.

May 27 Jimmy loans a wardrobe designed by William Burges, for an exhibition of the Victorian architects work at Knightshayes Court, near Tiverton in Devon. Jimmy, an admirer of Burges, who once lived at the Tower House in Kensington, also opens the exhibition.

May 30 Robert & SS play the Time Club, Bangor University, Wales.

May 31 Robert & SS play the Mountford Hall, Liverpool University.

June 3 Robert & SS play the Isle of Wight Festival, Seaclose Park, IOW.

June 5 Robert appears on BBC Radio 2's *Johnnie Walker Show* for an interview.

June 6 Robert & SS record a show for the VH-1 *Storytellers* TV series, recording a set at the Westway Studios in London.

June 10 Robert & SS play the Astoria Theatre, London.

June 21 Robert's new album, *Dreamland*, is released.
June 22 Robert & SS perform live on the *Richard Allinson* BBC Radio 2 Show from the BBC Studios, Maida Vale, London.
June 29 Robert and SS play the Acoustic Tent, Glastonbury Festival.
July 1 Robert gives an interview on BBC Radio 2 for *Simon Mayo's Album Show*.
July 13 Robert's *Storytellers* show is premiered on VH-1 in USA.
July Robert & SS again returns the States for tour dates that include support slots for The Who.
July 18 Robert performs on the *David Letterman* TV Show.
July 20 Robert plays the Rockfest, Cadott, WI.
July 22 Robert plays The Rave, Eagles Ballroom, Milwaukee WI.
July 24 Robert plays the Hammerstein Ballroom, New York, NY.
July 26 Robert plays the Tweeter Centre, Mansfield, Boston, MA.
July 2 7 Robert plays the Tweeter Centre, The Waterfront, Camden NJ.
July 29 Robert plays the Hersheypark Amphitheatre, Hershey, PA.
July 31, August 1, 2 & 3 Robert plays the Madison Square Garden, New York, NY.
August 18 Robert's *Storytellers* show is premiered on VH-1 in Europe.
August 23 Robert plays the Palace Of Auburn Hills, Auburn Hills, MI.
August 24 Robert plays the Tweeter Centre, Tinley Park, IL
August 25 Robert plays the Verizon Wireless Music Centre, Noblesville, IN.
August 27 Robert plays the Van Andel Arena, Grand Rapids, MI.
August 28 Robert plays the Polaris Amphitheatre, Columbus, OH.
August 30 Robert plays the P.N.C. Bank Arts Center, Holmdel, NJ.
August 31 Robert plays the Jones Beach Amphitheatre. Wantagh, NY.
September 2 Robert plays the Playhouse, Cleveland, OH.
September 4 Robert plays the Fabulous Fox Theatre, St. Louis, MO.
September 5 Robert plays the Memorial Hall, Kansas, MO.
September 7 Robert plays the Fillmore Auditorium, Denver, CO.
September 9 Robert plays the Berkeley Community Centre, San Francisco, CA.
September 10 Robert plays the Santa Barbara Bowl, Santa Barbara, CA.
September 12 Robert plays the The Greek Theatre, Los Angeles, CA.
September 13 Robert plays the The Joint, Las Vegas, NE.
September 15 Robert and his band film an appearance for the US *Austin City Limits* TV show taping at KLRU Studios in Austin, Texas
September John Paul Jones appears on Julie Felix's new album of Bob Dylan covers, *Starry Eyed And Laughing*. He plays mandolin on 'Mr. Tambourine Man', 'Subterranean Homesick Blues', and 'A Hard Rain's A-Gonna Fall'.
September 17 Jimmy attends Jeff Beck's gig at the Royal Festival Hall, London. He doesn't play but watches the whole show from the auditorium.
September 20 Jimmy opens the UK offices of the Brazilian children's charity he and his wife head, ABC at Bury St Edmunds, Suffolk, England.
October 4 Robert attends the launch of the Kidderminster Collage record label, Mighty Atom Smasher. Kevyn Gammond runs the project and Robert is a patron. The first release is a compilation of local bands that features a studio track by Priory Of Brion, 'Evil Woman'.

Robert undertakes his first full UK Tour with Strange Sensation.
October 8 Robert plays Exeter University.
October 9 Robert plays Cardiff Coal Exchange.
October 11 Robert plays Cambridge Corn Exchange.
October 14 Robert plays Norwich University of East Anglia.
October 14 *Dreamland* is repackaged with a bonus EP *Song For The Siren* (Radio Edit and a remixed version) plus two tracks from the *Richard Allinson* show.
October 15 Robert plays Birmingham Academy.
October 17 Robert plays Leeds University.
October 20 Robert plays Manchester Apollo.
October 21 Robert plays Newcastle City Hall.
October 23 Robert plays Glasgow Barrowlands.
October 24 Robert plays Sheffield Octagon.
October 27 Robert plays Portsmouth Guildhall.
October 28 Robert plays Bristol Academy.
October 30 Robert plays Hammersmith Apollo. Before this gig, Robert and his son, Logan, have a private viewing of the work in progress *Led Zeppelin DVD*.
November 5 Robert plays Vega, Copenhagen, Denmark.
November 6 Robert plays Rockefeller, Oslo, Norway.
November 8 Robert plays Globen Annexet, Stockholm, Sweden.
November 9 Jimmy, along with his wife hold a "Samba Party" at The Elysium bar in London, to raise funds for there Task Brasil/ABC Trust charity in aid of Brazilian children.
November 10 Robert plays Finlandia House Hall, Helsinki, Finland.
November 12 Robert plays Ice Palace, Sankt-Petersburg, Russia.
November 14 Robert plays Olympics Stadium, Moscow, Russia.
November 15 Robert's *Austin City Limits* show is broadcast (US only).
December 31 Robert appears on the New Year Eves edition of the *Jools Holland* show. He performs 'Boogie Woogie Roll' with Jools, 'Shake Rattle And Roll' with Soloman Burke and Tom Jones and helps with backing vocals on 'Hi Ho Silver Lining' with Jeff Beck, Solomon Burke, Tom Jones and Jools and his Band. This show was actually filmed two weeks previous. On New Years Eve itself, Robert performs at The Queen's Head pub in Wolverley, just north of Kidderminster.

2003
January 6, 7 & 8 Robert along with Justin Adams attends the *Festival In The Desert* in Essakane, near Timbuktu, Mali, Africa.
January 17 Robert Plant appears on BBC Radio 3 interviewed on the *Andy Kershaw* show, which was recorded at the festival in the desert in Mali. A version of 'Whole Lotta Love' with Justin Adams on guitar and some African drummers is aired plus a jam with Ali Farka Toure
February 28 Robert & SS perform Love's '7 & 7 Is' and 'Song To The Siren' for BBC3 TV *Re-Covered* show at Riverside Studios, Hammersmith.
March 2 John Paul makes a surprise appearance at the Queen Elizabeth Hall, London as a guest of Robyn Hitchcock. He plays during most of the second half of the set and the last couple of songs from the first set. Mainly he plays mandolin, but he also performs one of his own songs 'Ice Fishing At Night' on piano along with Peter Blegvad and Robyn Hitchcock on guitars.
March 8 Robert does two radio interviews today. The first on BBC Radio 2's *Jonathan Ross* show and in the evening he appears on the *Loose Ends* programme on BBC Radio 4 hosted by Ned Sheridan.
March 12 *Led Zeppelins Early Days Latter Days* is re-released in a double CD format. Issued at mid-price and featured on a TV campaign, it reaches number 11 on the UK chart.
March 17 Robert appears on BBC Radio 1's *Mark and Lard* show.
March 18 *Top Of The Pops 2* airs a special video of Song To The Siren. The track can also be heard on the closing credits of the new movie *Moonlight Mile*.
March 20 Robert & SS tape an appearance at the BBC Glasgow studios for BBC Scotland's *Live Floor Show* – 'Song To The Siren' and 'Gallows Pole' are duly aired on the March 22 show.
March 24 Robert releases a double A-side featuring 'Last Time I Saw Her' (a new remix with additional guitars from The Smashing Pumpkins James Iha) and 'Song To The Siren'. It fails to chart.
April 18 Robert's appearance on *Re-Covered* is aired.
May 8 Jimmy appears on BBC Radio 2 *Johnnie Walker Show* and is interviewed extensively about the forth-coming DVD and CD release.
May 15 Robert, Jimmy and John Paul all attend the preview of the *DVD* at The Empire, Leicester Square in London, simulation screening are held in seven other cities in the UK.
May 26 *Unseen Unheard Unearthed* pronounces the adverts that heralds the joint release of the Led Zeppelin double *DVD* and *How The West Was Won*, a live triple CD of Los Angeles and Long Beach shows from 1972.
May 27 All three members attend the preview of the *DVD* at Loews Theatre 34th Street New York
June 1 *The How The West Was Won* album enters the UK chart at no 5. The *DVD* enter at number 3 on the chart.
June 5 *The How The West Was Won* album enters the *Billboard* album chart at number 1. The *DVD* is top of the US video charts, having clocked up 120,000 sales in the first seven days of release, the largest ever sales for a music DVD release.
June 7 John Paul appears on the *Richard Allinson* show on Radio 2 talking about the DVD and live album.
June 28 All ten original Led Zeppelin albums are re-released in miniature sleeves as a 'Special 35th Anniversary Edition'.

APPENDIX 2: DISCOGRAPHY, 1991 TO 2003 *COMPILED BY GARY FOY & DAVE LEWIS*

The following discography chronicles the major official and promotional releases of Led Zeppelin and the respective solo projects of Jimmy Page, Robert Plant and John Paul Jones issued between 1991 and 2003 - and is compiled from initial research by Gary Foy. Though extensive, this discography does not claim to be totally comprehensive. All updates are gratefully received and will be duly documented in a future issue of the *Tight But Loose* magazine

---

LED ZEPPELIN: UK CD ALBUMS
Boxed Set 2
Atlantic: 7567-82477-2
(September 1993)
Tracks: Good Times Bad Times/ We're Gonna Groove/Night Flight/ That's The Way/Baby Come On Home/ The Lemon Song/You Shook Me/ Boogie With Stu/Bron-Yr-Aur/Down By The Seaside/Out On The Tiles/ Black Mountain Side/Moby Dick/ Sick Again/Hot Dog/Carouselambra/South Bound Saurez/Walters Walk/Darlene/Black Country Woman/ How Many More Times/The Rover/ Four Sticks/Hats off To (Roy) Harper/ I Cant Quit You Baby/Hots On For Nowhere/Living Loving Maid (She's Just A Woman)/Royal Orleans/ Bonzo's Montreux/The Crunge/ Bring It On Home/Tea For One.

UK chart position: No. 56 - 1 week on the chart.

The Complete Studio Recordings
Atlantic: 7-82526-2
(September1993)
De luxe box set re package of the original eight studio albums plus the posthumous *Coda* which has the following bonus tracks: Baby Come On Home/Travelling Riverside Blues/ White Summer-Black Mountain Side/Hey Hey What Can I Do

BBC Sessions
Atlantic: 7567-83061-2
(November 1997)
Tracks: You Shook Me/I Can't Quit You Baby/Communication Breakdown/Dazed And Confused/The Girl I Love She Got Long Black Wavy Hair/What Is And What Should Never Be/Communication Breakdown/Travelling Riverside Blues/ Whole Lotta Love/Somethin' Else/ Communication Breakdown/I Can't Quit You Baby/You Shook Me/How Many More Times/Immigrant Song/ Heartbreaker/Since I've Been Loving You/Black Dog/Dazed And Confused/ Stairway To Heaven/Going To California/That's The Way/Whole Lotta Love (Medley) Boogie Chillun'/ Fixin' To Die/That's Alright Mama/A Mess Of Blues/Thank You.

UK chart position: No 23 - 7 weeks on the charts.

Early Days - The Best Of Led Zeppelin Volume 1
Atlantic: 7567-83268-2
(November 1999)
Tracks: Good Times Bad Times/ Babe I'm Gonna Leave You/Dazed And Confused/ Communication Breakdown/Whole Lotta Love/What Is And What Should Never Be/Immigrant Song/Since I've Been Loving You/Black Dog/Rock And Roll/The Battle Of Evermore/When The Levee Breaks/Stairway To Heaven.
Includes enhanced CD video version of Communication Breakdown

UK chart position: No 55 - 1 week on the chart.

Latter Days - The Best Of Led Zeppelin Volume 2
Atlantic: 7567-83278-2
(April 2000)
Tracks: The Song Remains The Same/ No Quarter/Houses Of The Holy/ Trampled Underfoot/Kashmir/Ten Years Gone/ Achilles Last Stand/ Nobody's Fault But Mine/All My Love/ In The Evening.
Includes enhanced CD video version of Kashmir.

UK chart position: No 40 - 1 week on the chart.

The Very Best Of Led Zeppelin - Early Days & Latter Days
Atlantic: 75678-36195
(February 2003)
Tracks: Good Times Bad Times/ Babe I'm Gonna Leave You/Dazed And Confused/ Communication Breakdown/Whole Lotta Love/What Is And What Should Never Be/Immigrant Song/Since I've Been Loving You/Black Dog/Rock And Roll/The Battle Of Evermore/When The Levee Breaks/Stairway To Heaven/ The Song Remains The Same/No Quarter/ Houses Of The Holy/Trampled Underfoot/Kashmir/Ten Years Gone/ Achilles Last Stand/Nobody's Fault But Mine/All My Love/In The Evening.
Includes Enhanced CD video of Communication Breakdown and Kashmir

UK chart position: No 11

How The West Was Won
Atlantic: 7567-8-3587-2
(May 2003)
Tracks: LA Drone/Immigrant Song/ Heartbreaker/Black Dog/Over The Hills And Far Away/Since I've Been Loving You/Stairway To Heaven/ Going To California/ That's The Way/ Bron yr Aur Stomp/ Dazed And Confused/What Is And What Should

Never Be/ Dancing Days/Moby Dick/ Whole Lotta Love/Rock and Roll/ The Ocean/ Bring It On Home.
UK chart position: No 5

UK VINYL ALBUMS
BBC Sessions
Atlantic: 7567-83061-1.
Manufactured and distributed under license by Classic Records.
(November 1997)
UK issued vinyl Box Set on heavy weight vinyl.
Early Days - The Best Of Led Zeppelin Volume 1
Atlantic: 7567-83268-1
(November 1999)
Latter Days - The Best Of Led Zeppelin Volume 2
Atlantic: 7567-83278-1
(April 2000)
Note: The original ten album Led Zeppelin catalogue has been reissued on heavy weight vinyl by Classic Records.

UK CD SINGLE
Whole Lotta Love (edit)**/Baby Come On Home/Travelling Riverside Blues.**
Atlantic: AT0013CD (September 1997) UK chart position: No 21- 2 weeks on the chart.

VINYL 7 INCH PROMO
Whole Lotta Love(edit)**/Whole lotta Love**(edit)
Atlantic AT0031LC
(September 1997)
UK juke box seven inch promo.

NOTABLE CD PROMOS
Whole Lotta Love - A Tribute To Ahmet Erteugun
Atlantic Ahmet 1 (2000)
UK promo produced for the 2000 Music IndustryTrusts dinner to honour Atlantic founder Ahmet Erteugun. 2CD Compilation includes Stairway To Heaven and The Honeydrippers Sea Of Love
Led Zeppelin
Retro Active/Warner Chappell RA 003 3 (2001)
Limited edition 3 CD box set of studio tracks produced as a promotional item to attract interest to the Zeppelin catalogue for potential use in soundtracks/TV ads.
Tracks: Dazed And Confused/Good Times Bad Times/Communication Breakdown/Babe I'm Gonna Leave You/Whole Lotta Love/Ramble On/ Heartbreaker/What Is And What Should Never Be/Thank You/Immigrant Song/Celebration Day/Since I've Been Loving You/Hey Hey What Can I Do/Out On The Tiles/Black Dog/ Rock And Roll/Stairway To Heaven/ The Battle Of Evermore/When The Levee Breaks/Misty Mountian Hop/ Going To California/Over The Hills And Far Away/Dancing Days/The Rain Song/The Ocean/Houses Of The Holy/D'yer Ma'ker/No Quarter/The Song Remains The Same/Kashmir/ Sick Again/Trampled Underfoot/In The Light/The Wanton Song/Ten Years Gone/Nobody's Fault But Mine/ Achilles Last Stand/ Fool In The Rain/All my Love/In The Evening.
Stairway To Heaven/Good Times Bad Times/Kashmir
Atlantic 95289 (1991)
French promo CD single issued to

promote the *Remasters* album
Stairway To Heaven
Atlantic PRCD 4424-2 (1992)
In 1992 Stairway To Heaven was issued as a promo in a 12" x 8" card sleeve that when opened up revealed a pop-up hermit, complete with bundle of sticks, a CD single of Stairway and also a 7" vinyl single of the same track.
Baby Come On Home/Travelling Riverside Blues/White Summer-Black Mountain Side/Hey Hey What Can I Do.
Atlantic: PRCD 27 (1993)
UK four track promo, made available to tie in with the release of *Boxed Set 2.*
Baby Come On Home
Atlantic: PRCD 3 (1993)
USA one track CD promo.
Whole Lotta Love (edit)**/Baby Come On Home/Travelling Riverside Blues.**
Atlantic: AT4014CD (September 1997)
UK promo with promo sticker.
BBC Session Sampler
Communication Breakdown/The Girl I Love She Got Long Black Wavy Hair/ Whole Lotta Love.
Atlantic: PRCD-923 (1997)
UK promo.
The Girl I Love/Whole Lotta Led
(Historical Medley)
Atlantic: PRCD- 8351 (1997)
The "Whole Lotta Led" medley is a specially created chronological montage of every song Led Zeppelin recorded. US Promo
The Girl I Love/CD Rom of Whole Lotta Love Video
Atlantic: PRCD - 8376-2 (1997)
US one-track promo with a CD Rom video of Whole Lotta Love. US Promo
BBC Sessions - In Store Sampler.
Atlantic: PRCD - 8401 (1997)
Tracks: You Shook Me/I Can't Quit You Baby/Communication Breakdown/Dazed And Confused/The Girl I Love She Got Long Black Wavy Hair/What Is And What Should Never Be/Communication Breakdown/ Travelling Riverside Blues/Whole Lotta Love/Something Else/Communication Breakdown/I Can't Quit You Baby/You Shook Me/How Many More Times.
US promo.
Communication Breakdown
Atlantic: PRCD-8402 (1997)
US promo.
How The West Was Won sampler
Black Dog/Immigrant Song/Over The Hills And Far Away/The Ocean/ Heartbreaker
Atlantic PR301132 (May 2003)
US promo
Led Zeppelin interview disc
Atlantic PRCD-3011 (May 2003)
US interview promo for the *DVD* and *How The West Was Won.*

NOTABLE OVERSEAS/FOREIGN RELEASES - CD ALBUMS
JAPAN
Led Zeppelin- Minature sleeve
Reproduction CD re issues
In 1997 in Japan, the original ten album Led Zeppelin back catalogue was reissued on CD in limited edition minature card sleeves to the original albums. In 2003 these albums were again reissued in Japan and Europe as a 'Special 35th Anniversary Edition' and again were

very limited.
BBC Sessions
Atlantic: AMCY-2401-2
(November 1997)
Includes lyric booklet and Japanese text.

US CD ALBUM VARIATION:
BBC Sessions + Rare Interviews
Atlantic/Mastertone: 8307-4-2 + 8238 (November 1997)
Includes bonus extra disc of three interviews, BBC Radio-One Night Stand 1969/King Biscuit Flower Hour 1976-1977/The Publicity Interview 1990. Limited edition exclusive to the Best Buy chain.

SINGLES
JAPAN
Whole Lotta Love (edit)**/Baby Come On Home/Travelling Riverside Blues**
Atlantic: AMCY- 2403
(September 1997)
Good Times Bad Times/Communication Breakdown
Atlantic ASCD 181 (1997)
Whole Lotta Love/Living Loving Maid
Atlantic ASCD 182 (1997)
Immigrant Song/Hey Hey What Can I Do
Atlantic ASCD 183 (1997)
* Promo only 2 track CD's each in custom card picture sleeve repro of the original Japanese 7 inch picture sleeve. Limited edition of 100 of each title - only available by the purchaser of the miniature sleeve CD re issue series submitting relevant Obi strips from the packaging.
AUSTRALIA
Whole Lotta Love (edit)**/Baby Come On Home/Travelling Riverside Blues**
Atlantic: A4014CD
(September 1997)
Gold edition CD stickered "Limited edition Gold CD celebrating 30th anniversary".

NOTABLE UK COMPILATION APPEARANCES
Almost Famous Soundtrack
Dreamworks (2000)
Includes the Led Zeppelin track That's The Way.

OFFICIAL CD TRIBUTE ALBUM
Encomium - A Tribute To Led Zeppelin
Atlantic 82731 2 (March 1995)
Tracks: Misty Mountain Hop - 4 Non Blondes/Hey Hey What Can I Do - Hootie And The Blowfish/D'yer Mak'er- Sheryl Crow/Dancing Days - Stone Temple Pilots/Tangerine - Big Head Todd & The Monsters/ Thank You - Duran Duran/Out On The Tiles - Blind Melon/Good Times Bad Times - Cracker/Custard Pie - Helmet with David Yow/Four Sticks - Rollins Band/Going To California - Never The Bride/ Down By The Seaside - Robert Plant & Tori Amos

OTHER NOTABLE CD TRIBUTE ALBUMS
Kashmir - Symphonic Led Zeppelin
Polar Music 454 145 2 (1997)
Jaz Coleman's orchestral intepretations of Zep classics.
Whole Lotta Blues- Songs of Led Zeppelin
House of Blues 51416 1464 2 (1997)
A collection of original blues artists versions of Zep classics.

Led Astray: The Folk Blues Roots Of Page & Plant
Connoisseur VSOP CD 282 (1999)
A collection of original recordings of songs covered by Led Zep.
The Song Remains Remixed - A Tribute To Led Zeppelin
Anagram Records CDMGRAM 126 (2000)
Compilaiton of dance mix verisons of Zep classics.
Living Loving Played - A Tribute To Led Zeppelin
Reveberations LAK 33691 (2001)
Upcoming US female singer songwriters interpret Zep classics.
The String Quartet Tribute To Led Zeppelin Vol 1 and 2
Vitamin Records CD 1700 (2002)
String quartet versions of Zep classics.

LED ZEPPELIN VHS/ DVD'S
The Song Remains The Same
Warner Brothers D 011389(1997)
Also available on *VHS PES 61389*
The Old Grey Whistle Test
BBCDVD 1073
Features the 1975 Robert Plant interview backstage in Brussels with Bob Harris.
DVD
Warner Music Vision 0349 70198 2 (May 2003)
Tracks: We're Gonna Groove/I Can't Quite You Baby/Dazed And Confused/ White Summer/What Is And What Should Never Be/How Many More Times/Moby Dick/Whole Lotta Love/ Communication Breakdown/C'mon Everybody/Something Else/Bring It On Home/Extras: Communication Breakdown promo/Danmarks Radio/ Supershow/Tous En Scene/Immigrant Song/Black Dog/ Misty Mountain Hop/Since Ive Been Loving You/ The Ocean/Going To California/ That's The Way/Bron Yr Aur Stomp/In My Time Of Dying/Trampled Underfoot/ Stairway To Heaven/Rock And Roll/ Nobody's Fault But Mine/Sick Again/ Achilles Last Stand/In The Evening/ Kashmir/Whole Lotta Love - Extras: NYC Press Conference/Down Under/ The Old Grey Whistle Test/Promos
Also available on *VHS 0349 701983*
DVD Sampler
What Is And What Should Never Be/ In My Time Of Dying/Rock And Roll
Warner Music Vision PR 03945 (May 2003)
3 track DVD promo.

ROBERT PLANT - UK CD ALBUMS
Fate Of Nations
Fontana/Es Paranza: 514-867-2 (June 1993)
Tracks: Calling To You/Down To The Sea/Come Into My Life/I Believe/29 Palms/Memory Song/ If I Were A Carpenter/Colours Of A Shade/ Promised Land/The Greatest Gift/Great Sprit/Network News.
UK chart position: No 6 - 8 weeks in the charts.
Note: US version does not include the track Colours Of A Shade.
Dreamland
Mercury: 586-963-2 (July 2002)
Tracks: Funny In My Mind (I Believe I'm Fixin' To Die)/Morning Dew/ One More Cup Of Coffee/Last Time I Saw Her/Song To The Siren/Win My Train Fare Home (If I Ever Get Lucky)/ Darkness Darkness/Red Dress/Hey

Joe/Skips Song/Dirt In A Hole.
UK chart position: No 20
Note: US version does not include the track Dirt In A Hole
Dreamland - Limited Edition CD
Mercury: 063-025-2 (July 2002)
Tracks: Funny In My Mind (I Believe I'm Fixin' To Die)/Morning Dew/ One More Cup Of Coffee/Last Time I Saw Her/Song To The Siren/Win My Train Fare Home (If I Ever Get Lucky)/ Darkness Darkness/Red Dress/Hey Joe/Skips Song/Dirt In A Hole.
Limited edition Digi Pack foldout card sleeve
Dreamland - Collectors Edition
Mercury: 063-465-2 (October 2002)
Tracks: Funny In My Mind (I Believe I'm Fixin' To Die)/Morning Dew/ One More Cup Of Coffee/Last Time I Saw Her/Song To The Siren/Win My Train Fare Home (If I Ever Get Lucky)/ Darkness Darkness/Red Dress/Hey Joe/Skips Song/Dirt In A Hole/Song to The Siren-Radio edit/Song To The Siren-Alpha Mix/Morning Dew-BBC Radio 2 session/Funny In My Mind (I Believe I'm Fixin' To Die) - BBC Radio 2 session/Darkness Darkness - video.
Re-released with bonus CD and CD Rom video of Darkness Darkness.

UK VINYL ALBUM RELEASES
Fate Of Nations
Fontana/Es Paranza: 514-867-1 (June 1993)
Dreamland
Mercury: 063-094-1 (July 2002)

UK CD SINGLES
29 Palms/21 Years/Dark Moon/Whole Lotta Love (You Need Love) - CD1
Fontana/Es Paranza: FATED 1: (May 1993)
UK chart position: No 21 - 5 weeks in the charts.
29 Palms/21 Years/Dark Moon- CD 2
Fontana/Es Paranza : FATEX 1: (May 1993)
UK chart position: No 21 - 5 weeks in the charts.
I Believe/Great Sprit (acoustic)**/ Hey Jayne**
Fontana/Es Paranza : FATEX 2: (July 1993)
UK chart position: No 64 - 2 weeks in the charts.
Calling To You/Naked If I Want To/8.05 - CD 1
Fontana/Es Paranza : FATED 3: (September 1993)
No chart position.
Calling To You - CD 2 (5 re-mix special)
Song To Kalsoum Mix/Shookran Sah-Abi Mix/Always, My Heart mix/Artist's Valley/Per La Gente Mix
Fontana/Es Paranza : FATEX 3: (September 1993)
No chart position.
If I Were A Carpenter/Ship Of Fools (Live from Montreaux)/Tall Cool One (Live from Montreaux) CD 1
Fontana/Es Paranza : FATEX 4: (December 1993)
UK chart position: No 63 - 2 weeks in the charts.
If I Were A Carpenter/I Believe (Live from Montreaux)/Going To California (Live from Montreaux) CD 2
Fontana/Es Paranza : FATED 4:

(December 1993)
UK chart position: No 63 - 2 weeks in the charts.
Morning Dew/A House Is Not A Motel (Live)/Robert Plant Interview/Morning Dew- Video
Mercury: 582-958-2 (June 2002)
Song to The Siren - Radio edit/Song To The Siren-Alpha Mix/Morning Dew - BBC Radio 2 session/Funny In My Mind (I Believe I'm Fixin' To Die) - BBC Radio 2 session/ Darkness Darkness - Video.
Mercury: 063-861-2 (2002)
Last Time I Saw Her - Remix/ Song To The Siren - Radio Edit
Mercury: 077-933-2 (March 2003)

UK 7 INCH SINGLES
29 Palms/21 years
Fontana/Es Paranza FATE 1 (April 1993)
I Believe/Great Spirit (acoustic)
Fontana/Es Paranza FATE 2 (July 1993)
If I Were A Carpenter/I Believe (live)/Tall Cool one (live)
Fontana/Es Paranza FATE 4 (December 1993)
UK 12 INCH SINGLES
I Believe/Hey Jayne/Great Spirit (acoustic)/Whole Lotta Love (You Need Love)
Fontana/Es Paranza FATE 212 (July 1993)
UK 12 inch picture disc single.
Calling To You (LP version) Song to Kalsoum mix/Shookran Sah - Abi mix/Always my Heart mix/My Heart mix/Artisit's Valley/Per La Gente mix
Fontana/Es Paranza FATE 312 (September 1993)
UK 12 inch single.

NOTABLE US SINGLE
Darkness Darkness (radio edit)/Darkness Darkness long edit)/Darkness Darkness (album version)/Funny In my Mind (I Believe I'm Fixin' To Die)
Universal UNIR 20770 2 (June 2002)
US four track single.

NOTABLE FOREIGN ALBUM
BRAZIL
10 From 47
Es Paranza/BMG 670 8209 (1991)
Brazilian only official compilation issued to tie in with Plant's planned Rio Festival appearance
Tacks: Heaven Knows/Burning Down One Side/Tall Cool One/Big Log/In The Mood/Tie Dye On The Highway/Pink And Black/Ship Of Fools/Little By Little/Hurting Kind

NOTABLE CD PROMO ALBUMS
Fate Of Nations Interview Disc 1993
Fontana/Es Paranza FATE 1
UK Interview disc for syndicated radio play.
Head First
Mercury: No number (June 2002)
Tracks: Funny In My Mind (I Believe I'm Fixin' To Die)/Morning Dew/ One More Cup Of Coffee/Last Time I Saw Her/Song To The Siren/Win My Train Fare Home (If I Ever Get Lucky)/Darkness Darkness/Red Dress/Hey Joe/Skips Song/Dirt In A Hole.
UK Promo with original title.
Dreamland
Mercury: No Number: (June 2002)
Tracks: Funny In My Mind (I Believe

I'm Fixin' To Die)/Morning Dew/ One More Cup Of Coffee/Last Time I Saw Her/Song To The Siren/Win My Train Fare Home (If I ever Get Lucky)/Darkness Darkness/Red Dress/Hey Joe/Skips Song/Dirt In A Hole.
UK Promo.
Dreamland Interview Disc
Mercury DREAMINT 1 (June 2002)
UK radio interview promo
Dreamland - Advanced Sampler
Universal UNIR 20769-2 (June 2002)
Four track radio sampler.
Tracks: Funny In My Mind (I Believe I'm Fixin' To Die)/Morning Dew/ One More Cup Of Coffee/ Darkness Darkness.
US four track advance radio sampler.

NOTABLE CD PROMO SINGLES
29 Palms (Radio edit)
Fontana/Es Paranza PLANT 1 (April 1993)
UK promo.
Calling To You (edit)/Calling To You (LP version)
Atlantic/Es Paranza PRCD 5082 2
US promo.
If I Were A Carpenter (Radio Edit)
Fontana/Es Paranza): FATDJ 4: (July 1993)
UK promo.
If I Were A Carpenter.
Atlantic /Es Paranza: PRCD 5393-2: (July 1993)
US promo.
Morning Dew (Radio Edit)
Mercury: MORNCJ 1: (June 2002)
UK one-track promo.
Last Time I Saw Her (Remix)
Mercury LASTCJ1 (March 2003)
UK one track promo single

NOTABLE ROBERT PLANT GUEST APPEARANCES:
Knebworth The Album
Polydor 843 921 2 (1991)
Includes Robert on the tracks Hurting Kind, Liars Dance, Tall Cool One, Wearing And Tearing (latter track with Jimmy Page)
Waynes World 2 Soundtrack
Reprise 936245852 (1994)
Includes Robert on the track Louie Louie
Adios Amigo - A Tribute To Arthur Alexander -Various Artists
Demon Records (1994)
Includes Robert on the track If It's Really Got To be That Way
Alexis Korner On The Move
Castle CCSD 809
Includes Robert on the track Steal Away.
More Oar- A Tribute to the Skip Spence Album- Various Artists
Birdman BMR 023 (1999)
Includes Robert Plant on the track Little Hands
Afro Celt System Volume 3 Further In Time
Real World CDRW 96 (2002)
Includes Robert on the track Life Begin Again.
Primal Scream - Evil Heat
Columbia 5039232 (2002)
Includes Robert playing harmonica on the track The Lord Is My Shotgun
MAS Records - Various Artists
MAS 2002 (2002)
Sampler compilation produced by the Kidderminster Collage label - includes the Priory of Brion track Curse The Evil Woman

Jools Holland - Small World Big Band Vol 2- More Friends
Warner Music 09270 494192 (2002)
Includes Robert on the track Let The Boogie Woogie Roll.

ROBERT PLANT VIDEOS/DVD'S
Knebworth: The Event
Eagle Vision EREDV 273 (1999)
Freddie Mercury Tribute Concert 10th Anniversary Edition
Parlophone 492 8699
Includes Robert on the track Crazy Little Thing Called Love.

JOHN PAUL JONES UK CD ALBUMS
The Sporting Life - Diamanda Galas with John Paul Jones
Mute Records CDSTUMM 127 (1994)
Tracks: Skotoseme/Do You Take This Man?/Dark End Of The Street/You're Mine/Tony/Devil's Rodeo/The Sporting Life/Baby's Insane/Last Man Down/Hex
Zooma
Discipline Global Mobile DGM 9909 (September 1999}
Tracks: Zooma/Grind/The Smile Of Your Shadow/Goose/Bass N Drums/B Fingers/Snake Eyes/Nosumi Blues/Tidal
*Japanese version features extra track Fanfare For The Millennium
The Thunderthief
Discipline Global Mobile DGMO 104 (February 2002)
Tracks: Leafy Meadows/The Thunderthief/Hoediddle/Ice Fishing At Night/Daphne/Angry Angry/Down To The River To Pray/Shibuya Bop/Freedom Song

UK SINGLES
Diamanda Galas with John Paul Jones
Do You Take This Man?(edit)/Hex (La Diabia mix)/Do You Take This Man? (LP version)
Mute Records CDMUTE 127 (1994)

NOTABLE PROMOS
Zooma/Snake Eyes/B. Fingers/The Smile Of Your Shadow
Discipline Global Music DGMJPJ1 (1999)
UK advance promo sampler CD.

GUEST APPEARANCES/ PRODUCTION
Manu Katche- It's About Time
BMG/Ariola 262617 (1992)
JPJ appears on selected tracks.
Brian Eno - Nerve Net
Warner 9362 45033 2 (1992)
JPJ appears on selected tracks.
Raging Slab - Sing Monkey Sing
BMG 74321359902 (1993)
Features JPJ string arrangements
REM - Automatic For The People
Warners 9362 45055 2 (1993)
Includes JPJ string arrangements on Everybody Hurts, Drive, Nightswimming, The Sidewinder Sleeps.
Heart - The Road Home
EMI CDEST 2258 (1995)
Live recording featuring JPJ on bass, piano, mandolin, string arrangements and production.
Butthole Surfers - Independant Worm Saloon
EMI CDP 7987982 (1996)
JPJ production.
Elephant Ride - Forget
Columbia CK 67234 (1996)
JPJ production / keyboards.

Peter Gabriel - US
PGCD 87 (1996)
Includes JPJ on the track Fourteen Black Paintings
Julie Felix-Starry Eyed And Laughing
Remarkable Records RR7992 (2002)
Includes JPJ on the tracks Mr Tambourine Man, Subterranean Homesick Blues/A Hard Rains Gonna Fall.

JIMMY PAGE
UK CD ALBUMS
Coverdale Page
EMI Records: 0777-7-81401-2 (March 1993)
Tracks: Shake My Tree/Waiting On You/Take Me For A Little While/Pride And Joy/Over Now/Feeling Hot/ Easy Does It/Take A Look At Yourself/ Don't Leave Me This Way/Absolution Blues/Whisper A Prayer For The Dying.
   UK chart position: No 4 - 8 weeks in the charts.
Jimmy Page & The Black Crowes Live At The Greek - Excess All Areas
Music Maker .Com: (February 2000)
Tracks: Heartbreaker/In My Time Of Dying/What Is And What Should Never Be/Custard Pie/Celebration Day/Out On The Tiles/Whole Lotta Love/Nobody's Fault But Mine/You Shook Me/The Lemon Song/Your Time Is Gonna Come/Ten Years Gone/ Sick Again/Hey Hey What Can I Do/ Shake Your Money Maker/ Woke Up This Morning/Shapes Of Things To Come/Sloppy Drunk/Oh Well.
   CD only available on the Internet, the customer could choose which tracks and in what order required
Live At The Greek - Excess All Areas
SPV 091-72022 DCD: (July 2000)
Tracks: Celebration Day/Custard Pie/Sick Again/What Is And What Should Never Be/Woke Up This Morning/Shapes Of Things To Come/ Sloppy Drunk/Ten Years Gone/In My Time Of Dying/Your Time Is Gonna Come/The Lemon Song/Nobody's Fault But Mine/Heartbreaker/Hey Hey What Can I Do /Mellow Down Easy/Oh Well/Shake Your Money Maker/You Shook Me/Out On The Tiles/Whole Lotta Love.
   UK chart position: No 39 - 4 weeks in the charts.
   The Internet only CD now made available in stores, with one bonus track and some CD. Rom video footage. The Japanese version includes bonus tracks In The Light and Misty Mountain Hop.
Whitesnake - The Silver Anniversary Collection
EMI Records: 7243-5-81694-2 3 (May 2003)
David Coverdale/Whitesnake/ Coverdale best of CD that includes three Coverdale/Page tracks, Pride And Joy, Take A Look At Yourself and Shake My Tree

UK 12" PICTURE DISC SINGLE
Take Me For A Little While
(LP version)/Shake My Tree (guitar crunch mix)/Easy Does It
EMI Records: 12 EMPD 270 (June 1993)

UK CD SINGLES
Coverdale Page
Take Me For A Little While (LP Version)/Take Me For A Little While

(Acoustic Version)/Shake My Tree (The Guitar Crunch Mix)/Take Me For A Little While (7" Edit)
EMI Records: CDEMS 270. (June 1993)
UK chart position: No 29 - 2 weeks in the charts. Packaged in a Collectors CD single box set that included 3 colour prints.
Coverdale Page
Take A Look At Yourself (Album Version)/Take A Look At Yourself (Acoustic Version)/Take A Look At Yourself (with Girls)/Waiting On You.
EMI Records: CDEMS 279. (October 1993)
UK chart position: No 42 - 1 week in the charts.

UK 7 INCH PICTURE DISC SINGLE
Coverdale Page
Take A Look At Yourself (edit)/Waiting On You
EMI Records EMPD 279 (October 1993)

NOTABLE PROMOS
Coverdale Page
Take Me For A Little While (Edit)
EMI Records: CDEMDJ 270. (June 1993)
UK promo CD single.
Pride And Joy (LP Version)
Geffen Records: PRO-CD-4491. (June 1993)
US promo CD single.
Shake My Tree (LP version)
(September 1993)
Geffen Records PROCD 4504
US promo CD single.
Jimmy Page/Black Crowes Promos What Is And What Should Never Be
Music Maker.Com (2000)
US promo CD single.
Ten Years Gone
Music Maker.Com (2000)
US promo CD single.
Hey Hey What Can I Do
TVT 2142 SP (2000)
US promo CD single.

NOTABLE JIMMY PAGE PRE-ZEPPELIN RE ISSUES/ COMPILATIONS
The Yardbirds- Cumular Limits
Burning Archives Pilot 24 (2000)
Features Page era performances from 1967 - 1968 plus live footage from German TV.
The Yardbirds - Little Games
EMI Records 540 8132 (2003)
Re issue of the Yardbirds 1967 album with additional outtakes.
Jimmy Page And His Heavy Friends-Hip Young Guitar Slinger
Sequel NEECD 486 (2000)
Double CD of Jimmy's 60's sessions.
Jimmy Page - This Guitar Kills - More 60's Groups and Sessions
Castle CMEDD 741 (June 2003)
Additional double CD of more 60's sessions.

NOTABLE GUEST APPEARANCES UK Single
Puff Daddy featuring Jimmy Page Come With Me (extended edit)/Come With Me (radio version)
Epic/Sony 34K 78954 (1998)
UK chart position -number 2
Note* German CD single (Epic/Sony EPC 666026 2) also includes Come With Me live version recorded for Saturday Night Live with Page.

UK CD ALBUM
Godzilla The Album -Soundtrack
Epic/Sony 4896102 (1998)
Features Jimmy on the track Come With Me with Puff Daddy.

JIMMY PAGE & ROBERT PLANT UK CD ALBUMS
No Quarter - Jimmy Page & Robert Plant Unledded
Fontana: 526-362-2 (November 1994)
Tracks: Nobody's Fault But Mine/ Thank You/No Quarter/ Friends/ Yallah/City Don't Cry/ Since I've Been Loving You/The Battle Of Evermore/Wonderful One/ Wah Wah/That's The Way/Gallow's Pole/ Four Sticks/Kashmir.

UK chart position: No 7 - 13 weeks in the charts.
Walking Into Clarksdale
Mercury: 558-025-2 (April 1998)
Tracks: Shining In The Light/When The World Was Young/Upon A Golden Horse/Blue Train/Please Read The Letter/Most High/Heart In Your Hand/Walking Into Clarksdale/ Burning Up/When I Was A Child/ House Of Love/Sons Of Freedom.

UK chart position: No 3 - 6 weeks in the charts.
Walking Into Clarksdale
Mercury: 558-324-2 (April 1998)
UK limited edition digi pack.

UK VINYL ALBUMS
No Quarter Jimmy Page Robert Plant Unledded
Fontana 526 3621 (October 1994)
Walking Into Clarksdale
Mercury 558 025 1(April 1998)

UK CD SINGLES
Gallows Pole/City Don't Cry/The Rain Song - CD 1
Fontana: PPCD 2 (December 1994)
UK chart position: No 35 - 3 weeks in the charts.
Gallows Pole/Four Sticks/What Is And What Should Never Be - CD 2
Fontana: PPDD 2 (December 1994)
UK chart position: No 35 - 3 weeks in the charts.
Most High/Upon A Golden Horse/ The Window
Mercury: 568-731-2 (March 1998)
UK chart position: No 26 - 2 weeks in the charts.
Shining In The Light/How Many More Times (Live at Shepherds Bush)
Mercury: 566-086-2 (August 1998)
No chart position.
Shining In The Light/ Walking Into Clarksdale (Live at Shepherds Bush)/No Quarter (Live at Shepherds Bush)
Mercury: 566-087-2 (August 1998)
No chart position.

7 INCH SINGLES
Gallows Pole/City Don't Cry
Fontana PP2 (December 1994)
Most High/The Window
Mercury 568 751 7 (March 1998)

NOTABLE CD PROMOS
Jimmy Page Robert Plant No Quarter Unledded Radio Special
Fontana PP ID 1 (October 1994)
UK radio interview disc with cues.
Conversations with Jimmy Page & Robert Plant
Atlantic: PRCD 5987-2 (February 1995)
US Promo interview CD that includes

Wonderful One/Kashmir/Gallows Pole/ and Nobody's Fault But Mine, taken from *No Quarter.*
A Songwriting Legacy
Atlantic: PRCD 6061-2 (February 1995)
Tracks: Kashmir/Good Times Bad Times/Whole Lotta Love/That's The Way/When The Levee Breaks/No Quarter/Custard Pie/Tea For One/ South Bound Suarez/Poor Tom.
US Promo CD with one track from No Quarter (Kashmir) and one track from each of the Led Zeppelin CD's
Millers Genuine Draft Presents A Songwriting Legacy
Atlantic: PRCD 6061-2 (February 1995)
Tracks: Kashmir/Good Times Bad Times/Whole Lotta Love/That's The Way/When The Levee Breaks/No Quarter/Custard Pie/Tea For One/ South Bound Suarez/Poor Tom/ Wonderful One/Gallows Pole.

US Promo CD with the 1995 tour sponsors, Miller Beer's logo and this time with three tracks from *No Quarter* (Kashmir/Wonderful One/Gallows Pole) and one track from each of the Led Zeppelin CD's.
Jimmy Page Robert Plant TBA
Mercury ADV 1998 (February 1998)
UK Pre release advance CD for *Walking into Clarksdale* in card sleeve.
Jimmy Page Robert Plant Walking Into Clarksdale An Interview
Fontana PPTIC 1 (April 1998)
UK promo interview disc for radio.
Gallows Pole
Fontana: PPCD1 (December 1994)
UK one promo in brown keyhole cover.
Gallows Pole
Fontana: PPCDJ1 (December 1994)
UK one track UK promo in red key-hole cover.
Gallows Pole
Atlantic: PRCD 5921-2 (December 1994)
US one track promo in brown key-hole cover.
Kashmir
Fontana: PPCDJ 3 (February 1995)
withdrawn UK one track CD promo
The Battle Of Evermore
Fontana: PPCDJ 4 (March 1995)
UK one track CD promo.
Kashmir
Fontana: 1973 (February 1995)
French one track promo CD single.
Gallows Pole
Atlantic PRCD 5921 -2 (November 1994)
US one track promo includes rare Plant spoken outro.
Nobody's Fault But Mine/ Gallows Pole
Atlantic: PRCD 5954-2 (February 1995)
US promo.
Thank You
Atlantic: PRCD 6017-2 (February 1995)
US promo.
Wonderful One (Radio Edit)/
Wonderful One (LP Version)/What Is And What Should Never Be.
Atlantic: PRCD 6119-2 (April 1995)
US promo.
Four Sticks.
Atlantic: PRCD 6469-2 (September 1995)
US promo.
Most High (Radio Edit)/Most High
(Album Version).

Mercury: PPMHR-1 (March 1998)
UK promo.
Most High/The Window
Mercury: PY-901 (March 1998)
Spanish promo.
Shining In The Light (Radio edit)/Shining In The Light
Mercury: MERCJ-506 (March 1998)
UK Promo.
Shining In The Light
Atlantic: PRCD 8585 (March 1998)
US promo.
Sons Of Freedom
Atlantic: PRCD 8688 (May 1998)
US promo.
When The World Was Young (Edit)/When The World Was Young (Album Version)
Atlantic: PRCD 8726 (September 1998)
US promo.

NOTABLE FOREIGN RELEASES
USA
No Quarter - Unledded
Atlantic: 082706-2. (November 1994)
US version on Atlantic - does not include the track Wah Wah.
AUSTRALIA
No Quarter - Unledded
Fontana: 526-362-2 (November 1994)
Special edition exclusive to Virgin Megastores packaged in custom card sleeve.
USA
Walking Into Clarksdale
Atlantic: 83092-2 (April 1998)
USA version available on Atlantic reached No 8 in the *Billboard* charts.
JAPAN
Walking Into Clarksdale
Mercury: PHCR-1591 (April 1998)
Japanese edition with bonus track Whiskey In the Glass.

NOTABLE FOREIGN CD SINGLES
FRANCE
Thank You/ Gallows Pole
Fontana: 852-018-2 (December 1994)
French two track single.
Gallows Pole/ City Don't Cry
Fontana: 856-420-2 (March 1995)
French two track single.
Kashmir/ When The Levee Breaks
Fontana: 856-812-2(July 1995)
French two track single.
AUSTRALIA
Gallows Pole/ City Don't Cry/ The Rain Song.
Fontana: 856-421-2 (December 1994)
Australian three track single in special collectors signature edition slipcase.
USA
Wonderful One (Radio Edit)/
Wonderful One (LP Version)/ What Is And What Should Never Be/ When The Levee Breaks.
Atlantic: CD 5-85591-2 (April 1995)
US four track single.
JAPAN
Gallows Pole/ City Don't Cry/ The Rain Song/ What Is And What Should Never Be.
Fontana: PHCR-8316. (November 1994)
Japanese Four-Track Single.
Most High/ Upon A Golden Horse/ The Window.
Mercury: PHCR-8431 (March 1998)

Japanese Three-Track Single
Shining In The Light (Edit)/ How Many More Times (Live at Shepherds Bush)/ Walking Into Clarksdale (Live at Shepherds Bush)/ No Quarter (Live at Shepherds Bush).
Mercury: PHCR-8051 (August 1998)
Japanese Four-Track Single.

JIMMY PAGE & ROBERT PLANT GUEST APPEARANCES:
The Inner Flame - Various Artists
Atlantic 83008 2 (1997)
Includes Robert Plant and Jimmy Page on the track Rude World - Robert Plant and Rainer Ptacek on the track 21 Years
The Jimmy Rogers All Stars - Blues Blues Blues
Atlantic 83148 2 (1999)
Includes Jimmy Page Robert Plant and Eric Clapton on the track Gonna Shoot Your Right Down (Boom Boom)
Good Rockin' Tonight - The Legacy of Sun Records -Various Artists
Sire 311652
Includes Robert Plant and Jimmy Page on the track My Bucket's Got A Hole In It

JIMMY PAGE & ROBERT PLANT VIDEOS/DVD'S
VHS
Jimmy Page Robert Plant - No Quarter Unledded
Warner Home Video 8536 520003 VHS (1995)
Tracks: No Quarter/Thank You/What is And What Should Never Be/The Battle Of Evermore/Gallows Pole/ Nobody's Fault But Mine/City Don't Cry/The Truth Explodes/Wah Wah/ When The Levee Breaks/Wonderful One/Since I've Been Loving You/ The Rain Song/That's The Way/ Four Sticks/Friends/Kashmir
*Also issued on Laser Disc in Japan (AMLY 8077)
DVD
The Paris Concert For Amnesty International Concert 1998
Eagle Vision EREDV313
Includes Page and Plant performances of When The World Was Young and Rock And Roll. US version also includes Babe I'm Gonna Leave You.

BOOKS 1991-2003
GOOD TIMES BAD TIMES
EDDIE McSQUARE (BOBCAT BOOKS, 1991) 64 pages
HEAVEN AND HELL
C.R. CROSS & E. FLANNIGAN (SIDGWICK & JACKSON, 1991) 208 pages
LED ZEPPELIN LIVE. AN EXPLO-RATION OF UNDERGROUND TAPES
LUIS REY (HOT WAX PRESS, 1991) 275 pages
LED ZEPPELIN
WILLIAM RUHLMANN (MAGNA BOOKS, 1992) 80 pages
BREAKING AND MAKING RECORDS
ROSS CLARKE (KINGSFLEET, 1992) 224 pages
LED ZEPPELIN LIVE. AN EXPLO-RATION OF UNDERGROUND TAPES
LUIS REY (HOT WAX PRESS, 1993) 335 pages, UPDATED EDITION
ON TOUR WITH LED ZEPPELIN
HOWARD MYLETT (MITCHELL BEAZLEY, 1993) 176 pages
STAIRWAY TO HEAVEN LED

ZEPPELIN UNCOVERED
R. COLE + R TRUBO (SIMON & SCHUSTER LTD, 1993) 392 pages
THE LED ZEPPELIN BIOGRAPHY
RICHIE YORKE (VIRGIN BOOKS, 1993) 342 pages
GUIDE TO THE MUSIC OF LED ZEPPELIN
DAVE LEWIS (OMNIBUS PRESS, 1994) 175 pages
THE ILLUSTRATED COLLECTOR'S GUIDE TO LED ZEPPELIN
ROBERT GODWIN (CGP Inc., 1994) 560 pages
HAMMER OF THE GODS
STEPHEN DAVIS (PAN BOOKS, 1995) 376 pages
IN THERE OWN WORDS
PAUL KENDALL/DAVE LEWIS (OMNIBUS PRESS, 1995) 144 pages
THE PHOTOGRAPHERS LED ZEPPELIN
ROSS HALFIN (213.61 1995) 334 pages
GUIDE TO LED ZEPPELIN
FLORENCE RAJON (PRELUDE ET FUGUE, 1997) 132 pages
LED ZEPPELIN
TONY HORKINS (VIGIN MODERN ICONS, 1997) 94 pages
HEXAGONAL EXPERIENCE
C. LE PABIC & B. PASCAL C. (LE PABIC & B. PASCAL, 1997) 76 pages
LED ZEPPELIN LIVE. AN EXPLO-RATION OF UNDERGROUND TAPES
LUIS REY (HOT WAX PRESS, 1997) 552 pages
LED ZEPPELIN: THE CONCERT FILE
DAVE LEWIS & S. PALLETT (OMNIBUS PRESS, 1997) 176 pages.
LED ZEPPELIN THE PRESS REPORTS
ROBERT GODWIN (CG PUBLISH-ING, 1997) 500 pages
DAZED AND CONFUSED THE STO-RIES BEHIND EVERY SONG
CHRIS WELCH (SEVENOAKS, 1998) 160 pages
THE ILLUSTRATED COLLECTOR'S GUIDE TO LED ZEPPELIN VOL 2
ROBERT GODWIN C (GP Inc., 1998) 336 pages
WORLDWIDE GUIDE TO LED ZEPPELIN 45'S THE SINGLES
S. KETENJIAN & M. McFALL (SAMUEL KETENJIAN, 1998) 148 pages
LED ZEPPELIN FOLLOW THE LEGEND VOL 1: ALBION THERE AND BACK.
MACBAY & K. RHYS-GRUFFYDD (ADRI PUBLISHERS, 2000) 352 pages
THE MONTREUX CONCERTS
GILES CHATEAU/SAM RAPALLO (ELECTRIC MAGIC, 2001)
JOHN BONHAM - A THUNDER OF DRUMS
CHRIS WELCH & GEOFF NICHOLS (BACKBEAT, 2001) 192 pages
LED ZEPPELIN - A PHOTOGRAPHIC COLLECTION
NEAL PRESTON (VISION ON, 2002) 192 pages
LED ZEPPELIN A CELEBRATION REVAMPED EDITION
DAVE LEWIS (OMNIBUS PRESS, 2003) 240 pages